Longman bus

Edited by D. C. Hagu

Business administration

An introductory study

Owen S. Hiner

Senior Lecturer in Economics
in the University of Hull

Longman

LONGMAN GROUP LIMITED

London

Associated companies, branches and representatives
throughout the world

© *Longman Group Limited (formerly Longmans Green and Co Ltd)* 1969

First published 1969
Fourth impression 1978

ISBN 0 582 44025 4 cased
ISBN 0 582 44026 2 paper

Printed in Great Britain by
Lowe & Brydone Printers Limited, Thetford

To my Sister

Preface

I feel that I should perhaps try to justify this addition to the already large business literature, and I can only do so by saying that over the years my teaching of business administration to students of economics has made both them and me aware that there was room for a British text that provided a general introduction to the subject of the kind I had in mind to write. I have therefore aimed to fill what seemed to be a small gap in the literature, and by so doing to reduce in some measure our dependence on American texts in this field. Excellent though these works are in many respects they have a few disadvantages from the British student's point of view, including the fact that they describe a system and reflect the values of a culture which, although very like our own in some ways, are yet different enough to make a certain amount of 'translation' desirable to prevent readers here from being misled about the precise relevance of American company practice to our own.

America was the pioneer of large scale business education and remains the leader in the field of business research: the work done there has had an enormous influence on the way business studies have developed, and our great debt to it will be perfectly clear to any reader of this book. But British research has also increased rapidly in recent years, and some important case studies have appeared which now make it possible to use relatively more native material, so to speak, to illustrate some of the main theoretical ideas with which we are concerned. And as the number of British students of business is growing it seemed worthwhile to provide them with an alternative introductory text in which some of this material was incorporated.

I have tried to write a general introduction to business administration in which the major aspects of the subject are covered, although (partly for reasons of space) some of them are dealt with in a rather cursory way. Several problems are encountered in writing a book of this kind, of which two call for mention. The first is that different parts of the subject vary enormously in difficulty. Some of the things one wants to say about business, although important, come dangerously near to being so self-evident as to sound banal, while on the other hand the treatment of particular aspects ideally calls for fairly advanced knowledge in specialized fields. I have tried to avoid extremes, with what success the reader will judge, but I shall be happy to receive suggestions for ways in which the book could have been improved.

The other major problem is that business administration is a subject that has been built up from many disciplines, as I point out more than once, and in writing about it a number of technical languages have to be used, especially those of the social sciences. Although their use is unavoidable I have tried to write in a generally intelligible sense, and to explain technical terms where I felt that their meaning would not be readily apparent to the non-specialist. In attempting to present many, sometimes complex, ideas and theories in a reasonably succinct and straightforward way I have certainly over-simplified some, but I hope that the specialist accountant, psychologist, sociologist, or whoever he may be, will be tolerant of this so long as I have not been guilty of error, or of making misleading statements.

I have written with second or third year university students in mind, and hope that the book will be useful to a number of those reading for degrees in economics and commerce, or for papers in industrial psychology, industrial sociology and company law. People studying for business or management diplomas in universities, and in colleges of commerce or technology, should also find much of the material relevant to their courses of study. Beyond this I should like to think that anyone entering business from high school or university, irrespective of his specialism or the field in which he proposes to work, could get some benefit from taking this broad view of the enterprise, and be helped to a clearer understanding of the activities of his firm. I hope, too, that a number of people already in business might find this book of some interest and use.

In the course of this book I refer frequently to the company's primary task, which I define here to be the use of scarce resources to produce and sell goods or services profitably and efficiently in a socially satisfactory way. I have tried to provide a general guide to a large and rather complicated subject that will give the reader a modest base from which to explore in more detail some of the practical and theoretical ideas and problems to which he is introduced. I hope that he will do so and feel rewarded as a result. If he is deterred from further enquiry by what I have written I shall not have accomplished my own primary task.

I should like to thank Professor D. C. Hague and Professor T. Lupton, of the Manchester Business School, for their comments on a draft of the book which they read, and Mr A. I. Baker, of Baker Perkins Holdings Ltd, for information about the organizational history of his firm. I am also happy to acknowledge a debt of gratitude to my colleagues who gave their time to discuss problems with me and to read and criticize what I wrote, and especially to thank Mr H. K. Bevan, Mr R. J. Briston, Dr F. J. Bryant, Dr H. B. Miles, Mr R. J. Nicholson, Mr D. Rotheray and Mr J. C. Woodliffe for their help. Together they saved me from error in a number of places, and if errors remain they are mine alone. Lastly, I wish to record my thanks to Mrs Stella R. Geddes, who coped cheerfully and efficiently with all my imperfectly legible drafts and produced the final manuscript for the printer.

O.S.H.

University of Hull
July 1968

Contents

Contents

Acknowledgements

We are grateful to Tavistock Publications for permission to base figure 17, page 129, on figure 5 from Rice, *The Enterprise and Its Environment*, and to Heinemann Educational Books Ltd., for permission to base figures 21 and 22, page 135, on figures 1 and 2 from Brown and Jaques, *Glacier Project Papers*, Paper 8.

1

The business enterprise

1.1 The joint-stock company

The subject of this book is the business enterprise, which will be looked at mainly from an internal standpoint to see how it is organized and administered and what factors influence its operation as an efficient and progressive concern. But there are many forms of enterprise in Britain: economic activities are performed by sole traders, partnerships, cooperative societies, public corporations, municipal undertakings, statutory, chartered, and unlimited companies, companies limited by guarantee, and companies limited by shares. No less than ten different kinds of company can be formed under the Companies Acts 1948–67, although only a few of these are of much practical significance. Confronted with such variety there is a distinct advantage to be gained by taking one type of enterprise as a model for analytical purposes, and in a predominantly capitalist economy like our own the choice of such a representative business unit must inevitably be the joint-stock company, a company limited by shares.

The sole trader is typically precluded by financial or personal limitations from conducting his business on more than a modest scale, and partnerships generally are not well suited for many ventures where large amounts of capital are necessary or large risks are involved. Until recently banking partnerships were restricted to a maximum of ten members and other partnerships to twenty, but the Companies Act 1967 raised the limit for banking firms to twenty and removed it completely for firms of accountants, solicitors and members of a stock exchange. Nevertheless, because a partner is responsible to the whole extent of his personal fortune for the results of a partnership's actions this form of enterprise will probably continue to be confined to small numbers of people who can enjoy the fullest confidence in each other's integrity and skill. Before the introduction of limited liability the unincorporated company, which was a species of partnership, was sometimes formed to avoid the slow and costly process of obtaining a Royal Charter to trade, and some insurance companies retained their unincorporated status until quite recent times. None of these kinds of enterprise, however, was adequately equipped to sustain the increasingly large scale of operations demanded by changing technological and economic conditions, and it is clear that businesses would have been intolerably constrained in their attempts to raise capital and extend their activities if a more appropriate institution had not been devised.

The legal recognition of limited liability in 1855, after decades of controversy, marked the beginning of an era in which economic and social life has been transformed, for limited liability has made possible the growth of capitalist systems as we know them today. It is the foundation on which joint-stock companies have been built and expanded until they now play a major, if not a dominant, role in virtually every branch of industry, not only in Britain but in other countries throughout the world. The great importance of the joint-stock company can be agreed without accepting it as a perfect institution by any means. It is well known that limited liability has led to frequent abuse and that many of the problems created by private enterprise capitalism are among the most difficult and controversial ones to be solved. The outcome of the debate that capitalism has provoked is undeniably of concern to us all, but we shall not enlarge on the arguments for and against capitalism here. It is enough for our present purpose to show that corporations created to exploit the economic advantages of limited liability have such a widespread and preponderant importance that the joint-stock company is the natural choice as the model, or representative, business in our modern industrial state.

Companies are of prime importance because of the number of people they employ, the physical assets they own, the financial capital they command, the income they generate, and the volume of goods and services they produce. They have the power to affect our real standard of life and to alter the fabric of our existence by their efficiency in using scarce resources and their control over the rates of product and process innovation. And as we are to concentrate on the internal working of these companies it is also worth remembering that the administrative procedures and organizational structures which they have developed are similar in many respects to those of cooperative societies and public corporations, so that a great deal of what is learnt from a study of business administration in the company is applicable without much modification to these concerns as well.

Before going on to a more detailed consideration of the joint-stock company it is important to understand what limited liability means. A joint-stock trading company initially raises money, however small the amount, by the sale of shares and is authorized at any given time to obtain capital in this way up to a specified amount. There has been a movement lately in favour of the issue of shares with no par value, but the usual practice is still for shares to be given a nominal or par value, say of five shillings or one pound each, although they may be sold from the start at a premium and their subsequent price will almost certainly differ both from the par value and the price at which they were issued. If newly issued shares are sold at a fraction of their nominal value (which here does not mean at a discount) the capital is defined as partly paid up and the company has the right to call on shareholders for the balance of the nominal capital at a later time. It is much more common, however, for the share capital to be fully paid up at the outset, and when this is done anyone who buys X shares in a company with a par value of Y shillings each has a liability to that company which is limited to the nominal value of his shareholding, or X times Y shillings. No matter how great the indebtedness of the company he cannot be required to incur any further financial obligation to it himself. The shareholder in a company is always aware of the precise extent of his liability, and can make it theoretically as big or as small as he desires by varying the number of shares he holds. He can invest in one company or many and have a stake in enterprises in whose actual running he has no direct concern at all.

Public companies were originally the only ones to be limited by shares, but by 1908 it had come to be recognized that a number of the safeguards designed to protect investors in large companies were not needed when a company was small and operated as an essentially family concern, and the Companies Act of that year created a class of private companies, differentiated from public companies in three important respects. The maximum number of shareholders in a private company is fifty, excluding employees and former employees who became shareholders during the time of their employment; its shareholders have restricted freedom to dispose of their shares; and the company is not allowed to make a general offer of shares to the public. A public company, on the other hand, can have an indefinitely large number of shareholders; it can invite applications for newly issued shares by public advertisement; and its shares can be made freely negotiable on a stock exchange.

The idea that private companies could be identified with family businesses, implicit in the Act of 1908, became increasingly difficult to sustain when such companies were with growing frequency either bought up by, or formed as subsidiaries of, public companies. For this reason the Companies Act 1948 went a step further and created separate categories of exempt and non-exempt private companies to meet the changed state of affairs. The definition of an exempt private company was detailed and complicated and does not closely concern us here, but a major attraction of a company of this kind was its freedom from the obligation to file its accounts with the Registrar of Companies for public inspection. Many private companies constituted themselves as exempt corporations and at the end of 1965 71 per cent of registered private companies were of this class. But in 1967 the law was changed again: a new Companies Act stipulated that much fuller information about companies' affairs must be disclosed and the category of exempt private companies was abolished.

The company population is constantly changing as old companies cease trading and go into liquidation and new companies are formed. The aggregate of companies varies from year to year, but recent history shows some interesting trends. The number of registered public companies in Great Britain which were not in liquidation or in course of removal from the register fell from 17,125 in 1939 to 15,298 in 1965, while the number of private companies rose from 146,765 to 503,767. Not all of these companies were actually trading, however, and not all of them had issued paid up shares. The picture is significantly different if we take only those companies with a paid up share capital, about which there is comparable information for a slightly shorter term.

Table 1

Registered companies with paid up share capital (Great Britain)

As on Dec. 31	Public		Private	
	Number	*Paid up capital (£ m.)*	*Number*	*Paid up capital (£ m.)*
1939	13,920	4,117	146,735	1,923
1945	13,171	4,044	178,558	1,929
1950	11,920	3,898	235,307	2,198
1955	11,204	4,340	279,949	2,471
1960	10,806	4,726	363,663	2,659

(Source: Companies General Annual Reports for the years in question. H.M.S.O.)

There are several complementary explanations of the figures in Table 1. Most businesses start in a small way as unincorporated concerns and most of them stay so, but many of those that prosper find it necessary to change after a time from the unincorporated to the incorporated state and register as limited companies. The economic expansion after the Second World War and the fact that it was comparatively cheap and easy to form private companies provided a joint stimulus to the growth in their numbers, reinforced by the tax benefits which these companies enjoyed: even when the original members intended that a company should become public almost at once there were advantages in first registering it as a private concern. For the vast majority of private companies, though, the transition to public limited liability was either not feasible or not worthwhile and they continued to trade in their existing form.

The growth of the world economy, the expansion of international trade, and the development of new and highly capital-intensive methods of production have greatly increased the competitive strength of large scale enterprises, and many public companies have sought to grow quickly to consolidate their positions and to diversify their activities by acquiring, or merging with, others. The takeover and merger movement has not, of course, been confined to public companies, but it is their activities that have had the most striking effects on industrial organization and economic structure. This movement is the major reason, and the nationalization of industry is a subsidiary one, for the decline in the number of public companies and the increase in their size. The amount of paid up capital is an imperfect indication of size, but even so it is worth noticing that while the number of public companies with such a capital fell by 21·5 per cent between 1939 and 1960 the average capital per company rose by nearly a half. The public company's share capital in the latter year was, on average, sixty times larger than the private company's, whereas in 1939 it was only twenty-three times as great.

There is now such an immense difference between the very large joint-stock company and the very small that they seem hardly to belong to one genus, and this makes it extremely difficult in some respects to discuss 'the company' in generally applicable terms. The character of a large company is unlike that of a small in many ways, and the administrative and social problems arising in big units, and in the country as a result of their growth, are often different in both kind and degree from those of smaller concerns. We shall try to point out features of business administration that are common to all companies and features that are peculiar to some, but on the whole the discussion will be about medium and large sized companies rather than small. Business administration in these companies will be interpreted in a broad sense to cover a variety of aspects of organization, management and direction that are relevant to an understanding of the way a company operates, and of the reciprocal relations between its structure and methods of operation and the behaviour of the people it employs.

The main argument of what follows is that the company is a complex and many sided entity which cannot be properly understood without some knowledge of the theoretical and empirical content of a number of disciplines. If business administration can claim to be a subject in its own right it is as a synthetic subject founded on a multidisciplinary base, and one of the most vital factors in its development has been its increasing attraction to scholars in a large number of fields. The variety of different specialized talents brought to bear on the study of the business enterprise has grown steadily, and the benefit to the subject has been great, but as there is always a danger that too specialized an approach may lead to the formation of one sided impressions and biased judgments, it is most important to remember that from whichever disciplinary point of view the company is examined others, equally valid, exist. This book aims to provide a general introduction to business administration that places due emphasis on the many sidedness to which we have referred, but it is hoped that the reader will want to go on to read various discussions of a more specialized kind and that when he does so he will keep this caution in mind. To explore some of the current literature of business administration without remembering the essentially complementary nature of the contributions that have been made can sometimes lead one to believe that not a single animal, but a whole menagerie, is being considered, when this is not the case. As a means of illustrating this argument we shall devote the rest of the chapter to a series of short studies of the company, designed in the first place to convey some idea of the different

5

treatments to be found, and secondly to assemble enough information for us to draw a preliminary composite sketch of the company before we proceed to a more detailed investigation of its parts. The company will be looked at as a legal person, an economic unit, an example of formal organization, and an open system.

1.2 The company as a legal person

THEORIES OF CORPORATE PERSONALITY

All mature legal systems are characterized by the existence of a doctrine of corporate personality, although such a doctrine did not emerge clearly in England until the end of the nineteenth century, when the judgment in Salomon *v.* Salomon (1897) recognized the company as a legal person quite separate from the real persons responsible for its formation or occupied in the conduct of its affairs. The concept of corporate personality is important in a number of ways. The distinction made between a company and its shareholders, for example, means that the one may be solvent while the others are insolvent (and *vice versa*) and that people who form one company are free to form others if they choose. A company can lose its entire workforce and cease completely to trade, yet still survive as a legal entity. It is envisaged in legal theory as an incorporated group of persons associating under prescribed conditions to pursue a common object: it is a totality whose parts can change continually without affecting the continuity of the company itself.

As a legal person a company has certain rights, duties, privileges and powers, and can sue and be sued in its own name. The law endows it with a unique personality, but it remains an artificial creation which can only function if it has real persons to act for it and make decisions on its behalf. There has been considerable dispute about the true nature of corporate personality and several theories have sought to explain what it means. There is no need to discuss these theories at length, but a brief account of the more important ones will help to show the different ways in which corporate personality has been conceived. A long and interesting conflict can be traced between a tendency to philosophize on the subject and the practical demands for a clear definition and the improvement of the legal forms of business organization appropriate to changing economic and social conditions.

The Fiction Theory makes the proposition that the grant of legal personality to a company is a grant to an entity which has no mind or will of its own. The law imputes to a company a personality which is fictitious and determined solely by what the law prescribes: it is not a personality that enables a company to act wilfully or intentionally as real persons do. Since the company is endowed with personality by the law it has been argued that the company can only behave in lawful ways and cannot perform criminal acts in which a mental element is involved. The practical consequences of this doctrine would affront many reasonable people and, in Britain at least, it is clear that companies can not only do wrong, but be punished for doing so.

6

The Bracket Theory states that while human beings can have personal interests and individual rights a company can not: it is simply a legal device to enable certain complex relationships to be more easily defined and understood. When people form a company it is convenient to give them a collective identity and to enclose them, so to speak, in brackets to which a distinctive name is attached, but at any time it may be necessary to remove the brackets before the real position of the company can be known. While it is true that the veil of incorporation must often be lifted and the façade of the legal entity pierced in order to discover the true state of affairs, the full acceptance of the Bracket Theory would deny the feasibility and desirability of distinguishing between the rights, duties and assets of corporate entities whose creation is sanctioned by law and those of the persons who associate to create them. The conclusions that can be drawn from this theory have not commended themselves to British courts.

The Realist Theory is in direct contrast to the Fiction Theory, since it sees a company as an organism with a character and a spirit of its own, one part of the organism acting as the head, another as the trunk and others again as the limbs. It is argued that the reason we possess as individuals has its counterpart in the reason of an incorporated group and that the group also can have its own will, purpose and honour. But it has not been proved that the group has a unique mental unity outside the minds of its members, and if a company is compared with a human being, made the bearer of natural rights, and deemed to have a mind and will of its own, some strange results may follow. The Realist Theory suggests that it is morally wrong for one company to be used as the tool of another and this idea was indeed supported in Germany before the Second World War. It also suggests that a company should be treated with the same consideration as human beings and no more coerced or restrained than they, lest its dignity be injured or its freedom improperly curtailed. Presumably, companies should also be prevented from voluntary dissolution, since this would be tantamount to *felo de se*.

Some people have said that English law has been influenced more by one theory and some by another, while a different school has maintained that practical considerations have had the major influence on the courts' decisions. To an impartial observer it may appear that if any of these theories were to be inflexibly applied it would produce some nonsensical and harmful results. The implications of the Fiction Theory have certainly been rejected in one respect by making companies liable for the commission of certain acts, although there are obvious limitations to the kind of penalty that can be imposed on a company because of its nature as a legal person. It can be fined, its assets can be confiscated and it can be judicially 'killed' by depriving it of legal personality, but there are offences for which the penalty normally paid by a real person, such as imprisonment, would be inapplicable in the company's case. The general rule nevertheless seems to be that companies should be treated as real persons except when there are cogent reasons to the contrary. In deciding whether an offence has been committed by the company or by a person whom it employs, much depends on the nature of the act, the position of the employee, and other facts that are relevant to a particular case.

The endowment of a company with a unique legal personality raises the problem of the recognition of foreign companies, and theoretically it could be argued that a foreign company has no legal personality in England unless one is granted by English law, in which case the company would be two persons governed by two different legal systems. Common sense and convenience both require the personality of a foreign company to be recognized by our courts and that of a British company to be recognized similarly by courts in other lands. The residence of a company and its agents affects its treatment in different ways. For taxation purposes the English courts apply the Realist Theory and ask where the 'head and brains' of the company are situated, which is normally the place where the company is registered. In deciding whether a company has enemy character or not, however, it is the whereabouts of the actual controlling influence that matters and not the place of registration. A company is deemed to be domiciled in its place of birth and cannot move from its country of residence as a real person can, except by being dissolved and incorporated anew in another country as a different legal person. In this case, therefore, the Realist Theory obviously fails to apply.

Dicey asserted that 'whenever men act in concert for a common purpose, they tend to create a body which, from no fiction of law, but from the very nature of things, differs from the individuals of whom it is constituted'.[1] This is the case with companies, but in certain respects the difference between their personalities and those of their members derives from a fiction that creates one set of difficulties at the same time as it helps to overcome another. The separation of the legal person of the company from the real persons who form and operate it has led to anomalies that it is still not completely possible to avoid, and there is no simple formula for solving all the problems to which the concession of legal personality gives rise. None of the theories referred to is without weakness and none has been accepted fully in the development of English law. Our courts appear to have taken a generally pragmatic view of things and to have accepted that, while it is important for a group of people who form a company to enjoy reasonable freedom of action and have their just claims recognized, it is also necessary to acknowledge the fact that the granting of legal personality to the company may give rise to problems of an essentially economic and social kind. Their solution is not materially helped by the construction of legal theories based on questionable philosophical and psychological assumptions and divorced from the reality of the commercial environment to which they should apply.

The concept of legal personality is evolutionary, not static, and Paton submits that the tendency will be more and more to impute to the company itself the acts

[1] A. V. Dicey, *Law and Public Opinion in England,* 2nd edn., Macmillan, 1962, p. 154.

and mental conditions of the people who effectively control it.[1] In that case the question of who those people are becomes of fundamental importance and, unfortunately, it is not one to which an easy answer can be given. We shall try to provide an answer by stages in subsequent chapters, but some aspects of the matter will be touched on in a preliminary way towards the end of this section, after we have looked at some of the practical details of company formation under the present English law.

COMPANY FORMATION

A private company must have a minimum of two members, a public company seven, and each of the original members must agree to take at least one share in the company and subscribe his name to its memorandum of association, one of the essential documents called for at the time of incorporation. The memorandum regulates the company's dealings with the outside world and contains information which includes the company's name, the country in which its registered office is to be situated, the purpose(s) for which it has been formed, and the amount of its share capital in the different classes of shares that it is authorized to issue. The company's name must be approved by the Registrar of Companies at the Board of Trade and, apart from the fact that it has to end with the word limited, it must differ from the name of every other existing registered company. Care is called for in defining the company's objects, because in order to protect its investors and creditors it will be confined to what is stated in the memorandum: on this account it is usual to define the objects widely enough to embrace any of the anticipated things that the company may want to do. The memorandum of association can be altered subsequently in several important respects by the company, but to alter it might be troublesome if there were dissident shareholders, and a group of members with a sufficiently large combined shareholding could conceivably offer enough resistance for a court to set the alteration aside. The memorandum provides the company with its basic constitution and on it depend the company's powers and duties as a legal person.

The next essential document sets out the articles of association, which constitute a contract between the company and its shareholders and regulate the legal basis of the company's administration, so far as this is capable of being determined by the company itself. The Companies Act 1948 provides a model for the articles of association in Table A which applies automatically if articles are not registered, or to the extent that it has been neither modified nor expressly excluded. The matters dealt with by the articles are both varied and wide, and include such things as the voting rights of members, the powers of directors, the appointment and removal of directors, borrowing powers, and restrictions on share dealings. The articles are for

[1] G. W. Paton, *A Text-Book of Jurisprudence*, 3rd edn., ed. D. P. Derham, Oxford University Press, 1964. See Chapter 16 for a fuller discussion of the concept of legal personality.

9

the most part capable of being amended by the company itself, in ways which either the articles or the Companies Act 1948 prescribe.

In addition to these documents the company's promoters will also be required to produce a statement of nominal capital, a declaration of compliance to show that the statutory requirements of incorporation have been met, a notice of situation of registered office, and particulars of the company's directors and secretary. All these documents are submitted for examination to the Registrar of Companies, and so long as they are in order, and the company's objects are lawful, the certificate of registration will be issued on payment of the appropriate fee. From that time the company's existence as a corporate body begins.

Once its life has started the supreme organ of the company is the general meeting of its shareholders, but because it is often impractical for shareholders to deal with the day-to-day business of a company, or even to exercise a moderately regular oversight of its affairs, it is the common practice for a general meeting to use its legal authority to give the directors wide powers to act on its behalf. This is the first stage in an extensive process of delegation in the company, for the board of directors in turn may authorize one or more of its number to act in its name, and there is a further widespread delegation of authority to people below board level, which in many cases gives them considerable power. It is this dispersion of the power to make important decisions that has complicated the question of company control and led in some people's view to a state of affairs in which the law fails to conform to the facts of business life.

To describe a company as an association of members in pursuit of a common object can, it is said, be misleading in several ways. A sole trader can convert his business into a private limited company simply by bringing in another person as the necessary second member. That person may take no part in the affairs of the company and derive no personal benefit from his membership. Is such a company really an association of the kind envisaged in legal theory? At the opposite pole stand the vast, heterogeneous enterprises whose names are household words, whose shareholders are numbered in tens of thousands and whose membership is continually changing. In what practical sense can the individual shareholder in such a company be regarded as associating with all the other shareholders in running it, or in determining its objectives and the way they are achieved? The shareholders are treated in law as the controlling members of a company, while managers and workpeople are not members if they hold no shares: their relationship to the company is one of servant to master and this situation is criticized by those who see the employees' claims, and their interest in the company, as being more important than the shareholders' in many respects.

The members' power to dispose of a company without reference to the welfare of its employees is a major example of their ability to take action fraught with social implications, but this is something which company law has failed so far to take into account. This is a matter which can fairly be said to concern laymen as well as lawyers, and for other reasons also the outcome of the controversy about the nature of legal personality and the appropriateness of the current doctrine of association is of interest to others besides the legal theorist. The relevance of these issues to business administration lies in the fact that conclusions drawn from theoretical arguments may have important practical effects on the formulation and application of company law. A company is a legal creation working within limits which are partly determined by law. It is accountable to the law in a variety of ways, and changes in the legal conception of the company may have far-reaching consequences for the forms of business organization and the legally sanctioned behaviour of business concerns. For these reasons an appreciation of the legal aspects of the company and the substance of the legal debate is necessary for anyone who wishes to take a comprehensive view of this particular enterprise.

1.3 The firm as an economic unit

One of the pillars of economic analysis is the theory of value, which deals with the pricing of goods and services and of the factors used in their production–land, capital and labour, including managerial and organizing ability of all kinds. In an elementary form the theory shows how the interaction of demand and supply tends to create equilibrium positions in the different factor and product markets. When a market is in stable equilibrium price is at its long-run normal level and, so long as neither demand nor supply conditions change, any attempt to alter the established price/quantity relationship brings forces into play to preserve the equilibrium state.

The general theory of value explains certain aspects of macro-economic systems, such as national and regional economies, and a separate, but related, theory has been developed for the micro-analysis of the individual enterprise. This is known as the theory of the firm. 'Firm' does not convey the same meaning to the economist as it does to the lawyer, to whom it denotes a partnership; neither does it have the specific meaning of a company, although in the remainder of this book we shall use the words company, firm, business, enterprise and concern synonymously, for the sake of variety. The firm in the theory of the firm has no precise legal or organizational significance: it is an abstraction, an idealized business form, a rational but bloodless entity which exists for the purely economic purpose of satisfying a want by providing a good or service at a price. This firm is assumed to operate in a given environment and normally makes only one product. The dominant, indeed the sole, motive guiding its operations from the theoretical point of view is the desire to maximize profit, or minimize loss. It is taken to have full knowledge of its costs of production and to differentiate between particular categories of fixed and variable costs on the basis of their relevance to pricing decisions in the long and the short run. It is also assumed to know the critical portion of the demand schedule for its product, which shows the prices that consumers are ready to pay for different quantities of the good.

The firm can be regarded as a transformation unit which takes economic inputs and transforms them into economic outputs of a higher value. The desire to obtain the greatest profit leads the firm to seek the combination of inputs which will produce a given output at the lowest unit cost – the least-cost combination of productive factor units – and when this combination is found economic efficiency is maximized as well as profit. Profit, however, is a function of unit price and unit cost, and the relationship of both to the level of output has to be considered. In deciding whether to raise or lower the price of its product the firm is assumed to calculate the net increase or decrease in revenue associated with a small change in the quantity sold, and to compare this with the associated increase or decrease in costs. If revenue rises and costs fall the projected price change is clearly desirable. If both costs and revenue rise the change is desirable so long as the increase in revenue exceeds the increase in costs. And if costs and revenue both fall the change is still desirable if the decrease in revenue is less than the decrease in costs. This is a cumbersome way of stating the rules for price determination, but by using the calculus and thinking in terms of very small increments or decrements of price, cost and output, it is possible to see that a firm maximizes its profit by producing a certain output at which, in the economist's jargon, marginal cost and marginal revenue are equal. That output is the equilibrium output of the firm.

The economic theory of the firm, of which this is necessarily a skeletal account, is expounded by different economists in different ways, and several variants are to be found in the standard textbooks of the subject. The theory has been exposed to considerable criticism, but despite this, and the lack of unanimity on its content, it retains a central place in orthodox economic doctrine. If it were to be cast out it would leave a void which no alternative theory can at present satisfactorily fill, and it continues to appeal to many people on this score and on two other important counts as well. These are, first, that the theory is susceptible of very sophisticated treatment while also being suitable for presentation in a basically simple, yet logically satisfying, way; and, second, that given the assumptions on which it rests the theory is a tool for predicting the precise outcome of a particular course of action in specified conditions, which makes it attractive to those who assert that economics is a positive science.

In the early stages of its development the theory was restricted to a description of a perfectly competitive market in which no enterprise was sufficiently important to exercise a unilateral influence on the market price. This, in many cases, unrealistic assumption was subsequently made only as a starting point for analysis and the theory was enlarged to cover a wide variety of market conditions, including imperfect competition, in which elements of competition and partial monopoly are intermixed, and oligopoly, a prevalent condition of many industrial markets dominated by a few large concerns. The assumption of a single product is still retained for analytical simplicity, but it is not a severe limitation and product pricing in more complex models of multiproduct firms is also explicable in terms of the current theory.

The assumption of profit maximization, which is fundamental to the economic theory of the firm, is notoriously controversial and it would indeed be hard to argue convincingly that it is a valid one to make in the case of every real firm. Businessmen are undoubtedly motivated by other considerations, some of which are neutral in their effect on profit while others may actually weaken the profit drive, and the expected consequences of business behaviour which are weighed when pricing decisions are made are not all measurable in money terms. But if the concept of profit maximization is abandoned the situation becomes indeterminate and the predictive value of the theory is lost. It has become fashionable in some quarters to talk not of maximum profit but of satisfactory profit, and to substitute for the profit maximizer the (ugly word) 'satisficer', who is prepared to accept something less than the greatest possible financial returns. But whereas maximum profit can have an unequivocal meaning in a specified situation a satisfactory profit means different things to different people. 'Satisficing' is therefore incompatible with the normative theory of the firm as it now stands.

Leaving this matter aside, however, serious problems arise where the definition and measurement of profit are concerned. Should the profit that is maximized be gross or net? and if it is net what are the proper cost deductions to be made from revenue and what items of income should be added to sales receipts before a balance is struck? Should profit be measured as a lump sum, or expressed as a rate of return on the firm's turnover, its share capital, or the value of the assets it employs? If there is a conflict between profit maximization in the short and the long run how is it reconciled or a choice between them made? Does profit maximization have any significance except from a long-term point of view and how long is the long term taken to be? These are only some of the questions that bedevil the discussion of profits and there is no wholly satisfactory solution to the numerous difficulties that are raised. Profit maximization, which looks such a straightforward idea at first sight, becomes increasingly complicated the more closely it is examined.

It has sometimes been assumed that all rational decisions in the theoretical firm would conduce to profit maximization irrespective of their makers, but that in so far as there was one decision maker *par excellence* he was the entrepreneur, the source of organizing ability and innovating power, a member of a group which was sufficiently important to be identified by some theorists as a factor of production in its own right – organization, or enterprise – to which profit accrued as a distributive share in the way that wages accrued to labour, interest to capital, and rent to land. This simplified view of the firm has also been criticized for its failure to reflect reality. One sees that in many businesses there is no single entrepreneur, no single owner, who decides what to produce, what price to set and where to sell: neither is there one person to whom the profit goes as the uniquely earned fruit of his endeavours. Decision making appears as a shared process in which directors, chief executives, and managers at various levels all play a part, and in which committees and meetings have an increasingly important role. When profit is allocated the claims of shareholders and employees have to be weighed against the claims of the firm as a productive entity with an appetite for money to finance innovation and growth.

The list of things which could be taken into account when decisions are made, other than their anticipated effect on profit, is a long one which includes the desire to discourage competition, or government or trade union interference; the need to preserve the consumers' and suppliers' goodwill; the wish to improve working conditions; and the desire to command a certain share of the market, maintain a certain degree of liquidity, or keep control in the same hands. The urge to make a profit may be tempered by a liking for leisure, a perfectionist attitude towards production, or a desire to win social approval in various ways that are not consistent with pure profit maximization. To say this is not, of course, to deny the need to make a profit of some kind: this a firm must do, or soon cease to exist. In the last analysis decisions about prices, production and marketing methods, the recruitment of personnel, and so forth, must be made with profit in mind. In a money economy profit provides the principal test of a firm's performance and a standard for comparing one firm's achievement with another's. But all firms do not necessarily strive to maximize profit *ex ante* and can certainly not expect always to have maximized it when measured *ex post*.

The marginal analysis of price/output equilibrium positions has been objected to on the ground that it fails to explain either how firms actually behave in fixing prices or how they could act if they wished to obtain the greatest profit. Businessmen, it is argued, do not think in terms of marginal cost and revenue and could not give them precise values if they did. The economist translates cost and revenue schedules into smoothly continuous curves in his diagrams, whereas the real firm would have curves which were stepped, broken, and generally irregular in shape. The calculation of marginal revenue is made difficult by the firm's ignorance of the way in which the demand for its product fluctuates and by the fact that identical units of output may be sold to different buyers at different prices. Even in a firm making homogeneous goods the concept of marginal revenue is not easy to grasp, and still less is it so where output is made up of different products, completed and sold at varying intervals of time.

The difficulty of measuring marginal revenue is matched by the difficulty of measuring marginal cost. Modern accounting techniques make it possible to get a very accurate idea of the cost of an individual unit of output, but the calculation is dependent on the use of conventions and as these differ so may results. In any case, the economist and the accountant do not think of costs in an identical way. The economist emphasizes the consequences of choosing one course of action rather than another, and thinks of the true cost of a scarce resource devoted to a particular use as what is foregone by not using it in the most remunerative alternative way; in other words its opportunity cost. The conventional accountant, however, is primarily concerned with the measurement and recovery of historical costs, which are completely different from opportunity costs. The theoretical separation of costs into fixed and variable elements is inadequate to cover all varieties of cost in real life, because some costs are hybrid while others are attributable to more than one activity in a firm, and both affect marginal cost calculations when they are allocated in what may be an unavoidably arbitrary way. From different standpoints it is possible to have different views about which cost elements should properly be included in marginal cost and which should not.

If firms behaved in practice as the theory of the firm either implies that they should or says that they do, one would expect the forces of competition to reduce any marked differences in efficiency as firms strive to obtain the highest profit. Yet one of the salient features of economic systems is the tendency for these differences to persist. Another striking feature is the apparently unlimited propensity to grow which some firms exhibit, a propensity which the traditional theory of the firm is unable to explain. Indeed, the theory seems to postulate a limit to efficient growth due to the deleterious effect on profit of rising unit cost, falling unit price, or both. This may be true of the single-product firm, but a multiproduct firm is not similarly restricted, as Edith Penrose has persuasively argued in *The Theory of the Growth of the Firm*. The enterprise making many goods has potentially unlimited flexibility, for as the possibilities of one market are exhausted those of another can be explored. A company of this kind can branch out continuously into new fields by changing its product range and exploiting fresh opportunities to grow. It does not have to wait on fortune to present them; they can be systematically and continuously sought. Growth is a source of prestige and a means of satisfying managerial ambitions, and the increases in the firm's income which it generates provide the financial fuel for still more investment and growth in progressively rising sequence.

The criticisms to which the theory of the firm is open have led some economists of an empirical turn of mind to try to find out how prices are fixed in practice. They have made various discoveries, like that of the 'cost plus' method by which a conventional margin is added to prime (variable) costs of production to cover overheads and provide a profit, and on that count they claim to have found sufficient evidence to disprove the idea of profit maximization as a universal business goal. Their efforts have stimulated a vigorous defence of marginal analysis by other economists, and businessmen have also joined in the debate, some siding with the anti-marginalists and some maintaining that they really do operate in the way the textbooks describe.

The theory of the firm has not been attacked on economic grounds alone: it has also been accused of deficiencies shown up by developments in organizational, psychological, and sociological knowledge which have a direct bearing on our

15

understanding of the behaviour of actual concerns. When an economist looks at a firm he naturally sees it primarily as an economic unit and is interested in the efficiency with which it uses scarce resources to achieve economic ends. He can show why it is important that the least-cost and profit maximization criteria should be applied when decisions are made, and why, if these criteria are modified or rejected, the probable effect of doing so should be consciously assessed. It is impossible for most firms to ignore the economic consequences of their behaviour beyond fairly close limits, and so far as the improvement of our material standard of life is concerned it is undesirable that they should.

It is important to see the established theory of the firm in the context of a broader theory of value, and to appreciate that so long as the theory of the firm is used to explain the economic implications of using scarce resources in one way or for one purpose, as opposed to another, it is a valuable analytical tool. One can perfectly well argue that firms *should* maximize profit, if not that they actually try to do so in all cases in real life, or that they always act in a consistent way. There has been, however, a growing recognition of the fact that, in several respects, a business theory which is based on the assumption of profit maximization is unrealistic and incomplete, and whether or not the present theory of the firm continues to be used to explain the significance of different patterns of resource allocation there is no doubt that some other theory will find growing favour as time goes by. This new theory will almost certainly be more comprehensive than the old, and considerably influenced by the fruits of research into the nature of business operations that has now been undertaken for some time. An indication of the probable theoretical shape of things to come has already been given by more than one writer, but most of all, one suspects, by R. M. Cyert and J. G. March in *A Behavioral Theory of the Firm*, which appeared in 1963.

In this book the authors argue that a theory which takes the firm as the basic unit for analysis and purports to predict the firm's behaviour with respect to price determination, the selection of output volume, and the organization of the productive resources at its command must explicitly emphasize and satisfactorily explain the process of decision making within the firm. Cyert and March maintain that the idea of a universal profit maximization goal is untenable and that it is necessary to consider the complex organizational strategies which enable different and partially conflicting goals to be pursued, either simultaneously or in sequence, by individual managers, and by managerial coalitions which at the top of the company often act in the capacity that earlier theory ascribed to the entrepreneur. The refinement of a generally acceptable behavioural theory on these lines depends, among other things, on the development of satisfactory theories of expectations, choice, goal setting and control, and a great deal of work on these is now being done. Some of the main ideas of Cyert and March will be considered elsewhere in this book, especially in Chapter 9 where the process of decision making is discussed at greater length.

1.4 The company as a formal organization

SOCIOLOGY AND ORGANIZATION

Formal organizations are created to serve a variety of purposes and meet a variety of needs, and appreciable efforts have been devoted to classifying organizations and analysing their characteristics in the attempt to construct a comparative theory of organizations in the modern state. Much of this work has been done by sociologists, who have made valuable contributions to organizational studies, and two examples of their work have been taken here to give an indication of the methods used and the difficulties to which general classifications give rise.

The classification of organizations has been undertaken in a number of ways, one of the most common being classification by major purpose. This has led, for instance, to distinctions being made between religious organizations (e.g. churches), associative organizations (e.g. clubs), protective organizations (e.g. fire brigades), military organizations (e.g. armies), educational organizations (e.g. echools) and economic organizations (e.g. firms). P. M. Blau and W. R. Scott (*Formal Organizations*) have suggested an alternative classification based on the definition of principal beneficiaries, and they distinguish four types of organization on this basis. These are: (1) mutual benefit organizations, which are those like trade unions, political parties and professional groups, whose main beneficiaries are their own members; (2) business concerns (economic organizations), which are assumed to operate primarily for the benefit of their owners; (3) service organizations, which are defined as those whose principal beneficiaries are sections of the public in direct contact with the organizations, people on and with whom the organizations' members work – welfare agencies, charitable societies, hospitals and schools come into this category; and (4) commonweal organizations, which are those designed to benefit the public at large and include certain government departments, the armed forces and the police. The four types are not mutually exclusive and some organizations have a dual aspect: a university, for instance, is a service organization in one respect (teaching) and a commonweal organization in another (undertaking pure and applied research). The major problems associated with each type of organization are identified and this process leads to such conclusions as that, whereas in a voluntary mutual benefit organization with inherently democratic characteristics one of the main difficulties may be to secure an adequate degree of control over the members, the economic organization is likely to encounter its greatest problem in attaining a sufficiently high level of efficiency to ensure survival and growth in a competitive environment. However, it, too, will have problems to solve in devising appropriate methods of control over the resources at its command, including control over the employees.

Another basis for classification has been proposed by A. Etzioni in a book titled *A Comparative Analysis of Complex Organizations*. Etzioni makes use of a variable termed compliance, which he holds to be a major factor in the relationship between someone with power and someone affected by it. Compliance has both an inter-actional and a psychological component, because not only does power held by one person affect another's behaviour, but it also forces the other person to orient himself in a particular way towards the individual wielding the power. Power manifests itself in three different forms, coercive, remunerative and normative, which tend to be related in a systematic way to three types of involvement in different organizational contexts, these types being the alienative, the calculative and the moral. Etzioni argues that there is typically a close connexion between coercive power and alienative involvement in 'total' organizations like prisons; between normative power and moral involvement in organizations like churches and universities; and between remunerative power and calculative involvement in business firms. The associations between types of power and involvement are further related to differences in basic organizational goals; respectively order goals, cultural goals and economic goals in the cases of the three classes of organization that have just been defined.

It is difficult to devise a wholly satisfactory, comprehensive classification as these examples show, and in considering the company as a formal organization a number of qualifications have to be made where Blau and Scott's and Etzioni's analyses are concerned. The idea that the principal beneficiaries of a company are the owners is more likely to be true in the case of small firms than of large, and in the latter the legal owners (the shareholders) are often liable to find themselves denied the financial rewards which they had expected, either because of managerial ineptitude or because the divorce of ownership from effective control gives managerial groups the power to regulate the company quite as much to their own advantage as to the shareholders', a matter that we shall return to particularly in Chapters 2 and 3. Again, the company is assumed to wield a predominantly remunerative power over its employees, but it is important to remember that other kinds of power or authority are exercised also to ensure that people in a company behave in organizationally desirable ways, and it is apparent that in many cases both coercive and normative powers are used to produce the required results.

Remunerative power can be defined in a broader sense than the one that is literally implied, namely the power to offer a money reward, for a company rewards its employees not only by paying them salaries, wages and bonuses, but also by giving them status, prestige, political influence, satisfaction in work, pleasure in social relationships and opportunities for self-development. In so far as these non-financial rewards are not equally shared between the participants it is necessary to think of remunerative power as it affects one person (say a research scientist) as something different from the power that influences another person (say a temporary clerk). These matters are very relevant to the theory of motivation and an understanding of the human side of enterprise. By the same token the strength of the calculative involvement in the business organization varies from one individual to another, and some people undoubtedly feel moral or alienative involvement in different degrees. The goals of the company are taken to be primarily economic, but although this is something on which everyone would probably agree it should not be forgotten that other goals, cultural for example, can also be pursued by the firm, or that some goals, such as the desire to achieve a good standing in the community or a good record of fair dealings with employees, are not definable in purely economic terms.

Many other variables besides compliance are pertinent to the analysis of organizations, especially in the case of companies. Recent research has shown the importance of technology as an influence on organizational structure and processes, and for many years we have been increasingly aware of the effects on people's behaviour in organizations of the values, attitudes and aspirations which they bring into their firms, and of the actual pattern of formal organizational relationships which they are expected to maintain in their places of work. The bases on which formal structures are created, the ways in which responsibilities are determined and shared, the methods by which goals are decided and the means of their achievement controlled, the extent to which an organization is either flexible or adaptable, or rigid and resistant to change, all these are variable in greater or lesser degree and all need to be taken into account where the company is concerned. We shall consider these matters in greater detail as we proceed, and especially in Chapters 6 and 7 where Max Weber's concept of bureaucracy is introduced and the contributions of other sociologists like T. Burns and Joan Woodward are discussed.

SOCIAL PSYCHOLOGY AND ORGANIZATION

One of the most interesting and potentially influential analyses of organizations has been made by D. Katz and R. L. Kahn in *The Social Psychology of Organizations*, published in 1965. Katz and Kahn point out the danger of oversimplifying the analytical process by defining organizational types based on the presence or absence of a single characteristic, and suggest that it is possible to conceive of an indefinitely large number of typologies of this kind. They argue that particular characteristics vary in their importance for an understanding of organizations and that more than one of them must certainly be taken into account in every case. They also maintain that characteristics frequently have dimensions, so that an organization may exhibit more or less of a characteristic rather than all or none, and they themselves prefer to think of an organization, or one of its parts, as being high up or low down with respect to any one of its significant functional and structural dimensions. The basis of Katz and Kahn's own typology of organizations is a distinction between 'first order factors', which describe an organization's 'genotypic function', and 'second order factors' related to the first.

The genotypic function of an organization is its major activity as an institution within the framework of a larger society, or in the language of systems theory its primary task as a system in relation to its environment. Four broad classes of organization can be envisaged, with some differentiation of subsidiary types within each, in the following manner: (1) productive or economic organizations concerned with the creation of wealth; (2) maintenance organizations engaged in the socialization of people destined to occupy roles in other organizations; (3) adaptive organizations concerned with theoretical developments and the enlargement of knowledge; and (4) managerial or political organizations responsible for the work of adjudication, or for the coordination and control of people, physical resources and other organizations. An organization is normally specialized, but it may still contribute in fields other than the major one in which it is engaged, and organizations are interdependent, supplementing their own activities by drawing on each other's output as the need occurs.

The four basic functions can be further distinguished at the level of the individual organization, and the activities of people in a company can be thought of as taking place within productive, maintenance, adaptive and managerial substructures or subsystems. Activities concerned mainly with the handling, shaping, etc. of physical objects constitute the productive subsystem; those concerned with shaping the behaviour and attitudes of other people to ensure their participation in the firm's work belong to the maintenance subsystem; those related to the exercise of authority and to tasks of coordination and control are managerial activities; and those directed towards the solution of problems are adaptive. It will be noticed that productive has a more restricted meaning when applied to the subsystem than it has when used to describe a system. To an economist, at least, any activity for whose performance someone is prepared to make a payment is productive, and in that sense every employee of a company is a productive member of it, although in Katz and Kahn's terminology some of the employees only will play a part in the productive subsystem as they define it.

Once an organization has been identified by its genotypic function it can be described in more detail by examining its second order features. There may be many of these that deserve attention, each with its own dimension, but Katz and Kahn confine themselves to the consideration of four. These are the nature of the organization's workflow (with special reference to the distinction between organizations that process people and those that process physical products); the methods used to maintain a satisfactory input of human resources; the structure of authority and formally established relationships; and the type of equilibrium that the organization is able to achieve.

Every organization depends for survival on the involvement of people, on their commitment to it, and must find appropriate ways of holding them in its service. Many complex organizations rely on the operation of an 'instrumental cycle' of money payments made for work which produces an income from which another set of payments can be made for more work, and so on in a self-perpetuating sequence. The reward for work here is essentially extrinsic and must be enough to compensate, in the economist's language, for the marginal disutility of effort. It is also common, however, for an organization like the enterprise to combine the instrumental cycle with an 'expressive cycle' in which intrinsic rewards are enjoyed from the performance of work itself. The importance of the expressive cycle derives partly from the recognized motivational inadequacy of the instrumental cycle, and partly from a growing belief that more should be done to make work a socially and psychologically satisfying experience as well as the means of meeting economic needs. Behaviour in an organization is affected by three things in the main: the requirements of the tasks to be carried out, the enforcement of rules, and the pattern of shared values and expectations of the members. The offer of adequate extrinsic rewards is necessary to make people accept task requirements and submit to rules, but the intrinsic rewards have an increasingly important part to play the more fully basic economic needs are met. The theory of human relations has been much concerned with the limitations of a purely instrumental cycle and we shall examine these in more detail in Chapter 13, where the human problems of organization and some of the ways of dealing with them are separately discussed.

The structure of an organization can be studied in terms of its degree of openness, or exposure to environmental forces; its degree of elaboration; and the characteristics of its hierarchy, especially the ways in which the allocation of rewards to people at different levels and in different kinds of role is controlled. The less open an organization is the more stable and tightly structured it can be, and the more highly differentiated it becomes from other organizations the more elaborate and specialized is the structure it is likely to develop. The tendency to structural elaboration increases the more effectively the principle of the maximization of energic return is applied; in other words, the more successful the efforts to obtain a favourable ratio of inputs of energy to energy expended in the performance of organizational work the more elaborate is the organizational structure likely to be. The pursuit of efficiency, of a high productivity of resources, calls for considerable internal specialization of work (division of labour) and leads the organization to create increasingly complex and sensitive mechanisms for coordination and control, for planning and innovation, and for collecting, processing and transmitting information about the environment, the company as a whole, and the performance of its component parts.

Blau and Scott, it will be remembered, thought that the achievement of a satisfactory level of efficiency was the economic organization's major problem, but Katz and Kahn see it as the handling of human resources and their adaptation to the dominant needs of mechanization and the demands of the technological process, with the instrumental cycle playing a central part in reconciling people to the performance of what are sometimes highly uncongenial tasks. In its dealings with other firms an enterprise is assumed to prefer competition to conflict, and to seek to regulate the environment to its own advantage where possible by such means as product improvement and marketing campaigns, rather than by interfering directly in the affairs of other concerns or bringing force to bear on them by political methods or pressure-group tactics. Competition allows independent organizations to pursue what may be identical ends along parallel courses and avoid head-on conflict, but groups of firms may also take joint action to control their environment by regulating competition in a variety of tacitly or overtly agreed ways within the limits of the law. The degree of competition and the forms that competition take both influence the rate and nature of internal organizational development, and organizational structures must be adaptable in the face of environmental change if viability is to be ensured.

1.5 The enterprise as a system

An important development for the study of business organizations during the past twenty years has been the emergence of general systems theory, and the creation of an analytical framework within which a wide variety of different phenomena can be investigated and the behaviour of many apparently disparate entities logically related and explained. Systems theory in its existing form originated in the late 1940s when a group of scientists at Chicago University began to discuss the possibility of developing a general theory of behaviour capable of empirical proof. The disciplines represented by the participants ranged from economics to psychiatry, from history to mathematical biology, and it was essential to find a ground on which people working in such diverse academic fields could usefully meet. They eventually agreed that by thinking in terms of 'open systems' they could relate many of the concepts, the objects of interest and the investigatory techniques of their various disciplines in a potentially valuable way.

An open system may be generally defined as a conceptual or physical entity, or bounded region in space-time, consisting of functionally related, interacting or interdependent parts, with exchanges of energy between these parts and between the system and its environment. The universe can be visualized as a super system containing an infinitely large number of open systems of varying complexity, duration and size – such systems as molecules and cells, individual human beings and small groups, nations, and the solar system. The firm is one kind of open system, complex and humanly contrived to fulfil particular purposes and satisfy particular needs. Like other complex open systems it has subsystems of various kinds, and both systems and subsystems can be analysed in terms of the import, conversion and export processes on which they are fundamentally dependent for survival. The treatment of the firm as an open system undoubtedly promises to be of increasing value, but it is still in a comparatively early stage of development and more work has to be done before a satisfactory all-embracing systems theory of business is complete.

The use of systems theory in the study of the enterprise is complicated in at least three ways. Firstly, the question of where precisely to draw the theoretical boundary line that separates a firm as a unique entity from its environment admits of more than one answer. Secondly, a firm can be defined in different senses and envisaged as several different kinds of system, rather than simply as one. And thirdly, there is at present no general agreement about the number, nature and extent of the various subsystems that may be found within a firm: the basis on which subsystems are identified and defined appears to some extent to be a matter of personal choice.

We have seen that a company can exist as a legal person without trading at all, but as an active concern it is more usually visualized as a collection of assets (land, buildings, machinery, stocks, cash etc.) and a body of employees who use those assets and perform a variety of activities directed towards the achievement of specified company goals. A somewhat less orthodox view of the firm has been put forward by Chester Barnard, in *Organization and Management* and elsewhere, who maintains that any business is always more than a closed group of producers and must comprehend not only the acts of its employees, but also those of many people outside it who contribute to the fulfilment of its purpose. A single activity often forms part of several conventionally separate systems, and its true importance can then only be appreciated by knowing something of all the systems of which it is a part. In the ultimate sense a company is composed of cooperative acts whose number and nature constantly change, and there is inevitably some arbitrariness involved in labelling different aggregates of these acts as company A or company B. Any company remains the company it is not merely because it owns certain assets and employs certain people, but because its shareholders, directors, managers and workers cooperate with each other and with suppliers, distributors, consumers, bankers, trade union officials, civil servants, and many others besides, to form an intricate, variable pattern of interrelated activities which sustain the company's life.

This view of the enterprise undoubtedly stresses its open character and complexity, but probably to the extent of making it too amorphous for analysis at an elementary level. We shall regard our own model as bounded more narrowly and conventionally than Barnard suggests, and confine our discussion mainly to the shareholders, directors, managers and workpeople of the firm. Without a shareholder a joint-stock company cannot exist, and share ownership gives the investor legal rights in the company which may include the right to exercise some control over its affairs: but shareholders who are not employed by a company whose shares they buy can be envisaged as standing outside the system except when they take part in general meetings. Part-time directors are similarly occupants of marginal and occasional system roles, although their work can be of great value to a business as we shall see. The boundary of the system to be investigated here thus encloses, for most practical purposes, the full-time employees of a company only (and those who are regularly employed in a part-time capacity in operative positions). Other people can be thought of as attaching themselves to, and detaching themselves from, the system at different and irregularly spaced points in time.

The definition of a system's boundary makes it possible to classify system activities in three broad categories, in a manner suggested by A. K. Rice.[1] Activities which result in something being brought into a system from its environment are *import activities;* those which result in something being sent into the environment are *export activities;* and those which take place within the system itself and result in no transaction with the environment are *conversion activities.* The operations of every open system can be seen as a sequence or flow of import-conversion-export activities, and the efficiency of a system's work can be assessed by measuring the ratio of suitable values of exports to imports. The import-conversion-export flow can be studied at various levels and in various ways where a company is concerned, but in all cases in terms of its appropriateness to the achievement of the system's basic purpose or primary task. The more specific is the primary task the greater are the constraints under which a system operates, but the easier it is as a rule, relatively speaking, to design a system suitable for the efficient accomplishment of the task. If the primary task is not clearly defined, or not uniformly accepted or understood, or if there are joint primary tasks which conflict, the difficulties of operating a system efficiently tend to increase. The fundamental reciprocal relationship between an open system and its environment must always be remembered. The system's transactions with its environment vary with the type of work it performs, the resources it needs, and the state of the environment itself. Changes in the environment react on the system and may cause it, too, to change, but so may autonomous system behaviour alter the condition of the environment.

A joint-stock company imports finances which it uses to acquire human and material resources: together they are used in conversion processes that produce goods or services whose sale (export) generates an income for the firm. Some of this is used to maintain the flow of factor imports; some is exported as dividends, interest payments and taxes; some is needed to make good the wear and tear on the system; some may be stored in cash reserves; and some used to enable the system to grow. Different parts of the company can be studied in terms of the same import-conversion-export flow. A purchasing department, for example, could then be seen as buying (importing) materials and components, 'converting' them by grading, separating, examining, labelling and storing them ready for use, and finally exporting them to other departments in the firm. A research and development department, on the other hand, could be thought of as importing certain kinds of information, problems and ideas, which are subjected to conversion processes of analysis and scientific testing that result in the export of solutions to problems, or in new products and processes of value to the firm.

[1]A. K. Rice, *The Enterprise and its Environment,* Tavistock Publications, 1963; E. J. Miller and A. K. Rice, *Systems of Organization,* Tavistock Publications, 1967.

The import, conversion and export activities of different systems are not necessarily of the same kinds, or of equal number, difficulty, or importance in their claims on resources, but they must all be performed if a system is to live. Since every system except the greatest is part of another system the classification of any particular activity varies with the system level, and it follows that what is classed as a conversion activity when we look at a company as a system complete in itself may also be seen as an import, conversion, or export activity of one of its subsystems.

There are various ways of distinguishing the subsystems of an enterprise, one of which would obviously be to differentiate separate import, conversion and export subsystems, and the managerial subsystem which binds them together and regulates their work. Very simple firms, however, may have only partially differentiated operating subsystems and a single manager in charge, whereas large complex companies contain several operating systems with a number of subsystems in each. Johnson, Kast and Rosenzweig state that six key subsystems in every business are: (1) a decision making subsystem to produce plans and shape the activities of the enterprise as a whole; (2) a processing subsystem which imports information, materials and energy and converts them into saleable products; (3) an information handling subsystem specially concerned with the use of accounting data; (4) a control subsystem to ensure that major tasks are performed in accordance with plans; (5) a memory subsystem to store information and make it accessible when required; and (6) a sensory subsystem to measure significant changes in both the system and its environment.[1] Briggs also thinks in terms of sensing, information processing, and control subsystems or components, although his engineering approach to systems analysis leads him to define their work somewhat differently from Johnson and his colleagues. He also distinguishes an encoding subsystem, which converts information inputs into language intelligible to other parts of the system, and a maintenance subsystem performing a wide range of activities, from simple machine adjustments and repairs to the replacement of major physical system elements.[2]

Katz and Kahn offer yet another way of distinguishing subsystems, as we have already seen. They suggest that activities can be grouped into a production (or technical) subsystem; a managerial subsystem; a supportive subsystem, which undertakes import and export transactions with the environment; a maintenance subsystem concerned with the recruitment, training and indoctrination of employees; and an adaptive subsystem, which includes such activities as scientific and market research and economic intelligence, devoted to protecting and enhancing the company's position in face of environmental change.

[1] R. A. Johnson, F. E. Kast and J. E. Rosenzweig, 'Systems Theory and Management' in *Management and Organizational Behavior Theories*, ed. W. T. Greenwood, South- estern Publishing Company, 1965.

[2] G. E. Briggs, 'Engineering Systems Approaches to Organization' in *New Perspectives in Organization Research*, eds. W. W. Cooper, H. J. Leavitt and M. W. Shelly II, Wiley, 1964.

These three sets of subsystems cover a wide, but not exhaustive, range of system activities and there are obvious similarities between them, despite the fact that in some cases the same term (e.g. maintenance subsystem) is used in more than one sense. For certain purposes any one of these classifications would be useful, but it would also be helpful at times to think more conventionally of a company's departments and sections as separate subsystems, with additional managerial, planning, and control subsystems operating at different levels and cutting across their boundaries. It is possible in addition to think of all the formally created subgroups of employees, each with its own manager or leader, as an orderly pattern of subsystems linked together to form the unified system of the firm.

A company can often be looked at as a technological system with important characteristics of plant layout, equipment design, process integration and material flows. Indeed, in some enterprises, like steel works, vehicle assembly plants and oil refineries, the technological features are so dominant that they have an immediate and powerful effect on the mind. But whereas the technological component varies from one company to another, and is of relatively minor importance in some firms, every company has a social system which is of more uniform importance, although this is not necessarily so evident to someone from outside the firm. It was the research work of Elton Mayo and his colleagues at the Hawthorne (Chicago) plant of the Western Electric Company in the 1920s and early 1930s that led to the widespread recognition of companies as social organizations. Mayo's team actually set out to study the effects on workpeople's behaviour of changes in such physical variables as lighting, humidity and temperature, but they discovered some striking and unexpected differences between the ways in which these things were altered and the ways in which workgroups responded to the change. The researchers decided that strong social forces were at work, sufficiently powerful in certain cases to override the effects of changed working conditions, and concluded that the composition of primary workgroups and their treatment by superiors were factors of basic importance to the satisfaction derived from work and to the harmony and efficiency with which operations were performed. The seeds that Mayo sowed flowered into an extensive body of theories of human relations in industry, concerned with psychological motivation and patterns of individual behaviour at work, as well as with group attitudes and behaviour and their influence on the employees of a firm.

The technological component unquestionably puts a major limitation on the type of social system that exists in a company and on the satisfaction that people can derive from their jobs. The machinery and materials used, the kinds of skill and experience required, and the location of the plant all have a profound influence on the internal conditions of an enterprise. The idea of 'technological determinism', that technological demands impose unavoidable constraints on the pattern of activities, is widely held and in particular instances may be true, but in complex systems there is often an important element of choice in the shaping of organizational work structures, especially new ones, which affects the type of social system that can develop. The view of the company as a *socio-technical system* has influenced business studies increasingly during the past twenty years, and the work of Emery and Trist provides a good example of the insight gained by analysing the connexion between technological and social systems, and of the practical significance of organizational design.[1]

Their study of operations in the British coal mining industry, in a period of mechanization after the industry was nationalized in 1947, revealed the different effects of the composite and conventional long wall mining systems. In the composite system the basic tasks of cutting coal, loading it, carrying it from the coalface, and preparing for new cuts by fixing roof supports and extending the conveyor were all performed by small self-contained groups, while in the conventional system there was elaborate division of labour within workgroups and between shifts, which narrowed the task requirements of each miner and gave each shift only one part of the complete cycle of activities to perform. The superiority of the composite over the conventional system was evident in a number of ways. The former system was associated with a greater average amount of coal won from a daily cut, lower demands on supplementary labour resources, a much longer period without loss of a production cycle, and reduced absenteeism from all causes.

The main reason for this superiority was that miners in the composite groups developed close working relationships and a sense of mutual dependence, and each man was able to practise a variety of skills. Furthermore, the groups enjoyed a large measure of autonomy and self-supervision, instead of being closely controlled from above. Emery and Trist stressed the fact that their findings did not suggest that group autonomy should always be maximized, or that it was generally possible or desirable to minimize differentiation between tasks, but they did suggest that there was a strong case for examining different ways of organizing work in order to find the optimum fit between the technological and social systems. If satisfaction can be increased without loss of economic efficiency it benefits the people concerned, but there is a distinct probability that the discovery of the optimum fit will increase both social satisfaction and total system efficiency, to the advantage of employees and company alike.

In addition to this view of the company as a socio-technical system it is possible to see it as system of communications and information flows, and as a system for making and implementing decisions. It is also both a political and a status system. The political system embraces different interest groups of shareholders, directors, managers and workers which exert pressure on each other and often make conflicting demands. Individuals behave in political ways to promote personal ends, and compete for positions of power in which influential decisions can be made and

[1] F. E. Emery and E. L. Trist, 'Socio-Technical Systems' in *Management Sciences*, **2**, Pergamon Press, 1960.

control exercised over the activities of the firm. The satisfaction derived from work is to some extent positively correlated with status and the prestige conferred by the performance of certain kinds of work. A firm has one well-defined order of status related to the formal hierarchy and other status systems associated with its informal organization. Changes in formal organization, size and technology disrupt established status patterns, affect people's behaviour and create tensions that did not previously exist. The 'identification of one's own relative status, the appreciation of changes in status, and the definition of differences become, at times, of paramount importance' to the employees of a firm.[1]

Systems theory stresses the dynamic character of business enterprise, the interdependence of activities and the effects of different patterns of activity cycles. It treats the enterprise as a living organism with biological characteristics of adaptability and growth, and directs attention to the crucial relationships between the enterprise and its environment, and to the importance of different kinds of boundary control. It suggests that there is a tendency towards the establishment of fixed relations between the parts of a system, and the preservation of a steady state despite constant changes in the elements composing the system and the environment in which it works. The ability of open systems to resist and withstand change is essential to their survival, but it raises the question of when and in what conditions resistance becomes too great. Selective resistance is necessary to forces that threaten to damage or destroy the system, but blind resistance to changes that fundamentally affect the system's imports, the efficiency of its conversion processes, or the environment's ability to absorb its exports leads, ultimately, to failure to accomplish the system's primary task. There is no unique relationship of imports to exports, and the basic purpose of a system can be fulfilled in a variety of ways. The application of systems theory can help to clarify the definition of the primary task, identify the activities required for its completion, reveal the extent of organizational choice in ordering relationships between system components, and explain the dynamics of the environment and their effect on the system's capacity to work efficiently and attain its objectives.

1.6 The enterprise: a composite view

We have covered in this chapter a large amount of varied and possibly difficult ground in an unavoidably cursory way, and considered a number of ideas about the enterprise, some of a highly speculative and controversial kind. There were two reasons for doing this: first, to show in what different, but equally valid, lights the business concern can be studied and in what different guises it can be seen; second,

[1] T. Burns, 'Research and Development in the Firm', *Journal of the British Institute of Management*, I, no. 3, 1958, 187.

to provide enough material to enable a satisfactory composite picture of our model company to be drawn as a prelude to its more detailed investigation.

We see the joint-stock company as a legal creation designed to fulfil an essentially economic purpose, but with clearly marked technological, organizational and social characteristics of its own. In common with other persons and institutions in our society a company is affected by several branches of the law, but company law itself has a special bearing on the way this particular enterprise can act. Company law determines the process by which it is born, and defines the legal rights, duties and powers of its members, and of the directors whom they may appoint to act in their interests and as agents of the company. In certain important respects, therefore, company law establishes the formal basis of relationships between these two groups and affects the way in which control at the highest levels of a company is exercised and shared.

Many shareholders are prevented for various reasons from direct participation in the affairs of their companies, and this is one explanation of their need to delegate authority to others to work on their behalf. But even when shareholders choose to be engaged in running a company they find in most cases that the size and complexity of the task to be done obliges them to obtain assistance, and in appointing people to work with them they are again required to delegate authority and responsibility for the performance of subordinate jobs. The way in which the total task of a company is divided between its employees helps to give the company its unique organizational character, visible in part as an ordered pattern of interdependent positions and activities associated with them. When work is broken down in this way, and subsidiary tasks are grouped into organizational subsystems, the whole set of operations has to be controlled and coordinated according to an agreed plan in order to keep the system functioning in a balanced and efficient way.

An important aspect of the authority ascribed to each position in a company is the power to make decisions, and the organizational structure of the company is a major determinant of the distribution of decision-making power. Companies can be thought of as administratively more centralized when this power is concentrated in the upper levels, and more decentralized when it is shared in a wider fashion between people at all levels. It is necessary to examine the process by which decisions are made, the ways in which information is communicated and problems are solved, and the effect of different degrees of centralization on the behaviour of the managerial subsystem and the performance of the firm.

A company must provide sufficient incentives for people to work for it, supply it, and buy the goods or services it produces. Its employees are assumed to be primarily influenced by extrinsic (mainly monetary) rewards, but modern theories of motivation stress the variety and strength of non-monetary (intrinsic) rewards that a company can offer, and we must consider their nature and distribution within the firm.

29

Every company is essentially a creature of its environment, in which it lives and grows by virtue of its ability to perform repeated cycles of import-conversion-export activities. It is an open, but not a completely open, in the sense of exposed or defence-less, system. The degree of openness, or permeability of the system boundary, varies from one company to another, but some part of the energy expended by the enterprise is typically devoted to withstanding the pressures of external change and enabling the system to be adapted to change in ways chosen by the company rather than dictated by the force of uncontrollable events. Any study of the company must take some account of factors that influence the rigidity or flexibility of the system, since they are clearly relevant to its capacity to survive.

In this study of business administration the main subjects for consideration will be the division of a large and complex task into many subsidiary elements whose arrangement gives a company a distinctive organizational structure; the attributes of different kinds of organizational structure; the nature and extent of the authority wielded by different individuals and groups within an enterprise; and the human problems created by the demands of organizational work.

The next four chapters (2 to 5) deal with the work and influence of shareholders, directors, managers and foremen, all of whom exercise some kind of formal control over the actions of people in the company. Chapters 6 to 8 are concerned with various aspects of organizational structure, the definition and grouping of activities, structural types, organizational adaptability, organizational shape and principles of organizational design. In the five chapters that follow (9 to 13) we look in more detail at certain major features of business administration that will have been touched on in different places already. These features include the delegation of authority and the degree of centralization of decision-making power; the decision-making system; the effects of dividing managerial responsibility between 'line' managers and 'staff'; the importance of planning and control; the part played by committees and meetings; and the human problems that arise in a company and ways in which they might be alleviated or solved. Throughout the book we shall try to assess the extent of agreement or disagreement that exists about the various matters discussed, and in the process we shall consider a number of theories of organization and business behaviour, some of which have already been mentioned above. In the final chapter we shall draw the strands of the preceding argument together, review the main developments in organization theory that have influenced, or seem likely to influence, our understanding of the company and the behaviour of the people working in it, and reassess the nature of the enterprise that we have studied.

By dealing with these subjects in this order there is always a danger (probably unavoidable whatever method was used) that they may appear at times to be unconnected with each other, instead of being very closely interrelated as in fact they are. It is important always to remember that we are examining different facets of one thing, the company. Certain key words will appear repeatedly in different contexts – words like authority, control, coordination, decision making, delegation, organization, motivation and planning – and we shall try to show the relationship of these things to each other. Above all we shall try to show, also, their relationship to efficient business performance, because that is our fundamental theme.

2

Shareholders

2.1 Introduction

A joint-stock company is authorized to raise money by the sale of shares in the company to people who become its members. They buy shares in the expectation of income from dividends or interest payments, appreciation in the value of their holdings if the company prospers, and the return of at least part of their invested capital should the firm be wound up. A member's shareholding may also entitle him to attend and vote at the company's general meetings and take part in the government of its affairs. The nineteenth century view was that the shareholders in general meeting *were* the company and, although that view is no longer acceptable, the general meeting remains in law the supreme organ of the company and its ultimate source of control. The nature of many shareholding groups, however, makes them incapable of dealing regularly, quickly, or even at all with business affairs, and it is fundamental to the efficiency and continuity of the great majority of companies that the general meeting should be able to delegate some of its powers to the board of directors and make it responsible for a variety of important work. The division of power between the general meeting and the board means that for certain purposes either group may be thought of as the company, although as an identifiable legal person the company always remains separate from both. In the study of business administration it is necessary to ask how closely the conduct of company affairs at the highest levels conforms to theoretical possibilities and in what ways it differs. We need to consider the actual nature of the control exercised in modern companies, and the real effectiveness of the shareholders' role compared with what is often held up as the ideal, in order to understand what is happening and judge what improvement, if any, might be made in the shareholders' position.

Shares fall into two main groups, ordinary and preference shares, and each group can be subdivided into a potentially large number of classes, but in practice most small and medium sized companies issue no more than two or three classes and even very large concerns do not usually issue more than six classes of shares. Taking companies as a whole one finds a considerable variety of shares, however, including ordinary shares, preferred, deferred and non-voting ordinary shares, participating and non-participating preference shares, preference shares in classes ranked first, second and third, and cumulative, non-cumulative, redeemable and non-redeemable preference shares. A company can also issue loan stock (debentures), often secured by a charge on its property, carrying a guarantee of fixed interest payments and repayment at some specified future time of the capital sum borrowed. Several alternatives may therefore be open to a business which wants to obtain funds by selling securities. It can issue ordinary shares on which it pays a variable dividend out of profits; preference shares with a fixed rate of interest; preference shares whose yield combines a fixed interest element and a share of the profits; debentures; or some combination of securities in these four broad categories. The choice at any time is influenced by circumstances peculiar to a given company and the effects of economic and political conditions on the capital market, but as every company must issue at least one ordinary share it follows that an initial issue confined to shares of a single class must be of ordinary shares. Each limited company has an equity share capital, or equity for short, which is defined as its total issued share capital excluding the part(s) with no right to participate beyond a certain stated amount in the distribution of capital or income. In other words the equity consists solely of ordinary shares, or of ordinary and participating preference shares, and these are the major kinds of share that can be expected *prima facie* to carry voting rights.

2.2 Company meetings

An incorporated business is required to call an annual general meeting of shareholders once in each calendar year and must not allow more than fifteen months to elapse between one such meeting and the next. Extraordinary general meetings may also be called, and together with the annual meetings they provide opportunities for members to meet the directors and question them about company affairs. The ordinary business of annual general meetings conforms to a uniform pattern and typically covers the election of directors, the consideration of financial statements (a balance sheet and a profit and loss account), the ratification of dividends, and the appointment and remuneration of auditors. Business which does not fall under these headings is frequently termed special business and special, as well as extraordinary, business provides grounds for calling an extraordinary meeting whenever the directors consider it necessary. They are expected to give the shareholders enough information about the business to be transacted for them to decide whether or not they need attend, and the full terms of special or extraordinary resolutions must be sent to the members in advance. A company can also be required to convene an extraordinary meeting by its shareholders, the condition being that those members who demand the meeting shall hold not less than one-tenth of the paid up capital to which voting rights are attached.

Company meetings are attended not only by members, but also by people who act as members' proxies without necessarily being members themselves. It is common practice for the directors to offer to act as proxies and to obtain enough of the votes of absent shareholders to enable the board to carry any motion that it wants to have passed. A proxy must attend in person, but the way he votes may be left to his discretion or dictated by the member whom he represents. Proxy forms issued to members of a company with shares quoted on the London Stock Exchange must allow members to show whether they support or oppose the various proposals to be put to the meeting. The legal quorum for company meetings is modest indeed. Only two members of a private, and three of a public, company need be present at the start of a meeting for the valid transaction of business, and the Jenkins Committee recommended that the number should be two for all companies.[1] This minimum number can be increased by the articles of association, which also specify the classes of shares whose owners are eligible to vote.

Ordinary resolutions are passed by a simple majority, but special and extraordinary resolutions require a three-quarters majority (seventy-five in a hundred) of the voting members. A count is usually taken in the first place of a show of hands, allowing one vote for each member present irrespective of the number of shares he holds, and there is no legal obligation for proxy votes to be included when this is done. The normal run of business is despatched quickly and easily on a show of hands and it is not common for a poll to be held, except when special or extraordinary resolutions are being put to the vote. These are more likely to be controversial, or far-reaching in their implications, and something more representative of the voting strength of the members than a show of hands may then be demanded. A poll enables anyone who votes, whether in person or by proxy, to cast the full number of votes that his shareholding gives him, so that a member with 10,000 shares, for example, carries twenty times the weight of a member with 500 shares of the same class. If a motion put by the directors is defeated on a show of hands the chairman of the meeting can call for a poll, which means in effect that the board always has two chances of making its wishes prevail. A poll can also be demanded by any five members, or by a group of members holding not less than one-tenth of the voting shares. The first condition has prompted the suggestion that any member who feels that he may at some time want to demand a poll, and who cannot be sure of getting enough support to comply with the second, should take the precaution of splitting part of his shareholding between at least four nominees who can be relied upon to attend meetings with him and vote as he directs.

To restate what has just been said, each resolution at a general meeting must be passed by an appropriate majority of the company's members, or of the votes of those members, who are entitled to vote and who either go to the meeting or appoint proxies to attend and vote in their place. Many members do neither of these things

[1] *Report of the Company Law Committee*, Cmnd. 1749, H.M.S.O., 1962, para. 468(c).

and the number actually present at a meeting is often no more than a minute fraction of those eligible to attend. Time and time again company business is disposed of by sparse gatherings, and resolutions are approved by groups of members who together may own a comparatively small proportion of the voting shares. When this happens, for whatever reason, a company is being governed on the basis of effective minority control.

Shareholders' apathy to the transaction of formal business has come to be accepted as an inescapable and virtually universal fact of business life. Some companies have taken advantage of this attitude and have even used stratagems to prevent the few actively interested members from taking part in the discussion of company affairs. Their actions have helped to stimulate the efforts of energetic crusaders like Lewis Gilbert and Mrs Soss in the U.S.A., and the members of protesting groups in Italy, West Germany and South Africa, who have tried to increase shareholders' awareness of matters affecting their interests and make companies provide more information and better facilities for shareholders to go to meetings in reasonable numbers if they wish. Gilbert himself is said to have attended 3,000 general meetings and to have asked 15,000 questions, but there are not likely to be many shareholders as indefatigable as that.[1] Among British investors 'the spirit of faction', as Adam Smith called it, has not been strong and there has been no comparable militant movement for the reform of conditions here, where in any case the abuses against which Gilbert and his supporters campaigned have not been so marked.

.The great majority of company meetings are notable only for their almost unvarying adherence to an uninspiring order of business designed to ensure compliance with certain legal requirements of an incorporated concern. Of the small number of people who attend general meetings fewer still take an active part in affairs, and there has to be grave disquiet about a company's actions or prospects before shareholders make a serious effort to exercise their powers. The scanty attendance at company meetings may be deplored as depressing proof that members are supine and careless of their own interests in failing to use their voices and their votes, or hailed as evidence both of shareholders' confidence in the directors' ability to run their companies satisfactorily and of the general vindication of that confidence by results. Both reactions can be seen as partial reflections of the truth.

The fact that a general meeting is often little more than a formality should not obscure its legal importance or lead us to overlook the powers which it cannot delegate to any other person or group. Only a general meeting can change the articles and memorandum of association; sanction a change of capital; appoint directors and remove them from office, if necessary before their terms of office have expired; and resolve that a company be wound up. The significance of these powers is not to be disparaged and the formal authority of shareholders to make the final

[1] A. Rubner, *The Ensnared Shareholder*, Macmillan, 1965, p. 121.

35

decisions about a number of very important matters is clear. But the widespread failure of members to exercise control when they might do so means that the practical government of company affairs often departs considerably from the process that pure theory describes, and it is illusory in many cases to suppose that shareholders as a body have effective authority over the administration of an enterprise. On the other hand, individual shareholders and small shareholding groups may have a decisive influence on business behaviour, and to see why this is so we must look more closely at the forms that company control can take.

2.3 Aspects of company control

The word control is used in various contexts in the discussion of business administration and it is important to remember that at this stage we are concerned only with a power to exercise control which is derived from the ownership of shares. The diffusion of authority and influence in modern business means that many people who are not shareholders have control over employees and assets in a company by virtue of position, personality, knowledge, or some kind of skill. Managers exercise control over subordinates, but so do workers' groups control the actions of their own members. An outstanding feature of business organization in recent years has been the rapid increase in the number, complexity, and extent of their application, of procedures to control activities and processes of all kinds. We shall be looking at other manifestations of control in later chapters and, indeed, control of one sort or another is a subject to which we shall return often throughout the book.

LEGAL CONTROL

A company is legally controlled by any member or section of the members commanding a majority of the votes exercisable at a general meeting. In many small private companies legal control is held by one person, who may be regarded as the entrepreneur, or by a few people who are the proprietors or descendants of the proprietors of the original business from which a joint-stock company evolved. It becomes more difficult for an individual or small group to retain legal control as a company grows if it increases its share capital appreciably, and especially if it makes a public issue of voting shares. In cases where one member legally controls a medium sized or large company it is probable that the member is another company.

The capital structure of a business has a bearing on the way in which the power to control it is either concentrated or dispersed among the members. Concentration of power tends to be greater in a company with a high capital gearing than in one whose gearing is low, and greater still if high capital gearing is reinforced by high vote gearing. Capital gearing can be measured in various ways, using either the capital structure or the profits of the company as the basis for measurement. From the structural point of view the most satisfactory way of determining capital gearing is to use the formula

$$\frac{\text{market value of fixed-interest securities}}{\text{market value of ordinary shares} + \text{fixed-interest securities}}.$$

This tells us that a company which issues no security whose interest constitutes a prior charge on income has a capital gearing of zero, whereas a company whose capital is raised entirely by the sale of fixed-interest securities has a gearing ratio of 1:1. In practice, of course, gearing can never equal unity because of the obligation to issue at least one ordinary share. A weakness of this formula is that it does not allow for all possible fixed-interest commitments, such as mortgages and bank loans, and to that extent may give a false picture of the true capital gearing. But none of the formulae that could be used is without some weakness, and for our present purposes the qualifications are not of much practical importance.

The concept of vote gearing is complicated by the fact that some shares carry restricted voting rights and by the position of debenture holders, who are not members of a company and cannot therefore vote on special or extraordinary resolutions, although they may have considerable influence in other ways. In this analysis it seems appropriate to ignore these complications and define vote gearing simply as the ratio of the total number of issued shares to the number with unrestricted voting rights.

Let us now imagine that a company has an issued share and loan capital whose market value is £300,000, made up of £100,000 each of ordinary shares, preference shares and debentures. The capital gearing of the company is 0·66:1, and if the numbers of ordinary and preference shares were equal, and votes were given only to holders of ordinary shares, the vote gearing would be 2:1. The concentration of voting power decreases when vote gearing, as measured here, is reduced. If all the preference shareholders, for example, had votes the vote gearing would fall to 1:1 and, conversely, if the ordinary shares consisted of equal numbers of voting and non-voting shares the vote gearing would rise to 4:1 and the concentration of voting power would obviously increase.

The number of non-voting shares issued has risen since 1945 and firms of very different sizes have successfully offered these shares to the public. Their ability to do so has been greater when the supply of attractive securities was low in relation to the demand for them, and there have been frequent occasions when a shortage of stock has made investors eager to get a stake in a prosperous company, with or without the corresponding right to vote at its meetings. *The Economist* examined the position of ninety-one large industrial companies on 30 September 1955 and found that the nominal value of their non-voting shares (£69·7 m.) was well in excess of the nominal value of their voting shares (£45·4 m.). The current market values showed an even greater divergence, since they stood at £345 m. and £175·1 m. respectively. The concentration of voting strength varied from company to company: in J. Lyons & Co. Ltd, for example, the ratio of the nominal value of all ordinary shares to voting shares was approximately 7·5:1 and in Marks and Spencer Ltd it was 15:1.[1]

For some years the latter company provided a striking illustration of the way in which voting power can be concentrated in a large firm by means of a high vote gearing. According to the *Stock Exchange Official Year Book* 1965 the issued capital of the firm was £55·1 m., consisting of £1·35 m. preference shares in two classes, £0·6 m. ordinary shares and £53·1 m. 'A' ordinary shares. Preference shareholders had one vote per share which could be used only when their dividends were six months or more in arrears, when a resolution to reduce the capital or wind up the company was before a meeting, or when a proposal was made to alter the articles in

Table 2

Company	Nominal Capital (£ m.)		
	Issued	Ordinary	Non-voting ordinary
Associated Television	9·30	0·15	9·15
Montague Burton	20·91	2·23	15·68
Decca	4·99	1·75	2·45
Express Dairy	14·64	0·20	12·73
Great Universal Stores	50·70	1·36	38·32
J. Lyons	17·56	0·40	8·93
Rank Organisation	26·59	3·79	10·20
Thorn Electrical Industries	7·39	3·50	3·43

(Source: Stock Exchange Official Year Book 1966)

any way that was likely to affect the preference shareholders' rights. For normal purposes voting was confined to the ordinary shareholders who were given one vote for every two shares held. Their nominal £600,000 of ordinary stock thus gave them control over a total nominal capital more than ninety times as great. The holders of 'A' ordinary shares were enfranchised in 1966, but *The Financial Times* (4 February 1966) observed that before this happened the number of voting shares constituted only 1·1 per cent of the equity. Some examples of companies which continued to have a high vote gearing are given in Table 2. In some of these companies the preference shareholders had restricted voting rights and in some the shares in other classes carried votes, but the importance of non-voting shares in the issued capital is none the less plain.

The implications of the issue of shares with restricted or no voting rights were considered by the Jenkins Committee. In their favour it was argued that their

[1] *The Economist*, 14 April 1956, **CLXXIX**, 167–68.

prohibition would conflict with the freedom of contract, eliminate a useful method of meeting the demands of death duties, prevent new funds from being raised without a change in company control, increase the difficulties of making a capital adjustment by an exchange of shares between amalgamating firms, and narrow the investor's choice by denying him the possible alternative of a cheaper non-voting share to a more expensive one with voting rights. The main argument on the other side of the case was that the issue of non-voting shares contravened the doctrine 'that where the risk lies, there the control lies also – a proposition so important that it may almost be described as Capitalism's Golden Rule'.[1] There was the danger, also, that voting minorities in companies with non-voting shares might foist bad directors and managers on a majority of members who would have no alternative to an expensive court action if they wished to obtain redress. The same voting minority could, if it wanted, arrange for the disposal of the whole or the greater part of a firm's assets and the majority would be unable to prevent it. The Jenkins Committee finally decided that to prohibit the issue of non-voting shares would be too drastic an act, but three of its members wrote a note of dissent in which they argued that, except when the Board of Trade said otherwise, the quotation of shares with restricted or no voting rights should be prohibited, and recommended that all equity shareholders should be entitled to attend and speak at general meetings or appoint proxies to do so on their behalf.

Two more aspects of legal control are worth mentioning, one of them relatively unimportant so far as business administration in Britain is concerned, the other of much greater importance from the point of view of economic organization as well as a company's capital structure. Control may be exercised by a voting agreement or a voting trust, both of which are more common in the U.S.A. than they are here. An agreement between certain members to vote in the same way on some or all of the matters which are in the shareholders' power to decide may give them legal control of a company, but such an agreement needs to be formally set out in specific terms to be effective for any length of time and cover all relevant foreseeable contingencies. If it is not practicable or desirable for a formal agreement to be made an informal arrangement may be made instead, control being exercised on the basis of a gentle-man's understanding between the people concerned. A voting trust is created when the voting rights attached to a company's shares are settled upon trust and the trustees are given 'a joint irrevocable proxy with general or restricted powers' to vote at company meetings.[2] When a majority of the equity is settled in this way the trustees necessarily have legal control of the company.

The Companies Act 1948 defines a company as a subsidiary of another when the

[1] D. H. Robertson, *The Control of Industry*, Revised edition, Cambridge University Press, 1946, p. 89.
[2] M. A. Pickering, 'Shareholders' Voting Rights and Company Control', *Law Quarterly Review*, **81**, 1965, 248–75.

latter, the holding company, controls the composition of the board of the former or owns more than half its equity share capital, and in British industry the scope given to companies to control other companies in this way is of great practical importance. The holding company system enables chains of subsidiaries to be built up and large blocks of assets to be controlled by the owners of shareholdings which are relatively small in size. Legal control can equally well be exercised by two or more companies which together hold a majority of the equity in a jointly owned subsidiary, and circular control arrangements can be worked out between three or more companies linked by reciprocal shareholdings of appropriate size. For example, if each of three companies *A*, *B* and *C* holds fractionally more than 25 per cent of the voting shares in each of the other two, *A* and *B* together control *C*, *A* and *C* control *B*, and *B* and *C* control *A*.

EFFECTIVE CONTROL

It is quite possible for one member or a small group of members to exercise effective control while owning less than the number of shares necessary for legal control, and a minority whose position is not legally unassailable can often act for long periods as though to all intents and purposes it were. It must be remembered, however, that *de facto* control, unlike control *de jure*, can be wrested from one minority by another. In some companies a single member controls its affairs by virtue of his personality, knowledge, patently superior abilities, or long association with the firm; in others, effective minority control is exercised by members who form a small cohesive bloc and act according to mutually agreed plans. The significance of the power of these minority blocs was analysed by L. S. Penrose in a paper published in 1946.[1]

Penrose's argument related primarily to the voting behaviour of a political electorate, but it can also be applied in a modified form to the voting of shareholders in a company. The power of an individual vote was stated to be inversely proportional to the square root of the number of people comprising the voting population, each person having one vote, and some examples were given to show how minority groups of different sizes might expect to get their way in varying proportions of the number of issues voted on, assuming that the majority of people were indifferent and voted in a random manner. One resolute member could expect to get his way in 75 per cent of cases if he were one of a group of three in which the other two members voted at random; a resolute bloc of three could expect the same degree of success in a group of twenty-three; and twenty-three people acting as a resolute bloc could exercise a comparable influence in a group of a thousand. The associations between size of bloc, size of indifferent population and probability of success are shown in Table 3, which reproduces part of a table in Penrose's article.

[1] L. S. Penrose, 'The Elementary Statistics of Majority Voting', *Journal of the Royal Statistica Society*, **CIX**, Part I, 1946, 53–57.

Table 3

Size of indifferent population	Proportion of decisions controlled by a resolute bloc		
	84·1%	97·7%	99·9%
	Size of bloc		
25	5	10	15
100	10	20	30
10,000	100	200	300

Unlike parliamentary voters most shareholders have more than one vote and the influence exercised by a members' bloc is affected not only by the size of the bloc in relation to the total number of shareholders with votes and the indifference or random behaviour of the majority, but also by inequalities in the distribution of voting shares which mean that blocs of the same size may command shareholdings of widely different amounts. The more biased the share distribution the more likely it is, of course, that legal control will be in a minority's hands, but the power of small groups generally is enhanced when they consist of large shareholders rather than small. Given the size of its combined shareholding the effectiveness of a bloc increases with the ease of communication between its members and the extent to which their interests coincide. The most effective bloc is probably one consisting of directors with significantly large shareholdings in a company, and the smaller the company the stronger does such a bloc tend to be.

The statistical theory of the power of resolute blocs is clearly relevant to an analysis of company control. Coupled with an appreciation of the importance of a bloc's composition, and the aggregate number of shares in its members' hands, it reinforces the expectation that the habitual indifference of the majority of shareholders and the small individual proportions of voting capital that they own will make it relatively easy for small groups, particularly of directors, but sometimes of non-directors too, to sway events on many occasions and exercise the real control over company affairs, even in those cases where the law formally attributes power to the company's members as a whole.

2.4 The nature of shareholders' powers

Directors act as agents of a company with authority delegated to them by the general meeting and make many important decisions affecting the shareholders' interests: if their interests are adversely affected or threatened by what the directors have done or plan to do the shareholders have remedies that can be applied to protect their position. Their power to appoint directors and remove them from office gives the shareholders what appears to be one of their most important weapons, since it would follow that if shareholders are dissatisfied with the existing directors they can dismiss them and elect others in their place. We need to consider how effective in practice the exercise of this power is likely to be.

When a new company is formed the names of its first directors are stated by the subscribers to the memorandum of association or published in the articles. At the end of the first year all the directors offer their resignation and, although they may be returned to office *en masse*, the appointment of each director is then, and from then on, contingent on the confirmation of a general meeting. In established companies the usual procedure is for a proportion of the board members, conventionally those with the longest service, to retire annually, although any director can be declared in the articles a director for life and retiring directors are normally eligible for re-election. A board may be authorized by the company's articles to add to its number and to fill casual vacancies as they occur, the latter provision being a sound one because it enables a board to avoid even temporary loss of effectiveness due to a reduction in its strength. Whenever an additional appointment or an emergency replacement is made it must be approved by the next general meeting.

A shareholder can nominate a director by depositing a signed statement to that effect at the company's office not less than three, nor more than twenty-one days before a general meeting. If no such nomination is received the only people eligible for election are the retiring directors or other persons nominated by the board. The indications are that in public companies it is unusual for any but the large shareholders, institutional or private, to nominate directors and even they do so infrequently. This means that, given the small average size and wide dispersion of shareholdings, the lack of contact between members and their general uninterest in the details of company affairs, most nominations are made by existing directors. They can secure the election of their chosen associates with the ready acquiescence of the members actually present at a meeting or, if necessary, by command of the proxy votes, and most companies have almost entirely self-appointed and self-perpetuating boards. While there has been no indication of a widespread desire on the shareholders' part to march directors out of office their power to remove them was increased by the provisions of section 184 of the Companies Act 1948, which made it possible for the first time for directors (except certain directors for life) to be dismissed by an ordinary resolution of a general meeting. Section 184 naturally contains safeguards to prevent a director from being dismissed on a snap vote, in that special notice of the proposal to remove him must be sent to all members before the meeting and he must be given an opportunity to state his case. A director who is removed from office can claim compensation for wrongful dismissal if he proves that there has been a breach of either a formal or an informal contract of service with the company which entitled him to hold office for a specified length of time, or to be given a reasonable or minimum notice of dismissal which was not in fact given.

It has become increasingly common for executive directors (directors of a company who also hold managerial positions in that company) to sign service contracts which give them security of office for a limited period, often five or seven years, and guarantee their remuneration during that time. These contracts can be two-edged in their effects. They can be used to stabilize the composition of a senior executive group, and the fact that key executives cannot then easily be dismissed or leave voluntarily at short notice may increase their willingness and ability to plan ahead, and encourage the formation of efficient, closely integrated managerial teams which are of great importance to the development of their firms. But these contracts are made by the directors and can bind the company to an agreement without the shareholders' consent. When a director enters a service contract with his fellow directors the members' power to dismiss him, or at least to do so without paying possibly expensive compensation, is reduced. The use of service contracts means a partial limitation of the effectiveness of section 184 and makes it possible for boards dominated by executive directors to consolidate their position *vis-à-vis* the members.

An indication of the potentially injurious consequences of service contracts for members was given, and considerable controversy was aroused, by the action of a company in 1967. It amended the existing service agreements with executive directors and senior managers to provide that if the company were taken over against the advice of the board the agreements would be terminated automatically and the termination regarded as a breach of contract by the firm, but to discourage complacency advantage could only be taken of this arrangement if the company's results met minimum prescribed standards. The legality of service contracts of this kind has not yet been tested and it is possible that they would be rejected by the court if they were construed as attempts to discourage takeover offers and protect the executives' position at the expense of the shareholders, who might have benefited by accepting one of these offers had it been made.

Should the directors of a company fail to perform their duties with proper care, skill and loyalty, and the company suffers, or should they behave in an irregular or invalid way, it might be necessary for the company to take legal action against them. But the problem would then arise that a company can only act through human agents, who are first and foremost its directors. As it is hardly likely that directors would sue themselves it has been accepted that anyone connected with a company may start legal proceedings in its name. A shareholder could thus sue directors whose actions were *ultra vires*, as they would be if his rights were threatened or infringed; if the directors formed a controlling group which defrauded a minority of the members; or if they did something which could only be authorized by a special or extraordinary resolution and this was not properly passed. It has been suggested that the various possibilities could be summarized by saying that an ordinary shareholder may have cause to sue when the action complained of could not validly be approved by an ordinary resolution of a general meeting. A shareholder who sues the directors can expect them to challenge his right to do so, in which case proceedings are delayed until the general meeting has agreed to proceed with the suit. If the meeting does not agree to this the shareholder must bear the costs of the action alone, and his awareness of this risk would almost certainly deter him from suing in most cases where the directors were strong enough to command a majority of the votes.

When shareholders are unable to remove the directors, and have no case to take before a court, they may still invoke the use of another weapon, inspection by an official of the Board of Trade. Section 164 of the Companies Act 1948 gives the Board of Trade discretion to appoint an inspector if 200 members of a company, or members holding not less than one-tenth of the issued capital, satisfy the Board that good reasons for inspection exist. If a special resolution of a general meeting calls for an inspection, or a court orders one to be carried out, the Board must comply. In a number of cases, however, the Board has taken the initiative and conducted an inquiry into a company's affairs when fraud was suspected or some part of the company's membership was being oppressed.

The Board of Trade has been criticized on several occasions for not acting with sufficient vigour and for being too discreet in using its discretion to investigate a company's affairs. The run of failures by small insurance companies in the middle 1960s brought increased censure on the department and caused one member of parliament to say that the Board of Trade 'was always locking the door after the horse had escaped – in some cases after the horse had died of exposure in the public press'. In the Board's defence it was argued that its powers were too limited, and its restricted ability to act was compared unfavourably with the scope given to the Federal Trade Commission in the U.S.A. The Companies Act 1967 recognized the need to increase the Board's powers of inspection and authorized it to start an investigation when a company has been, as well as is, suspected of certain fraudulent activities; to require people to attend to answer questions and produce documents; and to obtain a warrant to enter and search premises where necessary documents that are not voluntarily produced are expected to be found.

Shareholders can also employ publicity to control directors' activities of which they disapprove. They can try to ensure that a controversial matter is aired in the press and they can engage the directors in a battle of circulars. If a serious difference of opinion arises between a board of directors and a section of the members the directors may seek to arouse support for themselves by sending shareholders a statement of their case. An opposing shareholders' group can reply in like manner, and since 1948 it has been able to use the company's machinery to circulate to other members the details of its argument, so long as the group holds at least 5 per cent of the votes or consists of at least 100 members each owning an average of **£100** of paid up capital.

In a paper war of this kind, however, the directors are in much the stronger position. They can fire the first shot without any expense to themselves, whereas the shareholders' group must pay to use the company's machinery unless the general meeting has said otherwise. In a company with many shareholders the costs of printing and postage would be high, but expense is not necessarily the main disadvantage under which opposition shareholders labour. More important is the restriction imposed by section 140 of the 1948 Act in setting an upper limit of 1,000 words to the length of any circular sent out by the company on the shareholders' behalf. This, together with the fact that the opposition would lose the tactical advantage of surprise by using the company's services, means that any group wanting to make the strongest attack on the directors' defences would usually find it prudent to forego the equivocal benefits offered by the law and bear all the expenses itself, because it could then print circulars to any length it desired and fight independently in the hope of winning enough proxy votes to defeat the directors in a general meeting.

The Jenkins Committee said that the Companies Act 1948 gave the shareholders 'powerful weapons provided they choose to use them, and even if practical considerations make them difficult for the small investors to wield the same cannot be said of the large institutional investors' (para. 106). The real effect of the 1948 Act was to increase the relative strength of large shareholders by providing weapons which they were more likely to be able to use than small investors, and although these were left in almost as ineffectual a position as before it was no longer true to say of shareholders as a body, as the Cohen Committee said in 1945, that their control was illusory.[1] But while it is certain that many small shareholders have very little idea of the nature of their rights and legal position, and lack the resources of time, knowledge and skill necessary to take decisive measures under any of the relevant sections of the Companies Acts, it cannot be assumed that large shareholders will exercise control with uniform or predictable vigour and success. Insurance companies are the biggest institutional investors and their investment policy is representative of the policies of other institutions holding shares in a large number of companies, in many of which a a single institution's shareholding, although absolutely large and possibly the largest of any member, represents only a small proportion of the voting strength. An institution with a diversified portfolio would find it difficult to take a close or continuous interest in the affairs of more than a small number of the companies in which it invested, although it might be represented on the boards of some of them and exercise a measure of control in that way.

The institutional investors (banks, pension funds and unit trusts, as well as insurance companies) can, of course, sell shares when their value declines as a result of bad direction or management, instead of intervening in a company's affairs to correct defective policies or change the composition of an erring board. A problem here, apart from any fiscal complications such as those caused by the introduction of a capital gains tax and its net effect on the buying and selling of shares,

[1] *Report of the Committee on Company Law Amendment*, Cmd. 6659, H.M.S.O., 1945, para 7(e).

is that if an institution disposes of a large block of shares in a narrow market it depresses the share price abnormally and reduces the proceeds of the sale. To the extent that institutional holdings grow larger, and it becomes increasingly difficult to opt out of membership because of the financial penalty incurred, the direct interests of institutional investors in efficient company operation may be sharpened. If we accept that large shareholders can sometimes exercise appreciable control it is arguable that a satisfactory situation exists so long as their actions accomplish for small shareholders what they cannot do for themselves. The strength of this argument increases in proportion to the effectiveness of the large shareholders' powers and the degree of common interest between owners of shareholdings of widely different values. If the interests of large and small shareholders diverge the former may use their strength to influence a company's actions to the detriment of the latter, and when the large shareholders and the board of directors act in concert the position of the small investors, should they be opposed to them, is weak indeed.

There is another factor in the shareholders' ability to play an influential part in business administration that is probably more important to the general run of investors than any of the matters mentioned so far; it is the information which shareholders are given, or can obtain, about what a company is doing, or plans to do, and how well it has performed. Shareholders cannot participate intelligently in business affairs, or make rational investment decisions, without a reasonably detailed knowledge of a company's current position and expectations. If knowledge increases power a well-informed body of shareholders should be able to exercise control to better effect than an uninformed one, other things being equal. Members obtain information in three main ways: from published material supplied by the company, from public media for the dissemination of news and opinion, and from answers to questions addressed to company officers. In the last case shareholders have often been refused the information they asked for, sometimes with a reasoned explanation of why it could not be given, sometimes with the reply that it was simply not the policy to divulge it. However free and extensive the discussion of company matters may be in the press many facts which shareholders need to know can only be provided in company reports, and some of the arguments for increasing their frequency and the amount of information they contain have now been accepted. The campaign to increase the information which shareholders are given, some fruits of which were reaped in the Companies Act 1967, produced results in advance of legal reform, for after the Jenkins Committee's proposals had been considered the Council of the London Stock Exchange urged all companies with quoted shares to produce reports half-yearly, and preferably quarterly, instead of annually as before, and to provide more details as well. The problem of information is not just one of quantity, however, for it is also important that the information should be presented in an intelligible form to investors without accounting expertise. It would be helpful if all statements of profit and loss, and all balance sheets, were accompanied by a lucid commentary in which the salient features were discussed and technical terms explained. A greater degree of uniformity in the presentation of company information would also help shareholders to make more intelligent comparisons of company performance.

The Companies Act 1967 required quoted companies to provide much more information than they were accustomed to give before, and by abolishing the status of exempt private companies it called for information about firms which were previously in that category and chose to retain their limited liability character. The information demanded by the Act is not likely to be of uniform help in strengthening the members' control, but as this was not the main purpose shareholders must feel grateful that some improvement in their position was still brought about. Companies must now give details of their own principal activities and those of subsidiary concerns; of the turnover attributable to each main line of business and the profit derived from it; and of any significant changes in their activities and fixed assets during a trading year. Not only must the ownership of subsidiaries be declared, but companies must also disclose any shareholding amounting to more than 10 per cent of the equity of a non-subsidiary concern and total shareholdings in excess of 10 per cent of the value of a non-subsidiary company's assets. The chairman's emoluments must be stated and the company must publish the numbers of directors whose emoluments fall within specified ranges of a prescribed scale: information has also to be given about all other salaries in excess of £10,000 a year. Separate up-to-date registers are to be kept, one containing details of shares owned in a company or its subsidiaries by directors, their spouses or their children; the other containing details of each holding of shares with unrestricted voting rights that amounts to more than 10 per cent of the number of shares in a class.

The Act of 1967 was regarded as an interim measure and a more comprehensive revision of company law was promised at a later time. It undoubtedly left anomalies that required correction and ignored a number of ways in which the shareholders' position could be further improved. But it is interesting to notice that in several respects institutional action has been quite as instrumental as parliamentary action in effecting reforms that benefit shareholders. The stock exchanges have done a good deal to promote more equitable relationships between companies and their members, and the formulation of *The City Code on Takeovers and Mergers* in 1968 was a notable outcome of joint institutional efforts to stop a number of activities that were contrary to ethical business practice.

Legislation could do still more, however, to curb directors' freedom to sell for cash or securities in another company the greater part of a firm's assets, or to use cash reserves to buy large amounts of shares or physical assets of another concern, without first getting the shareholders' consent. The aim of reform should be to increase the potential influence of shareholders by giving them new powers and, if possible, by reducing friction in the use of those they already possess. While some members have larger holdings or are more strategically placed than others there is bound to be inequality in the distribution of power, but the abolition of non-voting shares would be a major practicable step towards making more democratic what is always likely to be an inherently undemocratic state of affairs.

The legal theory of a company as a group of members pooling their resources and associating to regulate its affairs becomes increasingly remote from reality the bigger a company grows. The control of many companies today calls for the continuous application of knowledge, experience and skill that large numbers of shareholders cannot possibly possess. They must in numerous cases relinquish a large measure of control to boards of directors and managerial groups, whose job is to guide companies and provide the necessary regular supervision of the multifarious activities that have to be performed in complex functioning concerns. But this does not mean that shareholders should be encouraged, and still less obliged, to lose their opportunities to hold a watching brief over what the directors do. If shareholders degenerate into mere moneylenders enormous economic and social power will become concentrated into even fewer hands than is presently the case, and although companies are checked in various ways by market forces and by governmental and trade union restraints, the rationale of the joint-stock enterprise system is that shareholders themselves have a responsible, if practically limited, part to play in company control.

Shareholders have powers to protect their own interests and our argument is that these powers should certainly be preserved, and even reinforced, and that they could with advantage be more widely and intelligently used than they are; but their exercise does not, of course, necessarily promote or protect the interests of others. In this chapter we have been concerned only with powers that affect relationships between shareholders and directors, and if a more comprehensive, legally grounded system of checks and balances were to be developed there is an argument for strengthening the workpeople's position in a company which it is not possible to develop here. Some firms have already done a great deal to devise acceptable codes of industrial justice in which the rights of employees are formally defined and protected, but such schemes depend on the goodwill of the controlling groups in the businesses concerned and are outside the province of company law.

In modern companies *de facto* power lies with directors or senior managers, or with a combination of the two. Both sets of people are fallible in judgment and sometimes prone to the human weakness of misusing their power. The existence of shareholding bodies with opportunities to control them is not a sure guarantee that bad judgments will not be made, or that misuse of power will not go either unnoticed or uncorrected: it is a partial guarantee, however, that is worth keeping and strengthening. An alternative would be for the system of capitalist enterprise to be replaced by another in which shareholders as such ceased to exist, and the responsibility for controlling company operations could be taken from privately appointed directors and given formally to publicly nominated executive groups, state agencies, workers' committees, or representative bodies of various kinds. But if the joint-stock system is to be retained in anything like its present form, with shareholders investing their money at risk in ventures whose regular oversight they must largely entrust to others, their ultimate right of control should remain. Even a partially active body of shareholders can still play a useful part, not simply by curbing directors in a negative way, but by challenging and stimulating them to achieve better results. The most valuable role that shareholders can play is to make sure that as far as possible only people of high business calibre occupy directors' positions, and that they have the ability to select and work successfully with managers who possess the range of human and technical skills necessary to achieve a rising standard of performance in business today.

3
The board of directors

3.1 The director's position

DIRECTION AND MANAGEMENT

In many companies, both private and public, the shareholders entrust the running of the company to other people and intervene in its affairs only rarely, if at all, in their pure capacity as company members. The two groups of people mainly responsible for efficient company performance are directors and managers, and it is to a study of their activities that we now turn. There are some important differences between their work and responsibilities, although the precise line between direction and management is not always easy to draw and the full distinction can only be seen after both activities have been considered in detail. Attempts to define them concisely almost certainly lead to the oversimplification of both; nevertheless some generalizations at this stage may still help to prepare for the discussion that follows.

The directors of a company stand between the shareholders and the main body of employees and from their central position they exercise a general oversight of the company's affairs; control its finances; approve its policies; decide the major objectives to be achieved with the resources available; ensure that the firm keeps as closely as possible to its predetermined path; and give periodic accounts of their stewardship to the general meeting. In other words directors provide a business with its government and among them we normally expect to find the supreme source of executive (as distinct from legal) authority in the firm. The work of managers tends to be more detailed, more directly concerned with the actual job of getting things done and with supervising the human and material resources that are used to produce goods and services and translate policies and plans into effective action. Directors meeting as a board may do their work intermittently, but management is very much a day-to-day activity. The directors must see that a firm is well managed and they have the power to alter the size and composition of the managerial group for this purpose, but they need not necessarily be managers themselves. Company direction logically precedes management, and while good management can certainly reduce the harmful effects of bad direction it cannot entirely prevent them from

50

being felt. To be successful a company needs directors who do much more than merely discharge their minimum legal obligations: it needs people who will devote themselves diligently to its affairs and who are capable of meeting a variety of demands made on their intellects and energies by a continuous process of social and economic change.

Every public company registered on or after 1 November 1929 must have at least two directors and all private companies, in addition to public companies registered before that date, must have at least one. The directors of a company together constitute its board of directors and the board has important corporate responsibilities and powers. While a company exists its board is a permanent body whose membership can, within certain limits, be changed when necessary, and its own continuity enables the board to maintain the continuity of the enterprise it serves, which is its principal function. Individual directors come and go, but the company, like Tennyson's brook, can go on for ever (in theory at least) and its board provides, as an American judge once said, for 'a perpetual succession of individuals . . . capable of acting for the promotion of (a) particular object, like one immortal being'.

In the Companies Act 1948 there is a statement which is potentially misleading from an administrative point of view. It says there that a company's business shall be managed by the directors, and a very similar form of words is found in the United States where the law requires a corporation to be 'managed by a board'. This may imply that direction and management amount to the same thing and a false idea of their identification is further encouraged by the widespread existence of executive directors, who have a dual responsibility to discharge and two sets of duties to perform. The combination of the offices of director and manager can have both good and bad results which will be discussed later, but the point to emphasize now is that they are formally separate positions and anyone appointed to them should be capable of performing different duties on different occasions, and capable of performing all of them well. Because a man is a good manager he does not automatically make a good director, and someone who could give excellent service on the board might be quite unsuited for a managerial job. In a number of respects the criteria for appointing directors are different from those for appointing managers, and the qualities looked for are not entirely the same in each case. A firm that ignores this fact runs the risk of having poor direction, poor management, or both.

THE NEED FOR BOARDS OF DIRECTORS

From the earliest days of joint-stock organization there has been prejudice against this form of enterprise, concern at the opportunities for malpractice which it offered, and scepticism of the kind voiced by Adam Smith, who thought that the directors of a joint-stock company would inevitably take less care of other people's money than their own and that 'negligence and profusion' would, in varying degree, mark the handling of such a company's affairs. But despite the often justified distrust which it provoked the joint-stock company offered such great advantages that the number of companies continued to grow, especially after the Companies Acts 1844–1862. Since that time company law has been modified and improved by a series of statutes and judgments of the courts, which have done much to allay public suspicion and dissatisfaction. These changes in the law have increased the protection given to shareholders and resulted in the obligations of company directors being progressively more fully and carefully defined.

A company must have human guidance and is exposed to the danger, however small, that a director may be dishonest or of inferior calibre, or more interested in taking from it than contributing to its work. There are still occasional cases of directors who exploit loopholes in the law and trade on the shareholders' ignorance and inaction: indifferent directors are still appointed through nepotism or personal influence, or because of a misplaced belief in the importance of their connexions or the value of their names. It is virtually impossible to exclude such people entirely and any attempt to do so would probably cause more harm than good. Mistaken appointments are always liable to be made, but it is more important to ensure that the means of rectifying the mistakes exist than to go to exaggerated lengths to prevent them. For the larger limited liability company to operate there must be substantial delegation of authority by the members to a smaller group which administers the company on their behalf. A company is a legal person whose business must be superintended by agents–the directors–who have important functions to perform which in most cases could not be performed so effectively by anyone else.

QUASI-DIRECTORS

The director's office is an attractive prize to many people and the hope of winning it can provide a powerful incentive in a firm whose ladder of promotion reaches to the boardroom. In many such firms the number of people competing for office exceeds the number of places available and the larger the firm the poorer are the individual chances of becoming one of its directors, because the ratio of directorships to the total number of employees, and more significantly to the number of managers, tends to decline as a firm grows. The resultant competition for directorships may have a healthy stimulative effect, but it can also cause jealousy and resentment when people fail to achieve their ambition.

One way of dealing with this problem has been to introduce a variety of titles in which the term director is used in some qualified sense: the bearers of these titles are frequently not full directors at all, although the impression may be given that they are. In British public companies one can find such titles as alternative, associate, auxiliary, extraordinary, junior, local and special director, and this is only a partial list. There are companies which try to add distinction to managerial positions by calling their occupants by such titles as design director, personnel director, or director of research, and in large holding companies the scope for appointments to directorships is widened by the creation of subsidiary boards with limited autonomy, acting under the board of the parent company.

The spread of a rash of titles is unfortunate in some respects even when it causes no real harm, and if the practice were carried too far the meaning of directorships would be debased. But it seems unlikely that this will happen and the main danger is that a quasi-director may carry the weight of a full board member in his dealings with other people when he is not entitled to do so. His colleagues, subordinates and people outside the firm may accept his personal opinions as expressions of the opinion of the board, and there is a similar risk of confusion between the roles of director and manager where executive directors are concerned. It has been suggested that in the case of an executive director the separation of his two roles would be stressed by calling him (say) director and marketing manager instead of marketing director, but this by itself would do little to improve a situation in which a man was careless of the proper distinction between the two branches of his work.

LEGAL RESPONSIBILITIES OF DIRECTORS

There are comparatively few legal grounds on which a director may be disqualified from office, undischarged bankruptcy and conviction for fraud being two of the main ones. The normal retiring age has been set at seventy years, but a company can remove or vary this age limit if it desires. The articles can also state reasons for removal from office that apply in a particular company, such as persistent absence from board meetings or insanity. We saw in the previous chapter that the shareholders' power to remove directors from office was increased in 1948, but that owing to a combination of factors there remains a strong tendency for directors to decide who shall serve on company boards and for how long, and for most boards to perpetuate themselves as they choose. Thus, although directors have to justify their actions to shareholders and comply with the requirements of the law they typically enjoy a high degree of security as a body and considerable freedom to act in the way they think best.

The legal responsibilities and duties of directors are determined by a large body of case law rather than by statute. The view of the General Council of the Bar has been that it would be virtually impossible to define the director's task exhaustively and that to try to do so would in all probability lead to administrative inflexibility. In broad terms a director can be said to occupy a position of trust in which he is expected to behave honestly and diligently and exercise the same care and skill on the company's behalf as he would in his own affairs. If he fails to do this he could, in principle, be charged with negligence should the company's business suffer, but actions for negligence are seldom brought before the courts. They are particularly difficult to judge because of the complexity of the economic, social, organizational and other factors that influence business decisions and the nature of their results, but if a formal professional code were ever devised for and accepted by directors, as it has been for the accountancy and legal professions, negligence might then be easier to define and detect.

Directors are supposed to give regular, though not necessarily continuous, attention to a company's affairs and to safeguard the interests of its members, and fail to fulfil their obligations if they do not carry out their duties conscientiously. A damaging consequence of passivity or indifference on the part of directors is that one or more of their number may unduly dominate the company's affairs and turn them to private advantage. An example of this was seen in the case of a building society whose activities were investigated by order of the Chief Registrar of Friendly Societies in 1961. The Registrar's inspector was satisfied 'that for all practical purposes the society in the past (had) been run under the sole direction of' the former chairman who had used the company's funds for his own property transactions, and the other directors were censured for their failure to act effectively, which had undoubtedly contributed to the 'deplorable situation' in which the society was found.

A director, being in a position akin to that of a trustee, should not try to benefit himself at the expense of the company's members or put himself in a situation where his private interests conflict with his duties to the company, and if he acts as a director of several firms their interests should not obviously clash. He has an obligation to declare his personal concern in any contract of which he has knowledge that the company proposes to make, but in large firms many decisions affecting purchases and sales are taken below board level and a director's interests might be affected by a subordinate's action of which the director was not aware. It would be impracticable for every detail of business to be dealt with by the board and the danger of a conflict of interests arising must be treated in a common-sense way. A director would normally be doing his duty if he notified the board of his other directorships and of the way in which his material interests were likely to be affected by any contract which received the board's consideration. Professor Gower's opinion is that no matter how widely or narrowly a director's obligation to disclose his interests are defined he does not have to account for any profit he derives from a contract to which the company is a party so long as he fulfils it, and the contract is perfectly valid despite the profit he receives.[1]

A company's memorandum and articles of association establish the framework in which the board of directors acts and in most cases the board's discretion is wide. It is commonly given all those powers to act on the company's behalf which are not required by the Companies Acts, or by any of the articles, to be exercised only by a general meeting, and because these powers are so large the responsibility of the people who wield them is correspondingly great. Within the framework of its legal responsibility the majority of the functions of a company board fall into two principal categories, financial and economic on the one hand and social and personal on the other. There are differences of detail between one company and another, of course,

[1] L. C. B. Gower, *Modern Company Law*, 2nd edn., Stevens, 1957, ch. 23.

again depending particularly on the type of business and its size. The size of the firm has a direct bearing on the way a board does its work and on the kind of work it performs, and the board of a company with assets of a few thousand pounds can give attention to small and detailed problems in a way that would be impossible for the board of a large company whose assets were measured in millions. The board of a firm in the women's fashion trade has some quite different matters to deal with from those requiring the attention of the board of a shipping company: a firm selling only in the home market has different problems from those of a firm producing entirely for export, and so on. But despite the existence of these differences of detail the similarities in the work of company boards predominate and make it possible for us to consider the board's functions and powers in general terms.

3.2 The functions of a board of directors

POLICY MAKING

A vital function of any board of directors is to determine company policy. This is a fundamental task because the policy influences decisions and actions taken at all levels in the firm. It is possible to conceive of a board which neglects some of the other functions ascribed to it, but not to imagine one with no policy at all, for a company with such a board would be without real direction and little better than business flotsam. The policy of a firm can be thought of most simply as a statement of the firm's intentions, which can embrace both the objectives to be achieved and the methods to be used in their attainment. The policy of one firm often differs greatly from that of another and policies cover an extremely wide range of things. For that reason policy making stands apart from the two main types of function already mentioned. It can affect, and be affected by, all aspect of a firm's activities and need be neither purely economic nor purely social in character. There is no uniform mould in which policies are shaped: they may be simple or complex, specific or general, written or unwritten, short term or long, and broadly or narrowly defined. But in any enterprise a policy of some kind must exist to give expression to what Selznick has called the firm's 'mission', to focus attention on the primary task, and to provide a source of reference for employees as they carry out their work.

Although it is convenient to talk of a firm's policy in the singular one must remember that there are likely to be a number of policies relating to particular aspects of company operations such as production, marketing, research and finance, or to matters of organization, acquisition, product quality and industrial relations. 'The policy', therefore, often refers to a set of associated policies and in a composition of this kind it is important for the various parts to be consistent and form a balanced whole. A company's objectives and methods are always tending to change and its policy can seldom be regarded as immutable. A policy should be subjected to regular

55

review and one of the arts of direction is to recognize when modification is required. The board must try to define a policy which is both flexible and stable, since a flexible policy allows a firm to adjust itself more easily to pressures to change and a stable policy gives an added sense of continuity to the firm's operations. Once a policy has been adopted the people in the firm need time to become familiar with it and, having become so, they are quite likely to resist an alteration and to feel unsettled if alterations are frequently made. Hasty changes in policy are inadvisable for this reason alone and whenever possible the ground for change should be prepared in advance. This calls for foresight on the directors' part, the skilful exercise of foresight increasing the probability that changes will result from careful analysis of the firm's situation and reflect rational decisions whose implications have been adequately weighed.

If a board yields too easily to external influences, if it makes policy decisions on the grounds of expediency, or if it fails to look far enough ahead the firm may suffer from policy drift. The result of this might be that the firm would eventually find itself in a situation which had not been envisaged and with which the directors were not adequately equipped to deal. There were several cases of companies which adopted the fashionable policy of diversification during the 1950s without sufficient forethought, and which were later embarrassed because the businesses they acquired proved less profitable than expected, or made much heavier demands on the managerial resources of the parent firms than they were willing to meet.

When policy decisions are made they should observe a small number of elementary rules. They should be practicable and lead to effective action; consistent with earlier policy decisions or fully justified if they are not; intelligible to those who implement them; and acceptable to the people they affect. A policy has a smaller chance of being successful when imposed on a hostile group and more chance of being so if the policy-making process is shared instead of being reserved completely to the board. It is highly probable that senior managers who are not on the board will play an important part in policy making, both because of their responsibility for putting the policy into effect and because of the knowledge and experience which they can place at the board's disposal. It can also be argued that a company should give employees at lower levels the opportunity to contribute to policy improvement, and provide a system for eliciting their suggestions and bringing the best of them to the board's notice. This is one aspect of a wider problem of participation by employees which is relevant to their motivation and the quality of human relations in the firm.

A number of companies have produced documents in which their policies are set out in formal terms, and sometimes in considerable detail, but the value of these statements is not universally accepted. Some boards have doubts about the advisability of committing themselves in this way and even when the policy documents are printed their circulation (like that of organization charts) is often restricted to a small select group. A written statement of policy requires careful drafting and once it has been published there may be a reluctance to alter it, so that it develops a rigidity which it is desirable to avoid. Many directors feel that an unwritten policy gives them greater freedom, but Wilfred Brown takes the opposite view and maintains that a written policy can be more flexible than one which is orally defined.[1] When a firm has a written policy the nature of any change in it can be clearly seen, and there is less danger that people who ought to know about the change will not know than with unwritten policies, where ignorance of a change may result from faulty communication. A policy which is given full publicity allows all employees to see what the firm's intentions are, and it also enables people outside the company system to assess its qualities and judge for themselves to what extent the various parties with whom the firm deals are likely to be equitably and consistently treated.

The various aspects of company policy are seldom equally weighted, and it is often the case that one strand of policy is dominant to such a degree that it limits what the firm does in a large number of ways and subjects other parts of the policy to a major restraint. A business in which great emphasis is placed on a high quality of product, for example, is inevitably affected in its policy for the recruitment and training of labour, the type of machinery and materials used, and the methods of distribution employed. A large British manufacturer of transmission chains is a case in point. This firm is said to have made such a 'fetish' of quality that it refused to license other manufacturers and stopped its overseas subsidiaries from making products under its own trade name, because it felt that the local control of quality could not be guaranteed to meet the required standards. When a company has an unequivocal policy of this kind it is clearly a fundamental factor in determining the tone of the entire concern.

CONTROL OF OPERATIONS AND FINANCE

Much of the detailed planning and control of company work is done below board level, and the directors' responsibility is often of a more general kind. The board can be assumed to determine the firm's strategy and major tactics, and settle the plans by which operations are governed. It decides the way the company is to develop and ensures, as far as possible, that progress conforms to expectations and primary objectives are reached. This sometimes means in practice that the board satisfies itself that well-thought-out plans have been made by others for the directors to approve, and that there is appropriate control of activities throughout the firm. To a variable extent a board will itself exercise direct control over employees – over their number, the type of work they do, their distribution between jobs, their remuneration and their hours of work; over the physical assets which the firm uses – its stocks of raw materials, supplies of bought-out parts, transport, machinery,

[1] W. Brown, *Exploration in Management*, Heinemann, 1960, ch. 9.

and other fixed equipment; over output and costs of production; and above all over finance. No matter what other part of its authority it may delegate no board can relinquish its ultimate power to control the finances of the firm.

The fundamentally important financial matter with which any board is concerned is profitability. It must decide what it regards as a satisfactory rate of return on the capital invested and try to ensure that this return is obtained. The return need not be uniform in the different parts of a diversified company and it can be altered over time as conditions change. Risk is a major variable affecting the rate of return and a board has to define different acceptable returns on projects involving different degrees of risk. The board's willingness or reluctance to undertake risks has a direct influence on its use of finance, for whereas a cautious board might concentrate on investments in safe projects, like the replacement of equipment to supply a stable, guaranteed market, a bold board would be ready to innovate and break into new markets where the immediate prospects were uncertain but the potential reward was high. A balance between excessive boldness which may result in rash decisions and loss, and timidity which may lead to inactivity and a decline in competitive strength, is something which most boards try to secure, but it is clear that some lean more to one side than the other.

The board must decide, therefore, how the firm's funds are to be used and when and how they should be augmented by money raised outside. Changes in the amount of capital employed in the business, the type and value of any new share issue that is contemplated, the amount of money to be invested in new plant and equipment, the proportion of profit to be retained and the dividend which shareholders should receive are some of the important financial decisions that boards of directors must make, either alone or with the approval of the general meeting, on which they can usually rely. A board may conceivably wish to lay down financial policies affecting such things as the preservation of a given degree of liquidity, the ratio of the equity to fixed interest stock, or the maintenance of the valuation ratio (the ratio of the market value of a firm's shares to its net assets) at a level that would avoid the danger of an unwanted takeover bid. The financial information with which it is provided normally gives the board its principal opportunity to assess both past performance and the probable nature of future trends, and much has been done to increase the comprehensiveness of this information, the speed of its collection, and the quality of the tools used in its analysis.

Business finance in all its aspects is a large and important subject which can only be touched on briefly in a book of this kind. What is emphasized here is that the availability of finance is a major restraint on business actions and the skill with which it is used a major factor in business growth. Because the final control of finance lies in the hands of the board, and company success or failure tends to be measured in the first instance in money terms, the judgment of a firm's performance is largely a judgment of the directors' financial acumen.

APPOINTMENT OF CHAIRMAN AND MANAGING DIRECTOR

The directors normally elect one of their number to be chairman of the board and although this office has no legal significance it is important because the chairman tends to be looked on as the senior person in the company, and he presides not only at board meetings but at general meetings as well. In many companies the chairman has a considerable responsibility for making business and social connexions outside the firm. His position is on the boundary of the open system and his role, like that of other directors, but often to a greater extent, requires him to act as a mediator and help to maintain healthy relations between the company and its environment. Some companies have joint chairmen, possibly holding office in alternate years, more have a deputy chairman (or chairmen) who is formally authorized to act as chairman during the latter's absence from business. The practice of appointing presidents in British firms has also been adopted by a small minority of companies, but the term means something different in this country from what it means in the U.S.A. The president in Britain is not normally the chief executive, but is often an elder statesman of the company who has been given the title in recognition of former services after he has retired from active membership of the board.

The powers of a board of directors are given to it as a body, and its members exercise a collective authority and bear a collective responsibility for its actions. But if the matter rested there the board would be a much less valuable instrument than could be desired. A board is a committee which must put its decisions into effect through individuals, and there is an obvious need for delegation to some person, cr persons, to act in its name and on its behalf in board matters. Company law does not formally recognize the need for a chairman, but Article 109 of Table A of the Companies Act 1948 says that the members of a board 'may entrust to and confer upon a managing director any of the powers exercisable by them upon such terms and with such restrictions as they think fit'.

The articles of association of most companies empower the board to act in this way, and it is a widespread practice in limited liability companies to appoint a chief executive officer who is called the managing director and who occupies one of the most important positions of responsibility in the firm, if not the most important of all. The person appointed as managing director does not retire in rotation with the other directors and is more likely than they to be appointed for a fixed term with a renewable contract, or to be appointed for life. His security of tenure is thus typically greater than that of the general run of directors and should be so, because the unsettling effects of repeated changes of chief executive could be very damaging to a company's fortunes. The managing director can have such a decisive influence on these that his selection calls for one of the most critical decisions that a board must make. The fact that a managing director can be removed from office by depriving him of his directorship allows a mistaken appointment to be rectified, possibly at the expense of some adverse publicity and the payment of compensation, but boards can be expected to take great pains to avoid making a mistake of this kind.

There is not a great deal of evidence to show whether it is the more common practice to appoint managing directors from outside the company or within. It is reasonable to suppose that internal appointments are frequently preferred, not only because the possibility of promotion inside a firm provides an incentive to executive effort, but also because someone whose ability has been proved can be groomed, or developed, for succession to the managing director's post and bring to it a close working knowledge of the firm. This is an important matter which may be overlooked when a company's affairs seem to be going well, but ideally a board should have a good candidate for office whenever the position becomes vacant, so as to avoid the awkwardness of an interregnum and the temptation to make a hurried and possibly unsuitable appointment. There are times, however, when appointment from outside is either clearly preferable or cannot be avoided and the board must then decide where to look and what method of selection to use. It seems clear from the number of advertisements that appear that boards often do find it necessary to look outside their firms, and feel the need for consultants to help them make their choice. Young firms without an experienced managerial staff, or firms with a rapid turnover of executives, may be in this position, but even for large and well-established companies there may be a case for bringing in an outsider when, for instance, an infusion of new talent is desirable or when a complete reorganization is called for and drastic reforms have to be made. In the latter case someone who is unprejudiced by any previous connexion with the firm may do a difficult, and possibly distasteful, job with more success than anyone from inside.

The research workers who collected material for the P.E.P. report *Thrusters and Sleepers* found several instances of appointments made from outside because firms had no long-term policy for internal managerial development, or because crises had arisen which could not be adequately dealt with by existing managers.

The most drastic example of this was found in a subsidiary company of a large group where a new managing director had been appointed . . . to combat what was described as 'a million pound loss situation'. By bringing in a new management team the company was in the managing director's words 'cleaned and refurbished' and its commercial situation greatly improved.[1]

The introduction of a chief executive from outside the company will not lead to greater economic efficiency, however, if his methods have unfavourable consequences which offset the actual gains attributable to his reforms. A. W. Gouldner (*Patterns of Industrial Bureaucracy*) has observed that managers who inherit a difficult situation sometimes try to reduce inefficiency by tightening up controls and increasing the area of work subject to bureaucratic procedures, but only succeed in

[1] *Thrusters and Sleepers*, Allen and Unwin, for Political and Economic Planning, 1965, p. 55.

arousing hostility and provoking resistance to their efforts which actually worsen the situation they meant to improve.

An analysis of large public companies with net assets of £2·5 m. or more showed that in samples of 510 companies in 1955 and 704 in 1960 it was the practice for one person to hold both the offices of chairman and managing director in just over one-third of the firms, and if we add that, according to Brech, there is a similar tendency for these positions to be combined in medium sized firms as well, it is evident that the practice is quite general.[1] Yet despite its apparent popularity it has been the subject of a certain amount of justifiable criticism. The chairman, *qua* chairman, need have no executive authority at all, and a good case can be argued for making his an independent role when it enables him to give impartial advice to other members of the board. He can then help the managing director, particularly, by providing him with someone with whom to discuss problems and ideas. The chairman can be a source of encouragement, a stabilizing influence and an arbiter in cases of executive dispute. The larger a company grows the more likely it becomes that the executive responsibilities of the managing director will increase, while the need for the chairman to devote himself more fully to board matters and to outside relationships increases too, so that a formal separation of the offices has much to recommend it. But even in small and medium sized companies, where the same kinds of pressure may not be so strongly felt, the virtues of an impartial chairman, not forming a part of the executive group, should not be overlooked. In companies whose boards are dominated by family interests the danger of inbreeding arising from a lack of outside representation is specially marked, and a concentration of power can result from the holding of both positions by one man which may lead to autocracy in the direction of a company's affairs.

Another feature of the administration of large firms is the tendency for more than one managing director to be appointed. In the samples already mentioned it was found that there were joint managing directors in one-fifth of the companies in 1955 and in almost one-quarter in 1960. This practice seems directly to contradict one of the most respected principles of organization, which states that there should be only one clearly identifiable source of authority in a firm, normally that of a single chief executive. When two or more managing directors are appointed it appears either that the principle is being deliberately ignored or that the people concerned are not really of equal rank as their titles imply.

The most commonly found number of joint managing directors was two, but several firms had three or four and one firm was discovered with eight. An amalgamation of firms to form a new business enterprise may result in the creation of joint managing directorships for the chief executives of the formerly independent concerns, but in other cases the purpose of joint office may be to relieve a single chief

[1] O. S. Hiner, 'The Size of Company Boards', *Management International*, 7, no. 4–5, 1967, 69–81; E. F. L. Brech, *Organisation, The Framework of Management*, 2nd edn., Longmans, 1965, p. 342.

executive of part of his burden, although there are other ways in which this can be done. In some large companies each of the joint managing directors is responsible for the oversight of a major field of activity, such as manufacturing, finance or research, or of one or more of the subsidiary companies if he holds his office in a parent concern. They sometimes constitute a formally appointed managerial committee or managing board, or they may meet informally to discuss common problems and decide matters of mutual concern which have been entrusted to them by the main board.

Difficulties can arise when joint managing directors disagree, and if they cannot reconcile their differences or reach a compromise (which might weaken their actions in any case) to whom do they refer? One of them may be chairman of the board and accepted as the senior man, but if his will invariably prevailed the office could hardly be a genuinely joint one. If, on the other hand, there were an independent chairman he could only arbitrate between the managing directors or take a disputed matter to the board. Should the chairman actually be pressed for a ruling which the joint managing directors would accept he is being forced to make an executive decision for them and this would be an unsatisfactory result. There is too little information at present for us to judge how important these difficulties are, but it is clear that the danger of their arising exists.

SELECTION OF SENIOR EXECUTIVES

In many companies the board will also want to select the people for the senior executive positions immediately below the managing director(s), or to approve these appointments if the work of selection is delegated to the managing director(s) or a small committee of the board. It can reasonably be argued that the chief executive should have an important, possibly the final, word in this matter, since it is he who will have to work intimately with the managerial group, but the board ought to be satisfied about the quality of executive talent at the company's disposal and see that there is an appropriate balance of age and experience between the various managers. The need for continuity makes it desirable for at least some of these senior managers to be chosen with a view to their potential ability to move from the more specialized fields of business in which they may initially be engaged into the field of general management.

The Companies Act 1948 (section 177) requires each registered company to have a secretary and this officer is habitually appointed by the board. He is not automatically a director, but the nature of his duties is such that he must work closely with the directors and it is convenient to look briefly at these duties here. The secretary's work varies a good deal from company to company, but four main functions can be distinguished, any one or more of which may be performed in a particular firm. First, and obviously, there are the essentially secretarial duties which the title of the office implies – acting for the board as official correspondent, attending to all matters relating to the preparation of board meetings, keeping minutes of the meetings, and so on. Next there are various legal aspects of business administration to which the secretary may attend – for example, drawing up contracts, agreements and leases; ensuring that the formal requirements of general meetings are complied with; maintaining the register of shareholders; dealing with share transfers; and many other things of this kind. In the third place there are financial duties – supervising the preparation of accounts, dealing with major payments made by or to the firm, and possibly with wages and salaries. Lastly, the secretary may be given the oversight of the general office staff and act as the manager with direct authority over typists and other clerical employees. In a small concern the company secretary is quite likely to have all these responsibilities, although he would probably need to seek outside advice and assistance at times, especially in legal and accounting matters. Some separation of responsibilities becomes necessary as a firm grows, and it would be normal to find in a large company that a qualified accountant is put in charge of financial matters while the secretary concentrates on legal work and attending to the needs of the board.

SELECTION OF DIRECTORS

We have seen that boards tend to be predominantly self-appointed, so that the selection of new directors when existing members of the board retire (or when the size of the board is increased) is another important function. The chairman is recognized to play a large part in the recruitment of directors from outside the firm, while the managing director probably has greater influence over decisions to appoint executive directors. In all cases, however, it is obvious that people with the 'right' qualities must be chosen, although what these are is not generally agreed. An outside director may be selected for his title or his name, because he has a particular financial or industrial connexion, or because he can put certain professional knowledge at the board's disposal. The existing directors would almost certainly want to be joined by someone with whom they could expect to work harmoniously, and may go to considerable lengths to be assured of a candidate's suitability in this respect. A board may sometimes harbour misconceptions about the considerations that ought to influence a director's appointment, and nominate someone who is simply expected to provide cheap expert advice occasionally or offer special favours; an important shareholder may be put on the board to pacify or control him; and a titled citizen may be specially valued for window display. These are not necessarily reasons for not making a directorial appointment, but neither are they sufficient reasons when the person concerned lacks other qualifications which would strengthen the effectiveness of the board.

Board appointments made only, or even mainly, to preserve tranquillity leave much to be desired. The best boardroom is not always the one in which perpetual harmony reigns, for it may be the harmony of complete inertia. In a vigorous company there should be no dearth of occasions when lively and critical discussion is called for, with the directors challenging each other and asking pertinent questions which keep both the board members and employees on their toes and lead to a careful study of problems which might otherwise have been superficially dealt with or overlooked. A good illustration of what is meant here, and one which gives us another instance of the danger of one man's domination of a board, is provided by the case of a pottery firm whose chairman decided that it was pointless to invest in a new type of biscuit-firing oven because it would save very little fuel and hence have only a slight effect on the costs of production. A new director was appointed later who persuaded his colleagues to agree for the first time to a thorough cost analysis which showed the importance of labour costs in total expenditure to be considerable and that of fuel costs to be relatively small. It was then clear that the new oven would make possible a significant saving of labour, reduce operating costs by thirty per cent, and fully justify its purchase.

OTHER MATTERS

The protection of the shareholders' interests has always been regarded as a basic responsibility of a company board, but it has become increasingly recognized that the board must assume an additional responsibility for protecting the interests of other parties as well, especially those of its employees. The payment of a 'fair' wage and the provision of physically satisfactory conditions of work for employees are both taken (if sometimes incorrectly) to be normal features of an employer's contract nowadays, but the interests of workpeople are affected by much more than these. An enlightened and conscientious board will want to concern itself with a variety of other things affecting the employees' welfare, such as sickness benefits, pension schemes, severance payments, profit-sharing arrangements, joint consultation, education and training, recreational facilities, and more–the possible range is wide.

The managing director is expected to deal with a large number of organizational matters, although he normally delegates considerable authority to departmental or divisional heads to settle problems in their own subordinate spheres, but the board should be satisfied that the system as a whole is designed and operating in such a way that the primary task can be achieved. It must decide what information is needed to keep a check on the system's operation and see that the information is provided in the right detail at the right times. The board should thus aim to control the balance of the system, its long-run development and the direction of its growth, and guard against unwanted bias in the distribution of departmental powers. The nature of a company's dominant problem changes from one period to another and at different times production, research, personnel, sales or finance may give rise to difficulties that override all others and call for the concentrated attention of the board; but it is generally undesirable to allow one problem to absorb the directors to the exclusion of all others, or for one department always to dominate their view of the company's work. If a firm is seen as an open system in a continuous state of dependence on its environment and perpetually exposed to changing market forces, the board has the major responsibility for analysing the effect of these forces on the balance of the system and deciding when and how to resist them, adjust to them, or try to modify their nature and their strength.

3.3 The size of company boards

The majority of public companies have boards which are larger than the minimum permissible size, but many small private companies are believed to have only the one director that the law requires. The Jenkins Committee remarked on the 'irresponsible multiplication' of companies since 1945, especially of 'one-man companies' which were more likely than others to be small and undercapitalized. The term one-man company is rather misleading, since every company must have at least two members, and it must be taken to mean a company in which only one person is active as a director and who makes up the membership to the required number by appointing passive associates who will allow him to have complete charge of the company's affairs. To guard against continual abuse of the right of incorporation the Jenkins Committee recommended that every company should have at least two directors. Such a change would not, of course, entirely guarantee the prevention of abuse, because it would always be possible for passive directors to be appointed just as passive members are brought in now, but it could be argued that a net gain in terms of generally more responsible company administration would result.

An increase in the minimum number of directors can be supported on several grounds, for there are decided drawbacks to a system which allows a company to be directed by one person. There is an obvious danger with a one-man board (if the expression may be used) that the continuity of its activities will be disrupted by accident or illness. The sole director might have arranged for someone to carry on part of his work in his absence, but the firm would still be handicapped when things had to be done which could only be done by the director himself. A sole director is also less fitted to perform some of the functions of a board which have previously been discussed than a group of directors would be, and the addition of even one more director could usefully increase the sum of experience and interest devoted to a company's affairs and help to ensure that sounder and more balanced decisions were made.

Among public companies in Britain the size of board varies from two to over thirty directors and the same wide range has been found in the U.S.A., but there is reasonable evidence to show that in both countries a majority of the boards have from

65

six to twelve directors. One must be careful not to draw a fixed conclusion from these figures about what is the 'best' size for a board to be, because of the great diversity of business circumstances, histories and needs. To some extent a board may be judged by criteria applied to test the effectiveness of any committee and it could certainly be said that some boards would be stronger if they were larger, just as others would benefit if dead wood were removed. It is impossible to make a proper assessment of a board's merits without a full understanding of the conditions in which it works, and size is only one of the factors affecting its success. A board needs to be large enough to contain a group of people with sufficient knowledge and experience to enable the board to deal effectively with the normal run of business, which means that certain infrequent and unusual problems, and matters of a highly specialized kind, may require the board to seek outside help and guidance. It would be wasteful for every board to try to recruit enough directors to deal with anything that might conceivably arise, even if the people were available and companies could afford their services. It is fine for a board to be something of a polymath, but no one should expect it to be omniscient.

In many companies the board finds it helpful to carry out part of its work through committees of directors appointed to perform particular tasks, such as producing a report on a certain aspect of the company's activities or making a detailed study of its future needs. Much valuable preparatory work can be done by small groups on subjects which must later be considered by the whole board, and discussion at board meetings can be more easily concentrated on essential issues as a result. When the board is a big one there may be a strong case for the creation of a standing committee to act on its behalf and make decisions (within prescribed limits) in its name: such committees, made up of the chairman or managing director and one or two other members of the board, are normal features of the administration of large companies. A standing committee of this kind is very likely to be a management, or executive, committee which can meet easily and reach rapid decisions when required. Where the volume and regularity of business warrant it a board may decide to appoint permanent committees to deal with matters like salaries, promotions or pensions, in addition to temporary committees created to consider special problems as they arise.

3.4 The composition of boards

The results of a survey of 2,400 board members which *The Director* published in April 1966 showed that 89 per cent of them were executive directors and only 10 per cent were non-executive directors of companies. Rather more than 60 per cent of all the directors devoted more than 80 per cent of their time to the service of one company. This information confirms what was shown by earlier studies of a similar kind. G. H. Copeman, in *Leaders of British Industry*, stated that 80 per cent of the 1,243 directors who provided him with details of their positions in 1950 were acting in a full-time capacity for one firm, or for their principal firm when they served as a director of more than one company. R. Harris and M. Solly (*A Survey of Large Companies*) found that of 1,404 directors of 148 of the largest British companies in 1955, 70 per cent were full-time and 30 per cent were part-time directors. The correspondence between executive and full-time and non-executive and part-time is not perfect, and to some extent the way in which the terms are used depends on the size of the company. But the correspondence is sufficiently close for us to work on the assumption that in companies of all sizes the day-to-day control is largely in the hands of small groups of people who occupy the important executive positions and form majorities on their companies' boards. When this is the case the companies are governed by what are in effect executive boards, and the prevalence of this form of government makes it necessary to examine the advantages and disadvantages of boards of directors of this kind.

One advantage of executive directorships, as we have seen, is that they provide an incentive to managers in the firm, and if an executive has the right qualities for a director, so far as they can be judged, there is much to be said for this kind of appointment. The executive directors have an intimate knowledge of the various aspects of the firm's operations and its problems, and they are likely to be both competent businessmen and enthusiastic colleagues, anxious to promote the company's progress and improve its fortunes. Their presence on the board should ensure that no significant internal matter is overlooked when decisions are made, and if they form an amicable and balanced team they can take into the boardroom a mutual understanding and respect that facilitates discussion and simplifies their work. But which executives should be directors? Harold Whitehead has suggested that a strong case can be made for the inclusion of the heads of the production and sales departments in a manufacturing company, and of the secretary if he is qualified to deal with financial problems. These people, with the managing director, would form the essential nucleus around which a larger board could be built if desired. In most companies of this kind an understanding at board level of the problems of these departments would be of the greatest importance, but it could be obtained without necessarily giving directorships to departmental heads. Other activities in a company, like research, personnel, purchasing, design or marketing, may have equally good claims to representation and it is important to avoid making an appointment solely on the ground of departmental status. If it is thought vital to have a department represented on the board, however, a company can deal with the matter by taking care that the head of the department is chosen for his ability to manage and direct.

When directors are drawn from the executive ranks there is little danger of window dressing and not much likelihood that they will treat their duties in a casual way so long as the board works on a correct and formal basis; and since most executives may be assumed to be on the company's premises for the greater part of their working time board meetings can be held quickly in an emergency, if one should arise. Decisions can also be reached if necessary without convening a board meeting, and ratified later. A danger arises, however, that where a board consists entirely of executive directors it may neglect some aspects of its work because the members are meeting each other informally so often that the need for formal meetings does not seem to be great. The office chats and post-prandial conversations, valuable though they are in many ways, may become substitutes for the fuller, more widely representative and systematic discussions on which decisions affecting major issues should be based. Even when board meetings are held regularly there is something slightly Gilbertian in a situation in which a group of executives metaphorically don their director's hats and approve decisions that in many cases have been made already elsewhere. This is perhaps an exaggeration, but one cannot ignore the possibility that an entirely executive board will meet merely to put the seal of official approval on a series of *faits accomplis*.

A board of executive directors may become too narrow in outlook, and have too little information on which to base sound decisions, if all its members are so busy with matters inside the firm that they have little or no time to reflect on broad issues or take stock of what is happening outside. There is a real danger of parochialism when the board consists of departmental managers meeting in a different room. There is also a danger that the chief executive may so dominate the board that other directors have little effect on its actions. They are in the odd position of being subordinate to the managing director in their departmental posts, but ostensibly his equals at board meetings. A self-appointed and strongly entrenched executive board may also become dictatorial and act in ways that are inimical to the interests of the people to whom it is responsible. A board composed entirely of managers protected by service contracts may be specially prone to behave in this way, and although the chairman talks to the shareholders about 'your' company he and his fellow directors really think of it as their own. But the basic weakness of an all-executive board is that it may lack the detachment to carry out the independent review of company operations that should be one of its major tasks and, as Peter Drucker has observed, if it is not easily fooled by people outside it can still easily fool itself.

A board on which outside directors are represented is not by any means certain to be free from the potential defects of a board of executives, but there are good reasons for believing that the inclusion of outsiders helps to strengthen a board. The outside directors emphasize the distinction between direction and management: they bring more open minds to a study of the firm's position and can assess with greater impartiality than their executive colleagues the good and bad features of any suggestions that the executives make. The value of an independent chairman has already been discussed, but in cases where the chairman is also managing director the desirability of having outside directors is increased. By recruiting to the board from outside the firm it is possible to select directors from a much wider field and build a board that most closely matches the firm's requirements. There is no guarantee that a company will find all the talent it needs among its own managerial group or that, given that talent, it will get a board with a good balance of age, temperament and experience. In both large and small companies the outside director can, if he does his job well, act as a catalyst and help the executives to react more effectively on each other.

One can argue at length about the composition of an 'ideal' board, but even if it were possible to define one for a particular company it would be less than ideal for most others. One can press the special claims to board membership of people with this or that particular qualification, specialized knowledge or skill, but again it would be necessary to distinguish between the circumstances of different firms. The recently debated case for having scientists on company boards must be judged in this light. It is perfectly arguable that the boards of certain science-based companies have been inadequately equipped in the past to analyse scientific problems and that their firms' progress suffered as a result. But it would be incorrect to assume that all firms would be more efficient with a scientist on the board. A company needs a board capable of appreciating the different problems that it is likely to face, of recognizing their existence in the first place and then being able to decide their relative importance and how best to get them solved. The board should not necessarily be expected to solve them all itself.

It has been argued in America that the position of managerial groups *vis-à-vis* boards of directors is so inherently strong that to talk about a board's authority as we have done in this chapter gives a misleading impression, and it is claimed that in practice a board's influence is much weaker than theory suggests.[1] Managers are said to control the board's composition sufficiently closely to ensure that only people with managerial sympathies are appointed, and directors who assert their independence and challenge managerial decisions are soon removed. The managers' power is increased by their ability to determine what information is given to the board, and by their judicious selection of data and the ways in which they are presented the managers can persuade the board to pursue a course acceptable to the executive group. This argument applies to companies in which the board consists principally of part-time, or outside, directors, who are not in close touch with the internal affairs of the company and who must rely on the managers for much of the material on which boardroom judgments are based. These boards of outsiders are tolerated because they most easily help a company to comply with legal requirements and because the managers need a body to turn to when things go wrong. The board carries the final responsibility for what managers do, but managers themselves are in the main the arbiters of their own actions. This helps to explain why four-fifths

[1] B. J. Bienvenu, 'Boards of Directors Revisited', *Business Horizons*, 5, no. 3, 1962, 41–50.

of American corporations have indemnified their directors against the costs of a legal action taken against them for being insufficiently diligent in the performance of their work.

A suggested remedy for this state of affairs is that full-time professional directors should be appointed to strengthen company boards, but as only the largest companies could support a professional board it would seem that many such directors would still have to divide their time between a number of concerns in order to be fully occupied. If their professionalism gave them a better grasp of company problems than some of the present part-time directors are alleged to have the boards might indeed be strengthened, but because most of these directors would themselves be serving on a part-time basis in any one firm the managers would still have a considerable influence over company affairs.

The prevalence of executive boards in Britain means that criticisms of American directing groups are not so applicable here, and if there has been a decline in the power of boards in this country it is because the frequent combination of the executive and directorial positions has blurred a distinction between two aspects of business administration which it is important to preserve. If the board of directors did not exist it would be necessary to invent it, and the main question is how to compose a board which makes the greatest contribution to a company's efficiency and success. The exigencies of modern economic life seldom allow a company to be operated on an amateur basis, and boardrooms cannot be treated as exclusive clubs whose membership is decided by family connexions or attendance at a certain kind of university or school. Neither can boards of directors be expected to do their work properly if they consist largely of part-time directors meeting infrequently to make a show of deciding matters over whose selection and treatment they have only a negligible control.

It seems inevitable that managers will continue to provide the main source of recruitment for directors in most companies and that predominantly executive boards will continue to govern in the majority of firms. This seems to be a satisfactory arrangement in a large number of cases, but we repeat the desirability of leavening the executive directors with outsiders of the right calibre, so long as they are encouraged and assisted to make their best contributions to the board's work. In some large companies the magnitudes of the directing and managing tasks have made it necessary to create boards whose members are freed from the daily responsibility of supervising specialized activities to take the long view and devote themselves to studying the needs of the company as a whole. In other companies, also usually large, the executive directors are supported by staff groups who do much of the detailed work of examining alternative courses of action, make proposals, and prepare plans for the board's consideration. But in smaller firms the problem of finding sufficient time to escape from the unrelenting demands of managerial work and think about the company as a whole, as a director should, is a serious one which is not easily solved, and many companies suffer from this fact. If executive directors fail even to recognize that there is an identifiable set of tasks which make up the work of direction, and that direction and management are two different things, the situation is made still worse. For one reason or the other there is a danger in many joint-stock companies today that direction may receive less attention from preoccupied executive directors than its importance requires.

4

Business management

4.1 Managers and managerial work

A great deal has been written about managers and their work, and it is acknowledged that they are one of a country's most valuable resources and a crucial factor in business success. Yet, surprisingly perhaps, there is no generally agreed definition of a manager, and the distinction between managers and non-managers is not always clear. We saw in the last chapter that some confusion tends to exist about the differences between management and direction, and we shall see in the next that there is disagreement about whether foremen are managers or not. The failure to agree on a definition does not appear strange to everyone, since managers are, after all, a mixed group occupying many sorts of position in very different concerns. How, one may ask, could we expect to equate a research and development manager in a large electronic engineering firm with a bank manager in a small branch office? One answer is that despite differences of detail there are characteristics common to all managerial jobs that make it possible to distinguish managerial positions from the rest. It has also been said that all managers require certain basic skills, even though they are used in varying manner and degree, and that the identification of those skills enables us to differentiate managers from the members of other business groups.

A manager could be defined as someone who makes decisions about the use of human and material resources under his command with the aim of maximizing some economic function. The economist's theory of the firm assumes that he tries to maximize profit. It is usually agreed that a manager must have one or more subordinates and there are definitions which emphasize this fact, such as that management is a social process, personnel administration, or getting things done through other people. But these are all unsatisfactory definitions: there are social processes in business unrelated to management, and sole traders get things done through other people, such as subcontractors and accountants, who are obviously not subordinates. Some objections to the concept of profit maximization were considered in the first chapter and there is another that may be mentioned here.

Profit maximization assumes purely rational and consistent behaviour so far as the attainment of that objective is concerned, but this assumption has been criticized by H. A. Simon in *Administrative Behavior*, and by others, and many organization theorists think of rationality as being qualified, or bounded, by a variety of personal and social factors. They do not say that a manager necessarily behaves irrationally, but that his pursuit of the profit goal is affected by an inability to see the whole of many of the problems he has to solve, by a flawed understanding of what he does see, and by the fallibility of his own and other people's judgments. A manager is forced by the complexity of the real world, and the limits of time and ability, to simplify problems, to compromise and to act in a generally non-maximizing way: he is better thought of as aiming to achieve a combination of economic and non-economic goals at a satisfactory rather than a maximum level. It is argued that to remove the bounds from rationality and assume an objectively rational man is to reduce the content of behavioural theory to a logical exercise of no realistic value.

Another approach to the problem of defining a manager has been to isolate and classify the essential elements of his work. Various results have been produced by this method, a classic example being Henri Fayol's in *General and Industrial Management*, where he identifies power to command subordinates and responsibility to plan, organize, coordinate and control their work as the basic features of any managerial job. Some writers argue that organizing is part of planning, or that coordination is included in control, but Fayol's classification has received considerable support. It excludes other, alleged, aspects of management that fall into the category of things that can be done by non-managers too, such as decision making and implementing policy, and things that are the responsibility of some managers but not all, such as initiating and financing new activities and settling the course for a business to follow.

Planning, organizing, coordinating and controlling have both major and minor aspects in business, and apply both to the aggregate of operations and to the operations of quite small parts. These four activities may also be called for in a situation where someone deals only with material resources and no managerial work is done. Because a manager's job differs so much from one position to another we cannot define in much detail what planning, organizing and so on involve without destroying the general validity of any definition based on them. This is shown by Peter Drucker's statement of the fundamental tasks which he thinks all managers must perform.[1] According to him there are five such tasks: setting objectives, organizing, motivating and communicating, measuring performance and developing subordinates' skills; a list with a different emphasis from Fayol's. Whether or not this classification is complete its generality is certainly lost when Drucker elaborates its items. Organizing for him includes grouping 'units and jobs into an organization structure' and selecting people to manage the units; motivating is done partly through the manager's

[1] P. F. Drucker, *The Practice of Management*, Heinemann, 1955, ch. 27.

'promotion policy'; and measuring requires him to see that 'each man in the organi-zation has measurements available to him which are focused on the performance of the whole organization'. Clearly the work described here is not applicable to every managerial position, as Drucker maintains. Some of it would only be done by quite senior managers and possibly by no one but a chief executive.

The definitions considered so far give a broad idea of managerial work, but they do not provide a satisfactory answer to the question: who are managers and who are not? In a further attempt to find one we shall now look at the case made out by Wilfred Brown in his paper 'Organization and Science'.[1] The total amount of work done in a company is shared between people in different positions, in some of which no subordinate help is required, while in others the work is greater than the occupant can perform without subordinates to assist him. Brown maintains that only the second kind have a *prima facie* claim to be called managerial positions and that we need more information about them before we can say that in fact they are.

Every occupant of a potentially managerial position is responsible to a higher business authority for the performance of his group's work. He does not have unrestricted authority over his own subordinates, but acts within the limits set by company policy and by the formal organizational system of his firm. The fact that he is responsible for his subordinates' work implies that his authority should include some minimum power to select subordinates who are acceptable to him and to remove from his group the ones who are not, for if a manager has unsuitable sub-ordinates imposed on him who can act individually or collectively in ways which make it impossible for him to discharge his responsibilities satisfactorily they may force him from his position. Therefore, in order to discover whether a certain person, *X*, is a manager we have to ask five questions.

1. Is *X* personally responsible for more work than he is expected to carry out himself?
2. Is *X* responsible for the work that he has allocated to somebody else?
3. Does *X* have the authority to overrule the appointment of people to positions immediately subordinate to his own?
4. Can *X* require a person to be removed from an immediately subordinate position?
5. Is *X* authorized to make assessments of his subordinates' capacities and determine their differential rewards?

Brown argues that if the answer to all five questions is yes *X* is a manager, and that these questions enable us to discover whether the necessary and sufficient conditions for being classed as a manager have been met in any position.

Brown had previously defined a manager as someone with authorized positions subordinate to his own to which he could appoint people and decide their work,

[1] W. Brown and E. Jaques, *Glacier Project Papers*, Heinemann, 1965, Paper 1.

he himself being accountable for the way that work was performed.[1] This definition omitted any reference to the assessment of the subordinates' capacities and the determination of their rewards, but these matters were covered in the policy document prepared in Brown's firm, the Glacier Metal Company, where the manager's responsibility and authority were more fully defined. It was made clear that a manager was responsible, among other things, for appointing and training his subordinates; assigning an order of seniority to a sufficient number of them to make sure that work would be carried on properly in his absence; allotting tasks to them at levels consistent with the standards he set; ensuring that each subordinate was rewarded at a level appropriate to the work he was required to do; and deciding whether to retain a subordinate or secure his removal from the group.

Brown's five conditions provide a more objective basis for deciding who is a manager than any of the previous definitions, but his argument is not generally accepted and there is no doubt that if the test of satisfying these conditions were widely applied many so-called managers would fail to pass. We should certainly find that large numbers of operatives and clerical employees were not immediately subordinate to a manager as defined by Brown, and that the nearest 'true' managerial positions in his sense were two, or even three, levels above them.

The manager's right to determine both the composition of his own subgroup and its members' rewards is likely to be qualified in several ways. Attitudes to industrial justice have been changing in recent years and a number of firms now accept the view that an employee should not in all cases be dismissed without a proper consideration of his case. The situation is far from uniform, but the introduction of personnel policies with safeguards for employees has made it decreasingly common for individual managers, especially at the middle and lower levels of a firm, to hire and dismiss people at their own discretion. The decision to remove a man from his job is often reached by more than one person and efforts are frequently made to transfer someone who is unsuitable in one position to another, more appropriate, position in the firm.

When at least two managers are involved in making this decision one of them is usually senior to the other, although not necessarily in the same line of command. The involvement of two or more managers protects the subordinate against capricious treatment and enables wider company considerations to be taken into account. In a small number of firms an appeals procedure has been devised which allows a displaced employee to put his case before a tribunal, but this procedure needs to be worked out with care. Its purpose must be not only to defend an employee against the arbitrary abuse of managerial power, but also to give a manager confidence that he has sufficient influence over the selection, retention and removal of subordinates to maintain his authority and secure the required level of performance from his group.

[1] W. Brown, *op. cit.*, p. 50.

When there is a range of ability and work in a subgroup a corresponding range of remuneration is called for within which the reward of each subordinate can be appropriately fixed. Different ranges are needed at different levels and the final responsibility for seeing that these ranges stand in a correct relationship to each other rests with the chief executive. There is a danger of considerable resentment and unrest if they do not. The manager of a subgroup at a lower level does not usually decide the differentials between the limits of the salary range of his own subordinates and the limits of the ranges applicable to other groups, but he should, according to Brown's thesis, play a major part in deciding the differential rewards of his immediate subordinates within their own income range.

The conclusions reached from a study of managerial literature and business practice are that no completely satisfactory operational definition of a manager has yet been stated and that the criteria used to distinguish managers from non-managers vary from firm to firm. Managerial work also differs in content and emphasis from one position to another, but nevertheless these attempts to define it do, taken together, give a general impression of what it entails and point more clearly the distinction between direction and management that was made before. They bring out the economic, social and organizational aspects of the manager's job and indicate the kinds of skill that he is likely to be called on to practise. They do not, perhaps, sufficiently emphasize the outward looking character of his work, but systems theory helps to remedy this defect by reminding us that all managerial roles are boundary roles. Every manager operates on the boundary of a system or sub-system, endeavouring to control not only the actions of its individual parts, but also the relations between those parts and between the whole system or subsystem and its environment. Every manager is the intermediary between a smaller and a larger world, and his exposed peripheral position renders him peculiarly vulnerable to the play of opposing forces and conflicting needs as he deals with subordinates, superiors and peers.

4.2 General managers and specialists

Terms like top, senior, middle and junior manager are often used to indicate the level of authority at which a person is employed, but they are not very exact terms and need to be used with care, preferably in relation to a company whose organizational structure is known. Most firms have a single chief executive who is *the* top manager, but as we saw, a number of large public companies have joint managing directors who form a top managerial group, and other concerns may also have such a group, consisting of the chief executive and some or all of the departmental managers directly responsible to him. It is not always safe even to assume that the nominal top manager is the real leader of his firm, because research has shown that this may be someone in a lower position – an assistant managing director or a works manager perhaps. One must also remember the effects of the firm's size and technology on the size and composition of the managerial team and the kind of work done at each level, and not be misled into thinking that because *A* is a senior manager in one company his position is necessarily more influential, onerous or rewarding than *B*'s, who is a middle manager in another.

When we speak of a general manager we shall normally mean someone responsible for the organization, control, coordination etc. of the company as a whole, someone who in most medium and large sized companies has no direct responsibility for any specialized departmental group. Under the general manager there are specialist managers in charge of departments or subdepartments concerned with such work as production, sales, marketing, accounting, personnel administration, purchasing, research and development, design, transport, or any of the other kinds of work that may be done in a firm. The general manager is thus synonymous as a rule with the top manager, or chief executive, and is sometimes given the actual title of general manager, although in Britain he is more often called the managing director, and in America the president, of his company. His position is of great importance: he fills a critical boundary role and is frequently expected to make the largest single contribution both to the way in which policy and long-run plans are formulated and the way they are put into effect.

He must be satisfied with the nature of the firm's transactions with its environment, pay constant attention to environmental developments and make sure that appropriate internal adjustments are made to external change. He has to see that the work of his managerial subordinates is related to the primary task and adequately specified, accepted and understood. He must approve the major resources to be used under their command; keep a balance between conflicting individual, group and company needs; create a social organism capable of meeting the formal demands made on it; and define what Rice calls the 'span of considerations' (technical, commercial, humane, financial etc.) to be taken into account when decisions are made. In short he is the principal architect of the organizational structure, the major influence on the choice of goals and the main controller of conditions that determine whether or not the goals are reached. The 'success of the enterprise may well depend upon whether he infuses the whole hierarchy with energy and vision or whether, through ineptness or neglect, he allows the organization to stagnate'.[1]

In a small business the general manager often has direct command over one, sometimes more than one, specialized aspect of the firm's work and only emerges as a true general manager, freed from the encumbrance of detailed departmental commitments, as the business grows and becomes profitable enough for other managers to be appointed to take charge of specialized activities. Once that stage is reached his main interest in departmental problems should be their effect on the efficiency of the company as a whole: he should be thinking in company terms. But it does happen that a general manager who is promoted after long experience

[1] F. Harbison and C. A. Myers, *Management in the Industrial World*, McGraw-Hill, 1959, pp. 15–16.

of one department's affairs finds it hard to do this and refrain from interfering in the work of his departmental successor, and if he cannot cut his departmental ties the business may suffer from an unhealthy bias and from the frustration of the subordinate manager who is made to feel insufficiently trusted to take responsibility for his own group's work. Burns and Stalker remarked on this in some electronics firms, where the response to problems created by new market conditions was for the chief executive to assume responsibility for the sales manager's work, thereby preventing himself from exercising the same detached control over the sales department as he might exercise over others, and adversely affecting the critical value of discussions between the interests of sales, production, development and finance.[1]

In holding companies and large diversified firms with a number of subsidiary enterprises, or product or process divisions, the scale of operations in any one of the constituent parts may be as large as, or larger than, that of many complete concerns. In each subsidiary or division the manager in charge often has a general authority over his part of the entire company and is supported by his own team of specialized managerial subordinates. In these large business units there will then be a body of general managers at the second level of the hierarchy, coordinated by a super general manager, or a managerial committee, at the top. The scope for decision making of the second-level general managers is typically limited by the need to maintain a balance between the different parts of the entire concern, and is likely to be relatively restricted in the case of investment decisions and appointments to senior managerial positions, compared with the power of the general manager of a completely independent firm.

Without a suitable supply of general and specialized managerial ability a country's economic development is retarded as surely as by a lack of capital. Managers provide the enterprising force and organizing skill without which other resources are used ineffectively or not at all. As an economy grows and becomes more diversified the demand for managers tends to rise more rapidly than the demand for labour as a whole, and industrialized countries become increasingly 'management-intensive' as they expand. That is, they use relatively larger amounts of managerial and capital resources at a higher level of industrial development than they did at a lower one. This does not mean that every increase in the size of a business is accompanied by an increase in its managerial ratio, because much depends on the extent to which product range and technology are modified with increases in the scale of production, but the general tendency for the managerial ratio to increase is there. The effects of different levels of industrialization and technology on the demand for managers was well illustrated by the Chairman of Unilever Ltd in 1956, when he said that the managerial ratio in the constituent units of that enterprise ranged from three per cent in African plantation firms to fifteen per cent in industrial companies in the U.S.A.

[1]T. Burns and G. M. Stalker, *The Management of Innovation*, Tavistock Publications, 1961, p. 62.

There are wide differences in ability and outlook between managers at any one level or with any particular expertise, as well as between people at different levels or with different forms of specialized training, and these differences do much to explain the variability of business performance. All economic work tends to be carried out inefficiently to some degree, but this degree varies strikingly from firm to firm and two crucial influences on efficiency are the attitudes of a firm's managers and the nature of their skills, as the P.E.P. report *Thrusters and Sleepers* has shown. This study revealed a clear association between managerial attitudes and rates of company profit and growth, and although thrusting attitudes were not, it is true, always highly correlated with success, sleepy attitudes were a serious danger to a firm's position.

Two more matters that are relevant to a discussion of general and specialist managers must be mentioned here in advance of their fuller consideration later on. The first is that, given the importance of managerial attitudes and ability to business success, it is natural to ask what can be done to influence attitudes in ways favourable to the firm and improve managerial skills. This calls for an assessment of the scope and methods of managerial education and succession which we shall make towards the end of the chapter. The second thing is that, in addition to the separation of general from specialist managers, a further distinction is often made between line managers and staff, or as some put it between line managers and functional (specialist) managers. This is an important matter, but the use of these terms raises difficulties which are more conveniently considered in another context and we shall not attempt to discuss them here. The significance of the line and staff classification will be examined in Chapter 6 and the meaning of staff will be discussed in some detail in Chapter 10, together with the so-called line and staff problem in business concerns.

4.3 Authority and leadership

A manager exercises formal authority by virtue of his position in a company, an authority which ultimately derives from the general meeting of shareholders, but more realistically from the chief executive or board and, from the manager's own point of view, from his immediate boss. Both a manager and his subordinates are appointed on terms that define (with varying precision) the area in which and the extent to which authority is expected to be exercised and obeyed. The distribution of authority between hierarchically arranged positions makes it possible to speak of the formal structure of authority in a firm.

The arguments of Etzioni and of Katz and Kahn, which were discussed in the first chapter, showed that every business depends on its ability to offer sufficient inducements to secure the involvement of people and elicit the services they are required to provide. The basis of managerial authority is the firm's remunerative power (its control of an instrumental cycle) and the employee's involvement is essentially calculative in kind. But authority also has coercive and normative aspects when rules are enforced and sanctions imposed, and when employees are persuaded of the intrinsic merit of their work and accept the aims and values of the firm. The greater the inherent satisfaction of work and the closer the employee's identification with the objectives of the firm, the more favourable the light in which managerial authority is likely to be seen, although cause and effect are reversible here. At worst, authority will be tolerated only to the extent that it is in an employee's economic interests as a dependent member of a corporate body to do so.

The readiness to accept managerial commands is influenced to some extent by the generalized deference to authority inculcated from childhood onwards, and most men's instincts also lead them to prefer life in stable, organized social systems which legitimate authority and uphold the rule of law. But it must always he remembered that in the last analysis the use of authority is contingent on its acceptability to the people it affects, a view that was cogently stated by Chester Barnard in *The Functions of the Executive*.

He argued there that the effectiveness of authority is proportional to the degree of acceptance and that a subordinate will only accept a managerial command completely if four conditions are met. They are that the subordinate must know the meaning of any order he receives; he must believe that the order can be reconciled with the purposes of the business as he understands them; the order must not be incompatible with his dominant personal interests; and he must be physically and mentally capable of carrying the order out. Barnard believed that most cooperative activity rests on the fact that these conditions are widely met, but that there are, in addition, areas of indifference in which orders are accepted without conscious questioning or reference to criteria of acceptability.

Within a company, then, a manager has a legitimized authority associated with his position and sanctioned by his subordinates. His positional authority is normally reinforced by technical authority and an authority of competence to perform his work. The manager's technical knowledge and skill must be adequate for him to determine subordinates' tasks, guide them in the performance of those tasks, and help them solve problems that arise from their work. He also wins respect and strengthens his authority by demonstrating his control over the environment when coordinating the activities of his subsystem with those of others and negotiating on his subordinates' behalf. Lastly, a manager may exercise authority of a purely personal kind: he may have 'charismatic' authority, a natural gift of leadership endowed by grace, which makes people willingly submit to his command. But even without this natural gift he can still acquire a knowledge of human problems and develop a sympathy with his subordinates' aspirations that enables him to establish a *rapport* with them and gain their allegiance. When positional authority is combined with professional competence and with technical and charismatic authority the manager's influence is immensely strengthened, but these elements can be combined in different proportions which produce equally successful results in different situations.

Besides submitting to managerial authority subordinates submit to the informal authority of their peers. Group norms and values are established which may either be at variance with the objectives and values of the formal system or reinforce them, and where the group supports loyalty to the superior and penalizes disloyalty the manager's authority is again increased. Part of managerial skill lies in understanding the nature of informal group authority and identifying the aims of the formal and informal organizations, while part of managerial success lies in appreciating the fact that managerial authority is a convention that is accepted because organization on any but an insignificantly small scale is possible only if certain people make decisions about the work of others. The power to make such decisions is an outstanding feature of managerial work, but the real power to make them is ultimately given by subordinates whose behaviour is itself significantly affected by the decisions that are made.

Four dissimilar types of authority can be distinguished which are not to be thought of as totally unmixed in practice. Autocratic authority in its extreme form assumes a 'divine right' to absolute managerial control. The autocratic manager often tends to regard subordinates as mere labour units whose productivity is reduced by their inherent disinclination to work, and he reinforces the economic incentive with a variety of pressures that drive them to complete their tasks. Subordinates have minimal discretion and may be exposed to the arbitrary exercise of managerial power. Paternalistic authority may be little more than a humane development of autocratic authority. The manager may be just as strict and insist on his unilateral right to make decisions, but he takes more interest in his subordinates' welfare, even if he reserves the discretion to decide what is good for them and what is bad. In the early stages of industrial development paternalism led to considerable improvements in the physical conditions of work and some paternalistic managers forged strong bonds of loyalty and affection between their subordinates and themselves.

Autocratic and paternalistic modes of authority are both evident today, but they have been modified over the long term by a number of factors, such as the increasing strength of trade unions, industrial legislation, changes in social structure and social values, and the rise of the 'professional' manager relative to that of the owner-manager in modern industry. The combination of these factors has encouraged the spread of constitutional authority, which gives managers modified powers to enforce rules and determine conditions of employment. Finally there is democratic authority which recognizes the subordinates' claim to a share in the decisions that affect their work, and in some cases to make important decisions for themselves instead of having them made by a superior. Democratic authority does not normally mean authority exercised by majority vote, but managerial authority tempered by the subordinates' participation in varying degree in the decision-making process.

Modern human relations theory is to a large extent the product of a reaction against the kind of managerial attitude shown half a century ago by the man who said that subordinates had to be handled like unruly horses and whipped and curbed, and that the essence of management was knowing how to drive your team. In America, much more than in Britain, the reaction went too far during the 1950s and the most zealous reformers were advocating managerial behaviour at the opposite extreme from autocracy, implying in some cases that to issue a direct command was offensive to human nature. Extreme managerial behaviour in either sense is undesirable if it means acting on the principle that subordinates are to be treated like beasts or that complex enterprises can operate efficiently if no one orders anyone else what to do. In the first case authority is undoubtedly abused, in the second it is abdicated: a workable form of authority must generally be found somewhere between the two.

No matter what position a manager holds he must have some authority to command his subordinates when he thinks an order is required, although his authority may be tempered and exercised in a number of ways. He has a responsibility to see that the tasks of his group are properly carried out, and once he accepts it he cannot shuffle it off without failing as a manager. He does not have to behave dictatorially or bellow like an old-style gang boss; he does not have to know better than his subordinates in every case what ought to be done; but neither does he have to get approval for every decision by taking a majority vote. His authority need not deny his subordinates' desire for self-expression, or prevent them from openly reasoning why and offering views that are contrary to the manager's own. A good manager can understand and allow for the personal differences of subordinates; benefit from their willingness to make constructive suggestions; appreciate the significance and real causes of their problems and complaints; give weight to the nature of their aspirations; and allow for their expected reactions to the measures he takes.

Managerial authority, successfully exercised, can increase the subordinate's confidence and sense of security and help to convince him of the value of his work. The diminution of authority may be justified in certain cases, but carried too far it weakens the coordinated character of business activity and frustrates managers and managed alike. Contemporary theoretical opinion seems to be moving towards the view that a good manager needs to recognize the various ways in which authority can be exercised and their potential effects, so that he can behave in a 'reality-centred' way and choose the most suitable leadership style in each of the situations in which he is called upon to act. Different leader-follower patterns are appropriate to systems and subsystems with different primary tasks, and the higher his position the more important does it become for a manager to recognize this and to learn how best to influence the variety of managerial methods and attitudes that are necessary below.

4.4 Studies of the manager's job

L. A. Allen's statement that the manager was 'still one of the great unknowns in business' was justifiable at the time because of the lack of detailed knowledge about his work, and to a large extent it is still true.[1] But it is becoming decreasingly so as a result of the research being undertaken in the management field. In this section we shall look at some pioneering studies of the manager's job made by Burns, Carlson, Horne and Lupton, and Sayles, and compare their findings with those of Rosemary Stewart, which have more recently appeared.[2]

Carlson studied nine Swedish managing directors for four weeks and Sayles observed the managers in the engineering development department of a large American concern. Burns investigated the work of seventy managers in eight British firms (mainly medium sized) over periods of three to five weeks: they were high-level executives described as top managers in six companies and as members of self-styled top managerial groups in the other two. Horne and Lupton's survey embraced sixty-six middle managers in a very mixed sample of ten British companies of widely different size (from 170 to 40,000 employees), and the term middle manager was used elastically to apply to managers in positions at one level to four levels below the chief executive's.

There are obvious difficulties in investigations of this kind, because they cannot be conducted as fully controlled experiments. The investigator cannot watch managers all the time and must rely mainly on their cooperation in keeping records of their activities for him to use. Such records are unlikely to be free from subjective differences of opinion about what work was being done and how work of a composite kind should be listed, but the researchers felt that by discussing these problems carefully with the managers concerned the risk of error could be substantially reduced. Most managers found that with practice they could easily keep a continuous record of their work without interfering with their proper tasks.

The results showed that the hours worked varied widely. The Swedish managers worked from 42·5 to 57·5 hours a week, excluding time spent working at the weekend, and eight of the nine executives complained (as did their subordinates for them) that their burdens were too great. Burns's top managers worked from 37 to 47 hours a week, with a mean of 41·5 hours, while the British middle managers had a mean length of working week of 44 hours and a range of 34 to 56. Most managers seemed to have little time to be alone to think and they were seldom free from interruption for very long.

[1] L. A. Allen, *Management and Organization*, McGraw-Hill, 1958, p. 3.
[2] T. Burns, 'Management in Action', *Operational Research Quarterly*, **8**, no. 2, 1957, 45–60; S. Carlson, *Executive Behaviour*, Strombergs, 1951; J. H. Horne and T. Lupton, 'The Work Activities of "Middle" Managers', *Journal of Management Studies*, **2**, no. 1, 1965, 14–33; L. R. Sayles, *Managerial Behavior*, McGraw-Hill, 1964; R. Stewart, *Managers and their Jobs*, Macmillan, 1967.

The bulk of the British managers' time was devoted to current operating problems, and in Burns's firms the top managers were able to devote no more than a quarter of it to general managerial problems and external matters. Horne and Lupton analysed what the middle managers were doing in more detail by measuring the distribution of working time between four major tasks (Table 4). These were:

(1) formulating (F): assessing the future, defining short- and long-term objectives and specifying the resources needed to attain formal goals;
(2) organizing (O): creating and maintaining the right conditions for plans to be put into effect and deploying resources to ensure that immediate objectives were reached;
(3) unifying (U): coordinating the work of a group; and
(4) regulating (R): controlling resources on a continuous basis by means of various techniques.

The analysis showed that most of the time was spent on the last three and this could be interpreted as support for the idea that long-term planning and decisions about the future course of the firm are more likely to be the responsibility of senior managers than others. But the time spent on formulating did not necessarily decrease progressively down the hierarchy: it appeared to be affected less by the level at which a manager worked than by the size of his company, the technology on which it was based and the specialized nature of his job.

Table 4

Distribution of managerial time

	F	O	U	R
		(Per cent)		
Production manager	33	28	19	20
Sales manager	17	21	16	46
Personnel manager	14	15	18	53
Financial and administrative manager	15	10	15	60

The work of all managers naturally involved them in constant dealings with other people, but a significant fact discovered by Carlson and Sayles was that a fairly small proportion of time was spent with direct subordinates. In the case of the American managers it was about one-quarter of the total and of the Swedish less than one-third. There was a high frequency of contact, too, which seemed to increase as one moved down the hierarchy. One Swedish executive made 434 contacts in four weeks, 138 of them with a single person and 296 with two people or more. The average length of time devoted to each meeting was twenty-five minutes inside the company, but 150 minutes outside. Sayles quoted two cases of supervisors' work that revealed an extremely high rate of contact at the lower levels, since one supervisor made 387, and the other 457, contacts in an eight-hour day, giving an average duration of one to two minutes for each contact. If the senior manager was active in dealing with managerial subordinates and outsiders, the supervisors were hyperactive in dealing with their larger numbers of operatives and with people outside their subgroups.

A notable feature of managerial work in both the British and the Swedish firms was that communication was predominantly oral and much more concerned with giving and receiving information than instructions. The middle managers spent 57 per cent of their time in informative communication, compared with only 8 per cent devoted to making and confirming decisions and 9 per cent to issuing or taking orders. Burns found a positive association between the rate of environmental change and the amount of time spent in discussion. In changing conditions there was a need for a full exchange of information that resulted in a great deal of informal communication, especially at the lower managerial levels.

The results of Miss Stewart's study of a varied group of senior and middle managers in manufacturing firms were similar in many respects to those that have just been discussed. She found that managers worked on average $42\frac{1}{4}$ hours a week (the range was 35–60 hours), the tendency being for more hours to be worked the higher the position. Wide variations were observed in the amount of time devoted to paperwork and in rapidly changing companies the proportion of time spent on it was relatively low, discussion taking a proportionately bigger share. Discussion was largely informal, an average of 43 per cent of the time being spent in this way, whereas an average of only 7 per cent was spent in formal committees. Discussion time was almost equally divided between meetings involving only two people and meetings involving three or more, and appreciably more time (average 26 per cent) was devoted to contacts between the manager and his subordinates than to meetings between the manager and his own boss (8 per cent). The fact that only 2 per cent of time was given to reading literature originating outside the company suggested that managers had little or no opportunity for thinking about wider issues at work, or for relating non-company information to their own problems. The lack of time to think was also shown by the fact that during a four-week period the managers had on average only nineteen spells of half an hour or longer interrupted by no more than brief contacts with other people, and only nine spells without interruption of any kind. But it is important to emphasize that once again wide variations were found, and indeed Miss Stewart seemed more concerned to bring out differences between managerial jobs than to dwell on the unitary character of the work.

It is clear all the same that most of the managers in these samples had a very active job, involving frequent dealings with other people and calling for skill in communication, especially of an oral kind. General managerial responsibilities increased as

85

one moved up the hierarchy, but not in a regular and predictable way, and in the middle range of managerial positions the important requirements appeared to be a good technical and commercial knowledge of the manager's own firm, an appreciation of the relationships that would help him get his work done, and an ability to make easy informal contacts. A manager emerges from these studies as someone who is often unable to plan his daily work with much certainty and who must approach each day in an open-minded and flexible way, ready to meet a variety of unpredictable problems and solve them in predominantly informal ways. His job is not often of heroic proportions; its main features are uncertainty and variability in many cases, and the basic virtue lies in holding things together and keeping the business moving forward on a reasonably steady course. Patterns of relationships are never static and many problems are neither satisfactorily nor finally solved. The manager is exposed to conflicting forces and must resolve them as best he can: not even the chief executive is free to order his activities exactly as he desires. As one of Carlson's managers put it, he may find that he is not so much like an orchestral conductor, coordinating his forces from a lofty and aloof position, as he is like a puppet pulled by a hundred strings.

This method of research into the way a manager spends his time has increased our knowledge of managerial work, but it does not provide answers to a number of questions that could still be asked, and Marples has criticized its theoretical deficiencies and suggested other directions that empirical studies might usefully take.[1] If the manager's job is envisaged as a 'stranded rope' made of fibres of different lengths (of time), representing different issues which arise in a succession of observable episodes, it is necessary to ask how the average length of time devoted to an issue and the number of episodes per issue are affected by the level at which a manager works, or by the department or firm in which he is employed. Managerial skill may be found to consist of an ability to keep a certain number of issues in play at the same time, but one would want to know what kinds of issue they were, whether they were repetitive and routine or intricate and varied, where they originated and how they could best be resolved. Should a high proportion of the manager's time be absorbed in dealing with relatively few issues it would then be worth examining these closely to find out whether anything more could be done to settle them efficiently.

The object of further research, in Marples's opinion, should be to improve the effectiveness of managerial work, and this requires more information than that already yielded by analyses of how a manager spends his time. We need to know how much time is spent on problems which he has raised himself and how much on problems raised by other people; how much is devoted to high-priority problems and how priorities are determined; how managerial loads are allocated and how

[1] D. L. Marples, 'Studies of Managers–A Fresh Start?', *Journal of Management Studies*, **4**, no. 3, 1967, 282–99.

overloads are dealt with; and whether the revealed distribution of managerial effort is justifiable in terms of organizational needs. What has been found by these predominantly sociological studies of managers and their jobs has some relevance to educational and training needs, but has not so far made any significant contribution to raising the general level of managerial efficiency, and there is still a great deal to be learnt about the objectively measurable characteristics of managerial work.

4.5 Managerial education

Since managers are a scarce and valuable resource it is logical to look for ways of improving their supply and ensuring that it is adequate to meet expected needs. Several related matters arise here, especially the methods by which actual and potential managers are recruited and selected, the ways in which their progress is measured or appraised, the promotion pathways open to them, and the education and training provided to meet their needs.

Without a reasonably assured supply of managers a firm's continuity, efficiency and growth are threatened, and planning for managerial succession forces it to consider its future organizational development, its probable rate of growth, the prospective changes in its activities and techniques, and hence the numbers of managerial positions of various kinds that will exist at different times and the required qualities of their occupants. The expected demand for managers can be compared with the available supply of people in the company, their capabilities and their potentialities for promotion, and with the scope for recruitment outside the firm. What are known as 'manpower budgets' can be drawn up relating to different periods in a way analogous to that in which financial budgets are prepared, and the succession plans can be linked with programmes of recruitment and managerial development which ensure a suitable spread of ages and qualifications in the company, and provide some safeguard against the danger of sudden and disruptive changes in the composition of the managerial team. It is difficult in a dynamic environment to plan the managerial system for a long time ahead, but not appreciably more difficult than planning some other things. So far as research evidence shows, however, only a small proportion of firms, even of those which make long-term product innovation and investment plans, pay much attention to their future managerial needs, and many companies fail to look ahead at all. The imperfect predictability of future needs increases the value of flexible planning procedures and makes it necessary to revise succession schemes at regular intervals as new information becomes available about the progress of existing employees, and as new decisions are made about prospective organizational change. Uncertainty increases the desirability of having a varied supply of talent within the company if possible, so as to increase the probability that someone with the required qualifications will be available when a new position is created or an unforeseen vacancy occurs. This does not mean that firms should become closed, inbred communities, since managerial migration has much to commend it from many points of view; but morale is almost certain to be improved if people in a company believe that it is trying to make the best use of their talents in a consistent and equitable way, and not appointing from outside simply because it has not properly assessed the qualities of its own employees, or has failed to give them adequate opportunities to develop their abilities to the full.

The increasing scale and complexity of business organization, the proliferation of managerial techniques and the technological transformation of many branches of industry have caused more firms to take an active interest in managerial education and training than in appraisal methods and plans for succession, and there has been a rapid growth in the number of managerial courses and training schemes since 1945. Impetus to their development has come from governments, international bodies like the former European Productivity Agency, professional bodies like the British Institute of Management, universities, technical and commercial colleges, the National Economic Development Council, and the Industrial Training Boards. Courses are now offered for present and prospective general managers, staff specialists of many kinds, middle-level and junior managers, and newly recruited managerial trainees. There are courses which give an 'appreciation' of a wide range of subjects, courses to prepare people for entry to business, and courses to facilitate the transition from one position to another during their careers.

With all this activity there has been controversy about the aims of managerial education and how they can best be achieved, about the content of courses, their length, teaching methods, and the value of formal education and training from the firm's and from the manager's point of view. So far as the last matter is concerned attempts to isolate and measure the effect of education and training on managerial performance and development have not been very successful so far, and the difficulty tends to increase in proportion to the degree of generality of the course. It is easier to assess the benefits of a course devoted to a specific technique, like budgetary control, or to the improvement of a specialized set of skills, like those of personnel management, than it is to estimate the value of an extended course of business studies at the first degree or diploma level at one end of the scale, or an intensive general course for senior managers at the other.

The various ways of defining a manager's job and the numerous aspects of his work that we have already discussed provide some explanation of the variety of courses and educational objectives to be found. Courses are offered to improve skills in organization, planning and control; human skills in communication and motivation; and analytical skills in solving problems and making decisions. They are provided to develop powers of leadership; to improve a manager's ability to deal with arduous, complex and rapidly changing situations; and to enhance his capacity to work more effectively within groups. The effect of these courses depends on many factors, such as where they are held, how long they last, the skills of the teachers, the quality of the people attending, their attitude to the course, and the attitude of their superiors when they return to their firms and try to put what they have learnt into practice. The main emphasis has understandably been on courses teaching special skills and techniques, because it is usually easier to see the probable scope for their application. General courses have gained favour more slowly and the Acton Society Trust reported in 1962 that only one in five of the large companies, and virtually none of the smaller ones, were prepared to support these courses at the senior managerial level, which implied a good deal of scepticism about their worth.

Business education is no exception to the rule that all education is to some extent an act of faith, but managerial education has an element of fashion too, and the increased demand for it can be explained partly by the desire of companies not to neglect something that competitors do, and partly by the persuasiveness of the institutions providing the courses. But if a firm makes a perfunctory obeisance to education and training to keep in the fashion it is quite likely to send on courses the people who can most easily be spared, rather than those who are most likely to benefit, although careful selection by the organizers of reputable courses does much to prevent this from happening. Another danger is that the fashion-conscious firm may not have a clear idea about why it sent someone on a course in the first place, or what it intends to do with him on his return. Much frustration has been caused by managers' inability to convince their superiors of the relevance of what they have learnt.

Several of the assumptions on which managerial education rests are questioned in *Managers and their Jobs*, in particular the assumption that courses can be provided for people in some broadly defined category like middle managers, and Miss Stewart suggests that more analyses of job content might show the suitability of one type of course for managers at different levels. Greater emphasis might then be put on providing courses dealing with salient job problems, such as communication and human relations, and on meeting the needs of particular managers (e.g. in the export marketing field) where they are not adequately met.

It seems probable that courses devoted to specialized branches of managerial work will continue to increase and make a valuable contribution to business efficiency, but what of the more general type of course about which there are obvious doubts? Properly designed, a course of this kind can help most by making a manager aware of the problems he will find in a new environment when he moves from the boundary of one system to another, and by suggesting ways in which these problems might be solved. The perception of existing environmental features might also be improved where no movement from a position is planned. This does not mean an identical content for all general courses, obviously, because people with different

89

specialisms need their knowledge and experience to be supplemented in different ways. A basic problem in hierarchical systems is that the nature and requirements of the manager's job may change quite abruptly from one level to another, especially where the emphasis shifts from narrower tactical to broader strategic considerations, and appropriate training can do much to ease the transition, with beneficial results for both the manager and his firm.

5

Foremen and supervisors

5.1 The foreman's position in the firm

The problem of definition arises in the foreman's case as it did in the manager's and again this is due largely to the variety of positions found and the variety of work performed. Foreman is a well-established title in the manufacturing and construction industries, but supervisor is more commonly used in offices and service establishments and seems to be gaining in popularity in all trades because of the superior job characteristics and status it implies to many people. But there are not only foremen and supervisors: there are superintendents; senior, junior and assistant foremen; first and second line supervisors; leading hands and charge hands; even titles peculiar to an industry, like coal mining's overlooker, fireman and deputy. The work these people do varies from industry to industry and firm to firm, and also between the departments of a single concern. To analyse their activities and discuss their problems in a general way requires a measure of abstraction, and we shall concentrate on those who are principally engaged in supervising the work of others who have either insignificant or no supervisory authority themselves. Our representative foreman or supervisor is therefore found at the first level in the hierarchy above the operative, salesman, typist or clerk at which the superior member of an organizational subgroup only occasionally does the same work as his subordinates (to instruct them, for example, or in cases of emergency) so that it occupies a very small proportion of his time.

Much of what is known about the foreman has been learnt from studies of manufacturing (especially engineering) industry, which suggest that his work can be divided into eight main tasks. They are: (1) planning and organizing the activities of his group; (2) overseeing and correcting his subordinates' work and ensuring that his section functions in a normally satisfactory way; (3) giving technical assistance and solving technical problems; (4) inspecting tools, machinery and products; (5) coping with breakdowns, accidents, or failures in supplies; (6) performing clerical and administrative duties concerned with keeping records, preparing reports, and collecting data for managerial control; (7) dealing with personnel problems and matters of industrial relations; and (8) maintaining relations with people outside his group, especially his immediate superior, but also managers of other subgroups, clerical staff and specialists of various kinds.

Fayol's view of managerial work, at least, would suggest that people doing the kind of job that has just been described are managers, but in practice there is considerable inconsistency of attitude towards the foreman's actual position in the firm. The Institute of Industrial Supervisors has called him an executive, and the Industrial Welfare Society a member of the managerial team who directs the activities of a primary working group. In some of the larger British firms with complex technological systems the foreman is treated as a junior manager with scope for promotion to higher posts. Several writers, like Fraser and Bridges, however, prefer to treat the foreman as a special case, neither manager nor worker but someone with a distinctive position between the two.[1] Alternatively the foreman may be accepted as a member of the managerial group, but only as a separate part of it, because his work has special characteristics and problems of its own.[2] He has also been described as a managerial representative or assistant who translates managerial policies and decisions into action on the shop floor. In this respect an essential aspect of his job is that he takes responsibility for those components of operative work that could only be done by the operative himself if he were periodically to shut down and leave his machine.[3]

The ambiguity of the foreman's position is reflected in studies of his own reactions to his role, which show him as sometimes identifying himself with the workpeople, sometimes with managerial superiors and sometimes with his fellow foremen in a self-consciously isolated group. Placed as he is between two clearly separate sets of people it would be surprising if the foreman were not sometimes troubled by the ambivalence of his role, and various studies of his behaviour have revealed the 'role stress' to which he is subjected as the man in the middle, the bumping post, or the marginal man on the edge of the mainstream of industrial development who is excluded from taking a full part in the affairs of both 'them' and 'us'.

5.2 The foreman's status and influence

Many people believe that the foreman's status and influence have declined and that the real net advantages of his job are no longer so great or so attractive as they were.. The decline in status has not come about suddenly and has not affected all foremen to the same degree. It has been a long-term change taking place over several decades, but it has become more apparent since 1945 and its effects have been more marked in some branches of industry than in others.

[1] J. M. Fraser and J. M. Bridges, *The Industrial Supervisor*, Business Publications, 1964.
[2] National Institute of Industrial Psychology, *The Foreman*, Staples Press, 1951.
[3] W. Brown, *Exploration in Management*, p. 190.

The foreman often has a different kind of authority over workpeople today from that which he had a generation ago, and the difference is most striking where his power to hire and dismiss the members of his group has either been taken away completely or drastically reduced by being shared with other people in the firm. There are still companies in which the foreman takes on and discharges hands, but over a wide range of industry these decisions are now made by a superior manager or a personnel department's staff, often by a combination of the two. The foreman may be consulted about appointments that are made and his wishes met where possible, but he frequently finds himself with a reduced discretion to determine the composition of his own subgroup.

A high level of economic activity, with overfull employment in many of the post-war years, has meant that the threat of dismissal has lost some of the potency it once had, and the frequent general scarcity of certain grades of labour has put a higher premium on the retention of workpeople and affected employers' attitudes towards them and the way they should be treated. As we saw in the previous chapter the ethos of industrial justice has been changing also, and more firms are adopting codes of behaviour that allow the worker to appeal against dismissal and other disciplinary actions, and in some cases to be heard by a tribunal whose decision overrules that of the worker's own superior. The cruder authoritarian forms of management have been criticized and the modern emphasis is on more 'human' methods that require a leader to develop skills unknown to many of those who relied on blunt commands and sanctions to produce the required efforts from their subordinates. It would be not merely cynical, but untrue, to attribute these changes in attitude and practice solely to changes in the state of the labour market. It would also be naïve to imagine that new labour conditions have not played an influential part in bringing reforms about. Whatever their cause the foreman, as the person in direct contact with the worker, has inevitably been disproportionately affected by developments like these.

The greater number of jobs and wider knowledge of employment opportunities have affected labour turnover rates and, although the lack of official statistics makes it impossible to prove, there are good grounds for believing that labour turnover has been higher since 1945 than it was before 1939. A high labour turnover adds to the difficulties of the foreman's job in a number of ways. There are more unsettling disruptions of his work, more new recruits to train and more new personalities to study and understand. There is a constantly changing pattern of relationships to deal with and increased uncertainty due to the unpredictably fluctuating composition, not only of the foreman's own work group, but of the managerial groups above. A high rate of labour turnover is probably due in most cases to economic and social factors beyond the individual foreman's control, and the evidence so far certainly does not show a positive correlation between the currently accepted patterns of desirable supervisory behaviour and the rate at which the membership of a foreman's group is changed by the voluntary actions of his subordinates. Nevertheless, a foreman may still be sufficiently disturbed by a high rate of labour turnover to try to reduce it, and to feel that failure to do so is an adverse reflection on his own influence and skill. If specialist staff are made responsible for measures to reduce the turnover rate the foreman's ability to cope with the problems of his group is altered and he may believe that his formal status has been diminished.

The growth of trade union power has affected the foreman's influence and weakened his position in various ways, apart from its effects on managerial attitudes and the treatment of workpeople which have already been mentioned. Collective bargaining and the handling of disputes frequently rest upon intricate procedures, formal and informal, whose observance is jealously preserved, and a foreman can cause serious trouble if his actions contradict the letter or the spirit of these procedures and the agreements and company policies on which they rest. The workers can cohere to protect their interests and bring pressure to bear on the foreman which is different from, but not necessarily less than, the pressure of his superiors. Unlike his subordinates the foreman is not typically a strong trade union member himself. Sweden is one of the few countries in which there is a powerful foremen's union, and in America and Britain the collective strength of foremen is not so great. In many cases the foreman must fend for himself when caught between the opposing forces to which he is exposed.

Within the unions shop stewards form special groups whose power has tended to increase at the expense of the foreman's. Instead of taking grievances and claims to their foreman, as formal practice generally requires, workers frequently go first to the shop steward who may not necessarily raise matters with the foreman himself, but go straight to a manager at a higher level in the firm.[1] When this happens the foreman's authority is undermined and his ability to maintain good industrial relations is impaired. The tendency for the foreman to be passed by has been encouraged by the natural anxiety of senior managers to minimize discontent among the workpeople, and by their acceptance of the argument that a case should be taken direct to someone who can decide the issue himself. Managers have also felt obliged in self-defence to find ways of dealing with a variety of demands over time which avoid the dangers inherent in allowing similar claims to be settled differently by foremen acting on their own initiative in different groups. The importance of precedents, and the pitfalls associated with an unwitting acceptance of new standards that conflict with previous agreements, have increased the degree of centralization in this respect and raised the level at which decisions about industrial relations matters are made.

It is understandable that the foreman and the shop steward should see each other as rivals, and a complex relationship often exists between them not far removed from a state of perpetual duel. The shop steward who always takes advantage of

[1] W. E. J. McCarthy, *The Role of Shop Stewards in British Industrial Relations*, H.M.S.O., 1966.

direct access to a senior manager is sometimes able to establish closer relations with that manager than the foreman himself enjoys. Yet the steward who is not fully employed on union affairs is strictly an operative in a lower formal position than the foreman whose status his actions affect. Not surprisingly in these circumstances severe tension often develops between the two men. A further undesirable, and probably unnecessary, result of the shop stewards' influence with senior managers is that communication between these managers and the foremen may be weakened or break down. Decisions concerning the foreman's group can be made without consulting him and he may be unaware of their nature until the shop steward tells him what has been done. The extent to which this practice lowers the foreman's morale is unknown, but it is quite likely to have an adverse effect on his attitude towards the company and his job. Probably the best way of correcting such a state of affairs is to make sure that the foreman is involved in any discussion about his subordinates' problems that either a superior or a shop steward wants to hold, but if this is impractical it is essential for the superior to tell the foreman what decisions have been made without him, and why.

A foreman who is promoted from the workers' ranks sometimes finds that he is not adequately compensated for the disadvantages he incurs, and that the difference between his own real income and that of his subordinates is either negative or very small. In many situations workers paid by results, or for large amounts of overtime, earn more than the foreman, and successive flat-rate increases in time wages on related scales diminish the real margin between the worker's and the foreman's pay. The foreman may also suffer from the strain of divided loyalty after promotion and experience mental stress when he is forced to think in wider and more abstract terms than before. The problems of dealing with people also impose a heavier burden on many foremen than the problems they met when they only handled machines.

The foreman's authority in his group has been considerably affected by the growth of firms, which has led to the employment of larger numbers of specialist staff and the introduction of more, and more complex and remotely operated, techniques of planning and control. Specialists have taken over much of the responsibility for the organization and measurement of work and in a large plant the production planning department, the quality control staff, the work study section and the inspectorate largely decide what the foreman's subordinates will do, and carry out a number of the checks that show whether their work is being satisfactorily performed. In the field of direct production, therefore, as well as in industrial relations, the foreman's power has been whittled away and he often lacks the status of a junior staff specialist in the firm.

Changes in work methods and manufacturing techniques have affected the foreman's status by altering the skills that his subordinates need for their jobs. It is logical to suppose that the higher the skills of those working under him the higher the foreman's own skill must be and the better the qualifications and training required to do his work well. The converse is also likely to be true. These matters are closely related to technology, whose effects on the foreman's position are of considerable importance and call for discussion at greater length.

5.3 The effects of technology

The foreman has apparently been affected by technology in different ways, some more favourable to his status than others. His importance appears to be most strongly preserved in unit-production firms where goods are made to special order, and in process-production firms like those engaged in certain kinds of chemical manufacture and oil refining. In unit-production companies the proportion of skilled workers in the foreman's group is likely to be high and their skills varied. The workman is usually able to identify himself with the immediate objectives of production, appreciate the value of his own contribution to the firm, and derive satisfaction from the use of a variety of skills – perceptual, manual, conceptual and motor – in its performance. The foreman's position reflects the high level of abilities in his group, and in one special-order firm studied the foreman obviously made important judgments in balancing the use of productive capacity and the requirements of the sales department, which had a direct bearing on the success of the firm.[1] In complex process-production plants the foreman frequently has a high standard of education and training and considerable responsibility for the operations under his control, and this helps to raise his standing in the operatives' eyes.

Where goods are produced intermittently in small batches the foreman's situation is less happy, partly because of the strain he sometimes suffers in having to reconcile prescribed rates of output with satisfactory quality and the maintenance of standard costs. In more than half the small-batch-production firms in the Essex sample studied by Miss Woodward and her colleagues the foreman had to decide which of these things was the most important at any particular time, and the only way of doing so in some cases was to make his own assessment of the current political situation in the company by trying to gauge the mood of his superiors and the distribution of power within the senior managerial group. Considerable uncertainty attached to this exercise, and the foreman's reputation could easily be jeopardized by faulty intuition or misreading of the true state of affairs.

The more highly rationalized and mechanized the production system becomes the lower does the foreman's status tend to be and in the large scale mass-production companies, like some of the motor vehicle and television assembly firms, many of the problems of both foreman and worker are found in their most acute forms. The people who work on an assembly line have the speed of their work dictated by the insistent demands of the machines, and perform repetitive jobs requiring in many cases a minimum of skill. There is a high degree of division of labour and a determined

[1] J. Woodward, *Industrial Organization: Theory and Practice*, Oxford University Press, 1965.

pattern of work, so that often only superficial attention is called for and the discretionary content of each job is extremely small. For many operatives the scope for satisfaction in performing such work is, not unnaturally, extremely restricted and a possible result of this is restlessness and discontent with which the foreman must deal. The constant pressures of a competitive market lead to continuous efforts to simplify individual activities and standardize work still more, and the foreman increasingly becomes the leader of a group whose members, with their rapidly acquired semi-skills, are replaceable in the short run by other people of a similar kind, and in the longer run, possibly, by superior machines. The foreman himself is in danger of becoming almost as easily replaceable as his own subordinates in some modern plants.

The effects of high labour turnover and absenteeism are particularly serious for the foreman in the highly mechanized mass-production firm, for he must keep the assembly line moving and find substitute workers when required as quickly as he can. When his group is at full strength, however, he has little power to influence the members' work, apart from seeing that they are properly equipped and get prompt and effective help when they are in difficulty. He can still play a valuable part as a problem solver, and his status in the group will be favourably affected by his personal ability to deal successfully with the troubles of its members. For much of the time, though, he may have to act more as a policeman than a helper, and concentrate on controlling a set of activities designed to achieve objectives which he does little or nothing to decide. His virtual inability to determine the character of their work may lead his subordinates to treat him as someone in a relatively minor role, but not necessarily to blame him for any frustration they feel. On the contrary, the foreman may be identified with them as a fellow victim of a system which none of them can change.

It was hoped that as automation replaced some of the traditional methods of production on assembly lines the position of both foremen and workers would be improved, but there are fears that this hope may not always be fully realized and the prospects are rather hard to predict. A comparison of automated and conventional assembly-line plants has shown that automation does not invariably call for a higher level of operative skills, and that when greater numbers of skilled workers are engaged they tend to perform indirect rather than direct production jobs. To that extent, therefore, the status of the typical line foreman may not be significantly improved. Working conditions in an automated factory may be better, because they are cleaner, than they were in the previous plant, but this is more likely to be to the workers' advantage than to the foreman's, and if it is the difference between them will to that extent be narrowed.

The greater complexity and expense of much automated machinery emphasize the value of specialized knowledge required to keep it operating efficiently and the importance of avoiding the high costs of breakdown. The key people are therefore the technical experts and maintenance men, rather than the line supervisors and their operative teams where these do not themselves possess the skills needed to deal with the mechanical failures that occur. The foreman may also find that a change in outlook is called for if he is to accept the fact that when machines take over work that people did before the workers often appear to be less actively employed, without in fact slacking or neglecting their work. Since the subordinate/superior ratio at lower levels tends to fall in automated plants a foreman who is prone to exercise close supervision will have greater opportunities to do so, and the effects of this on the subordinates' morale might be adverse. However, it is unwise to generalize too freely about the consequences of automation until more research has been done, and in any case the number of occupations and people affected by automation is still relatively small, so that the problems raised for the foreman by other technological systems remain more relevant from an immediate point of view.

The discussion so far has brought out some of the less favourable features of the foreman's position, but the picture is not one of unrelieved gloom. Many foremen still enjoy considerable authority and prestige in their companies and are genuine leaders of their own work groups, with a material influence on the satisfaction which subordinates derive from their jobs. In groups like these the foreman is 'the boss' in the workers' eyes and his attitude towards them and the methods he employs may have specially significant implications for productivity and for the quality of human relations in the firm. Even where the foreman's position has been weakened in any of the ways referred to here his behaviour is still an important variable in the activities of his group, and has been the subject of an appreciable amount of research.

5.4 Supervisory attitudes and behaviour

Research into the effects of the foreman's attitude and behaviour on the members of his subgroup has produced some interesting results which suggest that differences in supervisory style have predictably different effects on the subordinates' own behaviour under certain conditions. Seven behavioural characteristics of the foreman have been identified as important in this respect. They are: (1) the closeness of his supervision; (2) the pressure he puts on subordinates to produce; (3) the interest he shows in subordinates' welfare; (4) the degree of democracy he allows in the group; (5) his strictness in the enforcement of discipline; (6) the time he spends in personal supervision of work; and (7) his ability to influence the group's environment. These variables are not independent and it is probable, for example, that a foreman who exercises close supervision will also press subordinates to keep up a high rate of production, and that he will enforce discipline strictly rather than leniently when rules are broken. Nevertheless, it is often helpful to consider particular instances of behaviour separately when analytical studies are made.

Close, as opposed to general, supervision means that the foreman controls subordinates by making frequent checks on their performance and issuing detailed instructions which severely limit their freedom to decide how work should be done. This kind of autocratic, directive leadership tends to impose rigid formal work patterns on the group and reduce the interest derived by its members from their tasks. A strict leader is not necessarily unjust, but he is unwilling to condone individual departures from the requirements laid down. He is more likely to go to a subordinate to correct, reprimand or instruct him than to wait for the subordinate to come voluntarily to him when problems arise. Studies made in an insurance company and a tractor plant in America, and in a telephone exchange in Sweden, showed that close supervision and autocratic behaviour reduced the satisfaction which employees found in their work.

A democratic foreman is one who grants his subordinates reasonable freedom to share in the running of the group: he allows problems to be discussed and is willing to listen to other people's ideas and suggestions and give them consideration before decisions are made. Instead of flatly commanding he explains his wishes and helps subordinates to understand the reasons for what they are asked to do. Experiments in democratic leadership indicate that subordinates are drawn more closely together as members of a team and enjoy greater self-respect, but some of these tests have been conducted in rather artificial conditions, without the organizational pressures and managerial controls that would be met with in an actual business concern. In practice, the benefits of an individual foreman's attempts to adopt a more democratic style of leadership can be vitiated by a directive and authoritarian atmosphere in the rest of the firm.

A foreman who continually emphasizes the importance of higher production, who regards his subordinates primarily as so many labour units, and who is absorbed in the technical aspects of his job is described as work, or production, centred. His attitude may simply reflect his own character, but it can also be reinforced by his training, and by the demands of production planning and operational control systems which impose strains on him that he transmits to the members of his group. Such a foreman is conventionally contrasted with the employee-centred leader who sees his job in human as much as technical terms, taking a genuine personal interest in his subordinates and supporting them when difficulties arise. This kind of foreman has often been found to have a sympathetic and employee-centred superior himself, and the evidence supports the view that all supervisory styles may contain an appreciable element of imitation.

When a foreman is either temperamentally disposed, or impelled by the pressures of his job, to be despotic and punitive a cycle of reactions may be started. A decline in production interpreted by the foreman as a sign of personal failure is quite likely to provoke corrective action in the form of demands for improvement, coupled with stricter control, more rigid discipline and closer supervision of the work. This kind of response by the foreman, however, increases the subordinates' awareness of his authority and leads to an increased state of tension in the group, to frustration and to a decline in satisfaction with the job. These in turn tend to have an adverse effect on production and so offset the expected consequences of the actions which brought them about, thus inviting still tighter control and a repetition of the cycle that had previously occurred.

There has been considerable discussion about the relationship between the foreman's behaviour and the productivity of his group, of which this is one example, and a number of experiments have been conducted to discover the nature and significance of the factors involved. Their results show that it is possible for variations in socio-technical systems due to differences in supervisory scope and style, subordinate/superior ratios, the manner in which workers are grouped, and the ways in which foremen are trained, to account in some cases for differences of more than twenty per cent in group output. Much greater increases in productivity have been obtained by the use of wage incentives, work study and more capital-intensive processes of production, but their initial money cost is often high, and even when substantial gains in productivity can be achieved by these methods the value of an additional, if relatively modest, increase due to inexpensive social improvements should not be despised.

General supervision and employee-centred supervision have both been found as a rule to be associated with high output and high workers' satisfaction with their jobs. Punitive methods of supervision tend to be associated with lower productivity, as do strong pressures to produce, but the correlation between democratic supervision and output is less clearly marked, partly because the size of the group is a relevant factor here and subordinates may tolerate a more autocratic attitude when the group is large than they would if it were small. A relatively high proportion of time spent on supervision has been shown to be positively correlated with greater worker satisfaction and higher productivity, so long as the time was devoted to helping subordinates overcome their problems and not to maintaining a close watch on their work. It is not enough, however, to think of production in terms of gross or immediate output alone, since a high gross output may be reduced by the rejection of inferior units to a lower net figure. The foreman's decisions can affect this net figure if he is responsible for inspection, and it is possible for a strict, production-centred leader to mitigate the adverse effects of his behaviour on gross output by allowing borderline cases to pass through and keeping the rejection rate as low as possible.

The various factors mentioned here have their greatest effect when combined in such a way as to be mutually reinforcing. Thus a democratic, employee-centred foreman could have a less beneficent influence if he enjoyed only a very limited power to decide matters in his group and satisfy his subordinates' aspirations in terms of promotion or financial rewards. One further aspect of behaviour that is believed to be important in terms of subordinates' reactions is the foreman's detachment, used here in two senses and not simply to mean that a foreman is remote or aloof. Detachment is used by some writers to denote calmness and consistency of behaviour that enables subordinates to predict how their supervisor will behave and enjoy a feeling of security in their relations with him. But it is often considered desirable, also, for a foreman to be detached in a way that prevents him from identifying himself too closely with his subordinates, becoming emotionally involved in their problems, and being too constrained by their reactions to what he says and does. He should be reasonably independent not only of subordinates but of his own superiors, too, and feel free to express opinions openly, knowing that disagreements will be respected, and resolved by discussion whenever possible. Where both kinds of independence were allied to good supervisory practices the effect on the subordinates' attitude to the foreman has been generally favourable.

These are some examples of associations observed between different kinds of supervisory behaviour and the productivity and satisfaction of work groups. Low absenteeism also appears to be significantly positively correlated with a democratic leadership style, although not with the other supervisory attitudes referred to here, but no clear association has yet been found between the foreman's behaviour and rate of labour turnover in his group. A widely drawn conclusion from available research evidence is that a foreman has considerable potential influence for good or ill on the members of his group, but it would be wrong to suppose that supervisory behaviour always offsets other influences to which subordinates are exposed, or that it has a stronger effect on productivity than conventional real rewards. It can, however, reinforce them or partially compensate for their absence. One could, of course, argue that hard-working subordinates with a high level of productivity inspire foremen to display good supervisory attitudes and that this is the true order of cause and effect, but in the present state of our knowledge it seems fair to infer that people often work more productively and enjoy greater satisfaction because they are supervised in one way rather than another. It is possible that other, quite independent, factors influence both a foreman's attitude and a group's response, but the nature and importance of these factors have not yet been experimentally proved. As things are it is reasonable to regard the foreman as a primary motivating agent in the firm and to treat his behaviour as an important influence on subordinates' behaviour and morale.

Our understanding of the effects of supervisory behaviour is, however, far from complete. Certain kinds of behaviour are now regarded, at least in theory, as generally better than others because they are associated with increased worker satisfaction and higher productivity, and the image of the happy productive worker is pleasing to behold. But happiness and satisfaction in work are not sufficient causes of high productivity and we cannot be sure that any particular style of supervision will guarantee their result. The existence of happy unproductive and unhappy productive workers, and the association of different effects on productivity with the same supervisory style, raise questions that still await complete and convincing answers. It is dangerous as yet to suppose that there is an ideal pattern of supervisory behaviour to which all should conform, and dangerous also to identify certain supervisory styles too closely with particular group types. Supervision is often shown as being good or bad in relation to a group whose membership is implied to be constant and of uniform character, whereas in practice the membership changes and each person in the group is a distinctive personality to be studied on his own. The real test of a supervisor's skill is therefore most likely to be his ability to cope with changes in a group's composition, reconcile disparate elements within it, and learn how to behave towards different individuals and deal effectively with different problems as they arise. He needs a variety of supervisory styles to meet the varying demands made on him in the ordinary course of his work.

5.5 The selection and training of foremen

The Hawthorne experiments of Mayo and his colleagues encouraged the belief that harmonious work groups are managed by people with superior skills in human relations, and the idea that suitable training could increase these skills led to a proliferation of training schemes in America in the 1940s and 1950s whose main purpose was to make the foreman more socially conscious, and aware of the effects of his actions on the feelings and behaviour of others, so that he could be taught to supervise in motivationally desirable ways. Enthusiasm for these schemes was not initially tempered by many serious attempts to discover whether they were actually producing their intended results, but when evidence at last began to accumulate the more ardent advocates of human relations training received an unpleasant shock, and many managers awoke to the fact that the schemes they had supported were far less effective than they had confidently hoped. Studies like that made in the International Harvester Company suggested that human relations training brought very small gains, and might even have a slightly unfavourable effect on the foreman's group. Research in the Detroit Edison Company showed that it mattered comparatively little what the foreman was taught, or how he was persuaded to lead his own subordinates, if he was not himself managed in a similar way. It was not sufficient to concentrate on supervisory training alone: human relations training had to start, and be effective, at the top of the managerial ladder before it could be really successful lower down.

Gradually, therefore, the lack of evidence to substantiate the bolder claims for training foremen along these lines led to greater caution and it was recognized that in some cases spurious human relations techniques had been propagated which did more harm than good. But although the emphasis on human relations skills is no longer so great as it was a few years ago it is still apparent in the contents of most training programmes for foremen today. So far as the foreman is concerned this is probably a good thing, for while the proportion of his time devoted to coping with human problems at work may look relatively small he often finds this one of the most difficult aspects of his job, and one with which he is least well prepared to deal without some assistance.

A satisfactory training programme cannot rest on human relations training alone; it must also pay attention to the technical and administrative aspects of the foreman's work. It is easy to draw up a long list of subjects about which the foreman should know something: business economics, labour law, costing techniques, decision-making techniques, work study methods, organization theory, psychology and industrial sociology are some examples. But it would require supranormal ability to acquire an effective knowledge of all these things, and given the foreman's previous education and the limited time he can devote to extending it a careful choice must be made, preferably with each foreman's special needs in mind. Since these needs differ from one person to another it is appropriate that a diversity of courses should be offered, and that complementary facilities should exist for training people in readiness for promotion to supervisory positions and to become more effective after experience has been gained; to prepare them for new problems that lie ahead; and to increase their suitability for subsequent promotion to still higher posts. The responsibility of senior managers to ensure that foremen are adequately trained is part of their wider responsibility for satisfying as far as possible the educational and training requirements of people at all levels in the firm. The value of training is reduced, however, if foremen are badly selected and attention to selection and training procedures should go hand in hand.

The criteria for selection are extremely varied. A foreman may be selected on grounds of age, technical knowledge or operative skill, or because he is strongly recommended by his own superior. It has even been said that his selection sometimes depends on his unpopularity with fellow workers, his religion, or his membership of a particular society or club. The more sophisticated firms may use interviews, group discussions and psychological aptitude tests to help them decide who is suitable for appointment, possibly with the assistance of an independent consulting body such as the N.I.I.P. Elaborate methods like these are also used fairly widely by the larger American and Scandinavian firms.

Interest in the selection and training of foremen had been growing, according to a Ministry of Labour report published in 1964, but it was still relatively low in many small and medium sized companies and expenditure on training was one of the first things to be reduced when company income fell. A number of businessmen no doubt remain sceptical about the value of training, and their attitude is understandable in view of the difficulty of measuring objectively the gains to be derived. It might help if formal and systematic, instead of informal and erratic, processes of selection and training were looked on at the least as valuable initiation rites which invest promotion to the foremen's ranks with more significance than it would otherwise have. The potentially awkward transition from worker's to foreman's role might then be more easily made and the foreman's status coincidentally raised.

5.6 Conclusion

There is ample evidence to show that the foreman's position is a strategically important one, placed as he is between managers on the one hand and non-managers on the other, and his situation between what have been called the upper and nether millstones of the firm is the cause of many of the problems that he has to face. He influences subordinates by his own behaviour in a variety of ways which can reinforce or offset each other with beneficial or harmful results. Some of these behavioural variables have been considered, but it is worth emphasizing in conclusion that although such factors as technology, the size of the group, the foreman's selection and training and his attitude are all highly relevant from the subordinates' point of view, the foreman himself is much concerned about the extent of his formal authority and the treatment he receives from his own superiors.

These have a close bearing on the way the foreman treats his subordinates and on his effectiveness in securing the cooperation of his group. The tone set at the levels above is important, because the foreman often takes his behavioural cue from the people whose requirements he and his subordinates must meet. The formal extent of his authority determines in large measure the control he can exercise over the group's environment, as well as within the group itself. When dealing with subordinates sympathy and consideration are certainly desirable, but employee-centred leadership is not by itself enough. The foreman needs to be able and willing to use his authority in ways which his group accepts as advantageous to its members, for if they perceive his authority as beneficial their attitudes towards him, the company and their jobs are, on balance, more likely to be favourably than adversely affected by what he does.

From the senior manager's point of view the foreman's role should be seen as one of special significance, because he occupies a boundary position in a subsystem composed of non-managerial employees whose aims, attitudes and abilities are likely to differ greatly from those of the executive members of subsystems at higher levels. The typical foreman has the unique task of acting consistently as an intermediary between managerial and non-managerial groups and interpreting the values, expectations and language of each group to the other. His success in carrying out this job has a direct and basic bearing on the efficiency of operations in a dominantly large part of most industrial concerns. Senior managers can do a great deal by trying to understand the nature of the foreman's problems and helping to solve them where they can. They can help by reducing conflicts between organizational demands on the foreman, by allowing him to share in the decision-making process as much as possible, by assisting him to prepare for change and by strengthening his authority in the firm. In such ways they increase the foreman's confidence and command over his job and materially improve his prospects of doing it well.

6

Formal organization (I)

6.1 The nature and purpose of organization

An appropriate organization of resources is essential for the achievement of a company's primary task, and in any business of more than very small size that organization must to a great extent be formally determined and not left to informal methods or chance. The result is that every firm of the kind we are studying will have a formal organizational structure, and it is to a study of the properties and significance of this structure that we now turn. The primary task, and decisions about the best way of achieving it, directly affect the company's organizational form and impose important restraints on the place, time and nature of the work done, and the resources used to perform it. Organizational structure is designed to meet a firm's needs: it is strictly a means to an end and not an end in itself. A change in the environment, or in the primary task and the subsidiary tasks related to it, may dictate a change in organization: structures which have apparently static characteristics in the short run cannot be expected to preserve them unaltered in the long.

Formal organization relates to the work of individuals, single subgroups, collections of subgroups, and the enterprise as a whole. It calls for definitions of the jobs to be done when the total task is shared between many people; the relationships between them; the authority which each person has over men, money, materials and machines; his responsibilities in the firm; the places in which different decisions should be made; and the channels of communication along which commands and information are to flow. Organization thereby helps to achieve objectives indirectly by providing a coordinating mechanism that unites a mixed bundle of productive factors into an operational entity. It has a synergetic effect which is seen in the form of a combined output from individual work efforts far greater than that obtainable from the performance of identical unorganized tasks. In fact, many jobs done in an organized situation would be done either less well or not at all if they were not logically related to, and coordinated with, others. Of the majority of activities in complex systems it is true to say that in organization alone lies their full meaning.

6 Formal organization (1)

In preceding chapters we examined the work of directors, managers and foremen, seeing how these groups are hierarchically disposed and how the members of each derive authority from a higher organizational plane. Ignoring the dispute about definitions we can envisage the chief executive, the managers and the foremen as elements of the managerial subsystem of the firm, the actual size and composition of the subsystem varying from one company to another. Together, these people have responsibility for the efficient day-to-day operations of the enterprise, the aggregate work of managing the business being shared within the subsystem. The sharing of the management process starts with the chief executive, who delegates to subordinate managers the power to command others and make decisions in specified spheres, authorizing them to delegate similarly in their turn. These acts of delegation should result in a known pattern of adequately defined, mutually appreciated individual responsibilities and tasks that enables policy to be carried out and the company's objectives to be reached. An organizational structure will then clearly and definitely exist and provide 'the framework of effective management', as Brech has called it, stressing the fact that the significance of organizational structure can only be grasped if one appreciates that the management process must always be an integrated one, although it has to be shared to allow a business to grow beyond a rudimentary state.

In the first chapter we considered Barnard's view of an organization as a changing aggregate of cooperative activities, and it has become increasingly common to talk of activities (or acts) as the true organizational fabric. People in a company act on materials and machines, and above all on other people. A minimum number of formal relationships must be maintained by the occupant of any organizational position, linking it to a certain number of others. A section foreman, for instance, may have regular formal dealings with a works manager, a production controller, an inspector, a maintenance engineer, a stores clerk and fifteen operatives, and his relationships with these twenty people constitute his *role set*. For each position there will be a comparable role set and the whole structure can be defined as a network of roles, or articulated role sets, and their associated activities.

In each role set there is normally a high proportion of predictable demands on a role occupant and a high proportion of predictable responses from the people with whom he deals. But, as we shall see in Chapter 9, there is controversy about the extent to which it is either possible or desirable to define a role in exhaustive detail, and organizational problems often arise from idiosyncratic interpretations of responsibility and unpredictable behaviour within the system, as well as from uncontrollable external change. Organizational behaviour is also complicated in varying degree by the multiple activities that have to be carried out in each role and by the fact that people at the intersections of role sets frequently suffer stress, as we saw in the case of the foreman. One role may form part of more than one subsystem (e.g. a role in the managerial subsystem may also be part of the main-tenance and supportive subsystems as defined by Katz and Kahn), and one person

106

may fill more than one role and have to reconcile the possibly conflicting requirements of his different role sets (e.g. the chief executive in Chapter 4 who assumed the sales manager's responsibilities). Nevertheless, the analysis of roles, role sets and role responsibilities provides a good insight into the way an organizational system works, and enables a helpful comparison to be made between formal organizational needs and the extent of their fulfilment.

In abstract terms the structure can be said to exist apart from people, for while a position may be vacated by someone leaving, or moving within the company, the position itself can remain, and even if roles are left unfilled it does not follow that the system breaks down, although its functioning might be altered or impaired. The work of a role may change in character without a corresponding change in the capacity of the occupant (and *vice versa*), and roles may be added or taken away. None of this means that people are irrelevant to the design of a structure, only that it can be treated for some purposes 'as an entity in itself', 'made the subject of explicit thinking, analysis, and alteration', and 'designed in its own right, bearing in mind that people subsequently will have to fill the roles set up within it'.[1]

This argument can be compared with L. F. Urwick's ideas in *Elements of Administration*, where he says that the organization planner should not imagine that human difficulties will not arise, or that the ideal design of a structure will not need to be modified to accommodate the human resources available. Job specifications have to be adapted to the people who can be appointed, but these alterations should be regarded as temporary departures from an ideal state. In any case, fewer adjustments to allow for personalities may be expected if the planner sets out to design a structure on a simple, logical basis which presumes the availability of ideal human material. If he plans the organization in this way the resulting 'machine' will operate with greater smoothness than if various 'human oddities' were first assembled and a structure then devised to contain them. A well-designed structure increases a firm's ability to attain its objectives in a socially acceptable and efficient way to the extent that it supports an appropriate system of authority, creates a low-resistance network of communications, enables correct decisions to be made in relevant positions, provides scope for self-expression and personal development, and conduces to an economical use of resources and to business growth.

Many organizational problems are common to a large number of firms and there are structural similarities in many cases between one company and another. How to secure complete coordination of the parts is a fundamental difficulty, as is the need to elicit the cooperation of employees. Personal and corporate goals are not always identical or even congruous, and managers must try to reconcile them and devise a system in which the individual can achieve his own dominant objectives while contributing fully to the achievement of the firm's. In all companies there is specialization and division of labour on both the horizontal and the vertical plane, and each

[1] W. Brown, *Exploration in Management*, ch. 3.

complex organizational structure contains so many levels and so many departments or sections operating side by side. Despite these similarities, however, each structure is unique to the enterprise for which it was designed and it is wrong to think of an ideal structure applicable to all firms, or to suppose that because a structure is suitable for a firm in one situation it will necessarily be so in another. Organizational structures cannot be cast in a standard mould; each must be tailored as closely as possible to the changing needs of one particular concern.

In this section we have combined some of the ideas of more orthodox, now often called 'classical', organization theorists (like Urwick) and 'modern' theorists (like Katz and Kahn), but this is an appropriate place to warn the reader of a considerable divergence of opinion, indeed of a fundamental difference of approach to organizational analysis, between some members of the older and newer schools, the nature of which will become clearer as we go along. One of our aims, however, is to blend theories as far as possible, rather than keep them rigidly apart, although their contrasting features will be brought out as well as the extent of their common ground. For the rest of this chapter we shall be mainly concerned with classical concepts and a rather stylized treatment of organizational structure: as the argument is developed subsequently these concepts will be examined more critically and the formal organization will be progressively humanized. We shall look at it increasingly in terms of the problems and behaviour of the people who occupy the positions in a structure and infuse the abstract administrative design with life, often modifying the intended character of the formal system in a number of significant ways in the process.

6.2 Formal relationships

If an organizational structure is seen purely as a network of formal positions the direct relationships between them can be partially defined in spatial terms. The basic relationship is a vertical one between superior and subordinate (Figure 1) and a series of linked vertical relationships creates an extended line of authority, or chain (Fayol's scalar chain) of command (Figure 2). In practice a line in which each superior had only one subordinate would be rare.

In a subgroup with several subordinate members the vertical relationships can be shown in various ways (Figure 3), with different possible implications that will be considered in a later section dealing with organization charts.

Horizontal relationships may exist between people on a common level who are members either of the same subgroup or different subgroups (Figure 4). The significance of broken and unbroken lines will also be dealt with later.

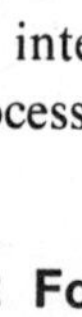

Figure 1

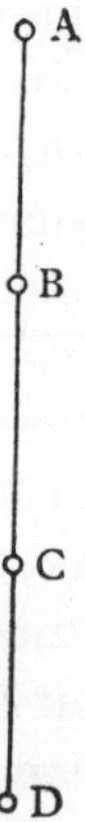

Figure 2

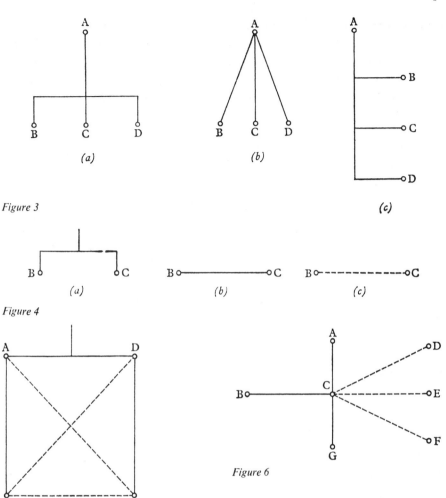

Figure 3

Figure 4

Figure 6

Figure 5

When vertical relationships are juxtaposed, diagonal relationships between people at different levels and in different lines can be established (Figure 5), and it is possible then for one position (*C* in Figure 6) to be formally linked in six different ways with others.

There is considerable terminological confusion in the organizational field, as this chapter will show, of which one needs to be aware. Unrevealing though they are in many respects the terms just referred to should at least be clear, but different terms are used by other writers, sometimes in an equivocal sense. Superior-subordinate relationships, for example, have been defined as direct, but if direct means without the intervention of a third person (and any other usage causes needless confusion) other formal relationships can be so defined. Even an alternative term, authority relationship, favoured by some Americans, is not entirely unambiguous, because an element of formal authority can exist in relationships other than vertical ones. Lateral relationship is a term sometimes used and Brech applies it to a limited category of horizontal relationships as we define them, but if spatial terms are to be used at all it seems helpful to make the important distinction between horizontal and diagonal clear.

Quite simply, it is pointless to try to devise an exhaustive catalogue of relationships, because the result would be too cumbersome to be of much practical use, and it is virtually impossible to arrive at concise definitions which are also complete. Vertical relationships tend to change in quality as one moves up the hierarchy; horizontal relationships between members of one subgroup may have quite different characteristics from those between members of different groups; and diagonal relationships can exist on a variety of bases between people in different 'line' or different 'staff' departments, as they will shortly be defined, or between people in both.

Whenever terms like these are used one must remember that they may have limited and peculiar meanings. They are often useful in theoretical discussion, but it is only possible to get to the heart of a formal relationship in practice by finding out why it was created, what results are expected from it, and how it is maintained in the complex pattern of formal and informal dealings in the firm.

6.3 Types of organizational structure

INTRODUCTION

Work can be organized on a process, product, time or territorial basis, or on the basis of a particular class of consumer to be served, but in practice it is often necessary to adopt more than one basis of organization in complex systems, and compromises will then be called for if different organizational requirements conflict. Each method of organization, considered separately, has potential advantages and disadvantages that vary in strength from firm to firm, and the basic problem is to discover the most appropriate method, or combination of methods, for the enterprise concerned. The matter is sometimes a complicated one, and the reader is referred to an article by E. J. Miller for a fuller discussion of the issues involved.[1] A few examples here may help, however, to indicate the kinds of difficulty that may be encountered when organizational structures are designed.

If work is arranged on a process basis, for instance, there may be scope for a greater development and a more intensive application of knowledge about the process, and for an economical use of process resources. Both managerial and operating economies can be enjoyed which would be lost or reduced if the resources were dispersed and mixed with others having a different specific use. On the other hand, the organization of resources in quasi-independent process-based units

[1] E. J. Miller, 'Technology, Territory and Time; the Internal Differentiation of Complex Production Systems', *Human Relations*, **12**, no. 3, 1959, 243–72.

may make it difficult to reconcile differences between the technical optima of related units, and require the sacrifice of some economies of scale to achieve an acceptable operational balance. Furthermore, although specialization is increased in one way it may be reduced in another. A typing pool is a process-based organizational unit whose members perform similar specialized work. But each typist may have to do a variety of work for different people and find it hard to acquire a close (specialized) knowledge of any one manager's requirements. If a manager's needs could be better met by maintaining a continuous working association with one typist, and if he has to wait for his work to be done by someone who is relatively familiar with his needs, his effectiveness and satisfaction are both likely to be less than they would be under a different system.

Organization on a product (sometimes called purpose) basis means that work related to the production of a particular good or service is grouped under the same command, and is a common arrangement in single-product firms. Multiproduct companies may have a number of identifiable product-based organizational units within the structure of the entire concern. This type of organization may, however, make uneconomical use of resources whose output is consumed by different units within the enterprise. An engineering company, for example, might have several plants making different goods, but all incorporating cast metal components. It has to decide whether to buy castings from outside, allow each plant to make the components it requires, or supply the plants from a central casting unit. Technical economies, especially, might be enjoyed by concentrating casting work in one unit, but set against these are possible problems of coordinating the casting unit's output with the variable needs of the production units, and the resentment that production managers might feel at the loss of direct control over an important part of their operations.

The departmental organization is essentially complementary to the two types that have just been considered. In either case it is possible to have a departmental distribution of work which allows a further degree of specialization to be enjoyed. But the allocation of departmental roles is a frequent source of difficulties. The danger of departmental bias has already been mentioned and is something that many companies fail to avoid, so that due perhaps to historical accident or a dominant personality one department exercises a disproportionate influence over the behaviour and development of the firm. Current theoretical discussions are tending implicitly or explicitly to push the marketing department into a pre-eminent position, on the ground that a company is a system driven by its market and that everything it does should be related to its ability to satisfy market needs.[1] This is fundamentally true, but it should not be allowed to obscure the importance of balance, or the fact that at particular times non-marketing matters may call for concentrated managerial attention for their problems to be solved. As Mrs Penrose has observed

[1] Cf. H. van der Haas, *The Enterprise in Transition*, Tavistock Publications, 1967.

in relation to this matter, strong marketing ability without technological competence and technological competence unsupported by effective marketing skills are equally vulnerable states.

A recurrent problem in departmental structures is to decide whether and when to locate resources in a newly formed or an existing department, and in the latter case which one. Is it desirable to remove all work identifiable with marketing from places where it is currently performed and create a new department? Should the provision of technical advisory services be a production, an engineering, or a sales responsibility? How strong is the case for a separate purchasing department? Should a statistical section be created, and should it be located in the economic intelligence or general administration department of the firm? These are hypothetical, but not unrealistic, questions of a kind often raised in business, and the answers to them clearly influence structural design, the nature of formal relationships, and efficiency. The position in which work of a certain kind is performed affects its cost and its real value to the firm. Often there is little difficulty in deciding where new resources should be located: their use may be confined completely or predominantly to one department, or a particular manager may have persuaded colleagues to give him an opportunity to prove their value and he takes control of them out of direct personal interest in their use. But in many cases such questions cannot be answered in an immediately obvious way, or by rule-of-thumb methods; they call for a careful assessment of a special situation and a comparison of the probable gains and losses associated with the choices that could be made.

Departmental organization in one form or another is the generally adopted basis for sharing work and we shall therefore look at it more closely in the next part of the discussion, where types of organizational structure are examined from a different point of view.

LINE ORGANIZATION
The simplest form of organizational structure consists of a single line of authority or a small number of lines in parallel. It is often referred to as a line organization, but without elaboration this term is misleading. Consider a business whose employees are grouped in departments concerned with particular aspects of company work, each with its own hierarchy. In all departments an identifiable line of authority and channel of authentic communication runs from the departmental head to the most junior employee, and the several lines come together at the position of the chief executive. Are all businesses based on such a departmental allocation of work line organizations, or only some? does it matter how many departments there are, or what kinds of work they do? To answer these questions by saying that, although each department has its own line of authority certain departments are line departments and others are not, leads to the apparent tautology that a line organization is one containing only line departments. Obviously, we must know what line depart-

ments are and why they are different from others. We shall first look at this problem of departmental classification and nomenclature in the way suggested by Joan Woodward and then compare her ideas with those of other writers on formal organization to see what agreement there is between them.[1]

Miss Woodward says that a firm's work can be divided into task functions and element functions. Task functions are the vital ones that must be performed if a firm is to operate as an effective unit and accomplish its primary task: they form the foundation on which the enterprise is based. Element functions embrace a potentially large number of activities, taking industry as a whole, and are intended to increase the efficiency of the task functions and so strengthen a firm's position. Task functions can be identified with what others have called line activities, and line departments are therefore responsible for the performance of task functions.

The task functions vary from one enterprise to another, depending on the size and nature of its resources, the way they are used, the industry in which the firm operates, and the goals at which it aims. Miss Woodward maintains that in the general run of manufacturing companies there are four task functions–production, sales (or marketing), finance, and product development and research–different names being given to them in different firms. Some companies may have less than four task functions, but in most manufacturing concerns the inclusion of production, sales and finance is virtually mandatory. In a retailing or wholesaling company, on the other hand, production in the conventional sense may not take place at all. Selling is a task function still, but purchasing may be another. Again, in businesses like advertising agencies, market research companies, and road haulage concerns the task functions include some which would be treated as element functions in other enterprises. The point need not be laboured; what matters is that in every business there are task functions on whose proper performance the business depends to a critical extent, and other functions of less fundamental importance. If a firm's activities are confined to the task functions, and resources grouped on that basis, it can for analytical purposes be considered as a firm with a line organizational structure.

Alternative names for task and element functions might be basic and auxiliary functions. Brech uses the terms operational and functional activities, although they do not correspond precisely to task and element functions, and when L. A. Allen talks about the functional nature of company activities he uses the word functional in a different way from Brech. However, granting for the present that there are grounds for differentiating activities on the basis of their relative importance to a company's viability, it may be better to postpone further consideration of terms and their meanings until the end of this section. Meanwhile we shall follow Miss Woodward in making the distinction between task and element functions the basis for discussion.

[1] J. Woodward, *op. cit.*

The most elementary form of line organization is that in which only one task function can be identified, as in the case of a small manufacturing workshop run by an owner-manager with a few operatives in his employ. This business might need no separate sales department because work was done on a contract basis and the proprietor had an assured flow of orders, but if selling effort were needed he would make it himself, besides supervising the manufacturing activities and dealing with the financial work of the firm. Alternatively, he could employ a foreman in the workshop and devote himself more fully to the other activities that were claiming his attention. This simple structure could be modified by sharing the task function of production between sections concerned with different processes or goods, in each case either with or without a concomitant division of the management process. The various possibilities are illustrated in Figure 7 and despite apparent differences the structures are essentially the same.

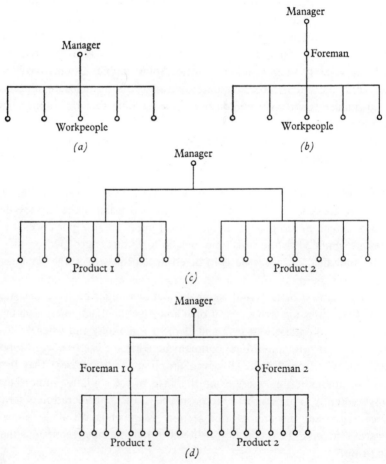

Figure 7

The next stage in the development of the line structure comes when more than one task function is identified and new departments are formed to deal with separate aspects of the work. A form of line organization is created in which specialist knowledge and skills are used in the performance of distinct task functions, the management process now being invariably divided. The upper levels of a structure with more than one task function (line) department are shown in Figure 8.

Figure 8

This structure could be elaborated by subdividing one or more of the task functions. For instance, work under the production manager could again be grouped on the basis of different products or processes, and sales tasks divided between home and export, or retail and wholesale, branches (Figure 9).

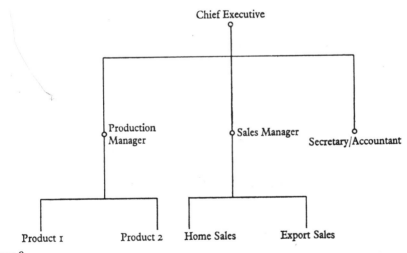

Figure 9

Another possibility, less likely in view of the organizational limitations assumed, would be for two (or more) quasi-independent companies to operate under a common board of directors, or an owner-manager with a controlling interest in each. The main feature of each company would be that its structure contained only task

115

function departments, which could be subdivided in the ways already suggested. The subsidiary companies might have identical structures, or different ones corresponding to different conditions and work, and it might be desirable for one task function, such as research and product development, to be undertaken in a single department serving the enterprise as a whole. Several possibilities exist, but once more they are in the nature of variations on a common theme. An example is given in Figure 10.

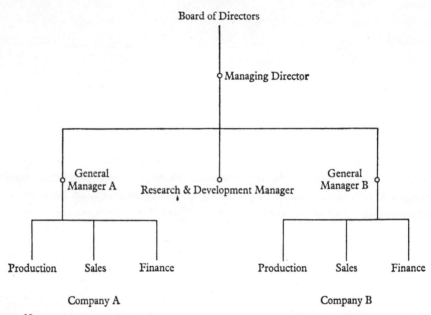

Figure 10

The line organization has a number of virtues. It is uncomplicated and easily understood; it can embody the essential functions of a business whose employees are accountable for well-defined activities and results within a few clearly marked areas of authority, and praise and blame can usually be allocated without much qualification to the occupants of the different roles. A reasonable amount of managerial specialization can be enjoyed and there should be relatively few barriers to communication, since managers can have a close personal contact with each other and departments are few enough for people in one to appreciate the work of the others and its value to the firm.

The very simplicity of the line organization suits it to enterprises of modest scope and also tends to limit its suitability to small or medium sized firms, although a company with a line organization and employing over a thousand people has been found. As a rule, the larger the scale of the enterprise the more likely it is that an unmodified line system will prove too restrictive. Growth and new operations impose increasing strains on the line structure, and the limited number of differentiated specialisms it contains reduces its ability to cope with the rising pressure of the demands to which the system is subjected.

Attempts by line managers to deal piecemeal with new and significant company problems within their own spheres may be not only wasteful of effort, but also inadequate. For example, although managers deal with personnel problems in their subgroups it could be undesirable for them to duplicate certain work involved in their solution, and they might in any case be less capable of doing it well than a trained personnel manager and his staff. It is logical and desirable for element functions to be separated from task functions after a certain stage of growth, so that managers responsible for task functions can devote themselves more fully to them and let other people with the requisite abilities take responsibility for element functions and increase the efficiency with which they are performed. When this happens the simple line structure no longer exists.

LINE AND STAFF ORGANIZATION

The term line and staff is often used to describe a particular kind of organizational structure or structural species, but it is not an entirely happy one because of the imprecision of the word staff in this context. We shall not go deeply into the complications associated with staff at this point, but merely observe that we are using a would-be technical term with no standard meaning. The line and staff structure, as it is most commonly thought of, is of such widespread importance and gives rise to such general organizational problems that it will be analysed more fully in Chapter 10, where the origin and significance of staff in business are also discussed. But this chapter would be incomplete without a reference to the structure and a short description of it is included here.

When a clear separation is made between task and element functions, and the latter are taken over, wholly or in part, by specialized individuals or groups in differentiated subunits, a line and staff organization can be said to be created. The separation may result in the formation of new departments responsible for element functions, the emergence of sections or subdepartments within existing departments, or a combination of both. The line organizational structure in Figure 8 becomes a line and staff structure: (a) if an element function department concerned (e.g.) with personnel is added; (b) if the sales department is modified to incorporate as distinctive activities (e.g.) advertising and market research; and (c) if both kinds of structural alteration are made. A purely line structure can be transformed to include, theoretically, an indefinitely large number of element functions, each system change creating a different pattern of interrelated, but organizationally distinguishable, sets of activities within the company which are designated task or element functions according to whether or not their contribution to the company's operations

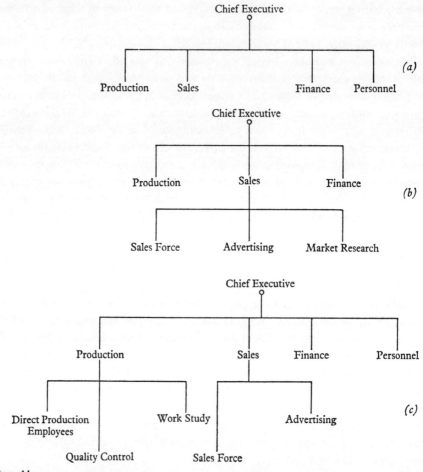

Chief Executive

Production   Sales   Finance   Personnel   *(a)*

Chief Executive

Production   Sales   Finance   *(b)*

Sales Force   Advertising   Market Research

Chief Executive

Production   Sales   Finance   Personnel

Direct Production   Work Study   Advertising   *(c)*
Employees

Quality Control   Sales Force

Figure 11

is of fundamental importance. The three possible line and staff structures just envisaged are shown in Figure 11.

FUNCTIONAL ORGANIZATION

The functional organizational structure (another controversial term) has more historical interest than practical importance today. The idea of functional organization is attributed to an American engineer, F. W. Taylor, who expounded it in his book *Shop Management*, published in 1903. Taylor was convinced that what he called the military (essentially the line) type of organizational structure, which was widely adopted at the time, suffered from serious defects that only radical change could cure. The main trouble was that the work of the foreman, or gang boss, in the engineering workshops that Taylor knew was so varied, and called for such a

118

variety of specialized skills for its proper performance, that it was almost impossible to find men who could do the job as well as Taylor thought it should and could be done. His solution was to share supervisory responsibilities between a number of foremen, preferably so that each was restricted to performing one 'leading function' in which he could develop a high degree of skill. A notable feature of functional foremanship, therefore, was that a workman no longer had a vertical relationship only with a gang boss, but received direct help and daily orders from different bosses concerned with different leading functions. The foreman's work was divided in the fully developed system of functional foremanship into eight activities, undertaken by the route clerk, instruction card clerk, cost and time clerk, gang boss, speed boss, inspector, repair boss, and shop disciplinarian. The organizational structure of a workshop operating on this principle is shown in Figure 12.

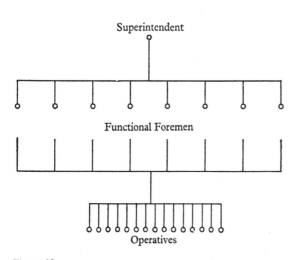

Superintendent

Functional Foremen

Operatives

Figure 12

In Britain, functional foremanship has had little appeal and seems likely to remain unpopular. Other methods have been found of dealing with the organizational problems that troubled Taylor, and their acceptance of the classical organizational precept of unity of command has made functional foremanship anathema to most managers of orthodox views. People who wish to avoid dual authority are unlikely to be enamoured of the idea of octuple command. Nevertheless, two examples of functionally organized companies were found in the survey of industrial firms in south-east Essex, although not strictly representative of the Taylor system. In one of the firms, whose organizational structure is shown on page 119 of Joan Woodward's book, there were five managers below the chief executive, responsible for five element functions, who had the titles of programming manager, chief chemist (quality control), maintenance engineer, personnel manager, and works accountant. Below them were thirty departmental supervisors, each of whom reported to and received instructions from all five managers. A modified version of this structure is depicted in Figure 13.

The supervisors in both firms enjoyed considerable independence and were more isolated from their immediate superiors than their counterparts in companies with a different kind of organizational structure. They were well qualified (in one company

6 Formal organization (I)

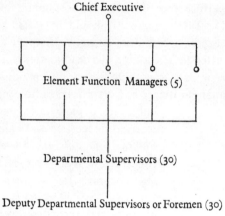

Chief Executive

Element Function Managers (5)

Departmental Supervisors (30)

Deputy Departmental Supervisors or Foremen (30)

Figure 13

all were graduates) and relied a good deal on each other for help and advice. But relations between senior managers and supervisors were good and no evidence of incompatibility of instructions, or of damaging conflict between managers, was observed. Neither did the supervisors try to play one superior off against another. A majority of the people interviewed in these firms were satisfied that the organizational system adopted was a good one and found no difficulty in adjusting to its demands, even when they had been accustomed formerly to working under a single superior. Uncommon though they are, then, and sceptically as they are often viewed, organizational structures similar to Taylor's model exist and are apparently associated with satisfactory economic and social results.

OTHER TYPES OF STRUCTURE

Organizational structures can be created with line and functional, or line, staff and functional characteristics, and illustrations of such structures are given in Figures 14 and 15.

In many large companies today the line and staff structure has been developed to a high degree of complexity that permits not only an elaborate managerial division of labour, but also the separation of different parts of a (possibly very) wide range of activities in semi-autonomous divisions within the enterprise, or in a number of individually incorporated businesses operating under common control. The term divisional organization has been applied to these structures, and although they differ in detail there are relatively few important distinguishing features to look for when a divisional type of structure is studied. These are the range of functions performed

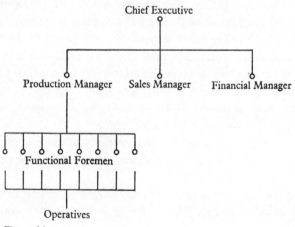

Chief Executive

Production Manager   Sales Manager   Financial Manager

Functional Foremen

Operatives

Figure 14

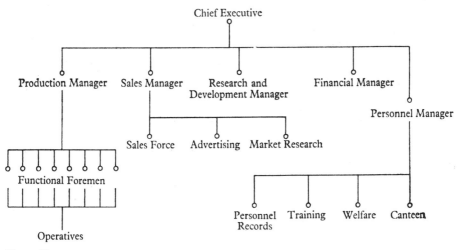

Figure 15

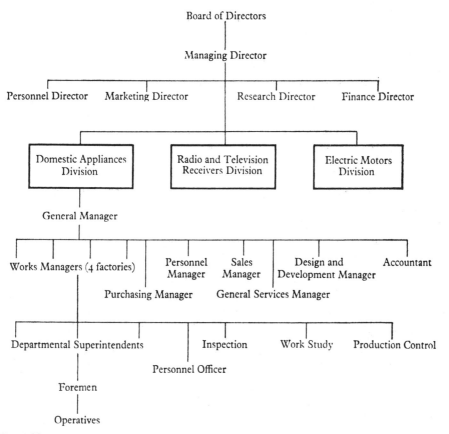

Figure 16

121

within the divisions, the functions performed by headquarters agencies or central staffs, the amount of divisional autonomy allowed and the form it takes, and the nature of the relationships between operational divisions and central departments.

It is possible, but uncommon, for each operational division or subsidiary company to be self-sufficient in terms of both task and element functions and to enjoy internal access to all the services it needs. In such a case divisions can be expected to enjoy substantial autonomy, and to be subject only to general oversight from a supreme authority to ensure that common policy is carried out, finances are efficiently used, and senior divisional managers of satisfactory calibre are appointed. More often the divisions are partly self-sufficient and lack the full range of either task or element functions required. They then rely in various ways on each other, or on central departments, for the services they cannot provide for themselves. For example, each operational division might have its own production and sales departments while the major financial and research services were provided by headquarters groups; or each division could contain the four task functions and leave to headquarters groups such element functions as advertising and market research. There might also be element function departments at headquarters to assist the chief executive and the parent company board in such fields as industrial relations, economic intelligence or company law. Numerous alternatives are open to firms with large, elaborate line and staff structures, and an organizational design like the one in Figure 16 is only a simplified example of what might be found in practice.

6.4 Organizational terms

The vocabulary of organization is, regrettably, neither consistent nor clear. The terms task function and element function which have been used so far are not particularly illuminating or apt by themselves, and while Miss Woodward rightly dwells on the difficulties created by the multiple meanings of function and functional in business literature she does not really justify her choice of task and element to distinguish two fundamentally different kinds of activity in a firm. But problems arise with some of the other labels that could be used, like primary and secondary, major and minor, or main and ancillary, because of the rather pejorative implication of the second word of each pair. Managers are understandably reluctant to say that they perform minor or ancillary activities, and still more reluctant to acknowledge degrees of importance of their work. If, for the sake of argument, manufacturing, selling, financial and research activities are singled out on the grounds of their basic importance, what remains is both varied and capable of many different gradations of importance in different firms. Is personnel management more important than purchasing? or work study than market research? The questions are pointless when asked in a general way because no general answer can sensibly be given. Classifying business activities involves a degree of arbitrariness, and although classifications may be analytically useful they are not necessarily accepted by managers as indicators of the relative value of their work, with the implication that has for their status.

Miss Woodward suggests that a major feature of task functions is that they lead to the achievement of specific end results, and can be performed largely independently of each other at different times and in different places. For instance, manufacturing premises and sales offices can be physically separated, and much research and development work is done in isolated laboratories and carried out in advance of the full-scale production of goods. Production can be broken down into subsidiary task functions, each separate in time and place and concerned with particular products or processes; task function work can also be performed by one firm for another.

Element functions enhance the efficiency of task functions: that is their justification and the criterion by which they are judged. They are often closely associated with the task functions and carried on in the same place, as production control, inspection and quality control normally take place in or near to production departments. But Miss Woodward also says that element functions are infrequently directed towards the achievement of specific and definable results in the way that task functions are, and that they can rarely be separated in time and place from the rest of the company's activities. Both statements call for qualification.

In attempting to increase efficiency many businesses have tried to make more specific the results at which element function departments should aim, and to bring the measurement of these results within the scope of financial control procedures that have been used in production and sales departments for a number of years. There is no insuperable reason why at least some of the work of, say, a transport or personnel department should not be regulated by specific objectives. The transport department could be required to reduce the number of hours per year lost through vehicle breakdowns to a prescribed figure; the personnel department could be told to do what was possible to reduce labour turnover to a level acceptable to the board. And so far as separation in time and place applies to element functions the word rarely is too strong. Using the same departments as examples again, one can envisage the work of repairing and servicing vehicles being done in a depot away from other company buildings at times when production is not taking place, and personnel staff conducting residential courses for employees out of working hours. The growth of headquarters service staffs in the larger divisionally organized companies has also increased the tendency for some element functions to be performed away from the main scene of productive operations.

Although four task functions are identified it does not follow that every manufacturing firm contains them all. Among nine firms studied in a later phase of Miss Woodward's research two were concerned only with manufacturing, two had their financial policies decided by holding companies, three had no marketing activities, and seven undertook no research. Not only does the number of task functions vary, but an element function, like purchasing, may assume such importance that it moves into the task function category. There is nothing universal or permanent about the distinction between task and element functions: it is essentially a convention and there is a paradoxical propensity for the distinction to become blurred the more one tries to make it too fine.

Brech argues that the division of the management process results either in the creation of self-contained operational units under managers responsible for the basic work of the firm, or in a combination of operational and functional groups which enables the latter to develop specialized services ancillary to the basic activities and make them available throughout the firm. Although he regards production and sales as the only true operational tasks in manufacturing concerns his classification is similar in principle to Miss Woodward's, but he maintains that the fact that functional activities are ancillary to operational ones does not mean that they are less important or of lower status, and this calls for comment. It would seem that the statement could be disproved by applying a crude but simple test to discover which activities, if any, could be eliminated without crippling a company or fundamentally changing its character. This would show, for example, that a manufacturing firm would not exist if production were permanently stopped, but that it could operate without a work study department, albeit with less efficiency; and from this one might reasonably infer that work study is less important than production. Some would say that this is self-evident, and a similar argument was certainly implicit in the writings of certain classical organization theorists who drew an analogy between an organization and a railway, and distinguished the principal line activities from subsidiary activities attached to them like sidings joined to the main line tracks.

In the early stages of their development the ancillary activities may indeed have a rather modest existence and be treated as distinctly secondary in importance, but as a business matures the line and staff (or operational and functional) activities become increasingly intertwined and interdependent, and as they do so it becomes correspondingly difficult to cut away a staff activity without serious detrimental effects on company work. In many cases the staff departments come to exercise a significant influence on the fortunes of the firm. Thus although it must be true that line tasks are more important than staff as the two are conventionally defined it is by no means easy in practice to prove that this is really the case, and probably not very profitable to try. The purpose of organization is to secure teamwork, the integration of managerial effort and the fusion of operational and functional ideas in the achievement of the primary task, not to divide the business into blatantly class-conscious groups. But this question of relative importance and status is one of the major problems of the line and staff system and we shall come back to it for a fuller discussion in due course.

When functional is used in a way that makes a functional manager synonymous with a specialist (or with a staff specialist in a different set of terms) it must not be inferred that an operational (line) manager, such as a production manager, is not specialized, whereas someone like a personnel manager is. The words operational and functional are used by Brech to describe the nature of managerial command and responsibility, not to indicate that someone is or is not specially fitted by particular experience or qualifications to do his job. A production manager is as much a specialist as his 'functional' colleagues so far as training and ability are concerned, although when these labels are used he becomes a specialist in one sense but not in another, which shows how confusing some terms can be and how necessary it is to use them with due regard to the different meanings attached to them.

These observations on the work of Miss Woodward and Brech are not made with invidious intent, but merely to illustrate a general problem in business administration. Other writers use different terms, or use the terms adopted by Miss Woodward and Brech in a different way, or have their own ideas about how many task functions (line activities) there are. Allen, for example, defines as a functional organization what many others describe as line and staff, and D. C. Miller and W. H. Form (*Industrial Sociology*) think that production is the only task function in a firm. The failure to agree about terms and their meanings partly explains why Brech questions both the value and the possibility of differentiating one kind of structure from another. He considers that the so-called line and staff organization is the normal one for any company that grows beyond a very small size, and that the interrelationship of operational and functional activities will continue to be the basic feature of organizational systems. Since it would therefore follow that virtually every structure would carry the same label the case for using it fails in his view, and he cannot conceive of a purely line organizational structure in any but the most rudimentary kind of firm.

The line and staff concept is central to classical organization theory, but in one of the seminal works of modern theory March and Simon have suggested an entirely different way of distinguishing organizations and defining their parts.[1] The organization is the entire system whose largest sections are departments, which can in turn contain subunits called divisions. The system embraces clusters of means-ends relationships related to an ordered sequence of operational goals, each cluster being separate from the others. (Operational here means capable of being objectively defined and measured.) If each cluster is peculiar to a separate department, and departmental goals are operational subgoals of the whole system, the departments are *unitary* departments and the organization is a *federal* one. If a cluster of means-ends relationships is contained in more than one department the organization itself is the smallest unit to contain it completely and becomes a *composite* one. Pure types are envisaged at the ends of a spectrum, with organizations having different combinations of federal and composite characteristics lying between. Line and staff organizations would be those in which the major departments are unitary in character

[1] J. G. March and H. A. Simon, *Organizations*, Wiley, 1958.

except for services provided by specialized organizational components serving the whole, or large parts, of the system. They resemble federal organizations the more nearly the line (operational) departments are self-contained, and composite organizations when staff (functional, element function) services are shared by more than one department in the firm.

In the welter of conflicting usage and contradictory terms one must often take one's own stand. If one accepts a legitimate distinction between task and element functions, and if these are identified with line and staff activities as they are often defined, Miss Woodward's evidence shows that significant differences between types of organizational structure do in fact exist. Of the hundred firms investigated in the course of her research thirty-five had predominantly line, two had functional (in a Taylorian sense), and fifty-nine had line and staff type structures, while four could not be classified. In none of the thirty-five line organizations did departmental specialization go beyond the four task functions mentioned, and neither the line nor the functionally organized firms were of very small size. If this sample is even moderately representative of contemporary organizational practice it suggests that different types of organizational structure may be widely spread and that some kind of distinction between them is worthwhile. Of course, if we think of line and staff *relationships* as opposed to activities it probably is true that all firms are 'line and staff', since there is always someone who assists or advises somebody else in a company and is thus in a staff relationship to him.

Whichever terms are chosen the important thing is to try to be as consistent as possible in the way they are used and to make it clear when their meanings change. The study of organizational structure in the ways outlined here can help one to understand better how companies operate, but it is necessary to remember that the language of organizational analysis is not always used in a company in its textbook sense, and sometimes it is not used there at all. The practical student of business administration is obliged to some extent to think and read in one idiom in private, and to talk and write in another inside a firm. Difficulties are unavoidable while the technical language of the subject remains unstandardized, insecurely established and imprecisely defined, and in consequence the danger of faulty communication is inevitably increased.

7

Formal organization (II)

7.1 Organization charts

Charts can be used to illustrate a number of the important features of a business. They can show the constituent companies or operating divisions of a large enterprise and the departments and sections in each unit. In a single firm a chart can make clear the structure of formal authority, the reportorial system, the number of levels and the size and number of subgroups. It can be elaborated to show the title of each position, the name of its occupant and the formal nature of the relationships between roles. If the company is small or medium sized one chart may adequately illustrate its main organizational characteristics, but several charts would be needed to give a good understanding of the structure of a large concern.

Although there is no standard set of symbols or way of drawing charts, certain conventions are quite widely observed. The use of unbroken lines to show vertical and horizontal relationships between members of one subgroup is general, and a broken line is often drawn to denote a direct relationship between people in different subgroups in which one person does not exercise formal authority over the other. Boxes containing the title of a position can be drawn in various shapes to indicate different kinds of role, such as chief executive, subordinate line manager, specialist staff manager and so on. The lines joining roles need not be solid or broken only, they can also differ in thickness and colour and convey still more about the system with the help of an appropriate code. But it is generally undesirable to crowd too much detail on to a chart: its value lies in being clear and easily understood, and a mass of symbols in a complex web of different kinds of line is as apt to confuse matters as to clarify them.

The ways in which positions are drawn and connected can suggest other distinctions besides those just mentioned. In the diagrams in Figure 3 a group of subordinates (B, C and D) under a common superior (A) has been represented in different ways, and diagram 3a might suggest that formal horizontal relationships exist between subordinates while diagram 3b does not. Both diagrams might show that subordinates are of equal status, because they are drawn on the same level, whereas in diagram 3c there might be an implication of inequality, with the possible corollary that although neither *B* nor *C* has formal authority over another member of the group each may enjoy informal power because of a difference in status. On the other hand, diagram 3c could be drawn as it is simply for graphical convenience and with no intention of indicating a significant difference in status between *B* and *C*, or *C* and *D*; which leads us to a controversial issue.

Organization charts have been blamed for exaggerating a preoccupation with, and disputes about, status differences and for making people abnormally sensitive about relative positions in the structure. The exactness with which formal status differences can be defined and portrayed in marginal cases is debatable, but assuming that fine distinctions are possible it becomes progressively more difficult to make them consistently as the number of roles grows larger and the variety of activities is increased. Concern over status is carried to absurd lengths if someone feels discountenanced because his position is drawn half an inch below somebody else's on the organization chart. If that danger exists it should be made clear to everyone concerned that the chart is drawn as it is for the sake of legibility or inclusiveness, and in no way purports to show minor differences in status. But there are chief executives who believe that the only safe course is to keep the chart secret and thus avoid agitating their subordinates unnecessarily with these problems.

The usual way of drawing organization charts is to put the chief executive (or board, or general meeting of the shareholders) at the top of the picture and show other roles at different levels below. But it is also possible, and sometimes preferable, to draw the chart sideways with the chief executive on the left, while another alternative is a chart in which roles at different levels are shown on concentric circles surrounding the central position of the senior manager or directing group.[1] One advantage claimed for the concentric chart is that its status implications are not so strong, and obviously some subordinate positions on an outer circle must often lie above a superior's position on an inner one. This chart is an interesting device, but it may not give so clear and direct an impression of company structure as other diagrams, and if it weakens the idea of being above or below someone, people may think of themselves as insiders or outsiders instead.

Systems theory has led to the introduction of new ways of portraying salient organizational features. Rice, for example, has a diagram showing the major import, conversion and export subsystems of a firm and the material and product flows between them and the environment. He also shows the managerial subsystem, with attendant control and service functions, in a diagram similar to Figure 17, which can be compared with the orthodox organization chart containing equivalent

[1]For examples of conventional organization charts cf. L. A. Allen, *Management and Organization* and E. F. L. Brech, *Organisation*. Examples of concentric charts are given in E. F. L. Brech, *ibid.*, Fig. 8, and in M. Haire (ed.), *Organization Theory in Industrial Practice*, Wiley, 1962, between pp. 58 and 59.

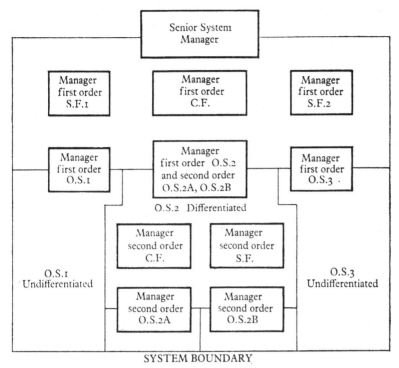

Figure 17

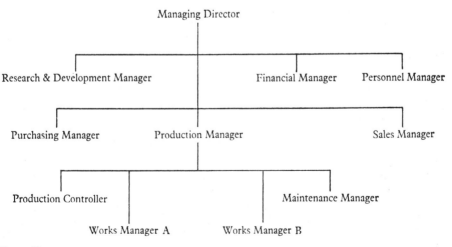

Figure 18

positions in Figure 18. Other examples of charts emphasizing system elements can be found in the paper by Johnson, Kast and Rosenzweig, and elsewhere, which suggest ways of looking at formal organization that are different from those discussed in the previous chapter.

There are many things an organization chart cannot do satisfactorily or at all, however comprehensive it is and however well drawn. It cannot show the full nature of a role with all the difficulties and problems of its associated work, or nuances of authority and responsibility. It cannot show how frequently the formal channels of communication are used or by-passed, and to what effect, or the extent and significance of the informal organization that exists in every group and often has a profound effect on its behaviour. An organization chart is a static representation of a dynamic system which may be changing even as the picture is made, and when it is drawn there is a danger that it may continue to be treated as evidence of a state that no longer exists. This would be not merely misleading, but worse if the chart acquired a sanctity that hampered organizational change, or made people talk as though the system in the picture still obtained while they acted according to a quite different pattern.

These drawbacks are enough to explain why organization charts are rejected altogether in some quarters, and treated in others as unconvincingly neat devices of which nobody takes much notice when non-routine matters arise. But a chart is often not to blame for the failings imputed to it. It cannot rationally be condemned as a source of confusion and uncertainty if they already exist in a company, or for aggravating mistrustfulness, raising social barriers between roles, and encouraging the pursuit of personal interests at the expense of one's colleagues or the firm. A chart is best seen as a tool for elucidating certain organizational features which is often best used in conjunction with other aids, of which one is the written definition of the work, responsibility and authority of each major role. The analytical work involved in chart preparation should throw light on some of the difficulties that a company has experienced, or may anticipate, with its existing structure, and suggest the probable consequences of choosing one pattern of relationships rather than another if the structure is changed. A review of the organization shows whether there are duplicated responsibilities, conflicts of authority, or important neglected areas of work; it shows, also, whether some people's burdens are too heavy and others' too light, and whether the qualities required in a role are matched by its occupant's. Periodic reviews of the organization in the light of changing conditions are important if efficiency is to be maintained, and the informed use of charts and diagrams can be a great help in solving problems of organizational structure.

An organization chart drawn as a purely symbolic design of points (representing positions) and connecting lines (denoting different properties of formal relationships) is a useful theoretical device. A firm can be depicted in this way as a communications network, or as a system in which the effects of alternative role patterns can be analysed by sociometric techniques. Graph theory can be applied to organizational analysis when diagrams of this kind are drawn, and developments in decision theory and communications theory have also helped to extend the range of potential uses to which suitably constructed charts can be put.

7.2 The shape of organizational structures

Hierarchical structures are frequently described as pyramidal and, although this is true only if certain conditions are met, the image of a pyramid gives a good general idea of the organizational outline of many firms. The shape will be pyramidal if employees are arranged on a series of common levels, so that the number of people at each

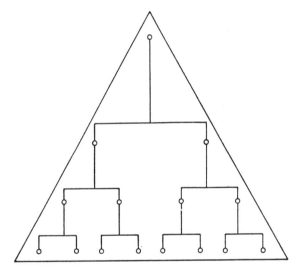

Figure 19

level increases from the highest level (occupied by one person) to the lowest. Otherwise the shape of the organization need not be strictly pyramidal, although it may be approximately so, and in any case to secure the resemblance to a pyramid a conventional pictorial arrangement of positions must be made, as in Figure 19.

An organizational structure, as we have seen, should enable work to be done in a systematic and cooperative way, and its value depends on the extent to which it promotes the achievement of organizational ends. The main task is invariably divided into smaller related tasks which can be divided into still smaller tasks if required, and employees are arranged in subgroups whose activities are defined in relation to a larger set of activities, and whose size allows each superior to maintain appropriate control over his subordinates' work. The management of subgroups is undertaken in roles of great importance in the formal communications subsystem of

131

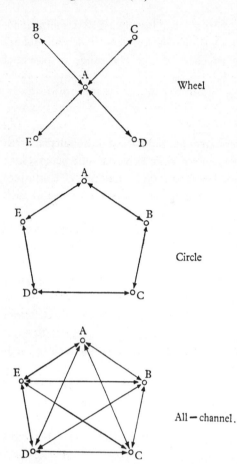

Wheel

Circle

All — channel.

Figure 20

the firm, and the relationship between the communications pattern adopted by, or imposed on, a subgroup and the group's structure and performance calls for further consideration.

Let us assume a simple situation in which five people are to work together to achieve certain objectives. The group is a small open system whose efficiency depends in part on its ability to receive, collate and transmit information, to make and transmit decisions, and to receive and act on decisions. If restrictions are placed on the use of communications channels they affect the group's organization and its ability to do its work. Three possible communications patterns can be envisaged, known as the wheel, circle and all-channel networks, which are illustrated in Figure 20.

In the wheel network there are four open channels and information can only be relayed to and from the hub position (A) along the spokes joining it to the outer positions (B–E), whose occupants are not in direct contact with each other. The organizational problems experienced in this group are reduced in some respects by the restriction on the number of channels to be used, and there is clearly a strong probability that A's position will be the decision-making centre. This arrangement constitutes a simple two level hierarchy. In the circle network the people in any three pairs of neighbouring positions send information to and receive it from each other, after which one member of each of two pairs communicates with the fifth person in the group, who occupies the decision-making position. This is a three level system in which, theoretically, decisions could be made in any of the positions: no one is more advantageously placed than another until nominated to make decisions by his fellow members, or appointed to do so by superior authority outside the group. There are fewer externally imposed restrictions on communication in the circle network than in the wheel, and none at all in the all-channel case. Here the members are all in touch with each other, and are free to adopt whatever pattern of communication they think is most likely to simplify the transmission of information and ensure that reasonably quick and satisfactory decisions are reached.

Laboratory experiments have shown that wheel groups quickly organized themselves hierarchically and devised a stable pattern of communications in which very few channels were not used consistently. The all-channel network groups were the slowest to evolve a persistent organizational pattern and were also more unstable than the others, more than half the available channels being used intermittently during the tests. Organizational efficiency, measured by decision-making speed, was increased by restricting the channels along which communications flowed, and decisions were made most swiftly in the wheel network, less rapidly in the circle and more slowly still in the all-channel system.

The reader will no doubt have noticed that the wheel is simply another alternative picture of the subgroup in Figure 3. It seems, therefore, that the practice of forming subgroups whose superior members supervise and coordinate the work of subordinates should result in communications systems that enhance the groups' efficiency as formal information-processing and decision-making units. But it must not be assumed that hierarchically organized subgroups necessarily adopt the wheel pattern on all occasions, or that the wheel is always the most suitable arrangement. Speed is not the only factor, and when decisions are complex or far-reaching in their implications, or when effective implementation depends on mutual understanding and acceptance by all members of the group, the wheel may not be the best system to adopt. The all-channel network, even if it slows down decision making, can improve its quality by allowing people to contribute collectively and exchange information freely, instead of between vertically related pairs of group members. The wheel network can eliminate uncertainty and confusion where unilateral decisions are made and transmitted as commands to other people: the all-channel group can achieve the same result through face-to-face contacts between all its members. Under different conditions, with different problems to solve and information to handle, both networks may be equally effective as purely technical instruments for reaching decisions. There are, however, potentially important human considerations to take into account when one network is formally preferred to another, which may affect the balance of advantage. This is a matter that we shall return to later, especially in Chapter 12.

In practice the pattern of communications often varies with changing group conditions, and is particularly influenced by the group's composition and organizational level. The same group may variously reach collective decisions using the all-channel net, organize itself spontaneously as a temporary hierarchy according to need, or act strictly as the formal hierarchy shown in the firm's structural design; and for different purposes different members may make decisions about the whole group's work. But in groups of non-managerial employees, as well as those which have a manager in charge, the tendency towards the hierarchical form is strong for a variety of social, technological and institutional reasons.[1]

The analysis of communicaticns networks and the behaviour of decision-making groups has helped both to explain and justify further the typical organization of firms and their components. The analysis emphasizes the part played by managers in the communications subsystem and shows how they promote efficiency by acting as rapid and accurate clearing houses for information flowing within and between subgroups. Managers can also be thought of impersonally as filters which pass on information and decisions from above in terms intelligible and applicable to subordinates, and prevent unnecessary information from passing upwards. Unnecessary information is defined here as information superfluous to what is needed by a manager at any level to perform his own work efficiently and exercise effective control over the work of others for which he is responsible. This process of correctly filtering the upward flow of communications could be described in classical terms as applying the principle of exception.

Another explanation of hierarchical structures has been suggested by Elliott Jaques, who bases his argument on the nature of the human resources available to a firm.[2] He says that a business system is a microcosm of 'the distribution of human capacity in large populations', capacity being defined here as time-span capacity ('the capacity to carry given levels of work as measured in time-span'). The levels of abstraction at which work is performed are related to different time-spans: at the first (lowest) level identified by Jaques a person's time-span capacity does not normally exceed two months and he performs mainly physical work, whereas a person at the fifth level should be able to construct and use theories, and have a time-span capacity of five to ten years. The frequency distribution of human capacity in this sense is shown by the positively skewed curve in Figure 21, the same information being conveyed in an alternative way in Figure 22 where the pyramidal resemblance can be seen.

The largest group in an industrial society consists of people who occupy the roles of semi-skilled worker or clerk at the lower levels, and individuals to the left of (or below) the line AB are taken to be unemployable within the normal range of economic activities. Assuming such a distribution, Jaques suggests that people whose potential time-span capacity falls within a particular band (stratum) can be regarded as forming an identifiable subpopulation, the total population being made up of a number of groups defined in this way. The actual number obviously depends on the widths of the time-span capacity bands, but Jaques suggests that it is seven. However, the whole concept of time-span capacity is controversial and so, inevitably, are its corrollaries; for example, that business organization tends to adapt itself to

[1] Cf. W. H. Scott and others, *Technical Change and Industrial Relations*, Liverpool University Press, 1956.
[2] W. Brown and E. Jaques, *op. cit.*, chs. 7 and 8.

provide work for the employable members of the population compatible with their time-span capacities.

Jaques maintains that if two rules were followed no structure need have more than seven levels. The first rule is that in all direct superior-subordinate relationships the roles should be in contiguous strata; the second is that the time-span capacity of each role should be such that they are one stratum apart. All organizations could then be fitted into a spectrum stretching from the one stratum business (the single trader) at one end to the largest enterprise with seven strata at the other. Some of the implications of this argument are discussed in a later chapter dealing with the size of subgroups, but it is worth noting here that many structures now contain more than

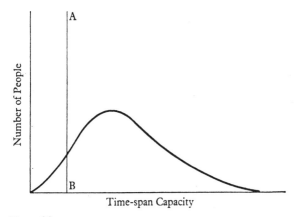

Figure 21

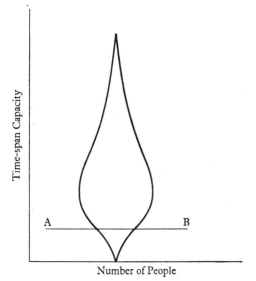

Figure 22

135

seven levels, and that if seven were the maximum a firm reaching that limit could only grow by increasing the numbers employed at existing levels. But it must be stressed again that these ideas only suggest some interesting possibilities to explore: Jaques's hypotheses have not been proved and extensive empirical tests would be needed to establish their validity.

There has been relatively little discussion about the intrinsic reasons *why* hierarchies exist in the forms they do: it is more common for hierarchical structures to be accepted simply as part of the nature of things. A hierarchy of some kind is indeed probably inevitable and preferable to other arrangements in many cases, but William Evan maintains that the assumption of an 'iron law' of organization is too facile, and that before it can be accepted with confidence we need to know a lot more about the causes and effects of different 'degrees of hierarchy' and the direction and extent of structural change.[1] To get this information a large-scale comparative study would ideally have to be made of organizations in different industries and in different countries, but for the present we have much more limited data to go on. Some of the research done recently, however, has yielded results which do much to strengthen the case that Evan has made. The work of Miss Woodward and her colleagues, which was along the lines suggested, has produced evidence of a potentially significant relationship between organizational structure and technology, first suggested as a possibility by Thorstein Veblen in *The Theory of Business Enterprise* in 1910. Miss Woodward classified firms by their production systems (in a more elaborate taxis than we need use here) into three groups of unit and small-batch production, large-batch and mass-production, and process-production concerns in that order on a scale of rising technological complexity.

She found that there was a significant tendency for clustering to occur around the median values of certain organizational properties in firms with similar production systems. For example, the number of managerial levels rose as technological complexity increased: 18 out of 24 unit and small-batch-production firms had three levels of management; 15 out of 31 large-batch and mass-production firms had four levels; and 7 out of 25 process-production firms had six levels, while 6 more such firms had five levels and another 5 firms had seven levels. The median value of the number of people reporting directly to the chief executive rose from four in unit production to ten in process-production concerns; the ratio of managers and supervisors to non-managerial employees rose from 1:23 to 1:16 and then to 1:8 along the technological scale; and the proportions of indirect workers and graduates employed also rose with increasing technological complexity.

These were not the only associations found between technology and organization, but they give an idea of the results which the south-east Essex studies produced. The differences between organizational-technological relationships in different

[1] W. M. Evan, 'Indices of the Hierarchical Structure of Industrial Organizations' in *Executive Readings in Management Science*, ed. M. K. Starr, Collier-Macmillan, 1965.

sorts of firm were accompanied by similarities too, especially at the ends of the scale. In both unit and process-production companies the average size of the primary working group was small, the number of skilled workers was relatively large, maintenance activities were important, and managers were less 'organizationally conscious' than they were in large-batch and mass-production concerns. In these, the line and staff system seemed to be more highly developed than elsewhere and executive responsibilities were more closely defined. Their organizational structures generally proved to be more mechanistic than organic in character, two terms that are explained in the following section. The fact that marked similarities were found between the organizational features of successful firms in each production group may imply that a certain kind of organization is most appropriate to a particular technology. The structure of the unit-production firms was characteristically short and broadly based, whereas the structures of the process-production firms were more often tall and narrow in shape. Further studies may cause Miss Woodward's hypotheses to be modified, but her work shows the value of comparative organizational analysis and indicates both the interest and the probable practical usefulness of the results hoped for if this kind of research is continued on an even larger scale.

7.3 Organizational change

As an open system the company is perpetually exposed to the forces of change, and although it may counteract them and try to reduce their disadvantageous effects it can never completely escape them, whether they be generated externally by governments, suppliers, competitors or customers, or internally by the ideas and ambitions of employees. A firm that wants to perform its primary task with continuously high efficiency must be able to recognize the strength and importance of these forces, and know when and how to adapt its organization to meet them. This does not mean that every environmental change dictates a change in the formal system: an effective structure should be flexible enough to allow adjustments to be made within the existing framework that are adequate to meet many of the changes experienced by the firm. But the greater and more permanent the environmental change and its effect on the basic import, conversion and export processes, the more probable will it be that a conscious change will be called for in the formal organizational design.

Analysing the organizational situation means seeing how well the existing structure accords with the firm's present needs and deciding what structural modifications are required: it also calls for an assessment of probable future trends and an estimate of how long the new system is likely to remain appropriate. The value of this analysis depends on the amount and quality of the data available and the competence of the people who interpret them. The time available for planning organizational change is also highly relevant to the case. Even a comparatively minor change may take some time to effect, and a major one often calls for a considerable period if it is to be properly carried out. When large companies merge, for example, several years are sometimes needed for the new structure to be devised, created and accepted. And the longer the time taken to accomplish the change the greater the likelihood that environmental developments will already have rendered the new system at least partially unsuitable for its work. In many companies there is an unavoidable tendency for 'structural lag' to occur, and often the best to be hoped for is that the most practicable solutions to organizational problems will not be too far removed from the perpetually elusive ideal.

Imperfect knowledge and lack of time often mean that extended organizational analysis and considered structural changes are difficult to make, but a general and probably more important factor still is the opposition to change that is likely to be met within a business at all levels. Any threat to the *status quo* introduces an element of uncertainty and insecurity into people's lives which many do not relish, and structural change is no exception when it involves the creation of new roles, the elimination of existing roles, the modification of established spheres of authority, the impact on settled minds of new ideas and values, and the disruption of stable patterns of relationships. Expectations are altered, new skills and methods of work may have to be mastered and old ones abandoned. It is virtually certain in these circumstances that resistance will be met, and if it cannot be overcome the necessary changes will either not be made or accomplished only with difficulty, and possibly with serious disturbance to the firm's activities. Even when organizational change is acceptable to those affected by it there will probably be a delay before the full beneficial effects are felt, because people in the organization (and often outside) have to accustom themselves to the working of a different system. A learning period is necessary before the new organization functions at its highest efficiency, and in the case of a major change this period may be long. Short or long it is always a factor that limits the frequency of practicable organizational change, whether resistance is encountered or not.

The managers responsible for organizational planning are sometimes disconcerted or resentful when the results of their earlier efforts are overtaken by events, and may be tempted to retain a structure that has lost much of its relevance to the company's needs. In small firms, especially, where senior managers must periodically add to already heavy commitments the burden of studying the desirability of organizational change and the work of initiating whatever change is required, there may be an understandable feeling that the existing monument to their past efforts deserves more permanency than circumstances warrant. Large companies can at least mitigate this problem by employing specialists to analyse the system's behaviour and recommend what structural changes should be made. The use of independent consultants to give advice on this matter has also grown considerably in recent years. The need for organizational change is shown by the unsuitability of a structure for the work a company has to do. If stresses are imposed on the structure that it was

138

not designed to bear, and if no formal alteration is made to the pattern of relationships and role content to meet them, employees themselves may try to modify the system to make it conform to their perception of actual needs. Their perception of what is required might still be different, however, from the organization that systematic analysis would show to be appropriate and it is, in fact, possible in any situation to distinguish several states of organization, as Wilfred Brown has shown in *Exploration in Management.*

He assumes to begin with that at a given time there is a formal statement of what the company's organizational structure is meant to be; a statement that is possibly made quite explicit with the help of organization charts and job manuals. Brown calls this the *manifest* organization of the company. A careful examination of what employees actually think and do might show, however, that they interpret the structure in various individual ways and act on the basis of an *assumed* organization that differs from the manifest. Analysis of the situation should show what the real, as opposed to either the manifest or assumed, organizational pattern is like and enable a picture of the *extant* organization to be drawn. This can then be compared with the *requisite* organization called for by the actual situation of the firm. The four organizations should desirably coincide, but it is probable that there will frequently be disparities between them, the more so if the environment is very dynamic and structural changes are slow to be made.

An elementary example will help to show how the four organizations might differ from each other in practice. Let us start with the manifest organization of a company in which a personnel officer is subordinate to the production manager, directly responsible to him and formally authorized to deal only with personnel matters in the production department. The personnel officer has valuable experience of industrial relations problems and when a trade union launches a campaign to recruit members among clerical workers in the sales department the sales manager, faced with some unfamiliar difficulties, assumes that he can obtain the assistance of the personnel officer as the person in the company best qualified to help him. The assumed organization is not strictly consonant with the manifest. The sales manager's request for help is granted by the production manager and the personnel officer agrees to assist. Having done so he becomes increasingly involved in the personnel problems of the sales department, and an analysis of the situation would show him acting as though he were formally responsible to two departmental heads instead of one. This would be the extant organization. The chief executive ultimately decides, after discussions with senior managers in the company, that the requisite organization calls for a separate personnel department to be created, whose head would report to the chief executive, with a staff capable of dealing with a range of personnel matters throughout the firm.

Burns and Stalker, as a result of their research into the structure and behaviour of firms in the electronics industry, have analysed the problems of change in different terms from Brown's, and an outstanding feature of their discussion is the contrast made between two diametrically opposed organizations which can be conceived of as pure types at either end of a range, along which stand intermediate structures exhibiting in varying proportions the characteristics of both.

The first of these pure types is the so-called mechanistic structure whose characteristics are basically the same as those of the bureaucracy described by Max Weber.[1] In his model of the bureaucratic organization the offices set up in the structure are governed by a legal authority and a consistent set of formal rules. The office holders derive status and authority from their positions and a sense of security and vocation from participation in the system. They discharge their responsibilities in an impersonal way, obedient to the institutional laws and rules of the system, and are expected to show loyalty to the organization itself and not to particular individuals or groups. The work of the bureaucracy is founded on a precise definition and separation of the authority and duties of different offices; the appointment of people best qualified to perform the activities associated with each one; and the arrangement of offices in a stable hierarchical pattern which provides a ladder of promotion for those selected on grounds of seniority, achievement and the satisfactory opinions of their superiors. Great importance is attached to the orderly preservation of information in the form of records in the office files. The ideal bureaucracy is a monocratic system transcending human weaknesses and whims: it is an inflexible, but none the less efficient and rational, instrument in certain conditions and has the virtues of precision, continuity, unity, discretion, unambiguity and low costs of operation per unit of output. It is technically very effective, because it ensures a close control of the work done and allows administrative specialization to be carried to its farthest extent. The failure of a bureaucracy to attain its ends efficiently has usually been blamed on some 'abnormality' in its working, variously believed due to infractions of the rules, irrational behaviour by office holders, or resistance to organizational demands by informal organizational forces.

The mechanistic organization, in the same way, has its own importance and values that transcend those of the people working in it. People are necessary for the organization to function, but they must adapt themselves to its demands and cannot expect more than a marginal adaptation of the organization to them. Work is highly formalized and responsibilities are narrowly defined: status is closely correlated with position in the hierarchy, and the pattern of communications emphasizes vertical rather than horizontal or diagonal flows. In fairly stable environmental conditions this system may be very suitable, the people in it enjoying a sense of security and predictability both with regard to future organizational behaviour and the progress of their own careers. So long as they do not object to close restrictions on their freedom to act within the organization they may be quite satisfied

---

[1] M. Weber, *The Theory of Social and Economic Organization* (translated by A. M. Henderson and T. Parsons), Oxford University Press, 1947.

with their roles. But the mechanistic structure is often so designed that it inhibits initiative in an indiscriminate way, making no distinction between initiative that would increase the organization's efficiency and ability to achieve its goals and initiative that would weaken them.

The organic structure stands at the opposite pole and is extremely flexible, with an inherent tendency to mould itself to meet changes in the environment. It can be contrasted in almost every way with the mechanistic organization. It is looser, less formal and allegedly more democratic; differences of status are less rigorously defined; there is considerable horizontal communication; and instead of being made to accept rules that give him little freedom of action in his role an employee has more scope to act independently, or in consultation with colleagues, to deal with different situations as he judges appropriate in the light of events. In the mechanistic organization there is a tendency for vertical communications to be treated by subordinates as instructions when doubt about their nature exists, and for communications to be accepted without argument or discussion. Communications within the organic structure, on the other hand, are likely to have a greater informative content and to deal with matters that can be challenged or discussed.

The people in the organic structure are said to have a high degree of personal involvement in the firm and to create without difficulty a relaxed and informal atmosphere conducive to good personal relations. A high degree of individual freedom is incompatible with a mechanistic system, but it may mean that in an organic system the definition of work and responsibilities is so vague or general in character that the shape of the formal structure is hard to trace with any certainty. Harry Miller, in *The Way of Enterprise*, mentions the case of a firm in which titles were scarcely used at all, the argument being that they were unduly restrictive and that a man's quality and right to exert authority would be shown by his achievements clearly enough for formal labels to be dispensed with. A loosely defined organic structure tends, however, to be not only flexible, but unstable too; uncertainty plays a larger part in the expectations of the people employed, and although change is more readily accepted they often experience considerable stress as a result of the pressures imposed on them.

In practice it is probable that most organizational structures, if not all, lie between the mechanistic and organic extremes. The precise characteristics of each firm are affected by a variety of factors, including the size of the business, the industry in which it operates, its past experience, and the temperaments and capabilities of its employees. Discussions about the influence of structure on individual satisfaction and social relations within the firm have often led to the conclusion that a highly formal system has prejudicial effects, but there are arguments on both sides and Brech, for instance, has stated that there is no generally valid basis for saying that a clearly defined pattern of formal relationships *per se* reduces adaptability and causes dissatisfaction, or for advocating the abandonment of a formal division of the management process in favour of an informal one. He maintains that a properly designed structure with many of the maligned features of the mechanistic system is quite compatible with the achievement of economic efficiency, social satisfaction and necessary organizational change.

Miss Woodward's findings partially support this view, but they also led her to remark that it has been customary in the past to take the large-batch or mass-production type of company as the representative business, to analyse it more fully than any other, and to generalize about business organization on the basis of information derived mainly from the study of this class of firm. She found successful companies (success involving more than the achievement of a high level of profit alone) among the large-batch and mass-production firms whose structures conformed closely to the mechanistic model and showed the influence of classical organizational ideas; but among the unit and small-batch, as well as the process-production, firms she found that success was often associated with a more organic structure. If the relationships between organization, the nature and stability of technology, and success eventually prove to be as significant as her study suggests, it might mean that certain predictable organizational developments should accompany particular alterations in a firm's technological system.

As the discussion of the socio-technical system in Chapter 1 indicated there are good reasons for questioning the idea that technological considerations should always dominate in the design of organizational structures. 'The problem of relating organizations effectively and stably to the environments in which they operate is one of trying to balance the economic, technological and socio-psychological advantages' which different methods of organization offer, and the optimization of a single condition does not guarantee an optimal set of conditions for the system as a whole if the others are not adequately met. This is Lupton's argument, and he is among those who reject technological determinism and call for a balanced judgment to be made of the relative importance of the several factors that influence, and are influenced by, organizational change. He stresses the importance of choice, and the need to estimate the potential consequences of alternative actions on the social structure of a company and on the 'role expectations' of the people it employs.[1]

Economic and technological factors are properly weighted more heavily than social ones when organizations are changed, but managers should also try to discover the social implications of their decisions and ask themselves whether they have the appropriate means of dealing with any prospective difficulties arising out of a change. There is always a danger that organizational change will increase real costs, of which costs of disruption, misused managerial energy, incorrect organizational choice and diminished human satisfaction are some. The main reason for analysing and weighting the major organizational variables when change is called for is that by so doing there is a better chance of making the organizational choice that

[1] T. Lupton, *Management and the Social Sciences*, Hutchinson, 1966, p. 44.

will keep these costs as low as possible. But what that choice will be in any real world situation must depend to a large extent on the kind of work to be done and on the personalities, attitudes, experience and values of the people employed to do it.

7.4 Principles of organization

The classical organization theorists had a normative aim and regarded their principles as a set of rules that would help the businessman devise a sound organizational structure for his firm. The ambitiousness of the claims made for these principles varied from one writer to another, but some people certainly believed them to be as valid as the laws of physical science. Mooney and Reiley maintained in *Onward Industry*! that the vastest conceivable organization would not be too great for the efficient leadership of one man if hierarchical and functional principles were correctly applied to its design. The improbability of an organization so great as this is not itself material, but the corollary of their assertion is, namely that since actual undertakings are smaller than the vastest conceivable one their efficiency can be assumed so long as the classical principles are respected.

These principles are of uneven quality and, while some of them are empirically based and stated in specific terms, others are little more than loose *a priori* generalizations. Whatever their ostensible value, the position before 1945 was that the central ideas of classical organization theory were never subjected to rigorous and systematic tests to discover the true extent of their applicability or see whether any important qualifications should be made. Latterly, however, numerous criticisms of the classical doctrine have been heard, and a substantial amount of research has been undertaken to ascertain how widely the principles are followed and the consequences of their application or neglect. In the attack on what they regarded as false gods some members of the modern behavioural school have overstated their case as much as any classical writer, and it has taken some time for the dust to settle on their iconoclastic handiwork and for a more balanced view of the merits and demerits of classical theory to be reached.

It is misleading in one sense to talk about 'the' classical theory of organization, because this gives an impression of a settled doctrine expressed in formally accepted terms, whereas one of the difficulties of the theory is that no definitive version exists. Successive writers in the classical tradition have defined new principles and restated old ones in a different guise, and the result has been such a proliferation of principles that selection is essential if discussion is to be kept within reasonable bounds. The differences between alternative definitions were often slight, but in some cases they were significant, as with the span of control principle discussed in Chapter 8 and the principle of the objective. In one form the latter principle says that 'organizational efficiency tends to increase as the work performed is directed towards the objective desired', a glaring example of dressing up the obvious to produce a pseudo-scientific

143

effect which has no practical value and does nothing to increase the respect in which the subject is held. Another version has more to recommend it by telling us that 'every organization and every part of the organization must be an expression of the purpose of the undertaking concerned or it is meaningless and therefore redundant'. Such a statement would be as acceptable to a systems theorist as to a member of the classical school.

There is a useful survey of the development of classical thought in Appendix I to Brech's *Organisation*, and the references there can be followed up by anyone who wishes to go into this aspect of the subject in more detail. There is no need to cover the same ground here; for our purpose it is enough to look at a synthesis of four sets of principles made by Puckey, which brings out very well the essence of the classical organizational view.[1] There are ten principles in this list, each of them being included in one form or another in the works of at least two of the writers from whom they were derived. In Urwick's terminology, which probably comes closest to providing a standard, the principles are those of the objective, authority, coordination, specialization, definition, responsibility, correspondence, balance, continuity and span of control.

It can be assumed that if these principles were correctly applied to organizational design the resulting structure would be eminently satisfactory from a classical standpoint. The principles are considered individually in different places in this book, although they are not always referred to by the names used here, but this is a convenient place to assess them in a body and bring out some of their ambiguous and debatable features. This can be done without undue repetition of what is said elsewhere.

The importance of defining a single source of authority in each business was emphasized by Fayol more than half a century ago and expressed in the principle of unity of command. Fayol advocated this in the interests of coordinative efficiency, and to prevent employees from being exposed to the possible receipt of conflicting orders from two or more people of superior rank. He argued that a company should have a single chief executive, and that below him each subgroup should also have a single leader who would stand in a clear chain of command stretching up to the supreme authority in the firm. The principle of unity of command has been variously stated, but in none of its forms is it free from difficulty in the matter of practical application. One serious problem is that it conflicts with the principle of specialization, which Taylor stressed when he advocated the use of functional foremen, and it is evident that the advantages of specialization are so great that the desire to enjoy them often leads, if only inadvertently, to situations in which dual authority is unavoidable even when it is not recognized formally to exist. This does not mean that an employee subject to dual authority cannot identify the person whose command must be obeyed, but it does mean that irreconcilable instructions from different

[1] W. Puckey, *Organization in Business Management*, Hutchinson, 1963.

sources may cause frustration, uncertainty and delay, which was precisely what Fayol and his supporters feared. In some firms the unity of command is knowingly broken. We saw that an appreciable number of large concerns have replaced the single chief executive with joint managing directors or managerial committees, and at lower levels also dual authority may be the preferred organizational pattern. There was an example of this in the General Motors Corporation when, to improve the coordination of financial work in the operating divisions, the divisional comptrollers were made responsible to their divisional general managers and to the chief comptroller of the company. The prevalence of dual authority was suggested by a study of a group of American foremen, seventy per cent of whom were found to have in effect more than one direct superior. In some situations it is obvious that undesirable results stem from weakening or breaking the unity of command, but in others there seem to be advantages in not applying the principle in a rigid way.

Principles regulating the pattern of formal communications can be read to mean that all such communications must be authenticated and sent along known channels which, in order to ensure accuracy, clarity and speed, should be as short as possible consistent with the need for a complete chain, or relevant section of a chain, of command to be followed. This is advocated to avoid confusion of orders and to obviate the danger that subordinates will act without their superior's knowledge and consent. But a literal application of these precepts might easily result in a communications pattern that was wasteful of resources. It is difficult to reconcile predominantly vertical communication flows with flexibility and technological change, and extensions to the range of specialized departmental activities emphasize the importance of horizontal and diagonal communication if swift and effective action is to be secured in many cases. However, there are undoubtedly problems connected with the adoption of multidirectional communications patterns that we shall look at in Chapter 10.

The principle of definition leads one to ask: what exactly is meant by saying that the authority, responsibility and duties of each position should be clearly defined in writing? Should the definition be as exhaustive as possible, or limited to a general statement that gives scope for a personal interpretation of his duties by the employee? The more detailed the definition the greater will be the danger of inflexibility and loss of initiative, but on the other hand if jobs are defined carelessly or not at all the result may be confusion, omission and duplication of work. Very detailed job definitions increase the bureaucratic character of a company and, like extremely formal communications patterns, they are not always appropriate in dynamic conditions. The principle correctly tells us that some definition is called for, but it does not tell us how much. We can see the need for definition, but a general assertion to this effect is of limited use when it comes to deciding what the unique definition of a particular job should be and where to choose between the equally undesirable extremes of excessive detail and no detail at all.

Taken together, the most commonly quoted principles do not constitute a true general theory of formal organization, and it has not been possible to prove a consistent relationship between the way they are interpreted and applied and the success which a firm achieves. There are examples of success and failure both among companies whose managers have heeded the classical maxims and those whose managers have not. Business success is not, of course, solely dependent on formal structure, and the difficulty of isolating and measuring other important variables makes it hard to assess accurately the significance of structure alone. The uneven and changing pattern of success in business does suggest, however, that principles of organization can at least be modified, and probably ignored in some cases, without necessarily incurring serious economic disadvantages. Some of the more recent studies of organizational behaviour give support to the view that both economic and social benefits may be derived from interpreting the principles in a liberal manner, and even from disregarding some of them almost completely.

It is not justifiable, however, to carry this argument to the point of declaring that classical theory is devoid of use. As aids to effective practice the principles are indeed of uneven value, but applied selectively, and with due attention to the peculiarities and needs of individual firms, they are useful guides to the design of a formal organizational structure. They at least remind us of the desirability of some clarity, logicality and order in organizational design. But, unfortunately, a number of principles do no more than indicate ends to aim at or directions to follow, and do not say how ends are to be achieved or how far in a certain direction it is desirable to go. These matters must be decided by the firm itself, and decisions about formal organization are often influenced by subjective as well as objective factors. There is no cardinal measure of the consequences of having a plural executive instead of a single chief, or of defining authority and responsibility with this degree of exactness or that. The test of an organizational structure remains its effectiveness in fulfilling the purposes for which it was designed and, although in broad terms these may be basically similar for all firms, they can be weighted in different ways and differ greatly in detail. A good structure certainly promotes economic efficiency and social satisfaction and a bad structure reduces them; but neither good nor bad has a unique meaning in relation to structural design and a good structure in one situation can often be bad in another.

Critics of the classical theory of organization have attacked it for its impersonality and alleged indifference to human needs and desires. They claim that formal organization is concerned with the achievement of purely economic ends and that some classical theorists only tolerated people as a necessary evil: people were required to make the system function, but prevented it from functioning in the most rationally efficient way. This interpretation of classical views underlies many of the sociological and psychological objections to the highly mechanistic organizations which have resulted when classical principles were rigidly applied. For their part the exponents

146

of classical doctrine have sometimes taken an equally extreme stand and accused their critics of being obsessed with the idea of personal satisfaction and making people happy, at the expense of sound business practice and organizational strength and efficiency.

We must not make too much of the extreme contrasts between classical and modern views, because the divergence of opinion is being reduced in several important respects, and as much emphasis is now placed on those elements of different theories that are reconcilable as on those that conflict. Organizational analysis has been broadened considerably over the years to take account not only of formal structure, but also of the effect of the composition of working groups on relations between their members, and of the connexions between structure, the nature of the firm's work, individual personality, group behaviour and total performance. Pugh and his colleagues have suggested a way of developing analysis still further on several planes by including not only structural variables, such as the number of levels and the size of subgroups, degrees of specialization, and distribution of authority, but also activity variables such as production, communication and control; contextual variables such as size, technology and location; and performance variables like productivity, profitability and market share.[1] In their view the aim should be to combine these variables in a complex model representative of real conditions, which places structure in perspective with many other factors that affect the company's character and fortunes. Development along these lines has much to commend it as a way of bringing together several strands of argument that are often developed separately and kept somewhat apart, and a theory related to such a model should be extremely valuable if a satisfactory basis can be found for combining and weighting the numerous and very different variables to be taken into account.

[1]D. S. Pugh and others, 'A Conceptual Scheme for Organizational Analysis', *Administrative Science Quarterly*, **8**, no. 3, 1967, 289–315.

8
The size of formal subgroups

8.1 Introduction

We return now to the question of organizational shape and look at the effects on the structure and behaviour of a firm of changes in an important variable, the size of the formal subgroup. The term subgroup has already been used quite frequently, but so far without being precisely defined. For the purpose of this discussion a subgroup is taken to be a formally constituted group of people in which one member is the superior and the others are his direct subordinates. Thus informal groups, and formal groups composed of people of equal rank, like a committee of managers on a common level, are excluded, as are formal groups like joint-consultation committees whose members are of different rank, but whose activities as members of the group are not governed explicitly by superior-subordinate relationships. The essential feature of the subgroups that interest us here is that they are command groups which cannot be subdivided into other groups in which formal superior-subordinate relationships exist.

In many businesses there is only one group of this kind and its members constitute the total number of people employed by the firm, but as firms grow beyond a small size it becomes necessary, as we have seen, for employees to be divided into two or more subgroups, and continued growth leads to an increase in their number, and usually in the variety of their composition and work. A subgroup may enjoy quasi-independence and develop a character of its own, but as part of a larger system it always depends in varying degree on the coordination of its activities with those of other subgroups, and on resources which only the firm as a whole can command.

The limitations to the size of subgroup do not apply equally to all groups at all times, but their existence gives rise to some fundamental problems of organization which have often been discussed in the literature, generally under a heading in which the word 'span' occurs. Koontz and O'Donnell talk about a span of management, for example, but Allen prefers span of supervision and Urwick span of

148

control.[1] In each case the span refers essentially to the same thing, the number of subordinates under a superior's immediate command, although different terms might suggest that writers viewed the problems of group size from rather different points of view.

Span of control is probably the most widely used term, but it seems to emphasize only one aspect of the manager's work as Fayol envisaged it, and one could also talk about spans of coordination, planning and command. Span of supervision is potentially misleading now that supervision is associated so closely with the oversight of clerical, technical and operative employees, and could be taken to imply a narrow reference to subgroups at the lowest level of a company, which Allen did not in fact intend. Brech has introduced yet another term, the span of (management) responsibility, but he makes it clear that this span refers only to subgroups in which all members occupy managerial positions.[2] Despite the fact that these authors stress different things they are all concerned with the same basic problems, and confusion between the spans can be avoided by using a neutral term which makes it clear that group size is the main point at issue. If the number of subordinate members is n the subordinate/superior ratio of any subgroup is $n:1$, and from now on we shall refer to this as the s/s ratio and use that term where possible in preference to any of the spans.

8.2 Relationships in a subgroup

In the article which appeared in 1956 Urwick told of his meeting in or about the year 1930 with an industrial consultant named V. A. Graicunas, and of the latter's preliminary exposition of a 'mathematical proof' that the number of subordinates reporting to a manager should be kept to a low figure. Their discussion led to the appearance in 1933 of a paper by Graicunas, 'Relationship in Organization', which is said to have had a widespread influence on business thought.[3] The essence of Graicunas's thesis was that in any subgroup of three or more people there are three possible types of relationship: (1) direct single vertical relationships between the superior and individual subordinates; (2) direct multiple (or group) relationships between the superior and two or more subordinates; and (3) cross relationships between pairs of subordinates themselves. In a group of three people A, B and C, A being the superior, the relationships are:

(type 1) A–B, A–C,
(type 2) A–BC, A–CB,
(type 3) B–C, C–B.

[1] L. A. Allen, *op. cit.*; H. Koontz and C. O'Donnell, *Principles of Management*, 2nd edn., McGraw-Hill, 1959; L. F. Urwick, 'The Manager's Span of Control', *Harvard Business Review*, **34**, no. 3, 1956, 39–47.

[2] E. F. L. Brech, *Organisation*, pp. 150–155.

[3] V. A. Graicunas, 'Relationship in Organization' repr. in *Papers on the Science of Administration*, eds. L. H. Gulick and L. F. Urwick, Institute of Public Administration, 1947, pp. 183–187.

Urwick sought to justify the apparently nice distinction between pairs of relationships of the second and third types by saying that the 'behavior of B in the presence of C and of C in the presence of B will differ from their behavior when each is with A alone', and that 'what B thinks of C and what C thinks of B constitute two cross relationships which A must keep in mind when delegating work on which B and C must collaborate in A's absence'.[1] A group of three people thus gives rise to six possible relationships on this analysis, but if a fourth member, D, were added the total relationships would rise to eighteen:

(type 1) A–B, A–C, A–D

(type 2) A–BC, A–CB, A–BD, A–DB, A–CD, A–DC,
            A–$B(CD)$, A–$C(BD)$, A–$D(BC)$,

(type 3) B–C, C–B, B–D, D–B, C–D, D–C.

It is not clear why Graicunas stopped at eighteen relationships here, and we could ask whether the argument would be pressed too far by saying that the number of cross relationships might also be affected by each subordinate's attitude to his peers considered not just singly, but in pairs, trios and so on. We could then conceive of other relationships in this group, such as B–CD, C–BD and D–BC. The larger the group the more numerous and complex would the possibilities be.

The addition of a fourth subordinate raises the total number of possible relationships to forty-four, and the size of the group was held at this point to approach a critical value. It is illuminating to quote Urwick once more.

The situation really gets complex when a fifth subordinate is added–even granting that many of the relationships will never need explicit attention. The superior again increases his direct relationships with individuals by 1–representing a 25% gain in his *power to delegate*. But the number of group and cross relationships he may have to deal with has gone up from 44 to 100–more than a 100% increase in the burden of *supervision and coordination*.[2]

The maximum number of relationships, as Graicunas defined them, in a group of given size can be calculated from the formula

$$R = n(2^{n-1} + n - 1)$$

where R is the number of relationships and n the number of subordinates. When the growth of R is calculated with respect to increases in n the results are dramatic, and by the time a superior has ten subordinates he appears to need phenomenal mental

[1] L. F. Urwick, *Harvard Business Review*, 1956, p. 40.
[2] L. F. Urwick, *ibid.*, p. 41.

agility to grapple with the 5,210 relationships that he might have to think about in managing his group. Even if relationships were restricted to simpler combinations of group members, and calculated on a minimum basis using the formula

$$R = 2^n + \frac{n}{2}(n-1) - 1$$

their total still rises sharply, from twenty-one when there are three subordinates to 1,068 when there are ten. The grounds for distinguishing between the maximum and minimum numbers can be seen by looking back at the group with three subordinates. The maximum number of relationships is eighteen, but the minimum excludes the relationships A–CB, A–DB, A–DC, A–$C(BD)$, A–$D(BC)$, C–B, D–B and D–C, which reduces the total to ten.

According to Urwick, Graicunas thought that six direct subordinates were as many as a superior could be expected to manage effectively, although the total depended to a large extent on the actual number of working contacts called for between the subordinates themselves. When in 1938 Urwick stated the desirability of limiting the span of control to a maximum figure as a formal principle of organization, he tried to make clear the importance of cross relationships as a fundamental restraint on subgroup size, and said that 'No superior can supervise directly the work of more than five or, at the most, six subordinates whose work interlocks'.[1] He had occasion later to stress the last three words because he felt that too often they were being ignored or misunderstood.

In an earlier article (in *Public Administration Magazine*, 1935) than the one already referred to, Urwick had suggested that an appropriate limit to the number of subordinates of a high level manager was four, and of a supervisor at a lower level, eight to twelve. The more general statement of the span of control principle that he made later caused some confusion when people were unsure whether he was thinking only of a chief executive's span or of spans at all levels of the firm. Some thought he meant one thing and some another, and the validity of a uniform span of any size was vigorously questioned. Fisch, for instance, argued that it would be totally wrong to impose the same limit in all subgroups, and emphasized the importance of allowing for the very different kinds of work that subgroups perform.[2]

The idea of limiting the number of subordinates to six or less, especially at the highest level of a firm, was not new, and views like Urwick's had already been expressed by Sir Ian Hamilton, H. P. Kendall and E. D. Jones, the last of whom suggested in 1926 that the ideal *s/s* ratio for a chief executive was probably 5:1. But Urwick reached a wider audience than any of these and his version of the span of control referred to here (it was not his only version) has often been quoted, with

---

[1] L. F. Urwick, *Scientific Principles and Organization*, American Management Association, Institute of Management Series no. 19, 1938, p. 8.
[2] G. G. Fisch, 'Stretching the Span of Management', *Harvard Business Review*, **41**, no. 5, 1963, 74–85.

and without qualification, and frequently with respect. Only in recent years has it been criticized for being too restrictive and not completely clear. The second charge is not so unfounded as might at first appear, because Urwick's 1956 article contains elements of ambiguity and contradiction. It also shows that he had decided to moderate the force of the principle of the span to the extent of conceding that it 'is not a rigid rule to be applied woodenly in all situations', but rather 'a very useful general principle and a valuable diagnostic instrument in cases where organizational weakness exists'.[1]

The significance of interlocking work as an influence on subgroup size is not hard to appreciate, for it is perfectly reasonable to suppose that the managerial burden of a superior whose subordinates work quite independently of each other will be lighter than that of a superior in another group of otherwise comparable composition and level, between whose subordinates' work there is interdependence. The span of control principle tells us nothing, however, about the absolute extent of the interlocking or interaction between subordinates' work that would require their number to be limited to five or six. It is not clear whether the work of each subordinate is assumed to interlock with the work of all others, or whether a smaller amount of interlocking is sufficient to make the limitation of size necessary. Neither is it clear that a given amount of interlocking might be associated with different degrees of difficulty in managing a group in different situations. In any study of group size we must ask how many of the potential relationships are both actual and significant from the superior's point of view in the light of the group's composition and tasks. We must also discover the frequency of contacts between group members and assess its effects. To talk only of potential relationships begs too many important questions whose answers are quite likely to differ from one situation to another and indicate the desirability of different values of the s/s ratio for different subgroups.

Several writers have pointed out that Graicunas based his formulae on too elaborate an interpretation of relationships between group members. The mathematical precision of his argument appealed to, but sometimes misled, people who welcomed the then rare application of quantitative reasoning to problems of business organization. Graicunas himself overstated the case when he tried to make a direct comparison between a change in the power to delegate and a change in the burden of supervision due to an increase in the number of relationships, but when this leads others to repeat solemnly that an executive will hesitate to increase the number of his subordinates from (say) four to five (by 25 per cent) because the total number of relationships in his group will rise by 127 per cent the result, as Mason Haire has observed, can be 'plain silly'.

The qualitative, and not merely the quantitative, aspect of group relationships must be borne in mind if the problems of management are to be fully appreciated. The significance of a given degree of interlocking is certainly affected by the attitudes

[1] L. F, Urwick, *Harvard Business Review*, 1956, p. 41.

of subordinates to each other and to their superior. He cannot force the members of his group to cooperate fully with each other if they are unwilling to do so, because there are many subtle and unobtrusive ways in which people can hinder each other's work. Wilfred Brown has given some good examples of the kinds of problem associated with collateral relationships (a more expressive term than cross relationships) between the subordinate members of a group. He says that a high degree of interdependence between subordinates makes it particularly necessary to have a clear policy governing their actions, and for the superior to determine whether decisions that cause disagreement between subordinates are decisions that the subordinates can be allowed to make. Harmonious collateral relationships governed by an acceptable policy and an appropriate pattern of delegation make the superior's job lighter. The persistent failure of subordinates to resolve their differences weakens the group's ability to perform its tasks and leads to continual requests for managerial arbitration. These increase the superior's burden and may necessitate either a redefinition of responsibilities within the group, in an attempt to change the pattern of collateral relationships, or a change in the group's composition.

8.3 Factors affecting subgroup size

It is now widely agreed that the diversity of subgroup situations invalidates the claim that a certain s/s ratio is the most appropriate one, either for groups at all levels in a firm or at the same level in all firms. It is, however, helpful to identify the more general influences on subgroup size and we shall do this before returning to the purely theoretical aspect of the problem.

The members of a group must make most of the contacts necessary for the performance of their work during conventional working hours, and if a group is one in which contacts between members need to be frequent, and the average duration of each contact is long, the number of members clearly cannot be as large as it might be if contacts were infrequent and short. Frequent contacts may be wanted by both superior and subordinates; by the former if he is unwilling to delegate or has to make regular checks on the subordinates' work, or if the nature of their work gives rise to numerous requests for his advice and assistance; and by the latter for this reason too, or because of their reluctance to accept responsibility. In some groups the subordinates may feel that prestige attaches to their ability to go directly to the superior when they choose, and they might resent an increase in the size of the group which reduced their opportunity to do so.

Anything that can be done without loss of efficiency to reduce the frequency of contacts between group members, and the burdens which the contacts impose, will enable the size of a group to be increased. Anything that can be done to simplify work, to speed the process of decision making, or to reduce the number of decisions that have to be reached will make larger groups possible. The location of group

153

members and its effect on the ease with which contacts are made between them is also an important factor, as are their attitudes to the various ways in which contacts are made. It is preferable for the simple and routine parts of the superior's work to be done by his subordinates, and an increase in the s/s ratio increases group efficiency if the right kind of addition to the group is made and the work is appropriately redistributed, despite the fact that the number of relationships is increased. This is presumably the logic of Urwick's case for employing general staff officers to relieve the chief executive of part of his burden, a matter that is discussed more fully in Chapter 10.

The amount of time available for contacts between a superior and his direct subordinates is affected by the frequent need of all group members to maintain contacts with people outside the group, both within and without the firm. The studies of managerial work referred to in Chapter 4 showed that some superiors spent a minority of their time in dealing with their own subordinates and made regular contacts with large numbers of other people. One of the chief executives mentioned by Carlson had eight direct subordinates, but had meetings with twenty-six people of subordinate rank in all. His apparent s/s ratio was thus considerably smaller than the actual one if his extended range of command were allowed for. Sayles's study of an engineering development services department showed that managers there had contacts with as many as thirty distinct subgroups in the company, several of which were managed by superiors at higher levels than that of the engineering services managers themselves. It is, therefore, obviously important to obtain an idea of the net time available to a superior for managing his immediate subordinates after the external (to his own subgroup) claims on his time, whether voluntarily or involuntarily incurred, have been met, and possibly to see whether these claims might not in some cases be reduced.

Urwick apparently supported the view that horizontal communication was desirable, and wanted 'lower level personnel' to be encouraged to develop cross relationships to the maximum, because there are 'many problems which can be solved quickly and satisfactorily at the subordinate level if the habit of communication and cooperation is accepted and promoted'.[1] This argument would be unexceptionable to many modern organization theorists, but it seems to weaken one of the mainstays of Graicunas's theory. It also seems to contradict Urwick's own assertion that the interlocking of subordinates' work is a principal restraint on group size, for if there is no interlocking what are the 'many problems' which the subordinates are expected to solve? And if there is interlocking how can the increased number of cross relationships be reconciled with Graicunas's beliefs, which Urwick apparently shared? To confuse the issue still more Urwick gives an example to support his case in which he advocates cross relationships not only between the subordinates of one group, but also between the subordinates of that group and those

[1] *Harvard Business Review*, 1956, p. 45.

of another. The effect of this interaction could only be an increase in the complexity of the superior's work in both groups if Graicunas's arguments were sound. But in practice the differences in the amount of time available for essential intragroup contacts and the way it is used, differences in the abilities and attitudes of group members, differences in the type of work done, and differences in the resources at the group's disposal all influence effective subgroup size and make it unwise to dogmatize about how many subordinates a superior should have.

The discussion of subgroup size in the past has mostly been about the potentially harmful effects of excessive size, but inefficiency can also result because a group is too small for a manager's relatively scarce ability to be fully utilized. In the real world the size of a subgroup must often be a matter of compromise, some groups being larger and some smaller than their hypothetical ideal. In the short and medium run it is often difficult to change the size of a subgroup, even when the need for a change has been seen, because of personal, technological, legal or economic restraints. A superior cannot be completely free to decide the number of his own subordinates, or who they shall be. Even the chief executive is subject to restrictions of money, space and labour-supply conditions, and lower-level managers are often limited further by their colleagues' needs, and reactions to proposed changes in the size or composition of subgroups other than their own. Managers may be too ambitious or too modest in their demands for subordinates, and their self-interest is not the best guide to the efficient use of resources, Group composition raises questions of balance and opportunity costs which must often be answered in the light of the anticipated effects of alternative decisions on the company's performance as a whole.

The fact that many influences affect the size of a group has led an increasing number of writers to modify Urwick's principle to the point of indeterminacy. Brech believes that the merit of any one figure for the most appropriate number of subordinates is questionable, although he maintains that for all but exceptional people it should be less than ten in wholly managerial groups with interlocking subordinate work. The policy document prepared for the Glacier Metal Company stated that each manager 'shall limit his immediate command to the number of people he can effectively control, and amongst whom he can maintain co-operation'. Allen suggests in comparably general terms that a manager should directly command the largest number of people he can control successfully, adding that in his view the s/s ratios in many companies are almost certainly too small.

The largest subgroup at the present time, and the widest and flattest structure, will bear no comparison with their organizational counterparts of the future if some recent prophecies are fulfilled. Modern capital developments promise to have a profound effect if carried to the probable extremes dictated by purely technical efficiency. The use of computers and other information-processing systems, elaborate and sensitive control devices, and automatic methods of communication make it easy to foresee the possibility of a great extension of managerial command at the operative level. Rice envisages situations in which several thousand worker-machine units will be directed by one person, with the aid of appropriate electronic and mechanical apparatus and the support of specialist staff assistants. This arrangement would have such powerful economic advantages that current systems, with their numerous levels of authority, would be redundant. But progress along these lines may be less easy than this suggests. Jaques has remarked on the psychological benefit which subordinates enjoy from contact with a good superior, and their frequent need for encouragement and praise. The splendid world in which s/s ratios are two or three thousand to one will be highly impersonal, and satisfactory ways would have to be found of dealing with the human relations problems that are almost certain to arise unless, of course, man's nature changes to such an extent that he is able to obtain sufficient emotional satisfaction from automatic transfer machines and processed-data outputs.

8.4 Subgroup size and managerial levels: theory

The connexion between subgroup size and the number of managerial levels could be stated precisely if the s/s ratio were the same for all groups. Two formulae would enable us to determine the values of any two variables in an elementary four variable model of the firm, provided that the other values were known.[1]

If M = the number of managers
W = the number of non-managers
S = the constant s/s ratio
and L = the number of managerial levels

it can be proved that

$$M = \frac{W-1}{S-1}$$

and that
$$W = S^L.$$

Using these formulae it is a straightforward matter to construct a matrix which shows, for different combinations of S and L, the numbers of managers and non-managers in a firm. A company with an s/s ratio of 4:1 and three managerial levels would have twenty-one managers and sixty-four non-managers, while in a firm in which S = 5:1 and L = 4 the values of M and W would be 156 and 625 respectively. A company in which S = 6:1 (the maximum suggested by Urwick for a chief executive

[1] Cf. L. J. Meij, 'Some Fundamental Principles of a General Theory of Management', *Journal of Industrial Economics*, **IV**, no. 1, 1955, 16–32.

whose subordinates' work interlocked) would require only six managerial levels (the number hypothesized by Jaques) in order to contain 9,331 managers and 46,656 non-managers.

The assumption of a constant s/s ratio is in no way supported by evidence of business practice, but it helps us to appreciate the relative expensiveness, in terms of the higher proportion of managers needed to run them, of companies with a low s/s ratio, compared with those in which the ratio is greater and the number of managerial levels the same. For example, the proportion of managers to total employment in a firm with two managerial levels is 30·8 per cent when $S=3:1$ and 16·3 per cent when $S=6:1$; with five managerial levels the proportion is 49·3 per cent when $S=2:1$ and 19·8 per cent when $S=5:1$.

Because the s/s ratio has no uniform value it is sometimes useful to calculate the average value of the different s/s ratios in a firm, using the formula

$$A = \frac{M+W-1}{M}$$

in which M and W have the same meanings as before and A stands for the average number of subordinates that each superior commands. Figure 23 shows the structure of a firm with four managers and sixteen non-managers, A being 4·75:1. The value of A can be reduced in either of two ways, with results shown in Figures 24 and 25. In each case the number of non-managers remains unchanged. The first structural change, shown in Figure 24, reduces A to 4:1, but the chief executive's own s/s ratio is increased by the addition of G, whose appointment makes possible a reduction in the size of the subgroups managed by D, E and F. In Figure 25 the value of A has fallen again, to 3·14:1; the chief executive's s/s ratio has also fallen to 2:1 and none of the subgroups managed by D–G has changed in size. But the number of managerial levels has increased by one.

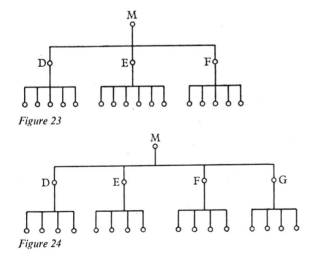

Figure 23

Figure 24

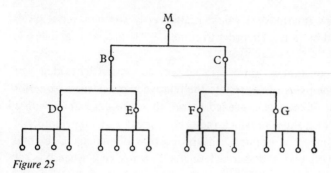

Figure 25

From these simple examples some general conclusions can be drawn. Given the value of W the value of A can only be altered by changing the value of M, but a change in M does not necessarily involve a change in the number of managerial levels. However, if M increases and the number of levels is not increased also, the fall in A must be at the expense of an increase in the s/s ratio of one or more of the subgroups. An appropriate increase in both the number of managers and the number of levels, on the other hand, makes possible a reduction not only in the value of A, but also in the s/s ratio of each subgroup, whatever the change in W. At the least, an increase in the numbers of managers and managerial levels enables the average s/s ratio to be reduced without increasing individual subgroup ratios when the number of non-managers is increased.

We can say, therefore, that unless a firm is able and willing to change its organizational structure and introduce one new managerial level or more, a reduction in the s/s ratio of the group(s) managed at one level can only be secured by increasing the s/s ratio of the group(s) managed at the level(s) above or below. This is true whether M and W increase or remain unchanged. Unless the circumstances in which the structure is designed allow no choice of action a firm has a range of alternatives open to it, wide or narrow as the case may be, and an opportunity to find the most acceptable combination of the values of S and L in the light of its own needs and resources. To some extent, however, structural solutions of this kind must involve a compromise which depends on the answers to such questions as: where in the firm is it most important for the size of subgroups to be altered? where will additional managers be found? what are the expected effects of increasing the number of managerial levels? and so on. Standard answers to these questions cannot be given.

MANAGERIAL COSTS

From a firm's point of view the costs incurred when the managerial ratio (the proportion of managers to total employment) is increased can be considered in both real and money terms. In real terms there are, for example, the effort and possible difficulty of finding suitable people to fill additional posts, the personal adjustments to be made by new and existing managers when they start working together, the disruptive effects within groups of changes in their composition, and the feeling of some managers that their work has reduced importance or that their hope of advancement has decreased. A rise in real costs due to factors like these could increase money costs as well for a time, but the firm would presumably expect that when the modified system settled down, and its members became accustomed to the new order of things, the eventual result would be an increase in efficiency which caused money costs per unit of output to fall. But if a firm has to compete with other companies for the extra managers it needs it may be forced to offer salaries above those already paid to managers in the grades to which new people are recruited, and hence to raise the salaries of existing managers to ensure comparability between their money rewards and those offered to newcomers. The total outlay on managerial salaries would then almost certainly be greater in the second case than in the first. But it does not follow that an increase in the managerial ratio must always lead to an increase in total managerial salaries, or that total salaries will fall when the managerial ratio is reduced, as has been suggested.[1]

Let us assume a firm in which the chief executive is paid £7,500, while managers at the second level receive £4,500, at level three £3,000 and at level four £1,500 a year. The number of non-managers in the company remains constant at 300. Different organizational possibilities are shown in Table 5.

Table 5

	Number of managers at level				Total managers	Total managerial salaries (£)
	1	2	3	4		
Situation A	1	2	8	21	32	72,000
B	1	4	8	20	33	79,500
C	1	2	6	24	33	70,500
D	1	3	17	–	21	72,000

It will be seen that, with given managerial salaries and suitable combinations of managers at different levels, a change in the managerial ratio of a certain order may be associated with a larger or smaller total of managerial payments, and that different managerial ratios can be associated with identical managerial costs. In many ways this is a very artificial example, of course, but it does emphasize the formal point that the exercise of organizational choice can have important and quite different consequences if one course is chosen rather than another. It also shows the danger of the uncritical use of an average s/s ratio, or total or average managerial salaries, when deciding the nature of organizational change, and the need to allow for other factors that affect both real and money costs when a change is made.

[1] R. E. Thompson, 'Span of Control, Conceptions and Misconceptions', *Business Horizons*, **7**, no. 2, 1964, 49–58.

8.5 Subgroup size and managerial levels: practice

Studies of business organization have shown that the *s/s* ratio and the number of managerial levels both vary widely in practice, even in firms of comparable size, and although this was probably predictable *a priori* the extent of the variations may still be a surprise. An illustration of the wide differences in the *s/s* ratios of chief executives is given by the results of a survey of more than 1,000 companies, published by the Research Institute of America in 1962.[1] They are reproduced in part in Table 6.

Table 6

Size of firm (Number of employees)	Number reporting directly to the chief executive	Median value
Under 100	2–7	4
100–199	2–12	5
200–299	2–23	5
300–499	3–11	5
500–999	3–17	5
1,000–2,000	3–11	5
Over 2,000	3–45	6

The tendency for the *s/s* ratio in the chief executive's group to increase as the firm grows larger was also noticeable in data collected by J. H. Healey, who studied plants in 620 manufacturing companies in the U.S.A. and found that when the number of employees was less than 1,500 the most common *s/s* ratio for the chief executive was 4 or 5:1, but that it increased to 9:1 when the firm employed 3,000 people or more.[2] In two-thirds of the plants the *s/s* ratio was 7:1 or greater, but there were differences between firms in different industries. Koontz and O'Donnell refer in *Principles of Management* to a survey made by the American Management Association which showed that in 100 large companies the *s/s* ratio in the chief executive's group ranged from 1:1 to 24:1, but that only twenty-six executives had six immediate subordinates or less. The median value of the *s/s* ratio in this sample was 9:1.

Joan Woodward has given us some of the most comprehensive and interesting information about the situation in British industry and her results, with the conclusions drawn from them, are worth quoting in some detail. She shows in the first place that the *s/s* ratios at lower levels tend, as expected, to be much greater than they are at higher levels. In a 100 companies studied the number of people reporting directly to the chief executive was 2–19, while the number of people under the command of a

[1] Quoted in W. Puckey, *op. cit.*, p. 160.
[2] Quoted in R. Stewart, *The Reality of Management*, Pan Books, 1967, p. 43.

first line supervisor ranged from 7–90. The variations in the *s/s* ratio of supervisors' groups in eighty firms are set out in Table 7.

Table 7

Average number of people controlled by first-line supervisor	Number of firms		
	Unit production	Mass production	Process production
10 or less	1	–	6
11–20	6	1	12 (*M*)
21–30	8 (*M*)	2	5
31–40	4	5	2
41–50	3	9 (*M*)	–
51–60	1	4	–
61–70	–	5	–
71–80	–	1	–
81–90	–	3	–
Unclassified	1	1	–
Total firms	24	31	25

(*M*) = Median value

Some interesting information about the number of managerial levels in these firms is presented in Table 8.

Table 8

Number of managerial levels	Number of firms		
	Unit production	Mass production	Process production
2	3	–	–
3	18 (*M*)	2	–
4	3	16 (*M*)	2
5	–	7	6
6	–	3	7 (*M*)
7	–	2	5
8 or more	–	1	5
Total firms	24	31	25

(*M*) = Median value

Miss Woodward's data indicate the effects of different production methods on average subgroup size and the number of managerial levels, the latter tending to increase as technological complexity increases while the former shows a propensity to fall. She also found that the managerial ratio tended to be higher in larger companies, with 3,000 employees or more, than in relatively small firms employing 1,000 people or less. But this conclusion conflicts with the evidence of other writers like Healey and Mason Haire, who maintain that as firms get bigger the average s/s ratio can be expected to rise. The full nature of the relationship between the s/s ratio and company size is not yet known and a possibly more significant result of Miss Woodward's study is the correlation between a company's success and its conformity to the median values of the s/s ratio and the number of managerial levels in firms with similar technological systems. Companies with below average performance were found to have structures in which the values of these variables diverged widely from the median values of the production groups to which they belonged. The practical implications of these findings should not be over-emphasized, but they suggest that, with due allowance for special problems, a firm might find it worthwhile to assess the suitability of its organizational structure if it were very different from the 'representative' structure of firms in the same technological group.

Herbert Simon has said that one of the troubles with principles of organization is that they sometimes come in contradictory pairs, and principles dealing with spans and the number of levels are a case in point. Urwick reinforced his principle of the span of control by asserting that 'in determining the number of levels which are necessary, prime regard should be paid to the span of control, not vice versa',[1] whereas a precisely opposite view is expressed by Rosemary Stewart in *The Reality of Management*, where she maintains that the most important thing to decide is how many levels of authority there should be. But to accept either rule as the dominant criterion of structural design is dangerous, for it could easily result in the creation of a structure that was unfit for its purpose. The test of fitness for purpose is the vital one, and it may show in one case that the average s/s ratio should be low even if the number of levels is high, and in another that the reverse of these conditions should obtain. A rather rough distinction can be made between structures with many levels and a low average s/s ratio and those with few levels and a high average s/s ratio, which can be labelled deep (or tall) and wide (or flat) structures respectively. Some of the general advantages and disadvantages associated with each type can then be considered.

The wide structure may improve communication in one respect, because of the short chain of command, and the small administrative distance between the men at the top and people at the bottom of the firm gives the chief executive and departmental heads a better chance to make their powers of leadership felt at lower levels and increase the sense of motivation and the morale of junior managers and opera-

[1] *Harvard Business Review*, 1956, p. 45.

tives. The higher average s/s ratio associated with the wide structure may result in managerial economies, and in the larger subgroups there may be an added incentive to greater delegation. But one must not assume a unique relationship between cause and effect here: the scope for greater delegation is as likely to result in bigger subgroups being formed as the existence of large groups to lead naturally to increased delegation. The much quoted case of the Sears, Roebuck Company in the U.S.A. should be interpreted to mean that the work of the retail-store managers in that firm called for little formal contact between them and the small amount of interlocking thus enabled their superiors to deal effectively with large subgroups. In other situations a large subgroup could as easily overburden a manager with the problems of maintaining contacts with his subordinates and coordinating their work, and compel him to seek refuge in greater formalism and restrictions on subordinates' discretion. Another danger of the large subgroups in wide structures is that they may fragment into several informal groups, with misunderstanding or conflict between them that weakens the formal system. The shorter managerial ladder may also have an adverse effect on promotion prospects and cause the nature of managerial work to change abruptly from one level to another, making the transition from job to job more difficult in some cases than in a longer chain of command.

The deep structure creates a greater administrative distance between senior managers and people at low levels which sometimes makes it difficult for the latter to understand and accept the firm's major objectives. But because the average subgroup is smaller when there are more managerial levels in a firm of given size there are opportunities for more direct and effective leadership within the subgroups, and for authority to be exercised in a more personal way without necessarily interfering in subordinates' work or reducing the degree of delegation. Work changes less abruptly from one level to another and long-term promotion prospects tend to be better in the narrow-structure firm, although ambitious junior managers who see little hope of reaching positions of importance without a long and frustrating delay may be tempted to seek promotion elsewhere.

It is easy, but unwise, to stereotype wide and deep structures and the generalizations that have just been made do little, unfortunately, to help solve practical organizational problems. Neither great structural width nor height is *necessarily* bad, and one type of structure is not inevitably associated with mechanistic and the other with organic systems. Fundamental structural alterations are possible in many firms which perceive the existence of organizational choice and are prepared to make what changes are required. In one Essex company a change in technology from batch to process-production methods was accompanied by reorganization that increased the s/s ratio of the chief executive, but reduced the average ratio in other subgroups; and in another case a firm reverted from standardized batch production to unit-production methods and was able to effect a dramatic organizational change that reduced the number of managerial levels from eight to four.

A further illustration of the connexion between subgroup size and the number of managerial levels was provided by the reorganization of the International Business Machines Corporation.[1] When America entered the Second World War the I.B.M. plant at Endicott had to raise its output substantially. The expansion called for a large increase in the workforce, the employment of a higher proportion of unskilled labour than before, and changes in production methods which reduced both the average production time per unit of output and the level of stocks. Before the reorganization there were five managerial levels, occupied by the works manager, divisional managers (the divisions were concerned with machining, assembly etc.), departmental managers, foremen and charge hands. The grades of charge hand and departmental manager were abolished and the number of foremen was increased fourfold, largely by promoting charge hands after intensive training. The average *s/s* ratio of the foremen's groups was reduced, and the tendency for the *s/s* ratios of divisional managers to increase was offset by the creation of more divisions and new appointments at the divisional managers' level. Heads of divisions were given more authority to decide matters without reference to the works manager, and he in turn was able to concentrate on tasks which only he could perform. The organization of the Endicott works was considerably altered and eventually there were fewer levels and significant changes in the size of subgroups at all of them. The fall in both the number of levels and in the foremen's *s/s* ratios was only obtained at the expense of greater *s/s* ratios at the upper levels, and this example illustrates in a particular way some of the general observations about group size and managerial levels that have already been made.

A final example shows not only how structural choices can be made, but also how factors affecting subgroup size may be quantified in an attempt to get closer to the optimum size in a particular case. The Lockheed Missiles and Space Company of California found some years ago that at the senior managerial levels of the firm the *s/s* ratio varied from 10 to 5:1; at the supervisor's level from 18 to 15:1; and at the middle managerial levels from 3·4 to 2·9:1.[2] The company decided that there were too many levels in the middle range, that subgroups there were generally too small, and that this situation resulted in higher managerial costs than were necessary, slower decisions, slower communications, reduced opportunities for superiors to develop their managerial skills, and 'over managing' of junior managers and supervisors which restricted their initiative and lowered morale. The experiments undertaken by the company were stimulated by the desire to increase the average subgroup size at the middle managerial levels.

Seven critical variables were identified as having a close bearing on the appropriate

[1] F. L. Richardson and C. R. Walker, *Human Relations in an Expanding Company*, Yale University Labor and Management Center, 1948.
[2] H. Koontz, 'Making Theory Operational: The Span of Management', *Journal of Management Studies*, 3, no. 3, 1966, 229–43.

size of the subgroups investigated. These variables, or factors, were the degree of similarity of the work (functions) of subordinate members; the location of sub-ordinates (the extent to which they were near each other or dispersed); the complexity of the subordinates' work; the amount of direction and control the superior had to exercise to ensure the satisfactory performance of work; the amount of effort he had to devote to coordinating his group's activities with the activities of other ele-ments in the company; the nature of the planning he was expected to do; and the type of organizational assistance a group received (e.g. from specialist staff employees or a personal assistant).

With the exception of organizational assistance, which was treated differently, the other six factors were assessed first in qualitative terms, and five categories were distinguished for each factor and arranged in ascending order of importance. The degree of similarity of functions, for example, was classified under one of five headings from identical to fundamentally different; the complexity of functions from simple and repetitive to highly complex and varied; and the amount of direction and control required from minimum oversight to close and constant supervision. To each of the five categories a numerical value was ascribed, so that for each factor there were five numbers, the range of their values reflecting the weight attached to the factor as an influence on subgroup size. The numbers relating to the five cate-gories distinguished for similarity of function, for instance, were in the range 1–5, whereas the numbers relating to the amount of direction and control were in the range 3–15. For each subgroup, therefore, a number was recorded under the appropriate heading for each factor and the numbers were added to give an initial weighted total for the group. This total was then adjusted by a multiplier to allow for the particular kind(s) of organizational assistance received, and a final weighted value was obtained.

A scale was constructed which related appropriate ranges of subgroup size to ranges of final weighted values, and when the weighted value for a group was known it was possible to see what the size of the group should desirably be. To show how the scale was constructed, a final weighted value of 40–42 indicated an appropriate *s/s* ratio of 4 or 5:1, while a value of 22–24 indicated the suitability of an *s/s* ratio of 8 to 11:1. This scale was devised only for the subgroups of middle-level managers, but it was thought that the same, or similar, techniques could quite well be applied in the preparation of scales for senior managers' and foremen's subgroups if required. Despite a number of environmental influences on the organizational development of this company after the analysis was made, the results obtained from it were thought to have contributed significantly to the reduction in the number of managers and to the increase in the average size of subgroups between 1961 and 1965.

There are, obviously, difficulties and dangers in making an analysis of this kind; a difficulty particularly in attaching sensible numerical values to the relevant factors, and a danger that the weighted total will be used in an inflexible or undiscriminating way. It would be undesirable to use such a scale without paying close heed to the peculiar circumstances of different subgroups which were not allowed for in the numerical calculations, or to assume that a subgroup can be made a certain size irrespective of other organizational conditions that need to be satisfied. Nevertheless, the Lockheed experiment was an interesting one, and empirical studies along these lines are more likely to help in solving organizational problems than general statements about 'correct' spans of control and numbers of managerial levels of the kind made sometimes in the past.

9
Aspects of delegation

Delegation is the fundamental process without which an organization cannot exist. The way in which delegation is carried out, and its extent, give each firm a unique character that has a direct bearing on its ability to achieve long-run success. The pattern of delegation gives the organizational structure its shape, determines the manner in which formal decisions are made and where, and hence affects the degree of centralization or decentralization in the firm. An understanding of the connexions between these three things, delegation, decision making and decentralization, is of major importance in understanding the way a company works, and in this chapter we shall try to make the connexions clear.

9.1 Delegation

Delegation takes place when one person gives another the right to perform work on his behalf and in his name, and the second person accepts a corresponding duty or obligation to do what is required of him. Delegation in business is a downward process which involves a sharing or reallocation of formal authority derived from a higher level. A superior may be entrusted to act on their behalf by his subordinates in some cases, and someone may accept an obligation from another person of equal status, but these are not generally true acts of delegation of the kind that concern us here. A subordinate cannot delegate to his superior the authority which the superior gave to him, neither can he formally transfer a commitment to someone of equal rank without his superior's consent, and almost certainly the consent of the other person's superior as well.

Literally speaking, delegation must always be an act to which both parties voluntarily subscribe, although in many business situations it would be idle to suggest that the voluntary element is large when the result of refusing to be a party to delegation may be removal from one's position in the firm or seriously reduced chances of promotion. The more voluntary the character of delegation, however, the greater is the likelihood of harmony between the people concerned and the better the prospects of efficiently performed work.

Successful delegation depends on the ability and willingness of a superior to give work to a subordinate and of the latter to undertake it. The degree of delegation can be defined in terms of the amount and type of work the subordinate is asked to do, and the discretion he has to decide how it shall be done. The greater his discretion the more responsible and rewarding does his work tend to be, but the superior's delegation is always limited, among other ways, by the subordinate's capacity to make organizationally acceptable decisions, in conformity with company policy and consistent with interdependent decisions made elsewhere in the firm. Delegation tends to be simplified when the subordinate's work is easily measurable by objective criteria and when it can be carried out with little danger of dysfunctional effects on the work of others, but tasks of this kind may be highly programmed, or subject to control by standard rules and procedures, and the subordinate's scope for discretion would then be small.

The stimulus to delegate can come from subordinates who are eager and qualified to undertake new or enlarged duties and exercise more authority, but the decision to delegate always rests with the superior. Managers vary considerably in their willingness to delegate, even when their opportunities for doing so are the same. Some are unable to delegate without great difficulty, and grudgingly allow subordinates a minimum of authority while retaining a close watch over what their subordinates do. A reluctance, or virtual inability, to delegate may be associated with an autocratic character and a disposition to treat subordinates as inferiors whose job is merely to obey orders. A manager may feel that subordinates with too much authority are a threat to his security, or he may believe that delegation is synonymous with the reduction of his power, and in each case be unwilling to delegate to the extent demanded by the situation of the subgroup he leads. The fact is that authority is not diminished by delegation, but exercised in a different way: a manager's responsibility for the work assigned to him is the same after delegation as it was before, although the mode of accomplishing the collective task is changed.

A manager who is neither autocratic nor jealous of power may still hesitate to delegate, in the sincere belief that a low degree of delegation is in the best interests of the firm. The most common reason for this belief is the manager's conviction that subordinates cannot do the work as well as he can himself, but if he persists in acting on this belief two undesirable consequences may follow. The first is that the superior fails to delegate when he could and carries such a heavy load that he cannot perform his work efficiently in all respects, so that some of it is neglected or inadequately done. The very fact that work is retained in this way may then actually reduce the superior's efficiency below what could be achieved by subordinates whose abilities he rates inferior to his own. The second consequence is that if the superior is at last forced to delegate more, his persistent doubts about subordinates' capabilities may cause him to supervise them closely and interfere frequently in their work to prevent mistakes, which means that they never learn to do their work in a confident and independent way.

168

In managerial subgroups greater delegation and job enlargement have an important long-run effect, because at the same time as delegation reduces managerial burdens to tolerable proportions at the superior level it creates opportunities for the development of managerial skills at the level below, where subordinate managers have the challenge of greater responsibility and the stimulus of more creative and interesting work to perform. The relationship between delegation and specialization is also worth noting, and here the economist's theory of comparative costs helps to dispel a misleading notion that is sometimes expressed. The theory shows the advantages of specialization in the production of goods entering international trade from countries unequally endowed with the factors of production needed to make them. It states that all countries can benefit if each one concentrates on the branches of production in which it has comparative cost advantages over the others, even although this means that the absolute cost of producing a good in one country is higher than it would be if produced in another. The analogy with the manager's group suggests that it does not matter if he can do the subordinates' work better than they can do it themselves, in fact it is often desirable that this should be the case, so long as the manager accepts the obvious fact that he cannot do their work in practice. If each subordinate achieves a satisfactory absolute standard the real product of the group is increased when task division allows each member to perform that part in which he has the greatest comparative advantage. The scale of comparative advantage is not, of course, fixed; a change in the nature of the work, and in the amount and quality of available resources, alters the scale and makes it necessary to modify the existing pattern of delegation.

The faulty allocation of work to group members has a harmful effect on efficiency for both physical and mental reasons. If the manager is overloaded the returns to his efforts fall, possibly with serious effects on the performance of the group as a whole, and subordinates who are under-utilized often feel frustrated and disgruntled, because they are prevented from exercising and developing their abilities to the full. If frustration is acute it may reduce the efficiency with which they perform even the inadequately demanding tasks they are given, and this in turn could cause an overburdened manager to try to reserve even more work to himself. It is conceivable on the other hand that a manager may delegate too much, and try to avoid responsibility by imposing burdens on subordinates that they are unfitted to bear. If the subordinates' efficiency suffers, and they are criticized for failing to do what was unreasonably expected of them, it would not be surprising again if morale declined.

One of the classical dogmas of organization that has provoked controversy is the principle of correspondence, which in one version states that in every position authority and responsibility should correspond, and in another that they should be equal. The ability to delegate goes with authority to get work done through other people, and when a superior delegates he defines his subordinates' authority to do their work. He remains responsible for the performance of the group, but the authority he gives to others to work on his behalf creates subsidiary responsibilities which subordinates accept. The way they discharge their responsibilities affects the way in which the superior discharges his own, and an integral part of superior responsibility is therefore to see that subordinate responsibilities are properly fulfilled.

Authority and responsibility should correspond in the sense that the amount of the former must be adequate for the efficient discharge of the latter; authority greater than this is dangerous if used in ways inimical to the activities of the firm, while inadequate authority imposes an unjust penalty and reduces the capacity for efficient work. Correspondence is thus desirable for reasons of equity and good performance, but attempts to make authority and responsibility equal are likely to have undesirable results if they encourage a narrow attitude towards responsibility and a refusal to undertake anything not clearly required by formal definitions of the work to be done. This is especially likely to happen in highly mechanistic systems where the discretionary content of work is small.

Although the authority and responsibility associated with each role must be prescribed to some extent the degree of detail in the prescription varies greatly from one position to another, and it can never be complete because all contingencies cannot be foreseen. The more narrowly defined the work the more difficult it is for the firm to adapt itself readily to the variable demands of day-to-day conditions. Everyone in a company has a broader responsibility than that nominally ascribed to his role, derived from participation in a social organization. Responsibility in this sense is frequently acknowledged, but is very difficult, perhaps impossible, to define in precise terms. It is quite clear, however, that there are many occasions when the spontaneous acceptance of undefined responsibility and the exercise of non-formal authority help to overcome difficulties and improve the firm's performance, and it would be undesirable to prevent displays of initiative which give a firm an organic character merely for the sake of achieving a very close correspondence, still more equality, between each person's authority and the responsibility he is expected to bear.

The extremes can be recognized plainly enough and rejected in most cases as equally unwelcome states. A company cannot operate effectively if people continually exceed their authority and conflict with one another as a result, neither can it maintain efficiency in changing conditions if employees are shackled by very detailed and inflexible definitions of work. In a general sense authority and responsibility should certainly correspond, although it is doubtful in what sense they can be truly equal, but the dynamics of business cause them frequently to diverge, and a variety of organizational and personal factors influence the effects of divergence in different companies at different times. One can only state the truism that what is tolerable and beneficial in one situation is not so in another, and part of the art of management is to decide how much divergence is acceptable.

An extensive lack of correspondence between authority and responsibility is likely to cause uncertainty, confusion, conflict and duplication of effort that increase the real costs of the firm, and it must be reduced as far as possible in the interests of organizational stability and cohesion. Evidence of a situation of this kind would show that something was badly at fault in the system and indicate the need for a change of organizational structure, one purpose of which would be to bring authority and responsibility more closely into line. But at the same time it would be necessary to remember that efforts to secure too close a correspondence would themselves run counter to a complex of organizational pressures and personal needs.

9.2 Decision making

In any role the nature of the decisions called for and the matters to which they relate are to a large extent formally determined by the definition of the work associated with the role and its position in the system, or in other words by the pattern of delegation. The capacity of employees to make these decisions has a vital bearing on a firm's ability to develop as a stable and prosperous enterprise, although its fortunes are affected not only by the decisions of people within it, but of others outside. One important function of decision making in an open system is to influence external decisions, like those of governments, customers and suppliers, to make them as favourable as possible to the firm, and another is to stimulate responses to unfavourable external decisions that minimize their harmful effects.

Organizational decisions are made individually by managers and non-managers, and collectively by groups, but many individual decisions are collective in a sense when they are made after consideration of other people's views and based on a synthesis of opinions. Employees are often required by organizational practice to discuss matters with colleagues before reaching decisions, and even when this is not the case there may be strong personal and social reasons that lead them to seek the counsel of others. A decision maker is often obliged to consult other members of the firm when this is expected to improve the quality of decisions, prevent conflict with other decisions, or ensure that as far as possible the decisions are acceptable to the people they affect.

Managerial decisions must frequently be made with a consideration of the needs and feelings of others, because if these are neglected too carelessly and too often the result is almost certain to be a deterioration in the morale, and possibly the efficiency, of the firm. Autocracy and coercion, unless supported by effective sanctions, fail when decisions are rejected by those on whom they are imposed, and this largely explains why many decisions are the outcome of discussion and compromise. There is nowadays a widely aired view that shared decision making is superior to autocracy in all circumstances on social and economic grounds, and in many companies there are attempts to broaden the basis on which decisions are reached. The idea that other people should be consulted and allowed to influence their decisions is still unpalatable to many managers, however, and democracy often makes a much stronger appeal to subordinates than it does to their boss. In practice, the scope for sharing in decision making (participation) varies considerably from group to group, and its motivational value is not uniformly or predictably high. We shall have more to say about this matter in the discussion of committees and meetings and in the later chapter dealing with human problems in the firm.

The tendency towards group decision making is most marked where the complexity of the matters to be decided, and the variety of specialized information on which decisions must be based, make it difficult for one man to decide, or take responsibility, alone. Many entrepreneurs in small businesses, especially when not obliged to defer to the suggestions of outsiders, can make all important decisions on their own, but in medium-sized companies, and above all in the large ones that dominate many industries today, the chief executive is powerless to do the same. When he is not required to discuss things with his board of directors he must often rely on other people, sometimes several levels below him in the hierarchy, to provide him with essential data on which his decisions are based, and in many cases he may look to his subordinates to make decisions for him, to which he gives approval and thus stamps them with his formal authority in the firm.

Decisions can be classified in various ways, and one suggested by Salveson is to divide them into decisions of understanding, recognition, action and enterprise.[1] Decisions of understanding are based on a knowledge of the environment and typically relate to tendencies and probabilities: a decision that a certain class of consumers constitutes a potential market for a good is an example of a business decision of this kind. A decision of recognition would identify a particular person or object as belonging to a class defined by a decision of understanding, as when an individual consumer is identified as an actual or prospective purchaser of a good. Decisions of enterprise, such as policy decisions, define the boundaries within which decisions of action are made. A policy decision may stipulate the quality of the product and the market at which it shall be aimed, after which numerous decisions of action are called for to settle the details of design, production plans, sales channels and so forth.

Decisions of action probably come most readily to mind where business is concerned, but while they may be the most numerous they are clearly not the only decisions to be made, nor always the most important. Some decisions of action are so straightforward as to verge on the automatic, like a decision to stop a machine that shows signs of abnormal behaviour and find out what is wrong: but others are more complex, like a decision to introduce a new method of distribution designed to supply customers in different parts of the country in a certain sequence to ensure the

[1]M. E. Salveson, 'An Analysis of Decisions' in *Executive Readings in Management Science*, ed. M. K. Starr, pp. 142–156.

172

lowest average cost of distribution per unit. Decisions of action are interdependent and frequently refer to the achievement of relatively near objectives. These decisions must be compatible with decisions of enterprise, unless the contrary is specifically allowed, and decisions of enterprise must also be compatible with each other to avoid confusion. Decisions of enterprise, being of a higher order than the rest, are made by boards of directors and senior executives, while decisions of understanding are often made by specialist staff: decisions of recognition and action, although varying greatly in importance, are made by people at all levels in a firm.

Decisions of action can start new actions, modify existing actions, stop them, or leave them unchanged. A decision to do nothing is a special kind of decision of action often open to the decision maker, and the inaction in which it results is just as likely to have significant consequences for the firm as action itself. People in business do not, of course, always decide their actions in a deliberate, conscious way. Numerous actions are performed from habit, or to conform to accepted rules and customs, and do not call for repeated decisions by those who carry them out. Group action is often affected by informal codes that dictate instinctive responses to particular circumstances which the group cannot control, but to which it has learnt to adapt in the way most likely to promote its own advantage.

The quantity and quality of available information are of great importance to good decision making and many decisions have to be made in conditions that are far from perfect, either because there is absolutely insufficient information or because the pressure of events allows too little time for information to be collected and properly studied. In many cases a compromise is necessary between the need for quick decisions and decisions of the highest quality, the problem of striking the right balance between these frequently opposed needs being met by people at all levels in a firm. It is one to which no simple solution can be found, but it becomes progressively less serious as the need for decisions is recognized earlier and more time is given for making them, and as information-handling techniques speed up the collection and analysis of data on which decisions are based.

The pressure of events often means that the first satisfactory solution to a problem is accepted instead of more time being spent to explore alternatives before a decision is reached. In small firms, especially, the demands of current activities and a lack of foresight sometimes lead to crises in which managers are forced to make rapid decisions for which they are not adequately prepared. They are often under a strong inducement to keep the costs of decision making as low as possible, and deterred by the paucity of information from extending their search when managers of larger firms might be disposed to search more widely for that same reason. The ostensible advantages of the existing state of affairs may also be great and, contrasted with the possible uncertainty and difficulty attached to a different course of action, provide a temptation to leave well alone.

Both the length of time in which a decision can be made and the amount of information to be studied before making it tend to decrease as one moves from the highest level in a firm to the lowest. The majority of foremen and junior managers have to make a relatively large number of quick decisions with short time-spans, often on the basis of strictly limited knowledge, to deal with situations as they arise in their own subgroups; but at the level of the chief executive or the board a high proportion of the decisions made affect the company as a whole, call for large amounts of information, and relate to long-term matters that do not have to be treated with the same urgency as the unpredictable daily problems that arise lower down.

Decision making has to do with both ends and means and, although it is often impossible to make a precise distinction between ends decisions and means decisions, it is possible to see which decisions are relatively more concerned with the one and which with the other. Ends and means are again decided at all levels, but at high levels the ends are sometimes remote and the means more broadly conceived, while at low levels the ends are frequently close and the means of achieving them minutely defined. If a hierarchy of decisions is envisaged in which decisions at each level are made for the purpose of achieving objectives that are largely, or wholly, defined at one level or more above, the decisions can be regarded as serially connected in a chain of cause and effect from its origin in the firm's primary task, and many decisions are related to one another in this way. But it would be wrong to suppose that decisions at level N are affected only by decisions made at higher levels $N+1$, $N+2$ and so on. A decision at level N is affected by other decisions made on the same level and by decisions made at lower levels as well, an extreme example of the latter being a decision of a subordinate not to accept a decision of his superior, which forces the superior to decide again or refer the matter to a still higher level to be decided there.

Some decisions are induced by changes in the environment while others are made spontaneously to bring such changes about, and investment decisions can be used to contrast the two kinds. An induced investment decision has to be made when machinery wears out, becomes obsolete, or breaks down beyond repair before the end of its expected life; and similar decisions are also likely to be made when competitors threaten a firm's market, or as a result of certain governmental actions, such as changes in the level of investment allowances or grants. A spontaneous decision to invest, on the other hand, might be made to diversify a product range, or to increase the scale of production and expand a firm's share of the market for an existing good.

The real cost of a decision to invest tends to be greater when a firm is considering the possibilities of a different kind of investment from any that it has made before than it is when the new investment is virtually a repetition of an earlier one whose problems and consequences are known. Investment of a completely new kind may call for a long and careful study of its probable effects on the firm's development, and of the organizational and social results it is expected to produce, and require the collection and analysis of a great deal of information which is not already

174

available within the firm. But the real cost of a decision can only be calculated if all its results are known, and in many cases this calculation cannot be made at all for individual decisions and only roughly for decisions in aggregate. Decisions made in different positions at different times act and react on each other and have cumulative effects, so that it is often impossible to disentangle the results of one decision from another, and when this is the case the problem of personal accountability is a difficult one to settle. The longer the period over which the results of a decision are felt the harder does it become to isolate them from the overlapping results of later decisions, and some of the firms investigated by Williams and Scott believed that the outcome of an investment decision could never be properly assessed.[1]

Considerable attention has been paid to decision making in recent years, and a great deal has been done to discover more about the nature of the process and improve the techniques that decision makers can use. Decision theory has a prominent place in modern behavioural theories of the firm and it is important to know something about its content. A number of the earlier models of the decision-making process were built on the assumption that a firm could be treated as a rationally controlled and motivated system seeking to maximize profit or minimize loss, in which decision makers had both sufficient knowledge of the environment to list the outcomes of alternative courses of action in precise order of probability, and clearly ranked preferences for different future states of the organization. Doubt has been cast on the complete validity of these models by theorists who detect flaws in the reasoning on which they were based. As we saw before, they doubt whether firms maximize and whether behaviour is always purely rational. The outcomes of alternative courses of action cannot, in their view, be ranked precisely, because 'pay offs' are not precisely calculable: outcomes can at best be ranked in 'bands of expectation' labelled fairly possible, quite probable and so on, and given approximate values depending on the strength of the expectation that they will occur. The rationality of decisions is weakened by people's frequent inability to see problems in their entirety, or soon enough for the right action to be taken to solve them: in other words, by limited cognitive capacity. The speed at which information can be selected, coded and used also imposes a restraint on rational decision making, as does the conflict between organizational and personal goals, and between subgoals in the organization, which leads to inconsistent decisions being made.

Cyert and March take the rational model as a basis for their own behavioural theory of decision making and modify it in a few, but significant, ways that allow them to introduce and explain the partial resolution of conflict, the avoidance of uncertainty, the search procedures for problem solution, and the effect of organizational learning.[2] The firm is viewed as a coalition of participants, each with his own order

[1] B. R. Williams and W. P. Scott, *Investment Proposals and Decisions*, Allen and Unwin, 1965.
[2] R. M. Cyert and J. G. March, *A Behavioral Theory of the Firm*, Prentice-Hall, 1963. For a shorter version of their theory see W. W. Cooper, H. J. Leavitt and M. W. Shelly II, *op. cit.*, ch. 16.

of preference about what should be done, and when and how. Often these individual sets of preferences are incompatible, and give rise to conflict which has to be resolved. Resolution is seldom or never complete, but several things can be done to reduce the incidence of conflict, including the setting of goals whose achievement calls for a lower level of aspiration than maximizing goals and hence imposes weaker demands on the coalition, and the sequential pursuit of goals by the firm. When claims on resources conflict, their order of importance can be settled by bargaining and they can be met in sequence: the firm is thus able to deal with major problems one at a time instead of simultaneously. Efforts are made to avoid or reduce uncertainty, particularly by the use of decision-making rules that tell participants how to act in specified conditions, and by the indoctrination of employees in the organization's traditions to make them behave in a 'loyal' and predictable way. The emphasis is put on short-run activities which can be planned and regulated by standard procedures, and controls are used that quickly show a difference between desired and actual results and feed the information to someone who can take corrective action. The firm also tries to reduce uncertainty by negotiating its environmental conditions, for example by making contracts with trade unions, suppliers and customers that increase the confidence with which it can plan its work.

When problems arise they set in motion a train of events designed to lead to their solution. A problem must, of course, first be recognized, and its nature and importance assessed, before a search for its solution begins, after which the search is expected to proceed along simple lines at the outset, cause being assumed to lie close to observed effect and new solutions to exist in the vicinity of old. Only when these rules fail to produce a satisfactory answer will the search become more complex and far-reaching, and more distant solutions be sought. Cyert and March suggest that in the context of coalition conflict the solutions most often accepted will be those that either enable the more powerful elements to preserve their position at the expense of the weaker ones, or which dispose of problems by taking up some of the slack that every system contains, and without seriously disturbing the existing organizational balance. Throughout, the firm learns from its experience. It learns which goals are acceptable and attainable, which means are satisfactory, which search procedures are effective and which parts of the environment can be safely ignored, and adapts its behaviour as required. The kinds of information needed to keep the organization functioning become increasingly well understood, and the firm can progressively improve the processes of collecting, coding and distributing the data on which decisions are based.

In this model, decision making is treated in systems terms; the input is a problem, the conversion process involves search, analysis, verification, comparison and choice, and the output is a solution. The whole enterprise is envisaged as a system for making decisions, and each subsystem is a decision-making component of varying independence, connected by feedback loops to other subsystems to ensure a high level of compatibility between their operations and goals. It goes almost without saying that in a theory of this kind decision making is looked on as the cardinal aspect of managerial work.

Modern theorists are at pains to bring out the effects of organization on decision making and the behaviour of the firm. The formal pattern of delegation, which determines departmental structure and the authority and responsibility of each role, plays a major part in shaping relations between individuals and groups and between the formal and informal organizations, and thereby influences the way in which decisions are made and implemented. Departmental structure affects the behaviour of the coalition and makes some solutions more conspicuous and acceptable than others: it also influences the selection of organizational goals and subgoals, and hence the long-run development of the firm. Organizational design settles the planning and control subsystems and these have a direct effect on the extent to which problems are identified and solved. The chosen structure results in particular search procedures being associated with particular kinds of problem, and major structural changes alter both the organization's need for information and the capacity to handle it: they also affect the firm's 'memory', and in extreme cases may damage it or destroy parts of it completely.

A variety of personal and institutional factors must be taken into account in a comprehensive theory of decision making, and theories like that of Cyert and March are illuminating in many ways that the purely rational theories are not. But behavioural theory has so far had more explanatory than predictive value, and the development of decision-making tools is at present of greater practical relevance to firms than the theory itself.

Probability theory and statistical analysis, mathematical programming, the theory of games, critical path analysis, production scheduling, market research, inventory control, budgetary control and discounted cash flow analysis are examples of the techniques that can be used to improve decision making in the firm. It is already possible to use some of these tools to help decide how much to produce, when and where to produce, and what combination of resources will achieve a given output at lowest cost; to decide prices and distribution methods; and to assess the expected profitability of different investments. In a limited number of cases it is possible to construct mathematical models of business systems to feed into a computer, which then shows, within the limits of any policy restraints imposed, what action should be taken to obtain a certain result. When connected to an electronic data-processing system the computer can detect when decisions are needed and what they should be, and issue instructions to an automatic production line which operates without human intervention. But electronic devices only solve problems that can be quantified, and managers must still make judgments and rely on personal experience when dealing with problems that can only be partially quantified, or not at all. The main virtue of electronic machines is to take over large

177

amounts of the routine work of decision making and do it at very high speed. Managers then have more time to consider higher-order problems and concentrate on decisions in which ethical, political or social factors play an important part.

The theoretical advances made in subjects related to decision making have already been impressive, but it cannot be said too plainly that there is an enormous gulf between theory and practice. The number of companies actually using these techniques is very small indeed, although their relative importance is greater than their number would suggest, and even in firms where decisions are based on the use of scientific methods the range of currently-applied techniques is generally rather narrow. Some of the new tools have hardly emerged from the experimental stage and need to be improved, and preferably simplified, before their widespread use is enjoyed.

A number of techniques are derived from advanced mathematical analysis and there is a shortage of people capable of applying methematical tools to business problems. It is not enough for techniques to exist and be known; managers must be able to recognize the kinds of problem for whose solution the techniques can be used, and firms must recruit people who can handle the tools and provide decision makers with intelligible and practical advice. At present it is not unfair to say that most managers have scarcely heard of many of these techniques, and relatively few can appreciate the extent to which they might advantageously be used. The introduction of an increasing number of mathematically-trained specialists into business firms, which seems certain to occur, is still regarded sceptically, even fearfully, in some quarters, and is likely to raise in an acute form some of the difficulties of mutual comprehension and cooperation associated with a high degree of specialization.

There is as yet no comprehensive theory of decision making, and what has been discovered so far shows clearly the multiplicity of elements in the decision process and the complexity of many decisions when they are analysed in full. A decision is influenced by the individual's perception of the enormously complicated real world, by personal interpretation of organizational requirements, by the personal goals of the decision maker, by his assessment of his own and other people's ability, by his propensity to cooperate or to act alone, by group loyalties and pressures, by the scope for the combination of different types of resources, by a particular selection of environmental data, by prescience in collecting and skill in processing information, by search patterns and by many other things besides. The future will bring further advances in the theory and practice of scientific decision making, but in the greater number of companies today most decisions are made in traditional and unscientific ways on the basis of personal judgment, intuition and experience, or result from elementary analyses of limited data and the use of rule-of-thumb methods of accounting.

178

9.3 Decentralization

THE MEANING OF DECENTRALIZATION

The study of a company's decision-making system shows how authority to make decisions is allocated, and hence the degree of centralization or decentralization in the firm. Essentially, one wants to know two things: the positions in which particular decisions are made and the importance of these decisions from the company's point of view. If all major decisions are made by relatively few people at the highest levels a state of centralization exists, but if extensive power to make important decisions is given to people at lower levels than these the firm has a decentralized administrative system.

Neither absolute centralization nor absolute decentralization is logically conceivable in companies employing more than one person. The sharing of work involves delegation, and as this requires the people to whom authority is delegated to have *some* power to make decisions, however limited, there must be a minimal amount of decentralization in any multiperson concern. Complete decentralization, however, would mean that everyone was free to decide his own work and how it should be done, which would be an anarchic and absurd situation. There must be central guidance and control to ensure appropriate uniformity of behaviour and coordinate the activities of the firm. What is interesting is the way in which elements of centralization and decentralization are combined, or balanced, and this is a matter to which we shall return.

There is no unique criterion of the importance of a decision, but significant information about the degree of decentralization can be obtained by measuring the time-spans of decisions and the degree of uncertainty to be coped with when they are made, and by finding out at what levels decisions are made about expenditure on equipment or materials; the appointment, promotion and dismissal of employees; the determination of wage and salary scales; levels of output; the kinds of resources used in production; the acceptance of orders; conditions of sale; and the use of external help. The greater the diffusion of power to decide matters like these at levels below the chief executive the greater is the degree of decentralization. This decision-making power should be thought of essentially as an independent one, of course, and as formally attributed to the persons concerned, not as an informally derived power, nor one to make decisions that only become effective after they have been approved by someone at a higher level.

CENTRALIZING AND DECENTRALIZING FORCES

There are always forces, external and internal, that tend to increase the degree of centralization, and others that tend to produce a more decentralized state, but probably the most important single factor in most cases is the character and ability of the chief executive. If he is autocratic and convinced of his own infallibility he will insist on making the major decisions himself and strictly limit his subordinates' freedom to decide things in their own spheres. But sometimes the top manager may be the only person competent to make decisions, and centralization results because the total supply of managerial talent in the firm is small and unevenly distributed. Given the chief executive's temperament and ability, however, the size of the firm is a most significant variable, and increases in size ultimately increase the senior manager's load so much that he either delegates more or accepts a decline in company performance when he is no longer capable of dealing effectively with all the major problems that have to be solved.

Growth and diversification tend to go together, and a large diversified enterprise often experiences managerial problems that are different both in order and in kind from those encountered in smaller firms, and different also from the problems of an equally large firm in which diversification has not taken place. Diversification frequently results in an organizational structure in which separate production units, possibly operating under different names, are controlled by an industrial holding company which is the parent of the group. Alternatively, a single enterprise may produce a variety of different goods in separate establishments or divisions under a single name. In each case a major problem is to combine, as one manager has put it, the strength of unity with the flexibility that diversity of operations can give. It is a matter of determining how much autonomy to allow the individual production units and what kind of authority to exercise over them from the centre. The outcome in many companies is a system of federal decentralization, in which considerable decision-making power is given to each divisional or unit manager to run his own part of the enterprise as far as possible on independent lines. This organizational development has been hailed by Likert as one of the most important social inventions of the present century and it has been widely discussed in business literature.[1]

Diversification and growth may eventually force the most reluctant chief executive to give more authority to divisional or subsidiary-company heads, and thus increase the degree of decentralization, but the movement sometimes goes no farther and the final result is that, although the top manager has divested himself of some of his power, the degree of centralization in the plant or division itself is high. If this happens it may simply mean that an oligarchy rules instead of an autocrat. The extent to which decentralization is carried in a diversified business must always depend a great deal on the attitude of senior divisional managers to whom substantial decision-making power is given, and if they are unable, or unwilling, to share that power with their own subordinates the limit to decentralization is quickly reached.

Business history provides many examples of the damaging effects of excessive centralization. It has been said of William Lever that the art of delegation was one

[1]R. Likert, *New Patterns of Management*, McGraw-Hill, 1961, p. 85.

he never learnt, and his extreme unwillingness to allow senior colleagues to make important decisions, or even to share with him the knowledge on which important decisions were reached, had an almost disastrous outcome when his fellow directors discovered the full implications of Lever's purchase of the Niger Company in 1920. The financial difficulties into which the parent concern was plunged by this acquisition led for the first time to a measure of external control over policy making that Lever deeply resented, but for the firm it proved in the long run to be a blessing in disguise.

The first Henry Ford had an equally exaggerated dislike of sharing his authority to make major decisions, and insisted on exercising it alone. He is said to have treated executives more as personal assistants than managers, and at one time he went to the length of arbitrarily demoting foremen a few years after their appointment, to prevent them from consolidating even their modest influence in the firm. A result of Ford's policy of centralization was that the company had almost no one capable of managing because no one was allowed to do so, and during the 1930s it lost ground in the American motor industry and made a deficit year after year. Towards the end of the Second World War Henry Ford was close to death, his son Edsel had already died, and the crown passed to Ford's grandson, Henry Ford II. Under his leadership, and helped by a strong transfusion of managerial talent, the Ford company was extensively reorganized and became a much more decentralized system, which certainly played a part in the restoration of its fortunes.

In so far as good decisions depend on the amount and quality of information available and the speed with which it can be put into the decision maker's hands, a number of improvements in communications systems have probably tended to make possible or strengthen a centralized state. Some of the recent developments in information-handling techniques and automatic control methods have for this reason helped to increase the centrality of decision making in the firm. But these developments can also be used to produce an opposite effect, since the more rapid collection and transmission of information enables improved data to be supplied to people in subordinate positions and used to make more important decisions speedily there.

When a business is in difficulties there is a frequently-felt need for stronger central guidance, and a greater number of important matters tend to be decided at the centre. Suppose, for example, that a company has a number of plants which use the same raw material, that the supply of this material suddenly and sharply falls, and that its price is increased: if plant managers had been allowed to buy their own materials in a normal market they might not be allowed to do so in the new situation. Decisions about how much to buy at the higher prices and how to share restricted supplies between different plants would almost certainly be made at a higher level than before. Anything that demands common action in different parts of a company, such as government legislation or trade union pressure, tends to raise the level at which decisions affecting that action are made and increase the degree of centralization.

The growing scale and complexity of business operations, although making it more difficult for a chief executive to decide all important matters alone, does not necessarily produce a steady movement towards decentralization. It may lead to the coordination of activities by a greater standardization of procedures and by rules to inhibit individual variations in behaviour, instead of to a wider sharing of decision-making power. The ratio of programmed to non-programmed decisions is thereby increased and by this means the people at the top are able to concentrate on the control of major variables, while the larger amount of routine work below is governed by a set of carefully integrated and highly specific plans. But if the desire to enjoy the maximum economies of managerial specialization leads to centralization in one respect it need not be incompatible with decentralization in another. A retail distribution concern, for example, may have a large number of branches situated in different parts of the country and catering in varying degree for different classes of consumer. The individual store managers could be given considerable freedom to decide the range of goods stocked in each shop, but required to order through a central purchasing department that bought in bulk for the firm.

Technology affects the degree of centralization by imposing restraints on the organization of work, but it does so in different ways. Extremely intricate mass-production systems, in which numerous parts are assembled in a precise order at carefully controlled rates, call for complex production programmes and continuous control, because a failure in one part of the system often has serious and widespread repercussions on the operations of the firm. Central decisions determine the layout of the plant and most of the details of work, and there is scope at lower levels to decide matters of only local and limited importance in many positions. Miss Woodward found a high degree of centralization in the more mechanistic mass-production firms in her study, but in process industries, on the other hand, where the technology was also complex, there was greater decentralization and managers in the plants had appreciably more freedom to decide things themselves. Senior managers in these industries apparently felt that subordinates could be relied on to make the same kinds of decision as people at the top, a feeling that owed much to the prevalence of scientific qualifications in the managerial groups that gave them a more homogeneous character than comparable groups in mass-production firms. The atmosphere of mutual trust, and uniformity of organizational attitudes, strengthened the bias towards decentralization in process-industry concerns.

Centralized decisions are by definition often made far from the positions they affect and, although they may be technically excellent, they risk the human consequences of imposing on people at lower levels decisions emanating remotely from above. Centralization may result in excessive detachment and lack of contact on the decision maker's part, a danger that would seem to have been present in an acute form in the case of one Orlando F. Webber, sometime chief executive of the Allied Chemical and Dye Company of America, who is reported to have run the company on the basis of monthly reports brought to him in his suite in the Waldorf Towers. With a decentralized system of administration a higher proportion of independent decisions can be made close to the points of action, if information relevant to decisions is available in appropriate positions. A greater number of subordinates can look to their immediate superiors for prompt decisions about their work, based on a first-hand knowledge of the situations to which they relate.

If managers are allowed to make and learn from their mistakes, before they become too costly for the firm to afford, a supply of progressively improved managerial ability becomes available within the company and this simplifies the problem of managerial succession. The challenge of having to decide things for themselves, and the prospect of promotion as a reward for proven ability, are both claimed to raise morale in a decentralized company and increase its attractiveness to the managers it employs. It has also been suggested that if subgroups at lower levels can be given a reasonably large measure of autonomy, and operational goals to achieve, their sense of collective responsibility is increased, their informal organizations are strengthened and more closely identified with formal aims, and the scope for the exercise of leadership by their superiors is widened.

It is not easy to estimate the extent to which decentralization has taken place, because the number of cases on which a conclusion can be based is relatively small and probably biased. Decentralization is looked on nowadays as a sign of progressiveness, and centralization as a sign of unwillingness to respond to the temper of the times. The larger companies that have increased the degree of decentralization in recent years set standards by which other companies are often judged, and there are many more publicized cases of decentralization than centralization in firms. Indeed, arguments in favour of the latter have become increasingly hard to find. The histories of some companies show that they have moved back and forth between centralized and decentralized states in pendulum fashion over the long term, but it is not always clear why they behaved as they did. One theory suggests that these movements are caused by successive reactions against the dysfunctional effects of carrying either centralization or decentralization too far, but it is equally possible that at different stages of growth, or in different environmental conditions, companies simply find one pattern of delegation more suitable than another. As managerial groups change, new ideas are introduced and new methods are tried, and this fact is probably sufficient to account for variations in the degree of decentralization over time in many firms.

THE BALANCE BETWEEN CENTRALIZATION AND DECENTRALIZATION
In any company there must be sufficient central authority to coordinate the work of the major subunits and prevent damaging inconsistency between the activities

of the firm. Central decisions usually determine the main subgoals of the organization related to the achievement of its primary task, the use of capital funds and cash flows, the appointment of senior managers and the way that common services shall be used. After that the scope for making important, independent decisions at lower levels varies greatly from firm to firm. But modern theory undoubtedly emphasizes the net advantages of a decentralized system and current managerial thinking seems increasingly to support the same view.

Decentralization means that as far as possible subgroup goals are set by agreement between subgroup managers and their superiors, largely on the former's initiative in many cases, although the amount of subgroup independence is affected by the type of work performed and the extent to which it complements or competes with the work of other subgroups, or with units outside the firm. In federally decentralized systems the granting of a high degree of autonomy to individual profit-making units is held to result in larger total profits for the enterprise, efficiency being increased by the incentive of having mainly self-determined objectives to aim at and measured by uniform financial standards which permit objective assessments of managerial performance to be made. A further virtue of federal decentralization is that the comparison of subunit results shows whether total resources are being allocated in the most appropriate way. The diffusion of responsibility for important operational tasks means that more managers have an opportunity to develop their skills to a higher level, and this benefits the firm in the short run because motivation is strengthened and in the long run because the supply of managerial ability is increased and improved. But if decentralization is to proceed to a significant extent managers at each level must be prepared to accept a change in the nature of their authority and the way it is exercised: the problem of personality is inescapable where questions of decentralization are concerned. A business that has been highly centralized for some time may find it difficult to decentralize, because managers at lower levels have not developed the competence to make important decisions and carry greater responsibility, and it may be hard to break the circle of cause and effect that encourages senior executives to retain decision-making power because they lack confidence in their subordinates, and prevents subordinates from developing in a way which makes greater delegation possible. Decisions of higher quality can often be made at the centre, it is true, but the real costs of getting information from lower positions and transmitting central decisions to (sometimes distant) points of action may be high. The advantage frequently lies in having a decision made at the nearest level to, or in, the actual place of application, even if the quality of the decision is not so good as it would have been if the decision were made higher in the firm. But the lowest level at which a decision can be made must depend in some cases on the number and organizational location of the subgroups which the decision affects, and this can be seen by looking back at Figure 25 on page 158.

The structure shown there contains seven subgroups, and in each one many decisions about the subordinates' work can be made by their immediate superior: thus decisions affecting *D* and *E*, for example, can frequently be made by *B*. Decisions affecting members of two or more subgroups on a common level can be made in one or other of two ways. The superiors of the groups concerned may agree a decision and put it into effect in their respective groups, and this is a satisfactory arrangement if there is no conflict of action, and senior managers whose work may be affected are told of the decision and approve what is done. Where conflict between subgroups is likely to occur, or where coordination at one level cannot be effectively secured by agreement at the next level above, the locus of decision making must be pushed still higher. In this example it is probable that some decisions to coordinate the work of *D*'s and *E*'s subordinates would be made by *B*, while decisions to coordinate the activities of (say) *D*'s subordinates with *G*'s would have to be made in some cases by *M*.

Decentralization has been discussed mainly with respect to large, complex, diversified companies in which the managerial burden that would otherwise fall on one person, or on a small senior group, makes a substantial sharing of decision-making power essential. It is a mistake, however, to think that decentralization is only relevant to large concerns, for the problem of finding an appropriate balance between centralization and decentralization is faced by companies of every size. The degree of decentralization has a bearing on power equalization, the speed and quality of decision making, motivation and individual satisfaction, and the methods by which coordination is secured, all of which affect the efficiency and profitability of the firm. Unfortunately, these variables are not all easily measured and the effects of their interaction cannot always be accurately foreseen. A company that wishes to decentralize may be deterred by what are sometimes high initial costs of change. These are money costs of training existing managers or recruiting new ones, and of a possible loss of efficiency while the change is being made, and real costs of uncertainty about the efficacy of the new system in the long term. What evidence we have suggests that firms do gain often from decentralization in greater flexibility and competitive strength, but the gains make take some time to appear. It is not suggested that firms should make a fetish of decentralization, but if one accepts the idea of an adaptable socio-technical system and the existence of organizational choice, the willingness to search for opportunities to decentralize would seem to be an appropriate form of managerial behaviour in many cases.

There is, in fact, no uniform answer to the question of how centralized or decentralized a firm should be, because so much depends on the organizational and psychological characteristics of individual companies, on their environment, and on their size, technology and rate of growth. Centralization and decentralization both have advantages and disadvantages of different kinds in different situations, and it is only possible to generalize by saying that in every company elements of both will be found. The most suitable balance between them is something that each firm must discover for itself, but an appreciation of the probable consequences of a bias in one direction or the other is necessary as a basis for analysis, and an assessment of their importance to an individual firm enables a more objective view to be taken of the design of the system than would otherwise be the case.

10

Staff problems in the firm

In Chapter 6 we considered some fundamental types of organizational structure, of which the most important was the line and staff organization, and we suggested that this term is not entirely satisfactory, because staff does not have an unambiguous meaning in business literature and there is no general agreement about the way in which an organization is, or should be, divided into line and staff components. The matter is not just an academic one, for if line activities have primacy and staff activities are ancillary to them, the distinction has important implications for the way in which formal authority is distributed and exercised, for the appropriate pattern of communication and for the character of interdepartmental and personal relations in a firm. In this chapter we examine the different kinds of staff in business and discuss some of the problems associated with their work.

Of the several meanings attached to staff two are not sufficiently relevant here to discuss at length. The word staff can refer to the whole body of people employed by a company or to one part of the workforce whose members are appointed on different terms and enjoy different conditions of employment from the rest. The staff in the second sense may consist only of managers, or of managers and foremen; but it may also embrace clerical employees, or be enlarged to include certain manual workers who by virtue of age or length of service, for example, are eligible for such staff benefits as monthly salaries, pensions, longer holidays, freedom from clocking on and off, or whatever they happen to be. The other meanings of staff are more important and will be considered in turn under the headings of general staff and specialist staff, each of which will be discussed in terms of the organizational roles of people in these categories and the nature of the work they do.

10.1 General staff

It is necessary to be clear at the start about the differences between an assistant manager, a deputy manager and an assistant to a manager. An assistant manager and a deputy each has authority in his own right and stands in a direct line of command between a superior and subordinates of his own; his position may be as high as assistant managing director or as low as assistant foreman and exist in any department of the firm. A deputy manager is normally assumed to take over his superior's responsibilities completely in the latter's absence, whereas an assistant manager may have a more limited power to act in place of his chief. An assistant to a manager has no formal managerial authority, although he may have a small number of secretarial subordinates, and no departmental responsibility. He is appointed to serve one executive in a direct personal capacity and constitutes either the whole or a

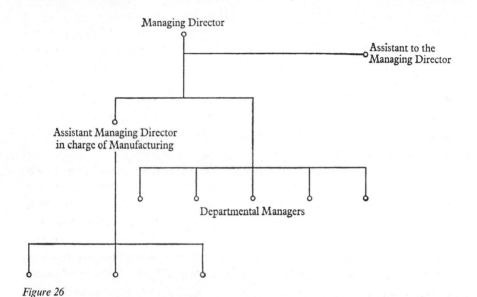

Figure 26

part of that executive's private staff. In diagrammatical form the difference between the positions of assistant manager and assistant to a manager is shown in Figure 26.

We deal first with assistants to managers as a staff group in their own right and within this group a distinction must be made between a personal assistant and a general staff assistant to a manager. Personal assistants are probably the more widely employed, but their status varies a great deal from firm to firm and in many cases they are little more than superior private secretaries to their chiefs. We shall exclude this kind of assistant here and concentrate on the one whose position is comparable to that of a General Staff Officer in the army, because this role is more interesting from an organizational point of view. It is perhaps worth noting in passing that the title of personal assistant is not used in a uniform way in business and is given to occupants of both low-level and high-level positions. Similarly, titles such as executive assistant and administrative assistant are given to assistant managers and assistants to managers, which sometimes gives rise to misunderstanding about the exact nature of the position on the part of people outside a firm.

The precise extent to which general staff assistants are employed is unknown, but they appear to be found more commonly in American companies than in British, and whereas in the U.S.A. they are employed in quite different sized firms, in Britain they are customarily appointed only in large concerns. The use of staff assistants in the United States has apparently become increasingly common since 1950, because Dale and Urwick mention a survey of 300 American companies which showed that 70 per cent of their chief executives had such assistants, most of whom had been appointed during the five years before the survey was published in 1957. The tendency for assistants to serve at a high managerial level was borne out by a further sample of fifty assistants, twenty of whom worked for presidents (chief executives) and thirteen for manufacturing vice-presidents or general managers.[1] The fact that most of our information about staff assistants, like most of the discussion about their use, relates to American practice need not prevent us from examining the possible consequences of their employment in broader terms. British industry has already shown its propensity to adopt American organizational practices, and staff assistants may become more widely employed in Britain if their value in America is proved more conclusively than it has been so far.

The case for their employment is most simply made by showing what staff assistants can do, taking it as self-evident that someone made assistant to a manager should be able to make a positive net contribution to the manager's work. He can do so by lightening the manager's load absolutely, or by taking over some of his existing work so that the manager is able to undertake new tasks of greater importance to the firm. A staff assistant can best help his superior by performing the whole, or he major share, of the detailed work associated with his role, and Urwick argues that the assistant should actually do all the paper work, relieve his chief of minutiae, and give him a greater opportunity to concentrate on fundamental company problems.

The assistant can act as a coordinator, making arrangements in his chief's name between other people in the firm and possibly assuming responsibility for the implementation of special projects on his behalf. He can collect, analyse and present information, especially information derived from outside the firm, and act as liaison officer between his superior and private consultants if their services are used. He can undertake special assignments and deal with problems which cannot conveniently be dealt with by the superior or his managerial subordinates. In all cases the assistant acts only for his chief and in his name, behaving rather like an extension of the superior's personality. His job is to understand, minister to and, when possible, anticipate the superior's needs. But experience has shown that assistants are not always appointed solely for their ability to give support of this kind. The assistant's

[1] E. Dale and L. F. Urwick, *Staff in Organization*, McGraw-Hill, 1960.

position is sometimes created as a reward or sinecure for a man with long service who is not easily found another role when an organizational change is made. The position may also provide temporary accommodation for an able person destined for promotion to an office which has not yet been vacated, and occasionally it is occupied by an experienced manager who discreetly advises a younger executive who is learning about his job.

It is desirable that the appointment of a staff assistant should not result from organizational weakness that the appointment itself perpetuates and conceals. If an assistant is wanted because a manager is excessively burdened it is necessary to ask why, and in what ways, his burden is too heavy. The load might be lightened by greater delegation to existing subordinates if they are not overloaded themselves, or by creating a new subordinate managerial position instead of the assistant's post. Established subordinates may feel angry and disturbed if work which they regard as falling naturally and acceptably within their own areas of responsibility is given to someone without their departmental experience or managerial authority. There is also a danger that the assistant's work will duplicate that of some specialist staff group, and an extreme possibility that he might be appointed at a high salary to do work that could be done by a competent secretary or clerk.

The assistant's position is such that he normally enjoys close relations with his chief, and if a confidential relationship is established between them the assistant may have access to important information which is not known to the firm's exe-cutives, and be aware of his chief's plans and proposals before they become matters of wider consideration and debate. The assistant's lack of managerial authority can therefore be counterbalanced by considerable authority of knowledge, which, if misused, may enable him to exercise an influence over his chief's subordinates that is not formally derived from his position. Without attributing Machiavellian motives to an assistant the situation could arise in which the superior deals more readily with him than with managerial colleagues, who find a barrier interposed between themselves and their chief. This would be a most undesirable state of affairs for the subordinates, and the assistant himself would be in a false position. Subordinates should always have the right of access to their superior, who must realize that one of the reasons for employing an assistant is to give him more time for dealing with them if necessary, not less.

Another danger attending the appointment of a staff assistant is that it may stimulate other managers to demand assistants for themselves. The danger is probably not so great if an appointment is made solely to support a chief executive, but if a manager at a lower level is given an assistant it is not at all unlikely that his peers will find reasons for wanting one also, a prime reason being that the status of a manager with an assistant will appear to be higher than theirs. But the worst possible grounds for appointing an assistant are to assuage managerial pride or decorate an executive position to increase the occupant's prestige. An assistant is placed in a difficulty if his appointment is resented and an uncooperative attitude is adopted towards him. He can always get access to people and information if his superior is the chief executive and so decrees, but his ability to do his job well is greatly affected by the nature of his relations with other people in the firm.

And what of the career prospects for a staff assistant? Should his job be a permanent or a temporary one? If it is temporary to what other position does he move? Dale and Urwick found that the average age of assistants in the smaller of the two samples mentioned was about thirty-six years, so that the people concerned were often at a critical stage in their business careers. It has been argued that an assistant can usefully extend his range of managerial knowledge by serving a senior executive, and enhance his own suitability for promotion to a managerial role as a result. Although his experience of management and managerial problems would be gained indirectly an able assistant could still profit from a close observation of the way in which a good senior manager worked. If the appointment of a staff assistant were taken as a certain prelude to promotion, however, it would undoubtedly affect attitudes in the firm, both to the value of the position and the person who filled it. Urwick suggests that a staff assistant should have managerial experience and be younger than the direct managerial subordinates of the executive he serves. He should also be appointed for a limited period, preferably two to four years, and at the end of that time should return to managerial work, probably with the prospect of early, if not immediate, promotion.

Dale and Urwick maintain that staff assistants can be of great help in small firms as well as large, a view supported by A. G. Hayek in an article in the *British Management Review* of 1950. But there might be difficulties in meeting Urwick's specifications of age, experience and future prospects when assistants are appointed in small firms and, indeed, Hayek's suggestions for the appointment of general staff assistants come close to being recommendations for appointing specialist staff who would work more effectively in newly created departments of their own.

American experience shows that where staff assistants have been unsuccessfully used the cause has often been a failure to safeguard against one or more of the dangers discussed here, but particularly a failure to define the assistant's duties plainly and clarify the nature of his relations with his chief's managerial subordinates. The misuse of assistants in general staff positions to do the work of specialists was another common source of trouble, as were the personal failings of some superiors who encouraged assistants to report on the activities of managers whose positions were higher than the assistant's own. Bearing in mind the qualities of self-restraint, managerial competence in a non-managerial position, discretion and analytical skill that are called for in a good staff assistant it is not surprising that unsatisfactory appointments have been made, simply because of the difficulty of finding all these qualities combined in one man who also has the appropriate technical qualifications for the job.

A misunderstanding of the true nature of military staff work and its relevance to business administration is said to be an important reason why firms are slow to employ staff assistants more widely than they do, but even if this misunderstanding were dispelled it would still be difficult in many cases to say unequivocally that these appointments should be made. The factor that is most likely to be decisive in this matter is the increasing size of enterprises that are already large, and the growing number of new large business units. The demands on senior managers in these big concerns have been increasing in consequence and will probably continue to do so, and in these circumstances chief executives who have rejected the use of staff assistants in the past may be compelled to change their attitude in the future. The short-term appointment of general staff assistants can be beneficial to managers and assistants alike, and a succession of these appointments would help to relieve managerial burdens over a long period. But the present indications are that in most companies alternative solutions to the problem of excessive managerial loads, in the form of a revised pattern of delegation and redistribution of work between a (possibly) larger number of subordinate managers, are likely to remain more acceptable than the introduction of general staff assistants.

10.2 Specialist staff

The employment of specialist staff is itself an inevitable result of this increasing scale and complexity of business operations, the widening scope for applying new knowledge in business, and changes in the nature and intensity of competitive forces. The need for a formal separation of line and specialist staff work is felt at different stages of growth by different firms, but although a company may exist satisfactorily for some time with a structure containing line departments only it must, if it is a dynamic and growing concern, almost certainly reach a point at which the transition to a form of line and staff system is essential. The attempt to increase a firm's efficiency and improve its competitive position by making this kind of structural change sometimes creates organizational complications, and problems of coordination and command, which must be solved if the advantages to be derived from greater managerial specialization are not to be weakened or lost.

The range of specialist staff work in modern companies is already great and seems likely to be extended as new specialisms reach the level of development at which it is profitable to apply them in the work of a firm. There is little point in trying to enumerate staff activities exhaustively, but to give an idea of their diversity they include such things as production control, quality control, work study, operational research, economic intelligence, statistical services, education and training, data processing and personnel administration. A complete list of specialist staff work would run to considerable length. In a book like this it is impossible to describe all these activities in detail and probably not very helpful even to select examples for detailed treatment. The work and responsibilities of staff employed in any of these specialized fields vary from firm to firm, but anyone interested to see how a specialist's duties can be formally defined should look at the representative illustrative schedules that Brech provides.[1] It will be sufficient for our purpose to consider specialist staff work in more general terms.

Specialist staff have the important job of giving advice and information to other members of the firm and helping them use it to the best advantage. The nature of the advice, the level(s) at which it is offered and the manner of its use all affect the way in which a staff department is set up and located. In some large companies there are central, or headquarters, specialist groups to assist the chief executive, or senior executive team, and the board, which might deal, for example, with legal matters or public relations. Alternatively, a staff department may be created to give advice and information to managers at lower levels and assist people in different parts of the company as required. A communication problem sometimes arises here which can be dealt with in different ways. Managers may be left to seek specialist advice and information when they think they need it, on the assumption that they know what they want and where to find it. They may know neither, and fail to use a staff department's services unless its members publicize the assistance they can offer and actively encourage managers to ask for their help.

In his limited role of provider of advice and intelligence the staff specialist acts as a repository of specialized knowledge and serves as an internal consultant who can be called for in cases of need. But a chief executive may decide that a specialist's recommendations are too important to be ignored or accepted at the subordinates' discretion, and require them to take advice and use information under conditions that are formally prescribed. When this happens the specialist's responsibility and the basis of his relations with colleagues in other departments are significantly changed, and to this matter we shall shortly return. Specialist staff can help by devising or developing techniques for managerial use, and three separate forms of staff responsibility can be distinguished here. The staff may be asked simply to develop a technique in a form suitable for managers or their subordinates to use; they may be asked also to make sure that the technique is used appropriately; or they may actually apply the technique themselves in the relevant departments or sections of the firm. When staff people devise new operating procedures with associated controls and apply the techniques, they clearly have some power over the people whom the controls and techniques affect.

Certain specialized activities, like production control, are performed in one department only and the staff responsible for such activities usually work in it themselves. (This example assumes a single production department, but if a business has several product divisions, or plants, there may be production control sections in each one and a central production control department to deal with matters relating

[1] E. F. L. Brech, *Organisation, The Framework of Management*, 2nd edn., Longmans, 1965.

to this specialism that affect the company as a whole.) Problems can arise when failure to distinguish between the line and the staff aspects of a particular specialism results in an unsatisfactory distribution of resources in the firm. Finance, for instance, may be considered the province of a line department so far as control of company funds and the preparation of published accounts are concerned, but the financial staff who calculate and check production costs or prepare budget statements provide a specialist service for other departments in the firm. Different kinds of financial work may call for dissimilar training and outlook, and while in some cases it is preferable to group everyone with a financial qualification under the head of the finance department it is not always the best arrangement to make, and the same argument holds true for other kinds of staff specialist in a firm.

To the staff activities already mentioned we should add the tasks of planning, controlling and coordinating work on which their specialized skills impinge. The specialist staff are expected to innovate and look for new opportunities for the profitable application of their knowledge, which means that a staff manager must convince his colleagues that the value of his department's services justifies their use. This is difficult at times, because the return on specialist services cannot always be quantified, their worth to the firm must often be assessed subjectively, and a potential cause of conflict between line and staff, of which more in due course, is the fact that line managers may feel they are judged by strict objective criteria while their colleagues are not. The central staff departments in some large firms are financed by levying a percentage of the annual revenue of the production divisions; in some companies the specialist services of one department are sold to the managers of others at agreed prices; and a third possibility is to impute the total cost of a specialist service as indirect costs of other departments on a predetermined basis.

Each method requires the acceptance of an accounting convention and will not necessarily equate the marginal costs and revenues attributable to the use of specialist services in different parts of the firm. When specialist staff provide services solely for one department it is still difficult to put a precise value on their contribution to departmental results, even assuming that these can be separately measured. If, as often happens, the staff of one specialist department serve several other departments whose activities have reciprocal effects, the staff's work will have not only a direct bearing on the efficiency of each department, but additional indirect effects on the general efficiency of the firm which cannot be isolated and measured. The purpose of employing specialist staff is to improve a company's ability to provide and sell goods or services at a satisfactory profit, and in the last analysis decisions to employ or not to employ staff, and to alter the range of staff services, must be made in the light of their estimated effect on the long-run profitability of the firm. But, as we have already argued, after staff specialists have been brought into a company, the longer they serve it the more closely interwoven does their work become with the work of others, and the harder it is for the firm to measure their true opportunity cost.

194

We have largely begged the question of what authority the specialist staff have, or should have, and the way that authority is affected by the nature of their work. There would seem, for example, to be an important difference between situations in which staff merely give information and advice, and situations in which they devise and implement plans, and control and coordinate the work of others. It is this question of authority that is usually in mind when people talk about the 'line and staff problem', and discuss whether or not there is an inherent tendency for conflict between line managers and specialist staff to exist.

10.3 Specialist staff authority

Classical theorists have generally argued that difficulties between line and staff employees are due mainly to bad organization, and that if the structure is properly designed and the work of each position clearly defined they need not arise, or create serious problems for the firm if they do. Modern theorists have been more concerned with behavioural variables, and maintain that personal factors associated

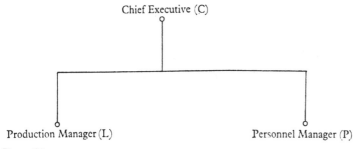

Figure 27

with the type of work done cause line-staff tensions, however carefully the structure is designed in the attempt to prevent them. Let us begin our examination of these views by considering a senior specialist staff manager's relationships with some of the people with whom he has direct contact in the firm. Figure 27 shows part of an organizational structure in which a line manager (*L*) in charge of production and a specialist staff manager (*P*) at the head of the personnel department are both immediate subordinates of the chief executive (*C*).

P has normal managerial authority over his own subordinates in the personnel department and they are responsible to him for the work that he allots to them, but *C* has the ultimate power to decide what is done by *P* and the other members of his department, subject to approval by the board. *P* derives authority from *C* and is responsible to him, but their relationship is something more than a simple vertical one in which *C* commands and *P* obeys. As chief executive *C* must be satisfied that the firm's work is satisfactorily done and its resources efficiently used, and part of

P's job is to assist him by giving specialized information and advice. When he does so his relationship with *C* is similar to that of a staff assistant whose position was discussed in the preceding section. *C* may be expected to rely heavily on *P* when solving problems in which personnel matters loom large, and when formulating general personnel policy. He will certainly expect *P* and his subordinates to do much of the practical work involved in translating that policy into action.

The relationship between *P* and *L* is more likely to cause difficulty than that between *P* and *C*, especially if we assume that *P* and *L* have equal formal status. If *P* is required to give *L* advice about the handling of personnel problems in the production department and recommend ways in which personnel matters should be dealt with there, and if *L* is free to accept or reject the advice as he pleases, *P* has no formal authority over *L*, although he may have an informal authority which we shall consider shortly. But is it probable that a board will sanction, or a chief executive propose, the creation of a specialist department and the appointment of a high-ranking specialist staff manager if his services to the company are to be used or not used as other departmental managers see fit? The answer is almost certainly no, for if the specialist's services are potentially important enough to justify the expense of staff employment the company cannot afford to let them be wasted. It is therefore reasonable to suppose that *L* (and other department heads who do not enter the story here) will be asked to conform to *P*'s directions in certain respects. How can this be unless *P* has some authority over *L*, and how does he exercise this authority as a member of a different department on the same managerial level?

The questions may be answered in this way. In his staff relationship with *C* the specialist can recommend the adoption of a policy or procedure that affects the work of *L*'s department, and of others within the firm. If *C* accepts the recommendation and gives it his formal approval he may decide that *L* should accept *P*'s ruling in matters relating to its implementation. If *P* can now be said to instruct *L*, and if *L* accepts his instruction, it is because both clearly appreciate that although the instruction comes from *P* it has the force of a command from *C*, and on this understanding *L* translates the instruction into action in his own department. This procedure leaves *L*'s authority unimpaired, in that he alone commands his own subordinates, but it is, of course, subject to restraint by this instruction from an equal in the name of a common superior. (The word instruction probably conveys too strong a meaning and would be inappropriate in many cases, but it is used here deliberately to stress the formal nature of the relationships in question.) If other specialists are authorized to instruct *L* in a similar way his scope for independent decision making is still further reduced, but he remains the undisputed head of his own department, and orders in it are given only by him or on his behalf.

To return to *P*; if he has to deal with other managers besides *L* he may be required to report to *C* any failure to carry out the chief's personnel policy, or instructions about personnel management practices in the firm. *C* may make *P* responsible for the coordination of these practices and for supervising the way in which personnel policy is carried out, asking only to be told of any failure in coordination or departure from policy that *P* cannot correct himself. It is arguable that *P* is then in the invidious position of bearing tales about his colleagues to their chief, but it is not necessary for this to happen and it should not happen often. So long as departmental heads know that a staff specialist acts in the chief executive's name, and what the chief's expectations are, they will accept an instruction from the specialist as an instruction from the chief. There need be no conflict at the departmental level and no uncertainty about the ultimate source of the specialist's instructions. A departmental head who disagrees with an instruction can contest it with the chief executive, but if the latter confirms it the manager must accept his ruling.

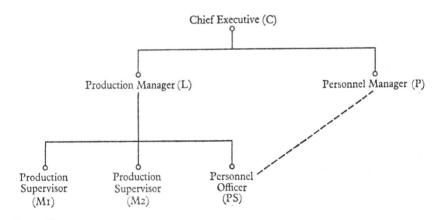

Figure 28

It would be unsatisfactory for departmental heads to disagree constantly and obstruct each other's work, and a chief executive would look with disfavour on subordinates who continually asked him to adjudicate on interdepartmental disputes. But there is no good reason why such a state should exist if everyone in the relevant managerial group helps to formulate common policy and understands why his personal authority is modified in certain ways for the good of the firm. The formal relations between line managers and staff specialists are defined when the organization is created and redefined as necessary when the organization is changed. If the prescribed content of the work of people like *L* and *P* in our example is clearly settled by a common superior, and each subordinate knows how his own authority affects, and is affected by, the authority of others, a major organizational cause of conflict should be removed.

Next we consider a case in which a staff specialist is seconded or attached to a line department in the firm. In Figure 28 the staff man *PS* is a personnel officer in the production department, and we need to ask what is the formal nature of his relations with L, with P, and with people on the same level as himself, like the production supervisors $M1$ and $M2$?

While working in this position PS is a direct subordinate of L, just as $M1$ and $M2$ are, but his responsibility for assisting L to deal with personnel matters in his department puts PS in a staff relationship to L analogous to that between P and C. L can command PS and reject his recommendations and advice if he chooses. However, we have assumed that the company has a personnel policy influenced by P and endorsed by C, and L must ensure that the policy as it affects his department is properly carried out. PS is there to help him do this, and we can expect that L will look to PS for advice about this aspect of the department's work and give it due weight. As the implementation of personnel policy affects the work of $M1$ and $M2$ they may be asked to accept instructions in L's name directly from PS, on the same conditions, and with the same safeguards for their own authority, as obtained in the case of C, P and L already discussed.

The relationship between P and PS must also be defined with care. Although they are both staff specialists in the same field, P is not his direct superior while PS is in the production department, but there must obviously be contact between them, because PS may encounter technical difficulties and special problems that can only be overcome successfully with P's help. Direct contact between P and PS should be quite acceptable to L so long as he knows of the major matters that are decided or discussed, and accepts their consequences for the work of his department. The broken line between P and PS shows that there is a formal channel of communication between them: it is not a line of authority but a link between two specialists, established on the understanding that what PS does in L's department is done with the latter's approval and in his name.

To summarize the argument so far, we can say that if the main problem of line and staff organization is to derive the greatest benefit from staff use without confusing the chains of command and weakening the authority of managers over their own subordinates, the procedures discussed here should provide the basis for a system of effective relationships which enables the line manager and the staff specialist to work in harmony, each aware of the things for which he is accountable and armed with the requisite authority to fulfil his responsibilities in a satisfactory way. This in essence is the classical view.

We must now examine the pattern of relationships when a staff specialist is not, as before, attached or seconded to a line department, but occupies a position in a staff department from which he can move about the company to wherever his services are required. We envisage again a production department and a personnel department with superior managers L and P and subordinates M and PS respectively, and start with the situation shown in Figure 29.

There is direct contact between L and P as common subordinates of the chief executive, but how and on what terms can M contact PS? Strictly bureaucratic methods of communication might require *M* and *PS* to deal with each other by following the scalar chains, so that all written communications between them had to pass by way of their departmental heads: oral communication would obviously necessitate a horizontal link to create the pattern shown in Figure 30.

If *M* and *PS* had to involve *L* and *P* every time they wished to make contact their superiors could easily be burdened with superfluous communications and valuable time would be wasted. Bureaucratic methods of communication are sometimes necessary where it is essential for superiors to be fully informed of subordinates'

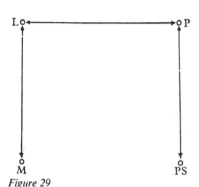

Figure 29

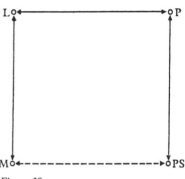

Figure 30

activities, and they may be economically acceptable where time is not a vital factor. But in complex changing conditions a more flexible system is desirable if efficient, uninterrupted operations are to be maintained.

Several writers have said that insistence on the inviolability of the vertical channels of communication is incompatible with the demands of modern technology. The emphasis must often be on diagonal and horizontal communication to find rapid solutions to the unpredictable problems that continually arise. For example, there was the case of a foreman on a vehicle assembly line whose main task was to get prompt help for operatives from people outside his own section, especially from specialists on or near to his own level with whom he could deal directly. Another study of a foreman, in a textile mill in which mechanization was taking place, showed that he had to by-pass managers at higher levels if he wanted to get quick decisions from specialists about his problems, and the successful operation of his subgroup seemed to depend more on the lack of line managers' intervention than on its effectiveness.

This suggests that opportunity for rapid direct contact with each other should be given to people like *M* and *PS*, and it is easy to see that it could have considerable economic and social advantages. There are dangers, however, in allowing diagonal

199

and horizontal channels to be opened up at will. Confusion, conflict of authority, duplicated communication and distortion of information flows are some of the possible consequences, which should not be tolerated if it is possible to avoid them. Thus, while *M* and *PS* might be authorized to make direct formal contact with each other it should be for purposes that are known to, and approved by, their superiors, at least in general terms, and subject to prescribed limits. It might be undesirable for various reasons for *M* and *PS* to have complete discretion to deal directly with each other. For example, *PS* might sometimes be faced with simultaneous demands for his services from managers at *M*'s level, and if *PS* himself decided the order in which these demands were met he would exercise an effective authority over people of equivalent rank in other departments and might be forced to make decisions with an important bearing on the balance of operations in the firm.

The difference between classical and modern views of these matters is not so great as it once appeared to be. Modern critics of rigidly hierarchical systems dislike excessive emphasis on vertical contacts and declare the virtues of multidirectional communication networks, but they agree that complete freedom of contact is neither feasible nor desirable: Urwick, personifying the classical school, has for some time favoured more horizontal contacts to increase the speed at which problems are solved, as we saw in Chapter 8. The attitude to formal relations between line managers and staff specialists needs to be empirical and the relations themselves adaptable to different situations. The appropriate pattern depends upon various factors, such as the type of work done by the line departments and the specialized assistance they require, the firm's technology, the range of specialist services available, the frequency with which particular services are demanded, the relative importance of the claims made on staff resources at different times, and the extent to which staff specialists are attached or seconded on the one hand, or operate from a common departmental base on the other. These are all relevant to the efficiency of the system adopted, and change in a developing concern.

The formal definition of line-staff relationships should ensure the line manager's requisite authority and make clear the ways in which it is modified by the employment of specialist staff. His authority is changed involuntarily when he has to use staff services, follow staff directions and take account of staff advice. It is also modified voluntarily when he asks for advice or assistance, and allows specialists to influence his decisions and the way in which work for which he is responsible is performed.

In some cases a staff specialist may exercise an authority of knowledge and experience that gives his recommendations such weight that they are tantamount to instructions. If a line manager's work suffers from what is demonstrably wrong advice, or inadequate assistance from staff colleagues that he is obliged to accept, the blame should fall on the staff; although a line manager who gets what he believes to be bad advice or poor assistance can appeal to the common superior and ask him to rule on the obligation to accept it. If a line manager voluntarily takes advice or requests assistance, and undesirable results ensue, the responsibility is his.

Classical writers have tried to define organizational rules that eliminate the danger of conflict between line managers and staff, their main purpose being to subordinate specialist activities to line needs and preserve line authority as the fundamental authority in the firm. The virtue of these rules is that they reduce ambiguity and uncertainty, and emphasize the relative importance of the different kinds of work to be done, but their rigid and uncritical application may neglect important personality and motivational factors, and create frictions that reduce the efficiency of the firm. They may also fail to reflect the reality of the situation in an increasing number of companies, where staff specialists hold the key to the understanding of environmental change, and control much of the information on which the really crucial decisions are based. As McGregor has observed, the modern business is to an ever-growing extent being run by the staff.

Research has shown, however, that there is still a marked lack of uniformity in the status, power and authority of corresponding line and staff departments in different concerns. In some cases the specialist staff do indeed have considerable formal and informal power, but in others they are little more than ciphers whose advice is seldom taken. Staff power is not necessarily related directly to position in the firm. A quite junior staff employee, like an accounting clerk, can sometimes exercise a form of authority over seniors; for example, by using his discretion to disallow an expense claim if company practice entitles him to do so. It is, of course, true that in the last analysis all staff authority is derived from someone in a line position, but this does not prevent many staff people from acquiring influence and authority over line managers whose consequences are sometimes profound.

The classical view of line-staff relationships rests on assumptions which have been criticized for being often invalid in practice. It assumes that specialist staff have no direct authority over line people, and that the latter will welcome the staff's suggestions and follow them whenever they can: any differences between line and staff employees are expected to be brought into the open and settled, either by the people concerned or at an appropriate higher level, in ways favourable to the interests of the company. If these assumptions are incorrect the logic of classical organization is faulty and the full beneficial effects of applying the formal rules will not be felt. A compromise view of the matter suggests that it is both necessary and desirable to define formal relationships, but to do so on the understanding that while the creation of a formal structure removes some obstacles to cooperation between line members and specialist staff it may raise others. Formal relationships are inevitably modified in a variety of ways, some important and some not. They can be informed and strengthened by understanding, confidence and mutual esteem, or weakened by suspicion, rivalry, misunderstanding and lack of respect. One must always look behind the formal facade to discover which condition exists.

10.4 Factors influencing line-staff relations

From a line manager's point of view the employment of specialist staff over whom he has no authority may constitute a potential threat to his status, and he may think that his competence is questioned and his position jeopardized by their work, the more so if the range of staff services is increased rapidly and the previously accepted pattern of organizational behaviour is extensively changed. Specialist staff who are keen to justify themselves often have a vested interest in change, whereas a line manager, while not conservative by definition, is often concerned to maintain a stable socio-technical system and, at least in the short run, to be suspicious of new methods that interfere with the established operations of his department. If he is hostile to the staff's ideas and seeks protection in formalism, the effect is to increase the degree of bureaucracy and the rigidity of the system that staff people are trying to change. This in turn tends to alienate them, because they have more difficulties to overcome in the performance of their work. Where the line manager is not expected to accept instructions from the specialist staff, or to seek their advice, he may simply refuse to use the staff services at all, although to do so would be to his advantage. He may adopt an uncooperative attitude in other ways, too, such as by making it difficult for staff people to get information which they need from his department.

Relations between junior line managers and specialist staff are liable to be strained if the latter are used to detect misinformation and report irregularities in operations to senior managers in the line departments. It is a well-known fact that line managers sometimes ignore company rules, soften their reports to superiors, and play down any deviations from plan with which they are having to deal. But senior managers who want accurate information on which to base decisions can cause trouble by using specialist staff to act as investigators and discover the information for them. And if an irregularity in line behaviour takes the form of altering or misapplying a control that a specialist himself devised he may feel quite unsympathetic to the fact that the line manager is under pressure from his subordinates or a shop steward to impose the control less rigorously than regulations require, or that he might do so without detriment to the efficiency of his group.

The specialist sometimes thinks and talks in a different language from that used by the line manager, and if his specialism is highly esoteric he may create prejudice by the incomprehensibility of his jargon and the complexity of his techniques. The line manager and the specialist need time to become accustomed to each other and develop a mutual appreciation of attitudes and ideals. When a new specialist service is introduced it sometimes takes several years before the people providing it are properly integrated into the organizational system and producing valuable results for the firm. Line and staff members must learn how to work together, the line managers discovering the most effective ways of using staff services and staff specialists helping to reveal the situations in which their skills can most usefully be applied. This calls for patience and goodwill on both sides, and a line manager who has both line and specialist staff subordinates can play an important part in persuading his line colleagues of the value of the contribution that specialists can make.

The specialist may have personal difficulties to overcome before he can make his best contribution to the company. He should try to avoid a narrow outlook on matters relating to his own specialism and remember that he deals with only one aspect of company operations. A line manager must often weigh several kinds of specialist advice and draw on a variety of specialized sources of information when making decisions, and it is his responsibility to assess their relative importance. The specialist should concentrate on giving practical advice that the line manager can understand and act on, and this may mean the deliberate rejection by the specialist of what is theoretically 'best'. Specialists trained in analytical disciplines, and used to thinking in precise or abstract terms, sometimes feel impatient if their theories do not apply neatly to the problems that business operations produce, and fail to accept the need for what to them are imperfect solutions and compromises. They may believe in the final authority of knowledge, and assume that everyone is equally rational and ready to accept new techniques and controls of demonstrable economic value, and when people act 'irrationally' and resist new ideas the specialists may condemn them as narrow-minded and obscurantist in their views.

A strongly placed specialist can possibly push a scheme through despite opposition, whereas if his influence is relatively weak he has to exercise much tact and patience to get his ideas accepted. But even a powerful staff manager's innovation has a better chance of success if it is adopted voluntarily instead of being imposed, and radical suggestions for changing the pattern of work are likely to be tolerated only if the staff specialist has been in the company long enough to win the line managers' confidence and respect.

Differences in age, education, social background, salary and rate of promotion cause friction between line managers and specialist staff which is intensified by organizational factors and by differences of status. Miss Woodward has told how the high status of line managers in a process-industry plant excited the jealousy of staff people, and how the creation of new departments added to antagonism between the two groups. In one case the members of the maintenance department acted as if maintenance was an end in itself, instead of a necessary service to the production department, and the staff manager devised a maintenance programme according to his own ideas of what should be done, which took no account of production needs. Crozier has also described the influence of maintenance teams in a bureaucratically-administered French tobacco factory.[1] The main operating problems there arose from the uncertain incidence of machine breakdowns, and the maintenance staff enjoyed considerable informal power on this account which strained their relations with production managers who were dependent on their help. Examples like these explain why line managers are anxious to control essential departmental

[1] M. Crozier, *The Bureaucratic Phenomenon*, Tavistock Publications, 1964.

services themselves, so that they can be used according to the line manager's own judgment of departmental needs. The greater the independence of specialist staff the more significant are their opportunities for affecting the line manager's work in ways that he cannot entirely direct.

Figure 17 showed a system containing both differentiated and undifferentiated operating subsystems, and control and service functions of different orders of importance. Rice suggests that conflict is likely to be caused when a manager in charge of an operating subsystem also has charge of a control or service function of the same order of differentiation. He gives an example of a firm where one manager commands both the financial and purchasing staff, and shows how in this situation circular recrimination can occur. Criticisms of quality from the sales department cause the production people to blame deficient bought-out materials: their deficiencies are attributed by the purchasing staff to an inadequate budget: and the financial staff respond by accusing the sales department of tolerating excessive overheads, and production of its lax control of operating costs. Where a system contains, as many do, either partially or wholly undifferentiated control or service functions the danger of conflict is often increased, because people performing these functions may either have a higher status than other managers accept as justified, or be relegated to an inferior position in the firm that injures their self-esteem. The systems theorist's ideal is for each operating subsystem to contain all the activities needed for efficient performance and no other, but in practice this is often impossible for reasons of scarcity of real resources, or expense.

Dalton gives an example of conflict between line and staff employees in an American chemical plant which was caused by differences in education and status. The chemically qualified staff worked in a laboratory away from the production plant, and were responsible for analysing samples taken by production workers and sent to the laboratory through pneumatic tubes. The tests called for no great analytical skill and the chemists' work was more manual than mental, but they had a strong feeling of professional superiority which affected their attitude to the samplers in a way that was hotly resented. Relations worsened when the samplers received an increase in pay which gave them a higher income than the chemists', and especially when they found a way of harrying the analysts which was most effective. On night shifts the chemists worked without a supervisor to protect them and the samplers started to send large numbers of specimens to be tested, while their own foreman made urgent demands for more materials to be checked. There were not enough samplers to do the work and chemists themselves were obliged to go into the plant and do the job they despised. The pressures to which the chemists were deliberately subjected resulted in wrong analyses, and the outcome of this conflict, which sounds petty enough in this baldly related form, was that impure goods were dispatched and had to be returned at high cost to the firm.[1]

[1] M. Dalton, *Men who Manage*, Wiley, 1959.

A line manager without an extended education, and with no formal training, may have acquired work habits and an attitude to his job that make him suspicious of the methods and behaviour of staff people. In a number of companies the specialist staff are said to be laxer than their line colleagues, to form a social *élite* and enjoy an enviable freedom from restrictions. These allegations are not necessarily just, but if they are believed they may colour a line manager's opinion in a way that was plainly shown by the comment of a chief executive after visiting an industrial research laboratory.

The place was like a civil service set-up with chaps just sitting about, chatting. Nobody seemed to have any responsibility–any feeling that he had a definite job to get on with and finish. . . . I have seen some of these long-haired types. They amble about in white coats, come and go when they think fit.[1]

Although it is clearly desirable that there should be harmonious relations between line and staff this does not mean that the aim should be to eliminate all friction and create a state of perfect peace. In a group of mentally vigorous people there will be differences of opinion and scope for constructive conflict that should result in the acceptance of new ideas and methods. The staff specialist who is not tied to routine can often provide the stimulus that prevents the managerial group from settling into a complacent and uncompetitive frame of mind. But because many of the specialist's ideas can only have practical effect with the line managers' support, it is essential for them to understand and respect each other's work.

There are reasons on both sides why line and staff interests and values conflict, but in different proportions and different ways organizational and personal factors combine to intensify conflict in this company and reduce it in that. It has become almost a convention to discuss this problem in terms of a clear-cut distinction between line and staff groups which is itself rather unfortunate, because it tends to exaggerate the differences that actually exist. We have already remarked that the distinction between what is line and what is staff is not always completely clear, and it is certainly true that neither line managers nor staff have a monopoly of blame where conflict takes place. Line departments conflict with each other (the scope for clashes between production and sales or marketing interests is frequently discussed) and conflict between specialists also occurs. Boundary disputes arise between departments of all kinds, and territorial struggles result in the stronger ones extending their boundaries and the weaker ones yielding ground.

It has been suggested that business staff should be divided on a similar basis to staff in the armed services, where one group deals with internal problems and the other with problems caused by environmental forces. The argument is that people who are qualified to maintain internal controls and services are not necessarily

[1]T. Burns, 'Research and Development in the Firm', *Journal of the British Institute of Management*, **1**, no. 3, 1958, 158.

equally fitted to detect environmental needs that call for the abandonment of accepted values and the redesign of a system that internally oriented staff specialists are employed, partly at least, to protect. Such a division would probably reflect higher managers' needs in many firms, but it would not guarantee a reduction of conflict, either between line managers and staff or between the staff groups themselves.

As companies recruit an increasing proportion of their actual and potential managers from people with an extended education some of the more crudely marked differences between line managers and specialist staff are likely to disappear, although more slowly perhaps at the foreman's level than above. Changes in technology tend to blur the border between purely line and purely staff activities and focus attention on the fundamentally corporate, as opposed to the departmental, view of managerial work. In organic systems there is said to be less emphasis on the sanctity of departmental ground, and a willingness to undertake new responsibility spontaneously as situations change, whereas mechanistic systems allegedly encourage a preoccupation with what is 'my' responsibility and what is 'his', and persistent efforts to make sure that the two remain quite distinct. However, there is no evidence to show conclusively that either system is generally associated with noticeably good or bad line-staff relations, although the inference is sometimes drawn that the organic properties of a system are in large part a function of the good relations between the people working in it.

As many firms are organized today there is still a conscious distinction between line and staff and a tendency for people to put themselves, or be put, in one of two camps. When that happens, however, there is no reason to suppose that either group will have all the virtues or all the defects. The staff specialist, like his line colleagues, may be narrow minded or broad, eager to make an impact on the firm or content to take a passive role, aggressive in promoting departmental interests or unambitious in his claims. These qualities are related to personality rather than to formal position in the firm, and lead one to suppose that, although organizational forces sometimes emphasize people's tendencies to behavioural extremes and intensify or reduce the line-staff conflict as a result, that conflict itself is best seen as part of a more general pattern of stress in which departments compete to increase output, obtain additional resources or cut down costs; managerial groups contend with organized workers; and individuals strive to improve their own positions in the firm. In short, a system in which a variety of personal and sectional interests are at stake and clashes are bound to occur.

The efficacy of a precise and formal organizational design to solve the problem of line-staff conflict has been much questioned in recent years, but the argument that behavioural factors should have more attention than they used to receive, which is now largely accepted, should not obscure the fact that vaguely defined organization and informal arrangements are not a remedy for conflict themselves, any more than the strictly military pattern on which early classical models were based. The line-staff conflict is a manifestation of the behaviour of people who seek to achieve a combination of corporate and personal goals by the complementary performance of differentiated tasks in complex systems, where both tasks and goals are influenced by the individuals and groups involved. Organizational change helps to diminish conflict in many cases, and organizational foresight prevents some forms of conflict from appearing at all, but neither completely eliminates the possibility that conflict will continue to exist. It will almost certainly do so, and firms face the continual challenge of minimizing its organizationally harmful consequences and containing it within tolerable bounds.

11

Planning and control

11.1 Planning

Planning is an exercise in foresight which should help a company to reach better decisions about the direction to follow and the pace at which to move than would be possible if no systematic preparation for the future were made. Intuition, sentiment and custom may be adequate grounds for decisions at times, but they cannot claim a general superiority over logical methods of analysis and assessment in complex conditions where the prosperity of a business is concerned. Uncertainty affects all planning in varying degree and the more distant the future the greater the uncertainty becomes. This is not a sufficient reason for refusing to plan for anything but the shortest term, since even a tentative guide to farther progress is likely to be better than none. Moreover, planning is an activity in which practice increases skill, and in time a firm should learn to improve both the premises on which plans are made and the decisions resulting from them. Confronted by a mass of information the firm must try to abstract the pieces most relevant to the plan it wants to make, and weight them according to their relative importance and the amount of uncertainty attached to each one.

Some firms respond to the uncertainty of future events by using more or less sophisticated forecasting techniques to provide refined information on which plans can be based. To merit their use the techniques should obviously produce results which on average are superior to those obtainable without them, but it is difficult to prove conclusively that they do so, if only because the results apparently achieved by forecasting may be affected by factors that the forecast failed to take into account. However, if forecasts have a reasonably consistent record of accuracy within acceptable limits there is a strong presumption that the techniques are satisfactory, and it may be possible for comparisons to be made, between firms and within them, of the results obtained by guesswork with those achieved by scientific techniques, which should help to establish their relative worth.

Forecasts can be based entirely on a firm's internal data; on macro-economic data, like those of national income and expenditure and international trade; on data

208

relating to a sector of the economy, such as an industry group or a single trade; or on a mixture of information obtained from many sources. Complex techniques like multivariate analysis can be used, which try to take into account the simultaneous influence of many factors on a particular result; or a firm can forecast by extrapolation from a simple linear trend or repetitive cycle. Sometimes it is possible to make good use of a single indicator, like an index-number series of the volume of wholesalers' stocks or import prices, if a close correlation has been found between movements in the index and movements in a critical variable in the firm's plan. There is obviously no ground for using a complex formula if a simple one will serve as well, especially as a complex formula used without sufficient care is liable to produce a significant cumulative error from minor errors in its component parts. But for many of the complicated forecasts that have to be made in large businesses, when numerous variables are involved which have a high degree of interdependence, a simple rule-of-thumb procedure would be inadequate and advanced methods should produce far superior results.

Forecasts are prone to error for a number of reasons. The relationships between variables may be incorrectly assumed; certain factors which subsequently prove to have been important may be omitted or undervalued when the calculations are made; information obtained by sampling may be biased or incomplete; the pattern of the past may not be repeated, yet a forecast will to some extent, and perhaps largely, be affected by a knowledge of what that pattern was. The more distant the future to which the forecast relates the more tentative it must be and the greater the possibility of error becomes. The very long term forecast can often say no more than that a particular trend is expected to move in a certain way, although as the period is reduced it becomes increasingly possible to forecast not only a trend but deviations from it. Yet important decisions must frequently be made about the long-run shape of the firm which would be impossible without a rational forecast of events. One of the electronics firms investigated by Burns and Stalker considered the possibility of entering the market for civil aircraft and examined aviation trends from the 1920s to the mid 1940s, when the study was made. It found that the number of passenger miles flown in British fleets had increased by more than 20 per cent each year and that there was a clear tendency to use relatively fewer and faster planes of increased capacity. This information helped the firm decide what type of aircraft it should build, and although the prospects of market penetration were far from certain it was clear that if the firm was to be in the new industry by 1960 the time to start preparations was in 1946.

Forecasting cannot eliminate uncertainty and should not be used to give an illusion of certainty where it does not exist, but it helps a company to cope better with the problems that uncertainty creates. The liability to error inherent in varying degree in the results obtained by forecasting suggests the unwisdom of allowing it to dominate the decision-making process, but does not justify its rejection. There is, rather, an incentive to improve the information on which forecasts are based and search for still better techniques. A firm cannot simply lurch from one short period to another without a plan and remain a competitive unit. It must always try to look beyond the end of the current order book and make provision for the longer term: the light that forecasting sheds on the future as it does so may be very dim at times, but as C. F. Carter has remarked, even a glimmer of moonlight here is preferable to total darkness.

Planning is necessary even when there appears to be no choice of course for a business to take, but more often it involves a consideration of alternative courses and alternative ways of pursuing them, from which choices can be made. The alternatives may present themselves fortuitously or they may be sought deliberately in the planning process, which is thus made to serve as an instrument of change. Innovation incurs real costs, however, and if they are high the impetus to change may be checked. It has been said that the effort devoted to searching for new courses will be inversely correlated with satisfaction with things as they are. The argument, presumably, is that satisfaction leads to complacency and dissatisfaction spurs firms to look for new ways, but while this may apply to some firms, it is not true of all. A satisfied company will still search if it has a vigorous managerial group and is continually alert to the possibility of new opportunities or adverse events: a dissatisfied company may be so absorbed in solving existing problems that it cannot spare the resources of time and mental energy to examine new prospects or think far ahead.

March and Simon have suggested a variant of Gresham's law of currency to the effect that planning is driven out by daily routine. In their language, managers who are tied down by the daily demands on their energy give programmed work priority over unprogrammed work like planning, which requires them to divert attention from the actual to the potential state of affairs; and in the majority of firms, without full-time planning staffs, this must always be a source of difficulty. It probably explains why plans are often made irregularly and not always at the most important times. But one of the serious dangers of preoccupation with the short run is that current activities will not be properly related to future needs. Planning for the long term forces a firm to question the implications of decisions made now and ask what needs to be done in the present to prepare for expected developments. For instance, a firm that plans to diversify must satisfy itself that it has, or can obtain, the resources necessary to support the additional financial, research and marketing burdens it will have to bear, and ask whether any modification is called for to its technological base. In making its plans the firm examines current activities and facilities more critically, and this helps to uncover problems which might otherwise be overlooked.

Ideally, a firm's plans should form a continuum covering as long a term as it is useful to foresee, with plans for different periods related to each other and suitably adjusted in the light of experience as the firm moves through time. Together, the plans should provide an integrated picture of the future development of the business, and within any period a major plan that is broken down into a number of subsidiary plans should be so devised that its parts are congruent and form a properly articulated whole. The construction of feasible and compatible plans and controls is fundamental to the coordination of activities.

Plans embody objectives of a general or specific kind, largely depending on the distance in time at which the objective should be reached, but all objectives eventually call for the definition of detailed means for their achievement. Specific, though, is perhaps a misleading word to use, for it is not always possible to define an objective with complete precision when it is clearly not in the general category. From a business standpoint an objective could be regarded as specific if there were reasonably narrow limits within which it could be attained. The general objective of operating at a profit could thus be refined into the specific objective of making a year's profit of X thousand pounds, plus or minus Y per cent. A truly specific objective is likely to be more difficult to reach than one which allows for some variation and enables an element of flexibility to be incorporated in the plan.

If the people who carry out a plan are given some room to manoeuvre they will probably find it more acceptable than being confined by a very rigid scheme. Similarly, a plan which seeks to achieve a satisfactory, as opposed to a maximum, level of performance is often likely to be more acceptable to those it affects. It is also generally desirable to establish objective criteria for measuring the success with which plans are executed, and to reduce as far as possible the element of subjectivity in judging results.

There is some disagreement about the desirability of changing plans once they have been put into action, although the weight of opinion seems to favour adhering to a plan for as long as possible, rather than altering it. But whether one can accept Schell's extreme view that it is better to persist with a poor plan than to shift a good one when it is in operation is doubtful.[1] It is more reasonable to argue that when difficulties are encountered the best policy is usually to hold to the course laid down and try to overcome them by the most effective available means, leaving adroit changes of course to the last if the difficulties are too great for progress to be made along the intended lines. Anthony maintains that while a plan should be followed unless there is convincing evidence of the need for alteration, it should not impose a strait-jacket on company operations.[2] There ought to be opportunities for rebuttal, and people should be able to suggest amendments which promise higher efficiency. It is easy to see that scope for flexibility of this kind might improve managerial morale, but individuals cannot be so free to change plans that unity of effort is destroyed. Striking the right balance calls for considerable managerial art, and managerial science cannot always offer a great deal of help in this respect.

[1] E. H. Schell, *Technique of Executive Control*, 8th edn., McGraw-Hill, 1957, p. 41.
[2] R. N. Anthony, *Planning and Control Systems*, Harvard University Graduate School of Business Administration, 1965.

11.2 Control

Control is assumed here to be formally and internally exercised over a firm's activities, and we exclude an important category of external controls imposed by governments, local authorities, trade unions and so forth, and another category of controls associated with informal organizations whose significance is discussed in Chapter 13. In other words, we confine ourselves to examining some of the features of formal control systems designed for use within companies and operated to help them achieve their ends.

A firm's current operations are frequently controlled by comparing actual levels of performance with standards that have previously been defined as necessary or desirable to reach, or which are dictated by the nature of the work being done. The control may be an automatic and mechanical one, such as a thermostat to maintain a steady temperature or a governor to regulate the speed of a machine, or it may be a humanly operated one, such as a check on production rates, the volume of materials in stock, or the level of cash reserves. Controls of this kind are used to ensure that immediate or short-term objectives are reached as the firm moves along its chosen course towards more distant major objectives. The proposed course can be marked with signs to show what progress should be made, and as each stage is reached a comparison of achievement with forecast result shows how closely the planned path is being followed. At the end of the course a further comparison, of the actual final result with the desired result, provides a measure of the success with which the preceding operations have in total been performed.

The effectiveness of a control is a function of the rapidity with which relevant and accurate information about an operation is produced and relayed to the control point, and of the speed and degree of completeness of the correction that can be made when a divergence between actual and desired levels of performance is revealed. Ideally, a control device should enable deviations from a desired standard to be prevented or kept within very narrow limits, but this is not always possible. Some activities are much less amenable to accurate control than others, and controls themselves vary greatly in sensitivity and directness of application. Production work, for example, lends itself more readily to close control than the work of a design and development department, and the quality of steel in an electric furnace can be controlled with far greater precision than the quality of a firm's managers throughout an extended programme of managerial development.

From a long-run point of view the ultimate purpose of control can be seen as survival, the achievement of a certain rate of growth or, most commonly, the attainment of a succession of satisfactory levels or rates of profit. In the pursuit of these aims the emphasis varies from firm to firm on different aspects of their work. Control in a manufacturing company may relate mainly to weekly output or the volume of unfulfilled orders; in a retail firm interest may centre on the rate of stock turn or income per square foot of shelf space; while in a capital-intensive process plant the managers may be most concerned to avoid the high costs incurred by shutting the plant down, and concentrate their control efforts on maintaining continuous operation. Because there is a great variety of things to control a variety of controls is called for, so that the most appropriate one can be selected for the job to be done, and satisfactory control rests on an understanding of the situation in which it is applied. Problems arise when controls are introduced without an adequate appreciation of the real state of affairs, and also when controls are allowed to proliferate unnecessarily. Irrelevant controls are likely to provoke resistance or to be ignored, and keeping them relevant and up-to-date in changing situations is a basic and continuous organizational responsibility. Each control should serve the purpose for which it is used as effectively and economically as possible, and when different controls are used simultaneously they should preferably complement each other and not make conflicting demands on the people who operate, or are affected by, them.

The nature of the control system has important implications for the distribution of power within a company. Formal organization theory has assumed that power to control is directly correlated with rank, and that as one moves up the hierarchy there is an increase in the amount of control exercised at each level. To a large extent this is true, but as a generalization it calls for qualification in a number of ways. The nature of control at a high level is so different from that at a low level that comparisons between them are not particularly revealing. In the former case effective control depends mainly on the selection of suitable subordinates to do the work of controlling lower down. The chief executive himself controls for the most part in an indirect way and relies on his knowledge of the people below him, and the information they provide, to decide whether the business is proceeding satisfactorily or not.

In so far as controls, and the information derived from their use, can be said to form a hierarchy the exception principle is expected to apply, and managers at higher levels need only be told when activities at a lower level are not producing the results called for in the plan. The stress here is on the selective upward transmission of information for control purposes, but it would be misleading to suggest that a control system can operate properly on the basis of this upward flow alone. The larger and more complex a business grows the more desirable does it become for control information to pass down the chains of command and sideways between departments if an adequate coordination of activities is to be achieved.

Control at lower levels is less general and more direct, and in particular instances it is often more important from an individual point of view than control exercised at the top. The board of directors in many companies can be said to control the long-run development of the enterprise, and hence to affect the number and variety of the employment opportunities it offers. An individual workman's position is therefore influenced in a very important way by the success of the board's control, yet for most of the time he would be much more concerned about the impact of the control exercised by his section foreman. The effectiveness of control at any level is dependent to some extent on the effectiveness of control at the levels below. The managing director does indeed have more control over the firm than a foreman or a departmental head, but the managing director's own ability to control is critically affected by the way in which those under him use their individual powers to control activities in their respective spheres of operation.

People's perception of the power to control others is closely associated with the formal distribution of authority among them and the way it is used. In an autocratically managed firm the chief executive's power appears to be very great, while that of employees in the lower ranks is relatively weak. In a more democratic company, on the other hand, the greater power given to people at lower levels increases their control, and the chief executive's is, rather, different in kind. If controls can be introduced and operated on a reasonably democratic basis they are less likely to produce unwanted side effects that impair their efficiency, because they will be more generally acceptable to the people they affect. Controls imposed autocratically tend to arouse hostility and create resistance, sometimes to the extent that effort is devoted to evading or attacking the controls at the expense of the work to be done. Some modern control techniques which call for sophisticated equipment or scarce abilities have to be operated centrally for reasons of efficiency, but where this is the case the control may appear remote and impersonal to people in lower positions, and have adverse effects on their morale if it fails to take adequate account of peculiar factors in individual situations, or makes demands on people that they are unwilling to meet. If it is possible to operate a control system on decentralized lines it is usually preferable on human grounds to one that is highly centralized.

The human consequences of control react on the operation of a control system and the efficiency of a firm in various ways, and stem from different causes. An uncritical reliance on the working of the exception principle, for example, brings two possible dangers in its train. By emphasizing things that are wrong it may fail to ensure that proper credit is given when all is apparently going well, but when satisfactory results have only been achieved by surmounting some uncommon difficulties. It also assumes a rational acceptance by people throughout the firm of objectives, methods and values that are often imposed on them without consultation, and one must recognize that some of the people at least may have different objectives and values, and prefer different methods, which will inevitably colour their view of control and the way it is exercised.

The ability to reach a given standard may be influenced by factors outside the control of the person responsible for the work which are not sufficiently allowed for. If the standard is felt to be too rigid and demanding, and sets a level whose potential attainment is not open to objective proof, the failure to reach it may cause frustration and the standard will be blamed for being unreasonably high. As an example, a departmental manager could be given a standard cost per unit to achieve which included an element of allocated overhead cost, and if he failed to meet the standard he might legitimately claim that the imputed cost element was too large. A situation is then created in which he could argue with other departmental managers or the financial control staff about the justification for the existing allocation of overhead costs, with ample scope for ill-feeing, and the expenditure of energy that might be more profitably devoted to other things.

A further danger is that when difficult standards are accepted, and with difficulty attained, they may be raised still more, and successful performance of the task could lead to more stringent requirements being made that took inadequate account of the strain suffered by employees in achieving the original result. Again, it may seem inadequate or arbitrary to try to measure performance in terms of ability to reach a single objective, so to increase the fairness with which his performance is judged a person may be assessed on his ability to reach several objectives and not just one. A problem arises here from the need to secure a balanced stress, for unless the objectives are equally important some kind of explicit or implicit weighting process must be used, and if the achievement of each goal is not measurable with equal accuracy and objectivity, personal judgments are called for when conclusions about the individual's capabilities are reached. Our departmental manager, for instance, might be judged not only by his ability to observe standard costs, but by the output of his section, the amount of waste material, the number of idle-machine-hours, the progress of his subordinates, or the frequency of the customers' complaints about the goods which his department produced. The blending of these related but distinctive elements into a composite objective would be difficult, and if it were not done carefully could lead once more to argument and discontent.

Planning requirements tend to be less emotive than those of control so far as information is concerned. When people know that information is being asked for to judge their work they may be tempted to say what they think would be favourable, rather than state facts as they are. Control procedures assume that correct information is provided and when this is not so the control is in danger of breaking down. An example of this was discovered by Dalton.[1] He studied a firm in one of whose plants the solution being made was supposed to have specific characteristics of strength, temperature and rate of flow through the vats. Controls had been set up to ensure that correct operating conditions were maintained, and members of the chemical staff were required to check the plant twice daily and report any deviations from the prescribed state. Yet the actual strength of the solution was three times what it should have been, the temperature was 10°C. above the standard level and the flow was twice the specified rate. The explanation of these radical variances

---

[1] M. Dalton, 'Conflicts between Staff and Line Managerial Officers', *American Sociological Review*, **15**, no. 3, 1950, 342–51.

was that production employees were forced to tamper with the plant in order to get the output required, while the chemical staff were sympathetic to the production foreman's problems and regularly reported that standards were observed. In return for this unofficial cooperation the production group concealed mistakes for which the staff people were responsible, and instead of reporting a fault to the chief chemist, as formal regulations required, the foreman gave his staff colleagues the chance to rectify it and ignored his obligation to make a report.

These are merely some instances of the potentially dysfunctional effects of control systems and the reader will notice that other examples have been given elsewhere in the book. They emphasize the fact that control is ultimately control over people, and that an effective control system must take into account not only the work to be done and the equipment needed to do it, but also the personalities, capabilities and attitudes of the employees themselves. There are reciprocal relationships between the kinds of control used, the way they are operated, the behaviour of the people who implement them and the behaviour of the people they affect. In any analysis of a company a knowledge of its formal control system tells us a great deal about the distribution of power and the nature of the power which one person has over another. It does not tell us everything, of course, because it excludes the pervasive and influential network of informal controls that is built up in every firm, but it still provides us with an important key to the understanding of organizational performance.

So far we have looked at some of the more obvious features of planning and control, considered as separate, but not independent, activities, and we go on to examine them from a different point of view and try to relate different categories of planning and control to each other. There are various ways of classifying planning and control activities which are not equally helpful. The length of time involved, the type of business department concerned, and the level at which planning and control take place all provide possible bases for classification. The choice of any one of them, however, would mean that many general characteristics would tend to be obscured. It is arguable that there is no classification which adequately combines comprehensiveness with simplicity, but one of the most satisfactory ways of analysing planning and control in more detail than we have attempted so far has been suggested by Anthony and, with some modifications, we shall use his categories of strategic, managerial and operational planning and control as the framework for the next part of our discussion.

11.3 Strategic planning and control

Strategic planning and control (which for convenience we shall refer to in a composite sense as SPC) is concerned with long-range objectives and the resources needed to reach them. It relates to a future which is sometimes very distant, and embraces all major aspects of company development – the long-run growth of production and sales, new marketing methods, diversification and the acquisition of subsidiary concerns, major capital investments, the supply of finance, technological innovation, personnel requirements and changes in organizational structure. SPC affects the entire physical, financial, organizational and human character of a firm's growth, and decisions reached as a result of work done in this field frequently create precedents and lead to a redefinition of company policy, within whose boundaries managerial and operational planning and control will then be performed.

Although SPC has long-term implications the actual length of time involved in putting a plan into effect is not a sufficient indication of whether SPC or some other kind of planning and control is concerned. A company could acquire, or merge with, another in less time than was needed to design and introduce a new model of a product which continued an established manufacturing line, but the former action would be the result of SPC and the latter could be a function of managerial planning and control. Annual operating budgets based on the maintenance of an existing set of activities could be projected, say, for a five-year period, but this again would be a matter for managerial planning and control, rather than for SPC.

SPC can concentrate on one aspect of a company's operations, or on one part of an enterprise composed of a number of quasi-autonomous firms. A plan to enter new markets with current products could be an example of limited strategic planning calling for decisions of fundamental importance. When the Volkswagen company decided to enter the North American market it did so knowing that its production policy was the antithesis, in one major respect, of the policy of the large American manufacturers with which it intended to compete. Volkswagen offered a vehicle whose appearance and basic design were not expected to change for many years, whereas General Motors, Chrysler and Ford competed by changing their model styles each year and this custom apparently enjoyed the approval of the American public. There was obviously a marketing problem to study here and an important strategic decision to be reached. The German firm based its plans on the conclusion that there were many potential customers for whom the guarantee of reliability and of swift and economical service would provide a sufficient inducement to buy its cars, and overcome the drawbacks of an unchanging style. It therefore concentrated on convincing the Americans that it offered a highly developed product whose buyer would be supported by a comprehensive system of service depots with adequate stocks of spare parts that would enable his requirements to be rapidly and efficiently met, and these depots, representing a large investment for the firm, were set up before the main advertising campaign was begun. However, while it may sometimes be appropriate, even essential, to devote the bulk of the strategic-planning effort to analysing and solving one problem of this kind, it is obvious that SPC must ultimately take account of the effects of change in one part of the company on the nature of operations elsewhere. Marketing strategy cannot be devised without considering

217

the consequences for production, purchasing, research, personnel and finance, and in the last analysis SPC must embrace the activities of the system as a whole. It is a comprehensive coordinating process with fundamental long-run implications, whereas other kinds of planning and control define and coordinate activities within parts of the system or during shorter periods of time.

SPC must take account of environmental factors and try to estimate the effects of such things as population trends, changes in social habits, governmental intentions and the anticipated behaviour of rival firms. It has a potentially large number of uncontrollable variables to deal with and the problems encountered may be very complex. For these reasons successful SPC often depends on the planners' ability to decide which factors are most vital from the firm's point of view and concentrate on trying to make satisfactory estimates of their effects. It is essential that the analysis of long-run problems should be as thorough as resources permit, and one of the main difficulties of SPC is that much desirable information about the environment is either not readily available, or only available in a general and unquantified form. Nevertheless, the responsibility for making long-run decisions in these conditions cannot be shirked, unless managers are prepared to put the firm's future in jeopardy, and the situation is precisely that in which business acumen is subjected to its severest test and high managerial quality most clearly revealed

Formal techniques are available to help the strategic planner, such as capital budgeting, mathematical model building, advanced forecasting procedures, and network analysis (also known as critical path analysis and programme evaluation review technique (PERT)). With the possible exception of capital budgeting these techniques tend to be either more suitable for planning in some industries than others, or restricted to the largest firms because of their costly and specialized demands on scarce resources. None of these techniques is used on any but a relatively limited scale in British industry, but if they could be assisted to understand and practise the methods of capital budgeting there is no reason why more firms, even of medium size, should not find it helpful in answering such questions as: should a new plant be built? should the existing works be expanded and modernized? where is the best place to build? and how should funds be allocated to competing projects?–all of which are important questions that companies of various kinds have to answer from time to time.

Capital budgeting calls for estimates of the profitability of alternative investment outlays. It means, in fact, that the firm must make profit forecasts for each investment and then apply some method of calculating whether an investment is worthwhile. It may estimate profits on the basis of pre-tax or post-tax book rates of return, or use a minimum expected payback period as the criterion; it can also make its calculations on the basis of discounted cash flows. Each method implies that the firm has a yardstick against which imputed profit rates can be measured and the last two also incorporate a weighted time element in the appraisal. Of the methods referred to, opinion increasingly favours the discounting of cash flows, which is helping to bring the accountant's and the economist's views of income more closely together. The yardstick may be the cost of borrowed capital, or an arbitrary figure below which a particular company feels that the commitment of investible funds would not be justified. The difficulties associated with capital budgeting are sometimes great, but if a firm is prepared to grapple with them its use of the relevant techniques of estimation has the great virtue of bringing into the open several aspects of the investment decision that are often either unrecognized or suppressed.

SPC is a high-level activity. Decisions to initiate it and decisions resulting from it are normally made by the chief executive and his colleagues on the company board, for whom SPC should be a basic responsibility. A very large firm may support a special staff group to undertake the detailed work of SPC, and in smaller, but still large concerns, one could expect staff people to be relatively more occupied in strategic planning matters than people with continuous operational responsibilities. To a great extent the work of SPC can be divorced from managerial and operational planning and control in the biggest companies, whereas it cannot so easily be separated in smaller firms. Even in the large company, of course, the short-run relationship between SPC and managerial planning and control can be a close one, although different sets of people are performing the two kinds of work. If it is decided, for example, that long-range marketing strategy calls for a present reduction in prices, or an immediate increase in advertising expenditure, this inevitably affects the current distribution of resources and the anticipated level of short-run income, both of which are in the province of managerial planning and control.

SPC is creative and analytical in character and should be the critical influence on a company's development and performance over the long term, so far as they can be consciously affected by the actions of people in the firm. Until it results in decisions to commit resources SPC is relatively neutral; it explores possibilities and examines expectations without necessarily defining objectives that have to be reached. It tends to be an irregular activity in most companies, calling for periodic bursts of concentration by senior managers and requiring them to take stock of the distant future more carefully than they are able or willing to do at other times.

The long time-span involved often makes it very difficult for the effects of SPC decisions to be accurately gauged, and it may only be possible to reach broad conclusions about the ultimate value of particular courses of action determined in the past. Planning is the dominant feature of SPC and control plays a relatively minor part, being mainly concerned with the need to keep to a planning timetable and produce the results of investigation and analysis as required. Control assumes much greater importance at a later stage when operations are being carried out within the framework which SPC has helped to create.

The fact that comparatively few people are engaged in SPC at any time means that communication problems are less serious than they are where other kinds of planning and control are concerned. The major problem of SPC is to ensure that managerial resources are devoted sufficiently systematically and often to the work. In the majority of firms the same people have to undertake both strategic and managerial planning and control, and the more obvious, measurable benefit to be enjoyed from the second, compared with the greater difficulty and less certain value of the first, reinforces the likelihood that if any aspect of planning and control is neglected it will be SPC rather than anything else.

11.4 Managerial planning and control

Managerial planning and control (MPC) is undertaken within the relatively fixed boundary of a system whose principal parameters of organizational structure, technology and production range have been determined by earlier decisions influenced by SPC. It has become the practice in many firms for MPC to refer to one year's operations, although there is no reason why a longer or a shorter term should not be chosen if desired. Taking a year, but not necessarily a calendar year, as a conventional period, the purpose of MPC is to define the principal objectives to be reached in that period, allocate the resources needed to achieve them, and operate controls to see that activities are kept in balance and satisfactory progress is maintained. Objectives are assumed to be desired objectives, so that MPC is not neutral in the way that SPC was said to be. The goals determined by MPC become standards by which managerial performance can be judged. The goals must therefore be congruent and acceptable, and give managers adequate motivation to seek their attainment. These conditions are clearly most likely to be satisfied where managerial self-interest and the interest of the company are simultaneously furthered if objectives are reached.

Once MPC has been incorporated as an integral part of a firm's activities it can be repetitively and rhythmically performed, and the work of planning and control can itself be planned and carried out on a timetable basis. In so far as MPC tries to cover all major aspects of company operations it is frequently appropriate to define both objectives and the information needed for control in common financial terms, but other units of measurement besides money are frequently used, either as alternatives to money values or additionally, to increase the clarity with which objectives are stated and results assessed.

MPC depends on the availability of much internal information, and in a well-established process there are arrangements for this information to be regularly collected, analysed and summarized, and sent to the people who require it in the performance of their work. The swift collection and dissemination of necessary data is an important part of the communications system as it affects MPC. More people are usually involved in MPC than in strategic planning and control and the former tends to raise more human problems too, so that good communication between the people involved is at once more difficult to accomplish and more important to secure.

The setting of targets in short-run plans calls for collaboration between the managers who must try to achieve them, and time must be allowed for discussion, revision and persuasion before the objectives are finally settled and the critical operating period beings. The main objectives will be those which the line managers are given to attain, and line activities are the foci of managerial planning and control. It is during the course of a short operating period, such as a year, that the problem mentioned earlier, of adhering to or modifying a plan, is likely to be raised in its most insistent form. Subject to the overriding need to keep the various activities of the firm in balance, it is reasonable to suppose that managers responsible for producing desired results should have discretion to make decisions which promise a better outcome than could be expected from a literal application of the plan. Managers need to respond to events that actually happen: the events expected when the plan was made may never in fact occur.

Planning and control are both important in MPC and contribute equally to the successful progress of the firm. Perhaps this can be better understood, and the nature of MPC more easily seen, if we look at one technique which, more than any other, has proved itself capable of encompassing the main activities of a company and meeting the principal requirements of a planning and control process in a reasonably satisfactory way. This is the technique of budgetary control.

BUDGETARY CONTROL

A budget is a statement in financial terms of what is planned or expected to happen: it is a forecast of an account and sets out the results aimed for, supported by details of the operational activities necessary for their achievement. The budget for total income and expenditure is normally the most important, but it can be supplemented by a capital budget and a cash budget, and if it is framed in the form of a master forecast it will need to be broken down into smaller, self-contained budgets for different departments, sections and subsections of the company, in whatever detail is needed for satisfactory control. The customary budget period of a year can be varied according to the firm's requirements, and five- or ten-year budgets are produced in some companies, while in others the budgets often contain forecasts for periods of less than a year.

Since in most firms the main financial items are income from the sale of goods and services, and expenditure on resources used to produce them, a sales budget and a production budget feature prominently in most systems of budgetary control. We have already discussed some of the problems of forecasting sales results, but we can add here that the difficulty of forecasting is increased when a wide range of products is made, especially if they compete with each other as well as with products of rival firms. A total sales forecast is obtained by the aggregation of separate sales estimates

221

for each product sold, and this enables the full implications of the sales plan for production, purchasing, transport, finance and personnel to be seen, and for sales quotas to be allocated to different sales teams and outlets. The sales budget clearly cannot be drawn up in isolation; it must take account of existing production facilities and commitments, of potential resources, and of possible changes in product quality or design during the operating period. Cost estimates are made in the budget as accurately as possible, although difficulties also arise here in the imputation of 'lumpy' costs to different sections of the firm. A distinction can be made between managed and non-managed costs, and improvements in budgetary control are closely concerned with decreasing the ratio of the former to the latter, since managed costs are those which are difficult to measure and call for personal judgments about the true amounts involved.

Accurate costs are important because they provide yardsticks for the measurement of performance, and failures to adhere to budgeted costs signal variances that show where correction is required. If information about the nature of a variance can be produced quickly and in adequate detail it indicates what kind of remedial action might be taken, and a simple example will show how the analysis of a variance illuminates the problem to be solved. Let us assume that the budgeted expenditure on material in Department A in a certain month was £4,000, based on the expectation that 4,000 articles would be produced, incorporating 4,000 units of material at a standard cost of £1 each. When the month's results are available their analysis produces the information contained in Table 9.

Table 9

	Department A			
	Production (units)	*Material Consumed (units)*	*Cost per unit (£)*	*Total cost (£)*
Budgeted	4,000	4,000	1·0	4,000
Actual production } Standard Cost	3,600	3,800	1·0	3,800
Actual production } Actual Cost	3,600	3,800	1·1	4,180

These facts are revealed: (1) the budget assumed that one unit of material would be used for each unit of production, but actual material consumption was greater than this: (2) the price of material has risen by 10 per cent above the standard cost: (3) production was 10 per cent below the forecast figure. The variance is £180, but simply to report this figure by itself is not sufficiently helpful. The data show that the fall in production should have reduced material expenditure by £400; that an increase of 200 units in the material consumed in producing the smaller output, compared with the budget expectation, should have increased material expenditure by £200 for that output at standard cost; and that the 10 per cent increase in the unit cost of material added £380 to the bill for material used in the actual output. The potential reduction of £400 was offset by a combined increase of £580 to give the variance of £180.

This analysis suggests four lines of enquiry to pursue. If the fall in production was due to manufacturing deficiencies these should be corrected, and if it was due to a decline in sales the cause of this should be attacked. In either case the reasons for the increase in material consumption need to be investigated and an attempt made, perhaps by seeking alternative suppliers, to reduce the cost of material to the budgeted standard cost. There is no assurance that any of these measures will yield successful results, but if the firm is unaware of the need to take them its chances of achieving the final budget objectives are inevitably reduced. Information could be produced on similar lines for labour variances, showing whether the amount of labour used was greater than allowed for in the budget, or whether labour costs had risen for any other reason, such as the employment of men at higher wage rates than anticipated. Variances in standard overhead costs might also be analysed to see if they were caused by differences between expected and actual degrees of plant utilization (capacity variances), or by changes in capital efficiency.

Variances reveal departures from plan but do not necessarily lead to certain corrective action, except where the feedback process conveys information to an automatic regulating device in a self-maintaining system. Variances show where particular effort to control costs is called for, but this kind of corrective action should be in addition to action taken under a sustained and systematic programme for long-run reductions in costs. The sum of positive and negative variances may be zero and profit satisfactorily achieved, but this itself is no reason for neglecting the signs of possible weakness that unfavourable variances reveal. One expects that these variances will occur and, although managers hope they will be comparatively small and easily remedied, they may be so great as to put in question the whole basis on which the plan was made, the extreme case being that in which the existing plan has to be abandoned and MPC started afresh. But because variances are not always unfavourable it is quite possible that opportunities for increasing net income above the budgeted level will be found, and these may also indicate the desirability of making alterations to the plan.

Budget revision raises difficult problems of timing and degree. If a firm persists in an obviously unsuitable plan there will be an air of unreality about the proceedings and morale is likely to fall, but if budget objectives are altered too freely when they look hard to achieve, much of the incentive which budgeting provides will be lost. There are several ways of dealing with this matter of budget flexibility. One, already mentioned, is to try to reduce the size of the problem by defining objectives as bands of acceptable values, and not in single-value terms. This gives room for tolerable variations to occur and, so long as it is not too wide, an objective band, so to speak, is more realistic than an objective point and a most-preferred value can still be aimed at within the band. Another possibility is to draw up alternative budgets and replace one with another as operating conditions dictate, while a small minority of firms undertake continuous budget revision and make running projections based on the most up-to-date expectations of events. In all cases a danger to avoid is that of metaphorically tampering too freely with the thermometer when it is the temperature that ought to be controlled.

There are other dangers inherent in budgetary control which should also be mentioned. One is the temptation to go into excessive detail and produce very complicated budgets, which are more liable to error and to limit subsequent freedom to act. It is too expensive to try to control in minute detail by budgetary methods and the means are liable to defeat the end. During the time taken to prepare a complex budget the premises on which the work was started might change so much that the calculations lose their value, and in striving to control everything the firm could fail adequately to control its essential tasks.

Budgetary control should not be used in situations where other controls are more suitable, nor should it necessarily be applied in the first instance to all departments of the firm. A wide coverage is certainly desirable, but some companies have found it satisfactory to start on a limited scale, concentrating initially on one or two crucial departments and then gradually extending the budget's scope as experience was gained. Care is needed not to let habit rule, for inefficiency may then be hidden: the fact that £X was allocated for a certain purpose in period A should not mean automatic acceptance of the same figure in period B. Budgeting also requires an atmosphere of mutual confidence and respect, so that managers do not feel they have to budget for excessive amounts in the hope of getting what they really want. And lastly, when departmental forecasts are accepted they should not be invested with sacred properties, otherwise the welfare of the firm might suffer if, for example, attempts to protect the production budget led to sales opportunities being lost.

Budgetary control is the most highly developed general technique currently available for managerial planning and control, but one must not exaggerate the extent of its use. It has been adopted by many of the more enterprising companies, which are precisely the concerns we should expect to be on the lookout for new ways of increasing efficiency and encouraging growth, but the limited evidence available suggests that British companies generally have lagged somewhat behind American firms in this respect. The National Industrial Conference Board found in 1958 that 89 per cent of a sample of 389 United States firms used budgetary control, whereas in a much smaller British sample, taken in a different enquiry at the same time, just over two-thirds of the companies used the technique. In both countries the adoption of budgetary control has been most rapid since 1945, although the first systematic treatise on the subject appeared as far back as 1922. Of the forty-seven firms actually visited in the course of P.E.P.'s research project (*Thrusters and Sleepers*) thirty operated a system of budgetary control, and the analysis of business attitudes showed clearly the importance attached to it by the thrusting concerns, which also used capital-budgeting methods in strategic planning and control. In the sleepy firms, which typically failed to use budgetary-control techniques, there was no attempt to make systematic forecasts; operations were only spasmodically reviewed and there was, in short, no adequate foundation for managerial planning and control of the sort that effective budgeting procedures can provide.

11.5 Operational planning and control

Operational planning and control (OPC) is concerned with the specific pieces of work which have to be done to achieve objectives set by strategic and managerial planning and control, and relates to the activities of individual employees and subgroups. The emphasis is on single tasks, or closely related sets of tasks, which can often be defined in detail, planned with exactness, and checked either during their performance or very shortly after the work has been done. OPC affects tasks whose time-span is measured less frequently in months or weeks than in days or hours. The information used for planning and controlling particular tasks is itself specific and detailed, as opposed to aggregative and general in the case of MPC. It is expressed numerically in many cases in non-financial terms, such as units of output, man-hours, weight, temperature, or volume. The work covered by OPC consists largely of standardized, repetitive tasks amenable to programming, predictable in their effects within narrow limits, and calling for a relatively small amount of personal judgment in either their planning or control. OPC is generally more objective and mechanical than other kinds of planning and control, and a good deal of the practice of OPC methods can be made the responsibility of employees at the junior manager's, foreman's, or operative's level.

Several techniques have been developed for application in the field of OPC, including production scheduling, work study, stock control, organization and method study, mathematical programming and inter-firm comparison, while a number of advanced mathematical and statistical techniques are employed which are subsumed under the heading of operational research. Some of these techniques demand a high level of academic and practical ability on the part of those who formulate and apply them, and are clearly exceptions to the generalization at the end of the last paragraph. On the other hand, however, a sophisticated technique can sometimes be used to produce a set of elementary rules, or indicate a straightforward pattern of activities, capable of being followed by people with little or no formal training in the techniques themselves.

225

It may be helpful to illustrate the nature of OPC with some examples of the techniques that are used, as these will show more clearly the kind of work involved and the difficulties encountered when OPC is performed. It would not be very illuminating to discuss complex techniques used by a small number of firms and the ones selected are both widely employed in an extensive range of industries. They are quality control and inspection.

QUALITY CONTROL

Although its solution varies greatly from one company to another the problem of quality control is something that no firm can entirely ignore. It must decide what quality standards to set and what resources to devote to seeing that they are observed. The quality of a good or service obviously cannot be allowed to deteriorate so far that sales can no longer be made, yet at the other extreme the preservation of the highest consistent quality may add significantly to unit costs. Above the level at which a good is unmarketable firms have varying amounts of discretion to decide appropriate quality standards and methods of control, and one would not expect that the same considerations would necessarily apply in ethical drug manufacture and the production of cheap plastic toys.

Quality standards and their control have important implications for inter-departmental relations, and for that reason the firm's attitude to quality should be clear, and should govern all the relevant aspects of its work from the design of new products, through the purchasing of materials and parts and the different stages of production and distribution, to the service provided after the product is sold. It would be illogical for a design specification to stipulate a quality of material that the purchasing department was unable to guarantee, or for that department to order unsuitable materials for production which resulted in excessive waste. It would also be inconsistent to use a more expensive material or process than was needed to meet an acceptable standard for the finished product, or to profess a respect for quality standards and then subject the production department to such pressure that the rate of output demanded could only be attained by sacrificing the quality of the good.

A product's quality is defined in terms of its ability to meet specified requirements with predictable reliability, but quality is a function of several variables and the control of quality may be concerned with one or more of such things as dimensions, weight, chemical or physical properties, appearance and performance. The essence of quality control is to determine the variables to be controlled, define standard values for them, and fix the limits within which deviations from the values are acceptable. When it has been decided where control should be exercised the quality control analyst can apply his techniques to produce patterns of results based on a series of measurements which show whether limits are being exceeded, and indicate the kind of corrective action that should be taken if they are. A great advantage of systematic quality control analysis is that it helps to determine what proportion of a quantum of material input, intermediate products, or final output needs to be examined to ensure a given probability that the whole amount will be satisfactory within tolerable limits. Sampling techniques form the basis of this method, and tables have been produced which enable average degrees of risk of error to be calculated when samples of varying magnitude are taken from batches of different size.

Quality control can be used to throw light on the efficiency of manufacturing processes and stimulate inquiries to discover whether the machines in use still have the desired capability for the work to be performed, and whether design changes or some modification of operating methods are called for. A natural response to increasing complaints of inferior quality may be to raise the proportion of output subjected to inspection, but to do this is often to treat the symptoms and neglect the disease. The works manager of one company responded in this way to customers' criticisms of his product and pressed for his inspection team to be strengthened. Before this was agreed, however, an intensive analysis of output was undertaken and for one week a 100 per cent sample was tested, from which valuable information was obtained.

Figure 31 shows what kind of situation was found. The number of units of output is measured along *O Y*, and on the *O X* axis values of a critical product variable are

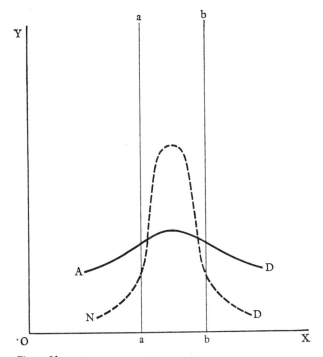

Figure 31

marked. The acceptable limits are shown by the vertical lines *aa* and *bb*. A normal distribution of output would be represented by the broken line *ND*, but when the curve of actual output was plotted it took the shape of the line *AD* and showed that an uncommonly high proportion of output was outside the permissible range of values. While this itself was not surprising it proved that although comprehensive inspection would certainly reduce the number of complaints it would do so by the rejection of such a large number of units that the fall in net output would threaten the profitability of the works. The trouble lay in the production process itself, and it was there that further investigation was needed before the problem could be solved.

Quality control techniques can also improve the operative's control over his own work. Straightforward pictorial devices like quality-rating charts and $\bar{X}$ charts provide information about output which tells the worker when attention to a particular aspect of the job is required. The efficiency of a metal-cutting machine, for example, affects the quality of the pieces turned out, a blunt tool producing inferior work. The operative knows this, but without some guidance he would not always know when the tool was satisfactory and when it needed to be sharpened or replaced. He might err on the side of caution and waste time in sharpening the tool more often than necessary, or he might underestimate the degree of bluntness and spoil some of his work. Using an $\bar{X}$ chart ($\bar{X}$ is the arithmetic mean of a number of values of X) he could be shown how to plot the critical values of the units produced by sampling output at prescribed intervals, and the data recorded would show when a limit was being approached and when attention to the tool was required. The need for subjective and possibly arbitrary judgments would be reduced and the scope of his work enlarged: the operative would enjoy more responsibility, and the greater control which he had over his work should be particularly beneficial to someone paid at piece rates according to the number of acceptable units produced.

INSPECTION

Quality control techniques can help to answer such questions as: what standards are feasible and desirable? at what stages should tests of quality be applied? is 100 per cent examination necessary? or can sampling methods be used? They can also help to answer other questions that continually arise: is this casting satisfactory? is this tolerance too wide? is the expected fatigue life of this component adequate? But they cannot tell us who should make the decisions called for when questions like those in the second group are asked. This requires an appreciation of the scope and formal importance attached to inspection, and raises different issues from those which have to be considered when deciding whether or not to use quality control methods themselves.

A firm must decide whether inspection should be primarily the responsibility of individual workers, their departmental superiors, or a separate inspection team, and if the third alternative is chosen the place of the inspection group in the organizational system has to be fixed. When inspectors are employed in the production department, as is often the case, there is a possibility of conflict between the demands of quality and output which the departmental head may often want settled in favour of the latter. In companies which emphasize high quality standards there are probably advantages on balance in creating a separate inspection department with a chief inspector, in a senior managerial position, who has formal authority to decide disputed matters of quality, or who can defend the case for a certain standard against colleagues on the same level as himself.

The appointment of inspectors tends to create a number of organizational and human difficulties, and the accuracy of inspectors, on which much of the effectiveness of quality control depends, is not so reliable as sometimes supposed. In the first place, physiological and psychological characteristics play an important part. Odd as it seems, inspectors whose work calls, say, for an examination of colours are not always tested for colour blindness before being employed. Much inspection work requires highly developed senses and acute concentration on the job in hand, so that dullness of these critical senses, boredom, frustration and stress are all liable to affect inspectors' judgments. Organizational and social factors also influence inspection work. The training inspectors receive is important, as are the conditions under which they perform their tasks, and the chief inspector's attitude is a further influence on the way they work. He may be more concerned with protecting his subordinates against criticism and hostility than in developing their skills and maintaining accurate standards, and it is often easier for him to avoid trouble by rechecking items which subordinates have examined than by remedying personal weaknesses in the inspection team.

Personal relations assume considerable importance for an inspector in a production department, in direct contact with operatives whose earnings he can affect and foremen of higher rank than himself over whom he has some measure of control. The ties that develop and the feelings aroused often influence the inspector's behaviour, but when inspection is undertaken in a separate place these social forces are felt less strongly and a more detached attitude can be taken by the inspector to his work. An inspector sometimes develops a fixed idea about an appropriate rejection rate, a corollary of this being that when the general level of quality rises or falls inspection standards become more severe or more lax. It has also been found that an inspector may fasten unduly on a particular fault, or a few faults, and pay little attention to others; or habitually pass or reject marginal items as the case may be.

The difficulties raised by inspection are not easily overcome. Multiple checks can be made by different inspectors to reduce the risk of faults being passed, but this process adds to expense without getting to the root of the inspection problems discussed here. The inspector's accuracy can be tested experimentally by asking him to check product samples containing known defects, but this does not guarantee that he will maintain consistent inspection standards in the plant. And a firm can arrange periodic meetings at which standards are discussed and different methods are analysed and compared, which may reveal weaknesses in the process that can be partially remedied, if not completely cured. Inspection problems have received increasing attention, especially from industrial psychologists and sociologists in recent years, but no entirely satisfactory solution to them has been found and this particular form of control must be recognized to be more than usually prone to imperfections inherent in the essentially human character of the work.[1]

11.6 Conclusion

We have tried in this chapter to show the importance of planning and control, and some of the problems they raise. It is helpful from several points of view to think of planning and control as separate activities with distinctive features and techniques of their own, but one must remember that the two things are intimately related in practice, or at least that they should be. There are firms in which the responsibility for planning and control is fragmented in such a way that a number of subsidiary planning and control systems are operated simultaneously with incongruent results, and this may go far to defeat the whole purpose of the exercise of welding the activities of the enterprise more closely together and ensuring greater harmony of operation. It is pointless in most cases to devise a plan without some way of controlling events after it is put into effect, and equally pointless to devise controls that are irrelevant to the execution of a plan. Together, planning and control make a vital contribution to business efficiency and are fundamental to all efforts to maintain or increase the real income of a firm. Their potential range of application is company-wide and the rewards obtainable from their skilful and intelligent use are large. They are important instruments of coordination and motivation, but their human implications, particularly in the case of control, must not be neglected, and one of the major organizational problems in the larger and more complex concern is to see that the dysfunctional effects of elaborate, impersonal control systems do not outweigh the undoubted advantages to be derived from their use.

The size of firm, the calibre of its employees, the markets in which it sells and its technology all influence the extent to which systematic planning and control are undertaken and the sophistication of the methods used. But the most important factors of all are managerial perception of the need for different kinds of planning and control to meet varying organizational requirements, and managerial skill in applying the chosen techniques to produce the greatest net gain for the firm.

[1] Cf. R. M. McKenzie, 'The Production-Inspection War?', *Metalworking Production*, **101**, no. 18, 1957, 771–72; R. M. McKenzie, 'On the Accuracy of Inspectors', *Ergonomics*, **1**, no. 3, 1958, 258–72; A. E. M. Seaborne and L. F. Thomas, *Subjective Standards in Industrial Inspection*, H.M.S.O., 1964; D. S. Pugh, 'Organizational Problems of Inspection', *Journal of Management Studies*, **3**, no. 3, 1966, 256–69.

Comparatively few businesses actually plan and control their activities on so ambitious a scale as that suggested here, but within their own limitations all would-be progressive companies must try to plan and control their operations to the best of their ability, and in so doing they should increase their feeling of autonomy by giving formal expression to the organization's most-preferred shape, and by taking positive measures to reduce the effects of restraints under which it must inevitably work. A firm which fails to plan and control its activities effectively is in constant danger of being left in an economic backwater to decay or of being destroyed by the forces of change.

12

Committees and meetings

So far we have looked mainly at relationships between people in pairs, superior-subordinate and line-staff relationships being the two most important examples, and at some of the behavioural characteristics of formal subgroups. But group activity needs to be considered in wider terms than those admitted previously, because a significant amount of organizational work is done by groups that we have not yet adequately discussed. We shall now examine the role of committees and meetings in business and assess their contribution to the efficiency with which company tasks are performed.

Committees and meetings are a pervasive feature of social activity and accepted instruments for dealing with a wide variety of matters in virtually every field of life. They play an influential part in company affairs, in national and local government, and in the administration of religious, educational and charitable institutions of all kinds. We have discussed boards of directors, which are a common form of committee in incorporated concerns, but there are other committees besides these in businesses of every size. Their number has never been calculated, but it is widely believed that their importance in the organizational system has increased considerably in recent decades. The distinction made here between a committee and a meeting is based mainly on the greater formality of the first as opposed to the relative informality of the second, although the degree of formality does not by itself always enable a clear distinction to be made. Many committees, such as company boards, are formally constituted, and if they are both permanent and important enough are shown on the organization chart. Such committees frequently have a constitution, a prescribed composition, regular meetings with prepared agenda, and approved minutes kept of their discussions. On the other hand, some committees are formal but impermanent, created to deal with problems *ad hoc* and disbanded when their work is done; they can meet irregularly and unpredictably as particular needs arise.

Meetings, too, are often highly formal in character, especially those in which an autocratic superior calls subordinates together to tell them about something concern-

232

ing them all, or issue instructions, and give them an opportunity to ask questions and remove uncertainty about what must be done. There need be no previous notice of what is to be dealt with at this kind of meeting, and members of the group do not come together on equal terms as they are ostensibly expected to do in a committee. There are many kinds of unofficial meetings, also, which may have an influence as great as, or even greater than, that of formal committees. These unofficial groups are not, however, explicitly defined as part of the organizational structure. Business committees have been described which dealt with general policy, or with a variety of specialized aspects of company operations such as product design, investment planning, marketing strategy, managerial development, internal auditing, and many other things. Meetings are known to take place at all levels from the executive directors' luncheon table to the gathering of departmental supervisors or the convention of shop stewards on the factory floor. On every working day meetings are held and committees sit, and they are an integral part of the pattern of business life. Yet they remain controversial, both from the theoretical and the practical point of view, and we must try to see why this is the case.

We first examine the general arguments for and against committees in business, with an emphasis on managerial committees, and on the plural executive as the supreme authority in a firm. This part of the discussion will be mostly concerned with formal committees, but later we shall consider the significance of less formal meetings in the light of contemporary ideas about the place of small groups in the organization of the firm.

12.1 The case for committees

A committee can be an efficient problem-solving body, capable of producing solutions superior to those found by individuals tackling similar problems alone. Meetings, of course, solve problems as well, but a committee formalizes the conditions under which they are presented, analysed and disposed of by its members when they contribute their knowledge, skill and experience to the common task. At its best the committee saves time by concentrating the known relevant information in one place and providing the means for an economical communication of facts and opinions between the people involved. March and Simon have suggested several reasons for the superior problem-solving ability of committees compared with that of individuals. They argue that the members of a group are not often likely to make the same error simultaneously, and by correcting each other's randomly distributed mistakes they achieve a higher average level of judgment than would be possible for any one of them alone. The proposals put to a committee vary in quality and should not be given equal weight: collective examination increases the probability that they will be ranked correctly and inferior ones rejected. This again helps to raise the standard of the committee's results. Proposals are made more carefully when people know they will be scrutinized by other members, and the confidence with which contributions are made to discussion supposedly reflects the depth of thought that has been given to them and favourably influences their chance of acceptance. However, one may be sceptical about this assertion that those most confident of their correctness are in fact most likely to be right.

A committee benefits from division of labour by 'factorizing' problems; that is it breaks them down into components suitable for specialized individual considera- tion. This sharing of work within the group should increase the speed at which it reaches decisions, because various facets of a problem can be studied at the same time and the information collected can then be synthesized to produce the final result. The ability to discover correct solutions oneself is believed to be less wide- spread than the ability to assess the correctness of other people's solutions, and the number of possible solutions produced by a group therefore tends to be greater than the number found by an individual. From the larger number of possible solutions a generally satisfactory one is more likely to emerge.

The committee is also favoured as a means of increasing the scope for shared decision making, for encouraging consultation and a democratic exchange of views, and hence for motivating people and enabling them to contribute more fully and effectively to the work of the firm. The Scanlon Plan, introduced by Joseph Scanlon between the two world wars and now adopted by a number of companies in the U.S.A., is a good example of the conscious use of committees for motivational reasons.[1] The plan has two main features: one is the calculation of cost reductions on an agreed basis, often the comparison of total employment costs with a financial measure of output such as sales revenue or the value added in production, and the sharing among all employees of the whole or part of any savings achieved. The other is the formation of committees to allow everyone to contribute his full mental as well as physical energy to the business. The basic purpose of these committees is to collect and assess ideas from any source which may improve the ratio of output value to costs. The highest committee has representatives of managers and workers among its members: it deals with matters that have wider implications than those dealt with below and keeps a general watch on the activities of lower- level groups. Departmental committees of workers and supervisors are normally free, however, to decide things that affect only their own operations. Formalities are reduced to a minimum and regular committee meetings may be supplemented by impromptu meetings on the shop floor to discuss ideas and adopt recommenda- tions if any group wishes to hold them. Minutes of formal meetings record what ideas and actions are approved, and allow the higher (screening) committee to keep in touch with developments throughout the firm. Supporters of the Scanlon Plan claim that it has led to some notable improvements in the efficiency and competitive strength of companies in which it has been adopted, and in the quality of relations

[1] F. G. Lesieur (ed.), *The Scanlon Plan*, Wiley, 1958.

between employees, but it seems to have had more success in small and medium-sized companies than in large concerns.

Committees and meetings provide opportunities for greater numbers of people to participate in decision making and problem solving than would be possible if each manager exercised the sole right to determine matters within his own subgroup. They also provide one means of communication between members of different subgroups. The ability to share in decision making affects individuals in different ways. Some people may feel that it increases their prestige and, especially if their suggestions are adopted, may identify themselves closely with the committee and work hard to achieve its aims. Group cohesiveness is consequently increased and the greater it is the more effective is the group likely to be. Cohesiveness can be strengthened progressively in a permanent committee with a reasonably constant membership, but is more difficult to secure when a group has a short existence as an assemblage of individuals from different parts of the firm. When a committee's decisions are accepted by the larger system of which it is part, its members may associate themselves more fully with the purposes that the organization as a whole exists to fulfil, and be ready to accept its norms. But the opposite effect is quite possible, however, for people whose ideas are rejected may feel alienated from their groups, and committees whose decisions are unacceptable to the larger system may feel that their status is impaired, and be less disposed to support its aims.

The connexion between business complexity and business growth is referred to in several places in this book and is clearly relevant to the use of committees in firms. A single executive is often faced with problems which he cannot, or does not wish to, deal with alone. He may feel that he has insufficient authority, knowledge or experience to handle a problem, or he may feel that, although reasonably sure that his proposed course of action is sound, he would still like to compare it with other people's proposals and hear their opinions of his own. A committee is not essential for him to do these things, but in some instances it is the best arrangement to make. In the case of formal managerial subgroups a meeting of the members enables a superior to discover the extent of agreement with his proposals and test the consistency of interpretation of policy directives or other commands from above. Meetings between managers from different levels help the senior person present to assess the effectiveness of delegation within the system, but only if what Rice calls the 'culture of the enterprise' encourages subordinates to speak freely in the presence of their chief.

Policy making and review are particularly likely to benefit from collective consideration, and often there are special problems that affect more than one department and call for coordinated effort in their solution. The individual committee promotes the coordination of its own members' activities, and a number of committees can extend the coordinating influence over a wider field if they are linked by interlocking membership. Examples of this arrangement can be found in many holding companies

235

in which members of the parent board serve on the boards of subsidiary operating firms. If a problem is of great importance to a firm it is possibly better dealt with by a committee than in an informal way. For instance, when a new product is being introduced, or a large special order has to be handled, and problems of production, design, marketing, finance, purchasing etc. have to be reconciled and solved, a committee of departmental managers may be the most effective way of seeing that the work is properly done.

A committee can help to lighten managerial burdens by reducing the strain of what W. G. Scott describes as 'executive loneliness'. In this sense it may satisfy psychological more than organizational needs, but be no less valuable for that, so long as it is not used to evade legitimate personal responsibility and made what I. K. Brunel, the great Victorian engineer, called a craven substitute for the exercise of individual authority where that would be more appropriate. Sometimes a committee is formed with the deliberate intention of limiting an executive's power, although it is arguable whether this is to be held in its favour or not. The system of 'collegial' management in Germany (the Vorstand) and Holland (the Directie) is said to have been designed to preserve the balance of power within senior executive groups and prevent the abuse of individual authority.

The committee appears, therefore, to be a useful body which can solve many complex problems better and more quickly than people working alone, increase the degree of participation in problem solving and decision making, motivate people to identify themselves with organizational goals, consolidate managerial authority, coordinate activities, and raise the general standard of the decisions that are made. As far back as 1928 Miss Follett argued that the opportunities given to employees to pool experiences and learn from each other are perhaps the most important feature of committee work, and she saw committees as a valuable aid to the exercise of leadership and the promotion of better relations within the firm. In her view these were cogent reasons for the spread of committees, despite the time they consumed and the additional burdens they imposed on some of their members.

The capable leader knows that in order to secure any lasting agreement between himself and the rest of his group, they must be made to share in his experience. This insight alone changes our whole conception of leadership. The leader knows also that any lasting agreement among the members of the group can come only by their sharing each other's experience. He must see that his organization is such as to make this possible.[1]

12.2 The case against committees

Although a committee can (in the best conditions) be an economical and effective problem-solving body it can also be costly, time wasting and inefficient. Managerial committees may absorb large amounts of executives' time, depending on the number

[1] M. P. Follett, 'Some Discrepancies in Leadership Theory and Practice' in *Dynamic Administration, The Collected Papers of Mary Parker Follett*, eds. H. C. Metcalf and L. F. Urwick, Pitman, 1941 repr. 1952, pp. 284–85.

of committees that exist, the number of managers serving on them and the frequency and duration of meetings. Even when committees are well run and do their jobs with dispatch, a manager who has to serve on several of them can become heavily engaged in committee activities, and his work outside the committee room may suffer if his committee responsibilities are great.

The danger of this happening is far from new. Hidy has shown that 'a galaxy of committees' existed in the Standard Oil Company of New Jersey by 1886, and the system of management by consultation and committee still operated in the parent company and its affiliates at the time he wrote, to such an extent 'that executives sometimes regard(ed) themselves as working members of a perpetual debating society'.[1] Brech gives a striking example of the burden of committee work in a firm of 3,000 employees with twenty senior and middle managers, in which there were nineteen committees meeting weekly or quarterly and dealing with overlapping subjects. Some managers were spending almost seventy hours a month in committee, or about one-third of their normal working time.

A formal, permanent committee with regular meetings generally raises few problems so far as attendance is concerned. Its members know they have these commitments at certain times and arrange their activities in order to be able to attend the meetings. Even if some of the members are prevented from being present a committee can still transact much, if not all, of its business so long as it has a quorum. In the case of a committee set up specially to deal with a unique problem it may be much more difficult for meetings to be fitted into a programme of work that already makes heavy demands on the members. The difficulty increases if the meetings must be arranged at times when everyone can attend, and an excellent instance of the problems that can arise was discovered in the course of Miss Woodward's research.

At a routine production-control meeting a question of manufacturing layout was raised which could not be answered immediately, although the necessary information was quite accessible and could have been produced in a matter of hours. Those present decided to consider the information together and tried to find a suitable occasion for another meeting. It proved extremely difficult to find a time when everyone could come and the next meeting was not held until six weeks later. The difficulty of finding a suitable date seemed to constitute such a challenge that the mere arrangement of the second meeting became a major end in itself, and when a time was at last agreed the sense of achievement was almost as great as if the actual manufacturing problem had been solved. The members dispersed, the problem was largely forgotten, and the manager who had been asked to get the information did nothing about it until just before the second meeting, which followed a very similar course to the first. The problem now appeared to be more serious than before and a subcommittee was set up to study it in greater detail. The arrangement of a sub-

[1] R. W. Hidy, 'The Standard Oil Company (New Jersey)', *Journal of Economic History*, **XII**, no. 4, 1952, 411–24.

committee meeting became another end in itself, and when that group finally settled down to work it was found necessary to report to the main meeting on several occasions. Twelve meetings of one kind and another, spread over nearly eighteen months, were held to solve the problem that set this train of events in motion, but the researchers were convinced that the long period was not due to deliberate obstruction or evasion of managerial responsibility. Indeed, the managers in this firm were advocates of greater efficiency and were quite unaware of the fact that they had dealt with this particular problem in an extremely inefficient way.

In this case a long time was taken to reach a final decision with the best of intentions, so far as could be judged, but delays can just as well be caused by deliberately obstructive tactics. The convention that certain people must be present for decisions to be reached gives those people power to control the pace at which work proceeds that may be abused. Within the committee the handling of business can be influenced by various political methods, such as raising points of order, appealing to precedent, demanding the clarification of procedural matters, proposing amendments and so on. Dominating individuals and minority blocs can often exercise control over the committee's behaviour out of all proportion to their relative numerical strength, as we saw in the case of shareholders' meetings. To some people, the playing of perfectly legitimate games within the limits of committee rules is a major source of satisfaction, and much more important than the accomplishment of a collective task. But it is not easy to generalize fairly about these things. Committee members are sometimes fully justified in their insistence on correct procedure, and the man who can always be relied on to discover a mistake in the minutes and correct his colleagues on a point of order may be doing the committee a service by helping it to avoid trouble at a later time, assuming that the rules adopted were sensible and acceptable in the first place.

Again, one cannot easily generalize about the relationship between the time spent on committee business and the efficiency with which business is done. One can only assess the relationship in a particular committee with a knowledge of its composition and work. There are psychological aspects of time spent in committee that should be taken into account. Members who make the effort to attend may feel cheated if business is disposed of too briskly, and complain of inadequate opportunity to express their views. On the other hand, when committees take a long time to complete their work there is a frequent tendency to equate time spent with value of achievement, and for members to feel a sense of virtue in proportion to the number of hours passed in the meeting. It is not always easy to settle on a happy mean between the perfunctory and subjectively pointless meetings of committees that act merely as rubber stamps, and the time- and energy-consuming meetings of committees that degenerate into largely-irrelevant talking shops.

A committee that is really a disguised form of command meeting can be most frustrating and a travesty of the ideal of joint endeavour. A committee whose members are of unequal rank often puts a strain on subordinates who find it difficult to speak as freely as they would like and make their fullest contribution, because of their feeling of restraint. Whenever people try to communicate with each other the problem of 'noise' may be encountered. Noise interferes with the transmission of information and ideas by reducing their strength or distorting their form, and makes them harder to receive. Committee discussions are often affected by noise and redundancy. Noise is caused by the introduction of irrelevant issues by members who are quite aware of the central problem the group wants to solve, but who still insist on importing problems of their own. It is also caused by differences in education, social convention and business background, and by feelings of superiority or animosity towards others. Redundancy occurs when there are repeated expressions of the same idea in different forms by different members of the group.

It is sometimes suggested that a strong chairman should eliminate or drastically reduce noise, and prevent redundancy, by limiting discussion strictly to the central theme, but it can also be argued that it is undesirable for him to try. There is a case for allowing people to generate noise, on the understanding that what they are doing will be pointed out to them, and in letting them be redundant. Noise and redundancy only reduce group efficiency if it is defined purely in terms of ability to solve *group* problems, and some psychologists maintain that this is an unrealistic view of things. A group satisfies personal as well as organizational needs and can help to solve the individual's problems in addition to those of the system: to the extent that it does so it serves a doubly useful purpose. If the efforts to eliminate noise and prevent redundancy are too successful the problem-solving abilities of the group may actually be weakened, because its members lose the incentive to contribute to its work.

A committee has an intermittent corporate personality, and when meetings end there is a danger that it may disintegrate into a number of individuals with different degrees of allegiance to the committee as a body and different feelings of responsibility for the decisions that were reached. Even when decisions are unanimous, or at least not openly opposed, there can be no certainty that all members supported them with equal conviction, or that they will all be prepared to carry out their own parts of the work of implementation with equal vigour. Some of them might be simply uninterested in what was done, while others are outwardly compliant but inwardly determined to modify a decision in accordance with their own views. This may be unreasonable, even unethical, but it happens all the same. Much depends on the way in which decisions are reached, and those based on a genuine consensus obviously provide the strongest motivation to abide by them.

Unanimous decisions may be reached simply for the sake of appearance, or after a process of bargaining which yields a poor but acceptable compromise. Pressure may be exerted on a minority to make it conform to a majority view, but there is then no reason to suppose that minority members will have such a strong sense of loyalty to the decision that was made. Where factions exist they can trade with each other if they have different, but not conflicting, major objectives that enable one faction to support another in a matter about which it is relatively indifferent, in return for support in a matter which it treats as important. Sometimes the whole collective decision-making process is wrecked by one person who is determined to have his own way and prevent any decision of which he does not approve. Sometimes people come to committee with their minds made up in advance that no decision shall be reached. Decisions must often be made with less information than the committee would like and in less time than it wanted to spend. But when business pressures impose no time limit the committee leader faces the delicate problem of deciding when the discussion should be closed. If he presses too hard for decisions he may antagonize people who are stopped from speaking, cause valuable alternatives to be overlooked, split the committee on a vote and possibly cause resentment among dissident members as a result. If the discussion is allowed to continue too long the committee may wander into byways or become so involved in seeking the optimum, but impractical, solution to a problem that it neglects to produce a feasible, satisfactory one.

For various reasons like these there is no guarantee that committees necessarily produce the best solutions to problems, and no assurance that the average quality of their decisions is always superior to that of individuals. Equally, there is no guarantee that committees ensure effective coordination, or provide the opportunities for participation, the sharing of experience, and the consolidation of authority expected under the best conditions. In view of the propensity of committees to breed committees, some people consider it essential to check their increase lest they debilitate the institutions that nourish them. Matters do not yet seem to have reached such a state in business as they appear to have done in government and universities, but the growth of firms encourages the growth of committees, and it would be comforting to know that every committee is looked at critically and dispassionately to ensure that it is really necessary and has the appropriate membership for its job, that its meetings are as valuable as they can be made, that none of its work could be done better by an individual or another group, and that it will cease to exist as soon as its work is completed.

12.3 Managerial committees

Broadly speaking in terms of the work they perform there are three kinds of committee in companies today. The first is the one whose main task is to deal with policy matters for the firm as a whole, and with major problems of planning, organization, staffing and finance that affect the long-run development of the concern. The board of directors, as we have seen, tends to be such a committee in many companies, but in the larger ones the board may delegate some of this work to subcommittees or staff groups. The second kind of committee is formed to deal with a special problem or set of related problems, or with a limited range of company operations. It might, for example, be a committee set up to consider the implications of the Industrial Training Act, the desirability of new methods of financial control, or developments in production techniques. Whereas general-policy-making committees tend to be permanent the other kind of advisory committee is often formed to deal with a non-recurring matter, but it is possible to combine the features of both quasi-permanent and temporary committees in the manner of Tube Investments Limited.

The growth of this company led to an increase in the number and importance of problems that had to be considered at the head office, particularly investment problems affecting more than one subsidiary concern. It was decided to form a coordinating and planning board to give these matters expert attention and prepare analyses of various subjects for the company's chairman. This board consisted originally of the chairman's personal staff, which was later broken up, and a number of senior managers in the operating companies. All the main interests in Tube Investments were represented and the intention was that the board should not act as a plenary group so much as a panel from which committees could be drawn as required, with authority to co-opt non-members of the board if they thought it necessary to do so.[1]

The third type of committee is the one with full executive powers. In some cases boards of executive directors are committees of this kind, but it is worth distinguishing such boards from other executive groups operating under larger boards of directors which may also have outside directors among their members. The groups envisaged here are appointed in most cases to support the chief executive, but in a few companies they have actually taken his place.

The system of management by executive committee in E. I. du Pont de Nemours was introduced in 1921 in an attempt to solve the problems caused by the diversification and complexity of the company's activities.[2] The feeling that has since been more explicitly stated was that when a company becomes so large and diverse that one man can no longer comprehend it as a whole the plural executive should be tried. An executive committee of the board was formed with the president and nine vice-presidents as its members, and they were relieved of operating responsibilities to devote themselves entirely to the general management of the company. The board reserved certain powers to deal with matters of finance, salaries and auditing, but otherwise the executive committee had wide authority to act for the board in the affairs of the firm. The committee's main tasks were to determine basic policy, select senior managers, and review their work using the most objective criteria available.

[1] R. S. Edwards and H. Townsend, *Business Enterprise*, Macmillan, 1958, pp. 222–3.
[2] W. H. Mylander, 'Management by Executive Committee', *Harvard Business Review*, **33**, no. 3, 1955, 51–58.

Each manufacturing department submitted monthly operating reports with forecasts of earnings and sales, and each departmental general manager met the committee, on average, four times a year to discuss work for which he was responsible. These general managers were empowered to decide production levels, prices and salaries within the limits of company policy, but capital expenditure above a specified amount required the approval of the executive committee or the finance committee of the board.

The executive committee was the court of appeal for interdepartmental disputes, although it showed its dislike of this role so effectively that it was seldom asked to act in a judicial capacity. Committee members gave advice in their individual fields of specialized knowledge and their influence here was indirect but powerful. The committee not only supervised the firm's current activities, but tried also to take a long view of events and encouraged departments to take a similar view. Weekly committee meetings were held at which the quorum was five, and four was the minimum number needed to support a resolution before it could be carried. The executive committee in du Pont had ten members because it was thought that a group of this size was not too large to be cumbersome, but large enough for the manufacturing, financial, technical and sales specialisms each to be represented by at least two people, so as to increase the probability that one of them would always be present when the committee met.

A similar group, known as the board of management, operated in the engineering company of Baker Perkins Limited from 1920 to 1963.[1] The boards of directors of the two companies that merged to form Baker Perkins were amalgamated in one body from which the management board was formed, with seven executive directors of equal status whose rights and duties as a board were defined by the articles of association. All major departments were represented on the management board, none with a majority, and the board was responsible for running the company, subject again to the reservation of certain powers by the full board of directors. The actual size of the board varied eventually from three members to eight, but five was thought to be the optimum. Formal meetings were held monthly, a few days before the meeting of the board of directors, and senior departmental managers were invited to attend when matters affecting them were discussed. Informal daily meetings gave members of the management board opportunities to consult, exchange information, and decide things that had to be settled before the next formal meeting, at which they would be ratified. Each member of the management board had authority over the day-to-day operations in a particular company sphere, and the members' mutual confidence enabled them to make emergency decisions about matters within the board's province, knowing that they could rely on their colleagues' support.

[1] B. D. Baker, *A Board of Management instead of a Managing Director*, British Institute of Management, Winter Proceedings no. 9, 1950.

The board of management was replaced by a group management of similar cast when a new company, Baker Perkins Holdings, was formed in 1963, and this body lasted until 1967, when changing conditions dictated a further reorganization of the concern. The work of the group management was taken over by two executive vice-chairmen, responsible for home and overseas operating units respectively, and divisions continued to operate under unitary managerial control in the federally decentralized system. The chairman himself was freed from executive duties to deal with long-range planning problems concerning the group as a whole. But although group management no longer exists in the same form as before, the experience of Baker Perkins, together with that of du Pont and the Indian chemical and textiles company whose experiment with a management board is discussed by Rice, provides valuable evidence of the pros and cons of the plural executive.[1]

Committee management tends to be more expensive than the conventional system of single managing director and departmental heads, and the chief executive can often make quicker decisions than the group. Work is duplicated when a number of people read the same papers and prepare the same ground, but this is true of committees of many kinds. Compromise, expediency and indecision are potential dangers in a management board, and its work is also adversely affected if there are serious conflicts of personality and ideas. Individualistic managers are sometimes frustrated by the need to conform to agreed modes of behaviour. Committee members with departmental responsibilities are liable to be overburdened, and although the importance of this problem is reduced by delegation there is an associated danger that delegation may be carried to the point of virtual abdication from a department, which severely limits a manager's accessibility to his subordinates. Someone responsible for a major company function, such as finance, might be unwilling to accept what he regards as incursions into his own 'territory' by other board members, and try to insist on the overriding importance of his own role in particular matters. Difficulties also arise when one member behaves outside the committee as though a policy decision had been agreed, when in fact no agreement was reached.

But set against these arguments is the fact that a plural executive enjoys the normal advantages of collective wisdom when complex issues are discussed, and by reaching decisions of high average quality it increases the security of the firm. There are benefits to be gained from mutual challenge, and a diminished danger that one manager will be allowed to develop a fixed belief in the infallibility of his ideas. The managerial committee also provides a safeguard against the possibility of a mediocre chief executive retaining his position because of inertia or misplaced sympathy on the part of the board of directors. A plural executive can often admit more readily to a mistake than a single manager, and find less difficulty (in terms of concern about lost prestige) in reversing a decision that is found to be wrong. The

[1] A. K. Rice, *The Enterprise and its Environment*, Tavistock Publications, 1963.

managerial group tends to be more objective on many matters, and certainly in du Pont the departmental heads preferred to discuss their ideas with ten people instead of one. A management board is sometimes the most appropriate body to assume command when no obvious successor to a chief executive can be found, and one of the greatest virtues of a plural executive is that the problem of succession is solved and continuity assured. This point was abundantly proved in the early life of the board of management in Baker Perkins where, in what may have been a period of abnormal misfortune, eight members were lost through death or retirement in as many years.

The prevalence of group management in one form or another is much greater than the small recorded number of formal plural executives would suggest. The tendency for managers to discuss problems with their colleagues, and take their opinions into account when decisions are made, results in a form of joint decision making at all levels in many firms, and there are signs that in a number of senior managerial groups this process has acquired such informal importance that the groups differ little from a true plural executive. Burns and Stalker found that the main feature of the managerial subsystem in one company they studied was the weekly meeting of senior executives to discuss production, market forecasts, sales strategy and new product designs. These meetings had their counterparts at all levels of the firm and were said to stress the interdependence of the company's parts and the dependence of the whole system on commercial success. People were diverted from their preoccupation with personal tasks and made to think about problems in company terms. In another, radio manufacturing, company the Monday morning meeting of senior managers was also a model for other groups in the firm, many of which exercised collective executive authority. The managers firmly believed that regular meetings like these were essential for the successful implementation of change.

Management by committee was found to be practised in thirty-three out of eighty of the south-east Essex firms and was particularly prominent in process industries, where four-fifths of the enterprises had some kind of managerial committee or executive board. Their highly rationalized production methods seemed conducive to joint decision making, and the committees were claimed to make a direct and valuable contribution to the attainment of both technical and social ends. Although the firms had single chief executives in the orthodox way, these men often acted more as chairmen of decision-making groups than as autocratic leaders of their managerial teams. In concerns outside the process industries, however, the management committees were not joint decision-making bodies to the same extent or in the same way: they appeared to serve political rather than technical purposes in most of these firms.

12.4 Group effectiveness

The use of committees and meetings to solve problems and make decisions is very much in tune with the ideas of a number of modern organization theorists, but they agree that businessmen's complaints about the inability of many of these groups to accomplish much useful work are often justified. They concede that committees can waste time, act indecisively, make mediocre decisions, and provide opportunities for confusion and evasion of responsibility. They accept that a committee may become an excellent setting for the play of personal animosities and the promotion of personal prestige; that it may encourage political manoeuvres and attempts to discredit opponents; that it may even transcend the people who compose it and become 'a mythical, mystic, mysterious, inaccessible entity whose decisions have the same force as an Act of God and are equally beyond appeal'.[1] But they also have firm ideas about the conditions in which groups like committees can be expected to act well, and about those in which they will act badly. Likert, whose recommended system of management calls for effectively interlinked work groups, is naturally interested in the behaviour of committees and meetings and, on the assumption that the greater the understanding of a thing the better it can be made to work, he is surprised that committees do so well in view of the small amount of analytical attention paid to their operations.[2] McGregor also remarked on the scanty knowledge of committee performance and the limited appreciation of the skills required of people undertaking committee work.[3] He suggested that together these were largely accountable for the persistent belief that individuals are much better fitted to make decisions and bear responsibility than groups, a belief that he was not inclined to share.

The task of reaching good decisions in committee is complicated at times by the tendency for objectives to be obscured, for personality problems to obtrude, and for faulty navigation to deflect a group from the path towards its main goal. A group, like an individual, must have a definite purpose and is liable to become confused if its primary objectives are concealed under a mass of side issues or weakened by the introduction of conflicting aims. Periodically, therefore, it is desirable for a group to take stock of its objectives and bring into the open any doubts and disagreement about the priority they should receive. Conflicts of personality cannot be avoided and are often the cause of poor communication and deterioration in the mood in which a group does its work. It may be useful from time to time for the group to give these conflicts a chance to be ventilated, in the hope that at least some of the more important differences can be reconciled. If a group gets deeply involved in a mass of problems the members may feel that no progress is being made, even when it is,

[1] E. Pawel, *From the Dark Tower*, Macmillan, 1957, p. 68; quoted by W. G. Scott in *Human Relations in Management*, Irwin, 1962, p. 181.
[2] R. Likert, *New Patterns of Management*, McGraw-Hill, 1961.
[3] D. McGregor, *The Human Side of Enterprise*, McGraw-Hill, 1960.

and lose enthusiasm for their work. It is appropriate for someone to see that the group does not lose its bearings and, even at the risk of unpopularity, to force the group to ask itself now and then if it is still quite sure where it is going and if the direction is one that it really wants to take.

The things stressed by contemporary writers, especially behaviourial scientists, are different from those stressed in classical organization theory, where plural executive committees might in any case be suspected of weakening the unity of command and obscuring the lines of authority. The orthodox treatment of committee procedure makes much of the formal nature of their meetings and the need for careful preparation of agenda, memoranda and minutes. Decisions are expected to be reached by majority votes and the role of the chairman is usually stressed as being of crucial importance. Nowadays it is more fashionable to argue that the atmosphere of a meeting should be informal and relaxed, that feelings as well as ideas should be freely expressed, and that excessive preparation may be undesirable, because it can lead to the prejudgment of issues which the meeting is called to discuss. A supportive atmosphere is required for solving problems, so that members can express themselves without fear of ridicule or hostile attack. In the ideal situation the chairman does not dominate the proceedings and, indeed, there need be no single leader of the group: different members emerge as natural leaders when different matters are discussed. Wide participation is encouraged, talk is pertinent to the business in hand, and when disagreement occurs the group tries to resolve it by equable debate. If it is impossible to resolve a matter in this way action may be deferred, or perhaps taken cautiously with an awareness of the need for reconsideration at an early stage. The tyranny of majority and minority is equally condemned and the group tries to reach decisions by consensus, with little in the way of formal voting. The group is also self-conscious in the sense that it examines its own procedures with a view to remedying any flaws in its behaviour. When decisions are made the members accept clear assignments for appropriate action.[1]

This idealistic picture of committee work may seem far removed from the reality to which many people are accustomed, and bring a wry smile to the faces of those who at one time and another have suffered all the afflictions that committee meetings can cause, from a sense of the total futility of the purpose for which the committee was formed to the fatigue of dealing with the aggressive member, determined to have his way in every matter, and the interminable talker, so enamoured of the sound of his own voice that he must speak to everything, to the infinite prolongation of business. The main reasons why the behaviour of many groups is so different from the ideal are, according to McGregor, that most people are prejudiced from the start by a low expectation of the group's usefulness, and that the autocratic exercise of managerial power, which emphasizes the superior's command and control over

[1] For a fuller discussion of these ideas cf. R. Likert, *op. cit.*, D. McGregor, *op. cit.*, and H. J. Leavitt, *Managerial Psychology*, 2nd edn., University of Chicago Press, 1964.

his subordinates, is still very common. Even in meetings of equals there is often a misplaced faith in the importance of a single leader, and in groups whose members have unequal formal rank it is very easy for feelings of subservience, suspicion, or hostility to be imported into a meeting, although they may be carefully concealed, and reduce the value of its work.

Business management calls for skills of personal leadership and skills of participation in group activities. The importance of the former has long been recognized in business literature and much has been written about them, but the earlier, and once almost exclusive, emphasis on the individual manager as the source of authority in the firm has been increasingly countered by the argument that success in achieving company objectives calls for a special kind of interaction between people that can only take place effectively in groups of the kinds discussed here. Systematic efforts have been made to discover generally applicable ways of increasing group effectiveness in business. Novel educational and training methods and experiments have been devised, like those of the National Training Laboratory for Group Development in the U.S.A., for whose 'T' (training) groups a marked success in improving social interaction has been claimed. As still more becomes known about the ways in which committees and meetings behave it may become possible to state with greater assurance what makes them most effective, and hence what should be done in order to increase their contribution to efficient organizational practice.

13

Some human problems of industry

13.1 Introduction

We suggested at the outset of this book that for many purposes the company must be treated as a particular kind of social system, and in discussing the nature and purpose of formal organization, and examining the main features of delegation, decision making, communication, coordination, planning and control, we have seen how the firm's operations are affected by reciprocal relations between organizational processes and employees' behaviour, and how a variety of personal problems are experienced by those taking part in the company's work. The reader will recall many of these problems: the problem of the foreman's status; the stress experienced by managers in their boundary roles; the difficulties caused by lack of correspondence between authority and responsibility, or by faulty delegation; the strains imposed by organizational change; the conflict between line and staff groups; and the problems created by control are some examples that will come readily to mind.

These problems, which vary considerably in importance, incidence and ease of solution, are due partly to the nature of formal organization itself and partly to the obvious fact that a firm is an assemblage of people who bring into it a variety of expectations, values and prejudices, and a mixed potential for understanding and misunderstanding, for conflict and peace. The factors affecting human relations in industry have received increasing attention during the last forty years and a voluminous literature has appeared in which the psychological, sociological, anthropological, political, economic and organizational aspects of the subject have been variously stressed, and interdisciplinary attempts to unify the more specialized analyses have also been made.

Human relations studies are concerned with problems of authority, leadership style, communication, motivation, participation, structural patterns, structural change, group composition and behaviour, interpersonal and intergroup relations, organizational size, uncertainty, and systems of penalties and rewards, and we must narrow this wide field considerably in order to limit our own discussion to a reasonable length. The matters on which we shall concentrate are the impact of formal

248

organization on the individual, the nature and importance of informal organization, the scope for job enlargement, and the case for wider participation by employees in decision making and the solution of company problems. We shall also consider some criticisms of the methods suggested for improving human relations in the firm.

Industrial relations form another large and important subject which is touched on only incidentally in this book, and it may be useful to point the distinction between industrial and human relations before looking more closely at the latter. The study of industrial relations involves an analysis of the structure and activities of formal associations of workers and employers. It deals with the development and influence of trade unions and employers' organizations, trade boards and wages councils; with the apparatus of collective bargaining, joint consultation, conciliation and arbitration; and with the statutory control of wage rates and conditions of work. Industrial relations are considered in local, regional and national terms and in any firm they are often mainly affected by external restraints, whereas human relations are to a much greater extent a function of conditions within the individual concern. A significant feature of industrial relations is the degree to which they are codified and regulated by law, and governed by a well-defined set of precedents and conventional courses of action, so that in many cases of industrial dispute the parties involved go through a predictable series of motions before agreement is reached.

To say that industrial relations have to do with material, and human relations with non-material, aspects of employment makes the contrast too crude, but the generalization contains a large element of truth. Industrial relations practices settle the basic conditions of employment, often at a minimum level only, and frequently leave scope for improvement in numerous firms: they do not touch many of the problems in the work situation with which human relations theory is concerned. Good industrial relations are certainly important, but they need to be strengthened in ways that an appreciation of human relations problems may suggest. They lay a foundation on which good human relations can be built, and the connexion between them is close enough for us to expect that an improvement or a deterioration in one will be associated with a similar change in the other. But there is not a one-to-one relationship between industrial and human relations, and good industrial relations, as indicated by an absence of overt industrial dispute, are not a sufficient guarantee of good human relations in the firm.

13.2 The effects of formal organization

The formal organization whose main features have previously been described has been criticized as a major cause of serious human problems, and to help in deciding how just these criticisms are let us recount briefly its salient characteristics. In doing so we shall define the organization in the extreme terms used by some of its more influential critics, not because it is suggested that all companies have structures of this kind, but rather because all structures are expected to exhibit in some degree the allegedly undesirable qualities to which much of the blame for poor human relations is ascribed.

An organization based on the classical precepts has a hierarchical arrangement of positions, or work roles, connected in chains of superior-subordinate relationships which form the channels of authenticated communication and command, and run from the supreme managerial position in the organizational pyramid to all positions at its base. The vertical relationships in the scalar chains are supplemented by formal horizontal and diagonal relationships which ensure cooperation between functionally separate departments and sections, and enable employees with the requisite knowledge or skill to contribute appropriately to the work of other people in the firm. The structure is designed to promote the achievement of the company's primary objectives, to which are related the formal subgoals of departments, individuals and groups. Competitive market pressures force firms to seek the least-cost combination of factor inputs, and the need to minimize costs typically dictates a high degree of task specialization, with differentiation of work between roles and standardization of work within them. The process of sharing the firm's total task between many people calls for close control from above of work at each level to ensure that activities are coordinated and correctly performed. The emphasis is on formal authority and on the formal definition of work and job relationships: individuals are expected to accept the goals of the enterprise and work for their achievement in a rational, logically ordered way. A structure of this kind stands well towards the mechanistic end of the spectrum envisaged in Chapter 7 and represents the application of engineering theory to organizational design, the business being conceived of essentially as an economic transformation system whose efficiency is measured by the ratio of the value of economic output to the value of the inputs of productive factor units.

With this model of the formal organization in mind let us look at the people who work in the firm, and consider their needs and aspirations and the traits of their individual personalities. One of the most influential writers on the subject of human relations, Chris Argyris, has made a number of attacks on the formal organization (for example, in *Personality and Organization*) on the ground that organizational demands are in many cases calculated to reduce the satisfaction of human needs. Argyris has argued that these needs are ranked in ascending order from the most basic physiological needs for food, clothing and shelter to what he calls the need for self-actualization, and McGregor (in *The Human Side of Enterprise*) self-fulfilment. Between the lowest and highest needs come the need for safety, social needs, and egoistic needs like those for self-respect, status and the esteem of others. It must be stressed that people are not necessarily motivated to satisfy these needs with equal intensity, or in the same order and ways, and they cannot satisfy them all by unaided effort, but the presumption is that someone who is either unable adequately to satisfy these needs, or is actively prevented from doing so, suffers ill-health as much as someone with an obvious physical ailment.

The development of personality is thought of as a progression from childhood to adulthood, in the course of which a person changes from a relatively passive to an active state; from total dependence to independence; from command of a limited range to command of a wide range of behaviour; from an ability to think only in terms of short time-spans to an ability to visualize distant possibilities; and from a state of subordination to one of social equality, self-awareness and self-control. The human relations school of which Argyris is a spokesman thinks of this progression as the normal one and treats any force that retards or arrests it as *prima facie* harmful. Conceding for the moment the truth of this argument, how does formal organization affect the ability to satisfy personal needs and how far does it recognize the employee as a mature personality? Obviously, much will depend on the work being done, the hierarchical position occupied, and the individual's character and attitude, which will themselves be affected by a variety of domestic, educational, political and religious forces external to the firm. Critics of formal organization are generally agreed that it is more inimical to people at the operative level than to managers, and the problems of the former group will be our main concern for the present.

The exercise of strict formal authority and the precise definition and close control of their work allow few employees the opportunity to show much initiative or develop their higher powers, and they are mostly required to perform short, simple, repetitive, programmed tasks. The worker is partially depersonalized by being integrated into a man-machine system, and his technological subservience is intensified by the fact that he is often unable to perceive the connexion between his own activities and the distant goals of the enterprise he serves. He is asked merely to concentrate on a limited task and not to interest himself in the larger design. The narrow confines of his work are an obstacle to self-fulfilment and prevent him from expressing himself as a mature personality. The conflict between the demands of formal organization and the demands of a healthy individual manifests itself in a number of ways, the most prevalent and easily recognizable of which are high rates of labour turnover, absenteeism, apathy, obstructiveness, disloyalty and aggression.

McGregor, in his celebrated antithesis of Theory X and Theory Y, has tried to show how the treatment of employees is influenced by some false assumptions about human motivation that underlie the design and operation of many formal systems. Theory X is a statement of traditional managerial views, the most influential of which is that the average person dislikes work and avoids it when he can. To overcome his reluctance to work he must therefore be offered sufficient material inducement to provide his labour, and managed by a mixture of compulsion, cajolery and controls to make sure that his work is satisfactorily performed. In other words, human effort within the enterprise is elicited primarily by a combination of bribery and threats,

251

and, although the proportions of the two ingredients differ from case to case, both are in some measure always used

Theory X says that managers defend their behaviour and justify their formal system by arguing that most people prefer to be directed, shirk responsibility, and have only a limited ambition to advance. The worker is expected to satisfy his higher needs outside the firm, and so long as he receives an adequate money reward the firm's side of the employment contract is kept. The employee is thus encouraged to think principally about his money income and to measure his satisfaction in money terms. Is it then surprising, ask critics of Theory X, that his hostility to the system manifests itself in aggressive demands for higher wages and other material benefits, or that he strikes when these claims are inadequately met? Yet greater material rewards only palliate the situation and cannot solve the fundamental problem of the inability to satisfy higher needs and achieve self-fulfilment.

McGregor argues that while Theory X explains some industrial behaviour it does not explain all, and he deprecates attempts to blame organizational failures on the deficiencies of workpeople alone. He maintains that there is a natural propensity to expend physical and mental energy in work, and that work in a properly organized firm can and should be a much greater source of satisfaction to the employee than is often the case. The average person, far from avoiding responsibility, would be ready to accept more of it if he could, and there is a large reservoir of currently unused imagination, ingenuity and creativeness to be drawn on in the solution of organizational problems. One of the main defects of modern industry is the failure to make the best use of human resources, because many managers have not succeeded in creating the conditions for greater self-fulfilment in work that would enable people to feel the same kind of enthusiasm for their jobs as they feel for activities voluntarily performed.

In contrast to Theory X McGregor offered the outline of an alternative, Theory Y, a theory of integration which rejects the idea of the natural or inevitable antithesis of the individual to the organization and tries to show that personal needs and organizational needs are not necessarily incompatible. McGregor believed that people could enjoy greater self-fulfilment than was possible in the existing conditions of many firms, without weakening the company's ability to achieve its primary task. Indeed, both he and Argyris, and many other writers in the human relations field, seek to prove that a closer integration of organizational and personal needs benefits the company as well as the individual.

An important part of human relations theory, therefore, rests on the premise that an excessively rigid application of classical theory has undesirable consequences and creates situations in which the achievement of organizational goals is made more difficult rather than less. This line of reasoning does not lead to the complete rejection of classical theory, but to the view that it should be modified to take more account of personal needs. There is no suggestion that authority, control and subordination are necessarily bad, but some of the ways in which authority is exercised and control applied are injurious to welfare and have serious dysfunctional effects on the firm. While organization planners fail to recognize these defects of the classical system, or do nothing to overcome them, employees will continue to react defensively, aggressively and regressively, and relieve their boredom, frustration and hostility by behaviour that is often inimical to the achievement of organizational ends.

In another book, *Integrating the Individual and the Organization*, Argyris defined what he thought were the essential properties of a company seeking to combine organizational and psychological success. They were: (1) that the organization should be created and maintained by the inter-relationship of its parts; (2) that people in the organization should be aware of the pattern of these parts; (3) that energy should be directed towards the attainment of objectives sought by the enterprise as a whole; (4) that the organization should be able to influence its internally biased operations in ways that it desired; (5) that it should also be able to influence its externally biased operations; and (6) that its three basic ('core') activities (achieving organizational goals, maintaining the internal system and adapting to environmental change) should be affected by anticipation of future, as well as by past and present, needs. Each property was envisaged as having a dimensional aspect, so that an organization might possess it fully, partially, or not at all. An organization with none of the essential properties would be dominated by one of its parts and by the pressure of present needs, and be unable to influence its internally and externally directed activities as it desired. People in the organization would see only its parts and not the whole, and each part would have its own goals which were put before the major goals of the firm.

The classical pyramidal structure, in Argyris's view, was notably lacking in the essential properties for psychological success, although he conceded that it was appropriate in several other respects. For example, it had merit when time was scarce and the decisions called for were known to be acceptable to the subordinates concerned; when organizational survival was at stake; when decisions were not likely to affect the distribution of power or the pattern of penalties and rewards; when the number of people to be influenced was high in relation to the time and space available for bringing them together for discussion; and when individuals did not want to achieve psychological success. Nevertheless, he argued, if it were possible to increase the extent to which an organization possessed the essential properties it would also be possible to increase organizational effectiveness by reducing the amount of energy dissipated in frustration and destructive conflict.

Argyris supported opportunities for the more widespread expression of subordinates' ideas and feelings, and approved of the Glacier Metal Company's plan for elected representatives from groups at all levels to contribute to certain aspects of the decision-making process. Project organization (or 'matrix organization' as it is sometimes called) was also believed to be a move in the right direction. In this system people are chosen as required from different departments or firms to form teams to work on particular projects, membership of a team being governed primarily by a person's potential contribution to the success of the project and not by his formal position or status. Teams are created and disbanded as organizational needs dictate and the system has considerable flexibility. Project organization is claimed to improve a firm's capacity to innovate and has been adopted with some success in certain branches of the construction industry, and in the American 'aerospace' industry in recent years. The system remains a controversial one as yet and its suitability for firms performing stable tasks may be limited: nevertheless, arguments have been put forward for its adoption in a wider range of industries where it has not so far been tried.[1]

Argyris hoped that many organizations would eventually outgrow the limitations of the rigid pyramidal structure, although he was unable to predict the rate at which this development might proceed. He looked forward to a time when employees would be able to accept more responsibility, exercise more influence, and feel a greater sense of commitment to organizational aims than is now generally the case, but he accepted the fact that as things are the social order produces many people who do not want psychological success, and it would be tragic for them to be forced into positions in which they were expected to achieve it. The effectiveness of a new organization possessing the six essential properties more fully than the majority of existing firms depends not only on changes in the formal system, but on changes in the individual as well, and to the extent that the latter require the antecedent reform of society they will be much more difficult to bring about than changes in the organization itself.

13.3 Informal organization

From the time of Mayo's studies in the Hawthorne works the importance of informal organization has been increasingly recognized and there has been much research into its nature and influence, and especially into the connexions between the formal and informal systems. The informal organization embraces all those activities within a company that are not specifically called for by, and included within, the formal organizational plans: it has a considerable bearing on the determination of formal objectives and, by way of elaboration and modification, on the ways in which, and the extent to which, they are achieved. The informal organization develops spontaneously as a complex system of its own, with a pattern of personal and group relationships that differs in varying degree from the formal pattern from which it derives.

[1]Cf. J. M. Stewart, 'Making Project Management Work', *Business Horizons*, **8**, no. 3, 1965, 54–68 and E. J. Miller and A. K. Rice, *Systems of Organization*, Tavistock Publications, 1967.

An informal group may be co-extensive with a small formal subgroup with similarities of social background or interest between its members, but if the subgroup is large, as in many cases it is at the lowest level of the firm, its members tend to form a number of informal groups on the basis of nearness, shared tastes, external acquaintance and so on. When the membership of a formal subgroup is diversified there is a stronger tendency for the people in it to join informal groups which cut across the subgroup boundary, but membership of any informal group is not incompatible with membership of another, either within the same formal subgroup or in a different part of the system. There are three generally accepted main grounds on which informal groups are formed, namely friendship, similarity of task and common interest, and these will certainly not confine informal groups within the boundaries of formally created subgroups at any level of the firm.

The friendship group is the basic element in the informal organization. Membership of a friendship group helps one to satisfy social needs and increases the sense of security in what might otherwise be a very impersonal environment. The ease with which friendship groups can be formed and maintained affects the stability of the workforce, and it has been noticed that where they are difficult to form, or liable to disruption by formal demands, the labour turnover rate tends to rise. There is no conclusive proof of a close correlation between productivity and the stability of friendship groups, but the possible negative effect on efficiency of breaking up such groups is a factor to be weighed when organizational changes are made.

Informal task groups of employees performing similar or closely related work have been found to exercise a significant control over work methods, quality, the relative compensation of group members and output. Task-group norms may be established to defend members individually and the group as an informal entity, but the latter is usually the more important purpose of the two. Work methods are affected by informal action in a variety of ways: for example, by periodic exchanges of jobs between members, by a temporary acceptance of a double task by one member while another is absent or rests, or by a change in the order in which tasks are performed which helps to reduce monotony and fatigue. These alterations of formal methods sometimes cause a fall in output, but may also lead to an increase. If formal organization recognizes an informal task group's potentially beneficial influence on work, and technological processes are designed to increase the group's control over its own activities, the sense of collective responsibility and willingness to produce more can be considerably enhanced. But control of output to a level below that dictated by formal requirements often remains a fundamental aim of informal task groups. It is done to protect slower members against exacting demands and to protect the group against the consequences of the high rates of output which the fastest members could achieve, the most undesirable of which would be an upward revision of formal requirements, a downward revision of the payment per unit of work, or a reduction in the size of the group.

A task group, probably more often than a friendship or an interest group, has a well-defined status system in which members defer to the judgments of an informal leader, or of leaders who emerge to deal with different issues. The jobs to be done may also be ranked in terms of their perceived desirability or importance, and allocated in accordance with the members' informal order of status. If the formal organization imposes a pattern of job allocation which differs from the one regarded as acceptable by the group, difficulties are bound to occur. If different jobs are associated with differences in earnings the group will normally expect that a more important or desirable job (in the group's estimation) should be paid more than a less important one; but labour-market conditions may require the firm to compensate the person in a less desirable job more highly than someone in a more desirable job, in order to maintain a balanced labour force in the light of formal organizational needs, with a resulting conflict between formal and informal goals.

The third important element in the informal system is the interest group. This also acts protectively, but is equally likely to seek ways of exploiting organizational situations actively to improve its relative position. An interest group may be composed of members from different sections or departments, drawn together by stronger bonds than those which attach them to their respective subgroups in the firm. Inspectors or work study engineers from different production departments might form interest groups of the kind we have in mind, or managers with different specialisms but a common objective, who see more hope of attaining it by collective than by independent action. Interest groups, particularly of the latter kind, tend to be less cohesive and less stable coalitions than task and friendship groups, and to break up and reform as the members' interests diverge and change. Loyalty to the group tends to be less pronounced, and the self-interest of members has a greater influence on behaviour in the interest group than in groups of other kinds. Interest groups are possibly more important at the higher levels of a firm and they often behave in a politically more sophisticated way than task or friendship groups, and pay more attention to tactics when dealing with other informal and formal elements in the firm.

In all cases the informal group is created in response to the demands or opportunities of the formal organization, whether the group is trying to defend its members against hostile forces or exploit a potentially favourable situation for its own ends. Since the informal organization exists whether managers want it to or not, the rational response is to attempt to discover its real nature and do what is possible to strengthen the identity of formal and informal goals. If the informal organization is resented and continually attacked the result will almost inevitably be a serious deterioration of morale. Managerial hostility to the informal organization intensifies conditions of conflict, and much damage can be caused by onslaughts on the sensitive mechanism which the informal organization develops in response to social and psychological needs.

There is no reason why the formal and informal organizations should always be antagonistic, and in fact they are not. To reduce antagonism where it exists is desirable, however, for this conduces to better morale, greater organizational stability, greater willingness to attain formal objectives, increased self-respect and respect for others, and better communications, because a greater degree of openness is achieved. When the strengths of the formal and informal organizations are combined the company's effectiveness and potentiality for development can be enormously increased.

It would be misleading to suggest that antagonism exists only between formal and informal systems, for there is an equal likelihood of conflict between different parts of the informal organization itself. It is quite possible for different informal groups to have conflicting norms, aims and methods, and for these to clash so severely that the whole structure is threatened. An informal group is integrated with the larger informal organization to the extent that they are mutually supportive, but just as complete integration of the formal and informal systems is rare, so is complete integration of the elements comprising the informal organization itself. We may normally expect to find a shifting balance between integrative and disintegrative forces within the informal system, and varying degrees of antagonism between different informal groups. These groups are thought to achieve a higher degree of integration with both the formal and the informal system in small firms than in large; in firms operating in small communities as opposed to metropolitan or large urban centres of population; and in firms with a high proportion of skilled workpeople and a small number of casual or part-time employees. Bigness has been much emphasized as a cause of human problems in industry, not least because large size so often tends to be associated with a more mechanistic and impersonal organization, and it is partly to reduce the seriousness of these problems that increasing efforts have been made to decentralize and to organize large enterprises as clusters of quasi-autonomous units, each of a size which enables employees to conceive of its work as a whole and aim for primary objectives whose significance is more clearly perceived.

Informal groups are a potent influence on individual attitudes, activities and goals, and powerful instruments of discipline and control, capable of offering inducements to, and imposing sanctions on, their members which are more effective in some cases than those of the formal organization itself. The informal group often ensures that work is done better than it would have been without the group's intervention, and sometimes the group's rejection of the literal interpretation of formal rules and procedures is what ultimately makes the desired output possible. The fact that the informal group can moderate the impact of autocratic management on its members is often mentioned as an instance of its beneficent effects, and this may indeed be so, but one ought to remember also that the group's authority may be quite as despotic as the manager's at times.

13.4 Job enlargement

In some production systems the technological processes impose severe restraints on individual freedom to control the way in which work is done, and the narrowness and social unattractiveness of many operative tasks has been a recurrent theme in human relations literature. It is argued that the inexorable routine of programmed work and the performance of one repetitive activity are primary causes of dissatisfaction, and hence of poor human relations in a firm. If jobs could be enlarged, the argument goes on, if work could be made more challenging and psychologically rewarding, a great improvement in the industrial climate would result. What then, is the scope for modifying organization to increase the satisfaction that workers derive from their tasks?

Opportunities for individuals to programme their own work vary greatly from one position to another, and there is, for example, much less scope for a vehicle assembly line worker to decide his activities than there is for many sales representatives or clerical employees to decide theirs. Without a fundamental change in technology it is difficult in many cases to give the employee greater independence, or control of work sequence and methods. It may be possible to move him from one job to another to relieve the monotony of concentrating on a single task, although this would often presuppose that each job called for minimum skill. The value of job rotation would in any case be small unless the worker wanted it, and preferably had a voice in deciding which jobs he did and the order in which they were done. A danger of job rotation is that it may disrupt the informal group, and if it is not practicable for the group to move as a whole, or to have different jobs brought to its members, the loss of satisfaction due to the disturbance of social relations might outweigh the gain obtained from performing a wider variety of work.

Some jobs allow more freedom of movement than others, and some are less dependent on the speed or sequence with which interrelated work is performed. Inspectors and maintenance workers enjoy greater freedom than machine-bound operatives with whom they have contact: someone who fixes a component to a television chassis is constrained by the work of people before and after him on the production line, whereas it often matters comparatively little in what order many office tasks are performed, so long as they are completed within an acceptable period of time. Where it is economically impractical to make more than marginal alterations to production systems there may be little scope for job enlargement, but in any case we must not be led to believe that every enlargement of work, every increase in the challenge it offers, and every reduction in its programmed (and hence predictable) content is necessarily correlated positively with greater satisfaction. We must also be careful not to apply uniform criteria of monotony or potential satisfaction, or impute low degrees of skill to jobs that the people performing them would not personally accept.

The probable gains to be expected from job enlargement must obviously be assessed in particular contexts, but given that it is welcome, and that technological limitations are not severe, there are grounds for saying that it would tend to increase personal satisfaction and improve human relations so long as it had no serious detrimental effects on the informal organization. Where close restrictions on the scope for job enlargement remain, alternative ways of improving relations must be found, and one of the more widely canvassed of these is increased worker participation in decision making. Before we discuss this, however something must be said about job enlargement from the managerial point of view as well as the worker's, which is the only one we have considered so far.

Managers, like workpeople, can be frustrated and demoralized by what they think are unjustified demands; by organizational inconsistencies and failures that hamper their work but are outside their control; by uncertainty about the nature of their responsibility or the extent of their authority; and by the behaviour of their own superiors. The idea of management by objectives, which was an important feature of Theory Y, has received increasing attention since it was first put forward, and underlies what will perhaps be one of the more widely adopted ways of improving managerial morale and performance in the future. The idea itself is straightforward, but its translation into practice has been found to require considerable time, and on occasion to be extremely difficult. Like many things that demand changes in traditional ways of thought and action, management by objectives calls for patience and understanding if it is to produce fruitful results. The purpose of management by objectives is to help the manager appreciate the essential parts of his job from the firm's viewpoint, and share in deciding the major goals he should aim for in a specified time. He is then given appropriate control over his own work and that of his subordinates to enable him to reach these goals, and receives regular information about his progress, and other guidance or assistance when required.[1]

Discussions between the manager and his immediate superior, frequently involving the manager's peers and a superior from two levels above, are intended to reveal the 'key results areas' of his work, which are those parts in which the quality of performance has the greatest bearing on the accomplishment of the firm's primary task. When these areas are identified the necessary conditions for achieving agreed results can be settled and indicators of managerial performance defined. The manager is encouraged to identify himself more confidently and fully with the attainment of his own formal subgoals within the system, or, in the modern jargon, to internalize organizational objectives. The process described is repeated at intervals as the nature of the work requires, and with experience it becomes progressively easier to maintain.

The introduction of management by objectives is time consuming, and this cost

[1] Cf. D. McGregor, *op. cit.*, and J. W. Humble, *Improving Management Performance*, British Institute of Management, 1965.

has to be set against the gains derived. It may also call initially for skills that some companies must temporarily import. It is an exercise that should start at the top in order to be effective, and be accepted as a valuable adjunct to the planning and control of activities throughout the firm. The main difficulty encountered is likely to be that of defining subgoals in terms that permit managerial performance to be measured objectively and fairly, and compared; but if this can be overcome, and the danger of allowing goals to become static is avoided, management by objectives has some important advantages. It should result in better communications, closer integration of work, and greater awareness of what must be done to achieve the primary task. Managerial morale is improved because managers have more control over their own work and operate in more equitable and predictable conditions. Above all, the consistent use of management by objectives means that all major parts of the firm are regularly analysed, with an increased probability that organizational weakness will be discovered and cured before harm is done.

13.5 Participation

Chester Barnard's definition of organization, which was considered in the first chapter, stated that an enterprise depends for its survival on the participation of various groups (e.g. employees, customers, investors, distributors and suppliers) who must all be offered sufficient inducements to make their contributions to the work of the firm. We are concerned here only with the problem of employee participation, which we shall discuss first in the light of the Barnard-Simon theory of the balance between contributions and inducements, and then in terms of participation in the decision-making process.[1]

The inducements which a company offers an employee can be thought of as a mixture of real advantages and disadvantages, which for him must have a positive net value. The money reward and the method of payment are fundamental parts of the inducement and its most important elements for the majority of people, but the satisfaction which an employee derives from his job is influenced by other things. It is desirable for job characteristics to conform to an employee's self-characterization in order for his satisfaction to be high. A man who attaches great value to security, for example, will not find adequate satisfaction in a very risky job, nor will an ambitious man be satisfied with one in which the prospect of advancement is poor. If we assume a general preference for less, rather than more, uncertainty, job satisfaction can be expected to increase with increases in the predictability of the major aspects of work and the relationships which the employee has to maintain in its performance. His satisfaction is also greater as a rule when the demands made on him by his job are compatible with demands made on him in roles outside the

[1]Cf. J. G. March and H. A. Simon, *op. cit.* and J. W. McGuire, *Theories of Business Behavior*, Prentice-Hall, 1964, ch. 8.

firm. The nature of the job should be as consistent as possible with his education and skill, the more so when the level of work is very low or very high. Satisfaction may also be affected in various ways by the size of firm, and by the size and composition of the employee's subgroup. Smaller units, it is said, normally offer more scope for satisfaction than larger ones, but on the other hand an employee may derive satisfaction from the prestige which a large enterprise enjoys, and from knowing that in it he has greater opportunities to move from one position to another. Within the workgroup the employee's satisfaction is acutely affected by the attitudes of his superior and peers, and by his ability to influence his conditions of work.

When he accepts employment in a company a person expects to receive a real reward (a real income of satisfaction) which is at least equal to the opportunity cost of the most favourable alternative open to him, and if the level of his reward falls below this opportunity cost he is motivated to move to another job. The ease of movement in general is governed by a number of factors, important among which are the employee's age, sex, education, skill, social status, family circumstances, and length and variety of experience, all of which must be taken in relation to the array of employment opportunities visible to him. The visibility of opportunities is affected mainly by the level and nature of the demand for labour, and by the individual propensity to search for and compare alternative courses of action.

While people normally try to find employment that gives them positive satisfaction, it does not follow that dissatisfaction will necessarily cause an employee to leave the firm. If he believes that the conditions of his job are both unsatisfactory and unchangeable, and if he sees a preferable alternative, he will be motivated to move. But he may decide that job conditions can be changed in his favour by negotiation or pressure on other members of the firm, and in these circumstances he may prefer to remain and try to increase the satisfaction obtainable from his present employment. The contributions which employees make to the firm's operations play an important part in determining the value of its output and hence its ability to provide them with adequate inducements. From the employee's point of view the inducement offered must be at least equal to or greater than the real value of his contribution, while from the firm's point of view it is viable (or 'solvent') only for so long as total contributions are large enough to allow appropriate inducements to be offered to participating groups.

We now look at participation in the second sense of the word in organization theory, namely sharing in the decision-making process of the firm. Above the level of zero participation, at which an employee has no share whatever in decision making, it is possible to visualize situations in which the superior listens to subordinates' views without feeling bound in any way to accept them, makes decisions himself and imposes them on the group; or situations at the other extreme in which a subordinate or a subgroup has complete freedom to reach a decision after discussion with the superior concerned. Between these limits various combinations of directive leadership and subordinate autonomy can exist. It has not been proved that more participation is necessarily better than less, or that the same kind of participation is equally effective in different cases, but the presumption of many human relations theorists is that greater participation increases both the inducement given to an employee and the value of his contribution, and strengthens his willingness to cooperate and identify himself more closely with the aims of the firm.

The subordinate's ability to affect his own work should at least decrease his resistance to the job and conceivably give him a more active interest in its performance, so that participation may lead to a desirable change of attitude from the firm's point of view and increase the employee's satisfaction with conditions of work. Participation also gives the informal organization a chance to exercise a legitimate influence in decision making, and helps to strengthen informal leadership within groups and increase the probability that decisions will be fully respected. This will be satisfactory to the firm so long as the informal leadership does not set goals that conflict with those of the formal organization, and there should be less likelihood of this with participation than there would be if decisions were made outside the group and threatened the informal system. Participation allows subordinates to express their ideas, problems and feelings more clearly, and since there are times when subordinates' ideas are better than the managers', participation could lead to a rise in the average quality of decisions.

The effect of participation on employees' performance is, however, somewhat uncertain. The success of participation depends to a large extent on the calibre of the people involved, and the way they are motivated by their share in decision making is affected by such things as their individual perception of the value of their skills, the extent to which technological or organizational restraints give them control over the work situation, and their desire to reach higher levels of achievement. Where skills are low or poorly valued, and where work remains inherently unsatisfying even when a subordinate is given more control over his job, participation may be relatively ineffective. Its motivating power may also be weak in large groups whose members feel that their personal contribution to decisions is insignificantly small, or in which there is not a unanimous acceptance of the decisions that are made.

Much of the discussion about participation implies that decision making should be a group process, and tends to understate the importance of participation which involves only a superior-subordinate pair. Yet participation is equally relevant in both cases and, as McGregor has pointed out, being closely bound up with the whole process of delegation it is significant at all levels of the firm. The informal group can, as we have seen, be a potent instrument of control over its members, and the relations between participation, group behaviour, individual motivation, satisfaction and performance must all be taken into account. Someone who shares in and helps to influence a group decision should become more closely identified with the group, his identification increasing in proportion to the acceptability of his ideas. But the converse of this is that if the group rejects his ideas he may become alienated from it. The association between participation and productivity is not entirely clear, and one cannot assume that participation invariably creates situations in which output can be increased from existing resources, but it may encourage a more concessible attitude and make the introduction of schemes to increase productivity less difficult than they would otherwise have been. Participation is expected to lead to closer personal involvement in the affairs of the enterprise and a stronger identification with its aims. It has democratic virtues, not necessarily or even frequently in the sense that majority decisions are reached, but in the sense that reduced managerial autocracy increases the individual's sense of being respected, and hence also his self-respect.

There are, however, several problems connected with participation that should not be overlooked. In the first place, inevitable limitations are imposed on its use by some production systems and by the need to make vital decisions affecting the employee's position without reference to him. When highly programmed work is unavoidable the most to be hoped for may be a situation in which the employee accepts the legitimacy of those decisions in which he cannot share, and the danger remains that if the residual area of shared decision making is small, or of minor interest to him, he may be unimpressed by the offer of participation and suspect an attempt to distract his attention from the problems that most concern him. Another difficulty is that the desire to participate may grow on what it feeds on, so that people have an increasing expectation of being consulted and feel disproportionately resentful when decisions are reached without them. Participation is time consuming and may slow down decision making to an unacceptable speed: it is necessary to weigh the higher real costs that participation may incur against the anticipated organizational and human benefits. Decisions which must be made quickly, which require specialized knowledge, or which are of a confidential kind often have to be made unilaterally, or at a high level, and decisions about remuneration or promotion are not normally of a kind in which the people affected by them are expected to share.

Participation is not a panacea for the human problems of industry, but it is a valuable weapon in the human relations armoury, and when used with care and understanding it can increase the individual's interest in the welfare of the firm and enlarge his opportunities for self-fulfilment by reducing his subjection to formal authority and increasing his sense of responsibility. The success of participation is affected by both managerial and subordinate experience and skills, and by the wish to participate: it may be necessary to educate all the people involved, to enable them to see what participation entails, in order to make it fully effective. Participation calls for managerial confidence in subordinates and a genuine desire to minimize the negative effects of formal authority by creating situations in which people have more opportunity to govern their conditions of work. The primary aim of participation is to secure a wider diffusion of decision-making power, without confusing organizational responsibilities or increasing conflict between organizational subgroups, and without diminishing requisite managerial authority, although the way in which that authority is exercised is necessarily affected when participation takes place. Participation can increase the challenge offered by work and create more 'human' situations, in contrast to the 'unhuman' situations in which work is tightly controlled from above and subordinates have minimal discretion. But unhuman situations cannot be avoided completely, and in many cases participation can only take the individual a small part of the way towards self-fulfilment in his job.

Managerial attitudes have a direct bearing on the nature and extent of participation, and the reader will recall that in earlier chapters a contrast was made between the employee-centred and the work-centred superior. The latter, it was observed, emphasizes high output and the control of costs, and supervises closely in order to get the desired results. He has an above-average propensity to retain authority and allows little participation in decisions affecting his group. If output falls the work-centred superior usually responds by imposing stricter discipline, and by so doing frequently harms the quality of human relations in the firm. The autocratic manager who is work-directed typifies the manager in Theory X who sees employees as lazy, careless and apathetic, and whose solution to the human problems of his group is to threaten, bribe, or both, as seems most expedient in a given situation.

The employee-centred superior is not necessarily weaker than his work-centred opposite, but he shows more consideration for subordinates' feelings, tries to understand their expectations and problems, and invites their participation so far as organizational restraints allow. He supports his subordinates, interferes as little as possible with their work once he is satisfied with their ability to carry it out, and tries to create an atmosphere of mutual confidence and trust. His methods are those of what some American writers call 'hygienic' supervision, because it is held to promote the health of the employees and the firm. The autocratic superior stresses the administrative, and possibly the social, distance between his subordinates and himself, whereas the employee-centred superior is more inclined to reduce it. There is a possible danger here, however, that the latter's behaviour may verge on paternalism, which is not at all sure to be appreciated by the people he commands.

13.6 Conclusion

Human relations and other organization theorists disagree about several of the matters that have just been discussed: for instance, the validity of the hierarchy of needs on which the arguments of Argyris and McGregor are in large measure based, and the extent to which it is necessary or desirable to change organizational structures to increase opportunities for self-fulfilment in work. There is disagreement also about whether greater importance should be attached to increasing the satisfaction of the individual or that of the group. The two are not incompatible in many cases, of course, but in so far as individual and group morale and satisfaction are not influenced in the same way by organizational action there is a divergence of view between those who stress the need for self-fulfilment and those who put more weight on the importance of group cohesiveness and the improvement of group tone. The one matter on which virtually all human relations theorists now seem to agree, perhaps defensively in some cases after attacks on their earlier views, is that the main purpose of work is not to make people always 'happy', which had sometimes been inferred. They also say that in urging that serious attention be paid to the potential value of greater partici-pation, changes in managerial attitudes, and non-financial incentives to work, they are not suggesting that managers should be 'soft', or abdicate their final responsibility for seeing that organizational systems function efficiently and that formal goals are achieved. They are stating their conviction that certain important, they believe crucial, industrial problems call for a reassessment of the values of mechanistic organization and a reconsideration of traditional managerial ideas and techniques. They think that the solution of these problems, even in part, would result in the greater satisfaction of human needs and the strengthening of the enterprise itself.

Much of the discussion about the human problems of industry is concerned with ways of reducing inequalities in the distribution of power in the firm. Employee-centred supervision, delegation, and participation in group decisions are all related to the question of power equalization, or power allocation as it is sometimes called, and the question is a controversial one that is often considered from a highly personal standpoint which strongly colours the observer's view. When human problems are discussed a lack of dispassion is understandable and acceptable, so long as we can assess the degree to which arguments are affected by emotions and preconceptions imported into the debate. But the subject of human relations is one in which ethical judgments are particularly prone to be made, and some of its critics maintain that human relations theory has been unduly biased by the normative assumptions of its authors. Certainly, the human relations field is one where it is most important to appreciate the subjective basis on which some of the leading propositions rest.

There are several important reservations about current human relations theory which ought to be kept in mind. The first is that there is no good ground for the sharp contrast sometimes made between the state of relations in modern industry and that of earlier times, or for the conclusion that human relations problems as we identify them today are a unique product of twentieth-century technology and organizational design. There have been narrow tasks and pressures to conform throughout the ages, and the individual now has more opportunity to obtain some redress against the evils of the system in which he is involved than he had even as recently as one or two generations ago. It is also arguable that in general the scope for the acquisition and application of skills has been widened, rather than narrowed, by industrial diversification and growth, and that we do not derive much benefit from a comparison of contemporary conditions with those of a cottage industry. Many jobs were highly programmed in earlier periods and there is no conclusive proof that workers today are more alienated from their work by boredom and inability to find self-fulfilment than they have been in the past.

A fundamental assumption, implicit if not explicit, of many writers on human relations is that the job ought to be the main source of satisfaction and provide the major opportunity for self-actualization. The extent and intensity of the felt need for self-actualization is itself open to question, as is the argument that work should be the primary source of self-fulfilment. Looking to a future in which industrial societies expect to satisfy material needs with progressively smaller labour inputs, will not the scope for self-fulfilment at work be affected by shorter working weeks, and probably by shorter working lives as the age of retirement falls, and will not the importance of finding self-fulfilment in leisure time increase as a result?

At any stage in industrial development there has to be a compromise between the satisfaction of material and non-material needs, and between the different ways in which satisfaction is achieved. Human relations theory has sometimes gone too far in understating the importance of financial incentives and material needs, and the ability of a higher income to compensate for the unattractiveness of work. The search for ways of satisfying non-material needs may indeed be intensified when material needs have been met, but there is no sign that this point has been generally reached, or that money rewards are not still the main incentive to work. In many cases inadequate money incomes remain a basic cause of dissatisfaction and bad human relations which ought to be removed before other ways of improving relations are tried. Another widespread cause of dissatisfaction is the inequity of the treatment of different people within a firm and the arbitrary nature of a great deal of industrial justice. A further criticism of human relations theory is that the emphasis on reducing conflict and competitiveness within the firm, and on increasing harmony and cooperation, is in many ways inconsistent with the stimuli to which people are subjected to behave more competitively outside the firm, and with the fact that organizations themselves are under continuous pressure to compete aggressively with each other in the struggle for markets. Nevertheless, despite these doubts about some aspects of human relations theory it is an important part of the theory of organization, and is concerned with problems which many managers and students of business agree deserve careful study. A large and growing body of evidence suggests that there are both good economic and social reasons for examining these problems as carefully as possible in the hope of reducing their importance, even if they cannot be completely solved.

14

Developments in organization theory

In this book we have looked at the principal organizational features of the joint-stock company, which was chosen as the representative large and medium-sized business unit in the British economy. Much of what has been said about the company would apply without significant modification to comparable institutions in a number of Western European and Scandinavian countries, in North America, and in countries of the British Commonwealth whose industrial and commercial organizations have been modelled on our own. It would be erroneous and dangerous, however, to generalize too freely from the analysis of a single institution in any country, and due allowance must be made for national differences in law, industrial structure, cultural values and social norms, since all of these affect the way a company (or its equivalent) operates, and the people in it behave, in different environments.

Having shown the company as a legal person, and how it can be visualized as an economic and socio-technical unit, a species of formal organization and an open system, we have tried to combine these conceptually different, but related, views of the enterprise in explaining how it develops and works, the nature and significance of its problems, and the methods by which those problems may be alleviated or solved. In the process we have referred to a number of theories of organization, and our main task now is to recall some of the more important ideas introduced in earlier chapters in a way that will help the reader to put these theories into perspective and assess their value, in addition to which we shall examine a few aspects of the contemporary treatment of organizations which so far have either not been brought out at all, or which have been dealt with only in an indirect or incidental way.

14.1 The evolution of organization theory

The term organization theory actually refers to a body of diverse and partial theories of organization, some complementing, some conflicting with, each other, and not to

267

a unified, comprehensive theory which satisfactorily explains and predicts organizational behaviour. There are, for example, theories which seek to explain the nature and purpose of organizational structure and the socio-economic properties of different structural designs. There are functional theories which describe how organizations operate as entities, and how their members and component parts perform their respective tasks. Some theories are concerned with the motivational factors that influence individuals and groups to participate in organizational activities, and with different patterns of contributions, penalties and rewards. Other theories deal with the behaviour of individuals and groups at different organizational levels, the relations between them, and their effects on organizational performance: certain of these theories are specifically concerned with such essential processes as communication, information handling and decision making. Comparative theories have been constructed to relate the common features of different kinds of organization, and by so doing to create a more general logical framework within which the study of organization can proceed. Systems theories are the latest addition to an extensive list and embrace many of the major aspects of the structural, functional, participative and behavioural theories which have already been stated in a variety of independent forms.

Organization theory covers a much wider field than that of business organization alone, but our interest in it naturally springs from its relevance to an understanding of the company, and it is with this aspect of theory that we have been almost entirely concerned. The theory of organization as it applies to the firm is essentially a product of twentieth-century discussion and research, and its development has been exceptionally rapid since the end of the Second World War. Over a longer term, however, its evolution has been marked by the emergence of a number of reasonably well-defined schools of thought which it is necessary to distinguish when the history of the subject is reviewed. But these schools should certainly not be regarded as individually homogeneous and mutually exclusive groups, for not only are there pronounced differences of emphasis and opinion within some of them, but also a number of similarities between their ideas, methods and aims.

SCIENTIFIC MANAGEMENT THEORY

The systematic examination of organizational problems in the firm received a great impetus from F. W. Taylor's studies in the 1880s of factors affecting the efficiency of manual work. Taylor's observation of current practice led him to conclude that there was a widespread failure to get the full potential value from industrial resources, and it became his life's mission to rectify what he considered a most undesirable state of affairs. He saw the workmen of his day as heirs to a body of traditional industrial knowledge which had been passed by word of mouth and practical instruction from one generation to another, changing haphazardly as it was transmitted, with no uniformity of development either within or between trades. Little

268

or no scientific effort had been made to discover the exact nature of the work to be done or the best way of doing it. Individual workers had their own ideas about methods and there were innumerable differences in the way that any particular task was performed. The worker's knowledge of his job was often much greater than the manager's, and the manager was dependent on the worker's readiness to exercise his goodwill, ingenuity and skill–in short, his initiative–on the firm's behalf. The manager's problem was how to get the best initiative from subordinates, how to elicit the greatest contribution of the good qualities looked for in his men.

The normal practice was to offer employees special incentives to motivate them to work as the manager wanted; incentives such as the prospect of quick promotion, shorter working hours, better physical conditions, welfare facilities, and piece-rate schemes or bonus payments related to increases in output. Taylor called this 'management by initiative and incentive', and argued that it was based on false assumptions and produced unpredictable results. His alternative was scientific management, which called for a fundamental change of attitude on the part of both managers and men.[1] The principal feature of Taylor's system was that managers should develop a science for each task element and for selecting and training the right person to perform each job, and he emphasized the need for continuous cooperation between managers and operatives to ensure that work was always carried out in the best possible way. The old style of management put too much responsibility on the worker and left him to settle things which were properly for the manager to decide. Scientific management was designed to produce a more equitable distribution of work by limiting the worker's responsibility to the accurate performance of a scientifically analysed and precisely defined task, the responsibility for analysis and definition being a managerial one. Taylor recommended that the principle of task specialization should be applied to the work of first-line supervisors and that functional foremen should be appointed to take over separate parts of the work that one foreman had previously performed alone.

Scientific task analysis was claimed to reveal the optimum method of work and enable standard operating procedures to be prescribed. Taylor was confident that scientific management would lead to progressive increases in the rate of work and of output through increased efficiency, and not because workers were driven harder than before. The worker would no longer be required to rely on his own fallible judgment, and individual variations in method would disappear. Taylor maintained that if a correctly designed task were carried out by a properly trained man he would thrive while working at the stipulated 'scientific' rate over a long term of years, and 'grow happier and more prosperous' in his job.

We see in Taylor a combination of practical engineer and idealist. He rose rapidly from journeyman to senior manager, but the time spent on the shop-floor as worker and foreman was long enough to convince him of the wasteful consequences of

[1] F. W. Taylor, *The Principles of Scientific Management*, Harper, 1923.

restrictive labour practices and industrial strife. He believed that the elimination of waste that his system could achieve was in the best interests of workers, employers, consumers and state, and he saw scientific management as the source of universal good. If people could only be persuaded to accept it, harmony and cooperation would replace individualism and conflict, and efforts would be directed to the achievement of a common desirable end.

Taylor was sensitive to the criticism that scientific management destroyed the worker's initiative and transformed him into a 'wooden man'. He compared a worker trained under his system with a surgeon, on the ground that both had to be carefully selected, closely supervised and minutely instructed during their training, armed with a body of systematically tested knowledge, and given the best equipment to work with when they had learnt their skills. He argued also that, like the surgeon, a worker should be able to contribute something new to the store of knowledge about his job and be rewarded for any practical improvement he might suggest. Scientific management was claimed to help the worker make more of his abilities, rather than less, and managers were urged to regard it as their 'duty and pleasure' to assist employees to attain the highest level of which they were capable.

Much of the odium that scientific management incurred cannot fairly be blamed on Taylor's methods when they were followed according to his own specific directions. The troubles that arose were more often the result of a partial adoption of his principles or the use of pseudo-scientific techniques by people who were not prepared, or not sufficiently interested, to take the time and care which Taylor insisted were necessary for the successful introduction of his scheme. His own way was to select one workman at a time, train him up to the efficient limit of his capabilities, and let his increased money income tell its own story to other members of the group. The whole body of workpeople could thus be induced gradually to accept the new basis of work, but patience was essential when persuading traditionally minded employees that fundamental changes were indeed for their good. The very large increases in labour productivity which task analysis achieved were a strong temptation to many employers to take a shorter route, and they ignored Taylor's warning that gradualness was imperative if the workers' confidence was to be fully secured. The effect of ignoring this advice was that in many firms scientific management came to be equated with exploitation and managerial sharp practice in the workers' eyes, and this created a resistance to the use of the techniques that Taylor and his followers devised which is still evident today.

But even without the misapplication of Taylor's methods by managers less idealistic than himself there were some dislikeable and unsatisfactory features of scientific management that made it difficult for many people to accept it in an unqualified form. It had an autocratic, or at best a paternalistic, tone. Activities which threatened the maximization of efficiency had, if possible, to be stopped, and because, in Taylor's view, purely social relationships were superfluous and tended to reduce efficiency, work gangs were broken up and operatives were separated so that they could not distract each other with idle talk. Several of the examples which he gave to prove the value of scientific management showed that it was calculated to increase the isolation of the worker from his peers, and Taylor apparently saw nothing fundamentally detrimental in this, nor did he consider that efficiency might be increased if social isolation at work were reduced.

Not surprisingly, the extreme application of scientific management has been sharply criticized by some of the human relations theorists for whom it is the antithesis of their idea of work as a source of social satisfaction and self-fulfilment, and by those who advocate job enlargement and greater participation by workpeople in decisions affecting their work. Scientific management raises problems for managers when there are differences between individual operatives' performance, particularly the problem of getting a balanced contribution from the members of a group. The difficulty of determining the optimum rate of payment per piece of work produced has been a notorious cause of trouble in the past, and is specially acute when changes in the level of demand are hard to predict, when other variables besides the operative's skill are liable to fluctuate and affect the amount he turns out, and when wage costs are a significant part of total cost per unit of output and hence particularly important to control. Tightly defined jobs and finely measured payments per piece have often subjected the worker to increased competitive pressure and intensified the strain of maintaining a satisfactory level of achievement. The employee's fear of rate cutting is often acute, the more so for having been justified on many occasions in the past, and scientific management has frequently created precisely those conditions in which the self-defensive behaviour of the informal organization is most likely to be seen.

Taylor's ideas have been described as physiological organization theory, and the acquired knowledge of physiology that he used in conjunction with his engineering knowledge undoubtedly led him to take a human-engineering approach to workshop problems. He gives the impression of thinking about work in essentially mechanical terms, and about people as human machines capable of producing a given output in the most efficient way only when their work is defined and regulated by an external agency to the most exact degree. His discussion understates the importance of non-economic incentives, and he does not adequately consider the factors influencing the equity or otherwise of the distribution of the larger real product obtainable with scientific management between different sections of the community. Everyone would benefit, but in what proportion and with what justification is not quite clear. Taylor's ideal economic world looks like a world of perfect competition where demand is always adjusted to a level at which increases in output resulting from an unremitting search for the highest efficiency of production can always be profitably sold. In the light of modern economic theory there is no difficulty in thinking of situations in which the maximization of efficiency would be detrimental rather than favourable to individual or sectional interests, and such situations existed in Taylor's day as well as our own.

Taylor's investigations were largely concerned with only a part of the total operations of the firm. Admittedly it was a major part, but there still remained a great deal more to discover about business processes, and many important non-manual activities were not illuminated by Taylor's work. In certain respects, in his emphasis on the formal definition of work, on the need for correspondence between authority and responsibility, and on the advantages of specialization, for example, Taylor was a forerunner of the classical theorists and influenced a number of their ideas. But the main significance of his work lies in the fact that it demonstrated the possibility and importance of a systematic analysis of business operations, and showed the scope for and the value of scientific investigation in an almost uncharted field. He was also instrumental in creating techniques for increasing efficiency which, despite the controversy they aroused, have been progressively developed and are in widespread use at the present time.

CLASSICAL ORGANIZATION THEORY

To what extent the classical theory can be said to have its origins in the work of any one man is doubtful. As we have just seen, Taylor has an incontestable claim to be numbered among the pioneers of the classical school, but it is more usual to regard Henri Fayol's *Administration Industrielle et Générale* as the work which formed the foundation of classical organizational doctrine. This book was first published in France in 1916, although a major part of its material had been contained in a paper which Fayol delivered to an industrial congress in 1908. The first English translation appeared in a small edition in 1929 and had a considerable impact on the ideas of L. F. Urwick, who became one of the most influential and prolific members of the British classical school. It was largely as a result of Urwick's advocacy that Fayol's ideas came to be as widely appreciated as they were.

Fayol described what he considered to be the essential characteristics of organization, not only in business but in governmental, educational and other kinds of institution as well, and stated a number of principles which he believed could usefully be applied by all managers in the performance of their work. He dwelt on such things as the nature of managerial authority and responsibility, the significance of different degrees of centralization, the scalar chain, and the importance of unity of direction and unity of command. He also analysed the content of managerial work in terms of five main constituents (planning, organization, command, coordination and control) and discussed the importance of each one. His search for general principles was stimulated by a conviction that without them the administrator was in 'darkness and chaos', but although he believed in their universal applicability as general rules he also stressed the fact that there was an art in knowing how to use each principle correctly and emphasized the need for a flexible interpretation in different organizational contexts.

Several of Fayol's ideas became recurring themes in handbooks of business organization and management, but whereas he was rather more concerned with the nature of managerial activities the later writers devoted increasing attention to formal organizational structure, conceived of as a framework within which those activities were performed. The years between the two world wars saw the most important developments in classical theory take place, with people such as Sheldon, Elbourne and Urwick in this country, and Mooney, Reiley and Gulick in the U.S.A., making notable contributions to the widening and deepening of classical thought. To Mooney and Reiley has been given the credit for producing the first comprehensive analysis of organizational structure in *Onward Industry!*, which was published in 1931. Gulick's theory of the assignment of departmental activities was an important addition to the body of classical ideas which appeared in 1937, and Urwick refined his own concepts of organization in a series of books and papers from the late 1920s onwards. It may also be mentioned that, although no direct connexion between their work at the time has been established, Max Weber produced his theory of the ideal bureaucracy while the classical theory of organization was taking shape. We saw earlier that distinct similarities between the bureaucratic structure and the mechanistic structure of classical theory were subsequently found to exist.

The number of principles of organization increased as the number of treatises on business organization grew steadily larger, and selection from this mass of precepts became a necessity in order to preserve the classical theory in a reasonably succinct form. In 1938 Urwick wrote a paper, *Scientific Principles and Organization*, in which the fundamental classical views were embodied in only eight principles. These were the theoretical core of his work and the classical doctrine assumed there a shape which has not since been radically changed. Urwick himself revised and elaborated his argument, notably in another paper, *Notes on the Theory of Organization*, in 1952 and various writers have attempted subsequently to modify the classical theory in marginal ways, without materially altering its essential character.

Criticisms of the classical theory and its expositors have not only been frequent in recent years, but also severe and even acrimonious at times. The cardinal fault of the classical theorists is said to be that they failed to submit their theory to adequate empirical tests. Many were practising managers, or people closely concerned with the day-to-day aspects of managerial work, who are accused of generalizing too freely about organization on the basis of their limited personal experience, and of making no serious attempt to verify their propositions by rigorous scientific methods. Their theory, according to some of its critics, is little more than a collection of general precepts of unequal practical value, some of them being little better than 'pompous inanities' while others are mutually contradictory. The classical theorists have also been censured for taking too narrow and mechanistic a view of organization, for being excessively interested in organizational anatomy and insufficiently concerned with such major organizational dynamics as decision making, goal setting, problem solving, motivation, information handling and communication. Their assumption that man was a rational, materially-stimulated creature was an over-simplified estimate of his true nature that led classical theorists to neglect many of the human problems created by formal organization and to be unaware of their possible dysfunctional effects. Not all classical writers, of course, are said to be equally guilty of all these deficiencies; they are ascribed collectively as deficiencies of the school.

Nevertheless, in spite of the assertions of a number of modern organization theorists that the classical theory is variously irrelevant, misleading or incomplete, it continues to command a wide measure of respect, especially among members of the new management theory school, such as Koontz, Dale, Allen and Brech, and classical ideas and values are prevalent in business itself. Although the area of business knowledge has been greatly enlarged since the classical theory matured, it is still possible to claim with justice that an appreciation of the structure and functions of formal organization as defined in that theory helps us to get a better understanding of the firm than we could get without it. There is unquestionably more to an enterprise than the anatomy with which the classical school was largely, although by no means exclusively, concerned, but as a human being tends to function imperfectly if he is anatomically impaired so a company's behaviour may be affected adversely in a variety of ways if it is structurally unsound. We need to know about organizational anatomy in order to have an adequate appreciation of the way a firm works. Classical theory does not tell us everything we need to know about the company, but because it helps to clarify certain aspects of the formal organization and processes within business it deserves a place in any more comprehensive theory of the firm.

HUMAN RELATIONS THEORY

The early members of the human relations school started their investigations of business behaviour when the classical theory was just beginning to be shaped, and they were not at first very critical of the assumptions on which that theory was based, or specially conscious of the possible influence of formal organization on the quality of human relations in a firm. Mayo and his colleagues were initially invited by the Western Electric Company in Chicago to study the effects of variations in physical conditions of work on the operative's performance, and it was not until some significant differences appeared between their experimental results and their expectations that the research workers were induced to delve into the complex personal and social factors at work in the firm.[1] They began then to form a picture of the company as an integrated social system in which the informal group was an element of fundamental importance, and the observation and analysis of small-group

[1] Cf. F. J. Roethlisberger and W. J. Dickson, *Management and the Worker*, Harvard University Press, 1939.

behaviour, which became a major feature of the Hawthorne experiments, has continued to absorb much of the energy of human relations theorists down to the present time. The discoveries made by the members of Mayo's team led them to recognize and stress the interdependent nature of the parts of the firm's social system, and the need to balance a variety of conflicting formal and informal interests and objectives within the firm. Increasingly they came to identify group harmony and stability as major sources of personal satisfaction in work and essential conditions for the viability of the company. When the classical organization theory crystallized it was possible for human relations theorists to study the implications for the achievement of personal and social goals of the kind of formal organization that classical theory prescribed; to consider in more detail the relationship between formal and informal organization; and to assess the social effects of such structural properties as subgroup size, task specialization, and the number of levels, as well as the effects of different patterns of formal delegation, different ways of exercising formal authority, and different methods of formal control.

Two of the major themes in the development of human relations theory have been the tendency towards conflict between the formal organization and the individual, and the organizational significance of small informal groups. The impact of the organization on the individual has been studied in the light of theories of personality and human needs, and attempts have been made to show what changes are called for in formal organization theory and practice to enable the individual to achieve self-fulfilment in his work. Research into group dynamics has been undertaken to elucidate the total field of forces acting on the group's members: to explain, for example, how leaders emerge, how group goals are selected, how decisions within the group are made and how group equilibrium is secured. The group's cohesiveness is a matter of special interest, and is treated as an important dependent variable affected by a combination of centrifugal and centripetal forces, some generated within the group (e.g. compatibility or incompatibility of temperament and attitude, social differences, competition between members) and some imposed from outside (e.g. managerial behaviour, recruitment and training practices, technological requirements, organizational change). Sociometric techniques have been designed for the analysis of group behaviour which have shed light on the efficiency of different communications networks and the optimum location of decision-making centres within groups. Group dynamics and sociometric experiments have contributed jointly to an increased knowledge of the consequences for human relations of such things as group composition, methods of motivation and participation, leadership style, and the degree of congruity between personal, small-group and formal organizational goals.

Their belief in the importance of harmony and stability has coloured many of the writings of human relations theorists, a number of whom held that an understanding of the forces producing harmony and stability in the small group would show how to secure them in the large. But doubts have been cast on the soundness of inferences about the behaviour of large units drawn from the analysis of behaviour in small groups, and the tendency to treat conflict as an aberration, and its appearance as a pathological symptom, has been criticized. Some theorists in the human relations field have been accused of harbouring distorted ideas of organizational reality which, as Sherman Krupp has put it, led them to try to describe a jungle in terms of a theory of the farm.

The classical theorists, as we have already remarked, were censured for not undertaking empirical research on the scale necessary to test their thesis: the human relations theorists, on the other hand, have been attacked for excessive, and often 'trifling', empiricism, for having too narrow an outlook on organizational problems, and for neglecting important environmental factors by treating the firm as a closed instead of an open system. They have also been criticized for 'woolly' and impractical idealism, and for an apparent willingness to sacrifice economic efficiency to a doubtful notion of personal satisfaction. Their proposed methods for dealing with human problems in the firm have sometimes been misused by managers who employed human relations techniques to manipulate subordinates, while professing a spurious concern for the values that human relations theorists were anxious to promote. In this respect human relations theory has to some extent suffered in a similar way to scientific management theory in an earlier period.

But despite the fragmentation of work in the human relations field, the diversity of the inquiries pursued, and some arguably misguided sentiments and dubious theoretical assumptions, the cumulative result of over forty years' experimental research and analysis is both impressive and important. Much more is known now about many human aspects of industry that were previously unrecognized, insufficiently considered, or inadequately explained; and a number of useful tools have been provided for managers who want to understand more about the nature of human relations problems and solve or mitigate them if they can. Human relations theory (or neo-classical theory as some prefer to call it) has added a new dimension to organizational knowledge, amplified classical theory in a number of important respects, and contributed much to the humanization of the formal organizational structure.

MODERN ORGANIZATION THEORY

There are several similarities between the ideas and interests of the human relations and modern organization theorists. The line drawn between the two schools is more than usually tenuous in places, and a number of contemporaries (people like Argyris, Leavitt and Likert, for example) can be said to have a foot in each camp. Modern theorists have taken a close interest in such matters as communication, goal setting and decision making, which also interested a number of human relations theorists; but the modern theorists have tended to treat these things as processes to be analysed in the context of the whole system rather than in the small group. There has been a distinct shift of emphasis in modern theoretical discussions from micro- to macro-organizational analysis, and although their concepts and methods are quite different the modernists have this much in common with the classical theorists of whose work they have taken a generally critical view.

The field of modern organization theory is less precisely defined than that of either classical or human relations theory. The impact of the behavioural sciences on the ideas and methods of modern theorists has been profound, as it was on those of the human relations school, but the range of disciplines influencing the modern theoretical treatment of organizations is wider than ever before. The concept of organization has also been modified and the area of theoretical and empirical activity increased. Whereas most classical and human relations theorists were only interested in the organization and internal problems of the firm, the modern theorists study a larger number of organizational types, and a good deal of their research has been carried out in hospitals, welfare agencies, trade union branches, military units and government departments. The modern theorists are collectively interested in all kinds of organizational behaviour and deal much more with processes within the organizational structure than with structure itself. Their idea of structure is not so much that of an orderly arrangement of formally connected positions and stable tasks as of a complex dynamic pattern of interdependent, interrelated, and changing activities.

Organizational participants are not assumed to behave in a consistently rational, economically motivated way, nor to identify themselves predictably with the achievement of organizational ends. Their rationality is bounded and adaptive, their behaviour is influenced by an amalgam of formal and informal pressures, and in certain situations they respond more strongly to non-economic incentives than to economic ones. The company is a complex socio-economic organization which does not necessarily try to maximize profit, or indeed devote itself exclusively to maximizing any single, unchanging function of its work. It has multiple goals, varying from one period to another and typically defined in terms of satisfactory levels of achievement. Having many goals is quite consistent, however, with having a major goal whose achievement makes the first claim on organizational resources, and multiple goals may be perfectly congruent and capable of simultaneous pursuit. The normal expectation is that the selection of goals, and their order of priority, depends on bargaining and the resolution of conflicts of interest between persons and groups within the organization, and between one organization and others in its environment. The organization contains shifting coalitions of participants, each of whom contributes to its operations in return for a composite reward whose real value to him must at least equal the perceived opportunity cost of participation. An organization is viable only for so long as it can offer sufficient inducements to elicit the contributions it needs.

For a number of modern organization theorists the most important and closely related organizational processes are problem solving and decision making. Indeed, as we saw in Chapter 9, some theorists regard the firm essentially as a system for making decisions, and a wide variety of factors that influence the decision-making process have been studied as a result. Statistical forecasting techniques, probability theory, the nature of expectations, and attitudes towards risk bearing are examples of these. Work has been done to discover how the recognition, ranking and treatment of problems bear on the maintenance of organizational efficiency. The need for a systematic analysis of problems has been stressed to bring out the significance of particular problems for different subunits of the firm. By factorizing problems it is possible for specialized attention to be given to their component parts and for better solutions to be found. Efficient communication and procedures for selecting, coding, storing and retrieving information are highly relevant to the economy and success of problem solving and decision making, and to these aspects of system operations much attention has also been paid.

It would be impossible to do justice to the variety of topics in modern organization theory in such a short survey as this, and what has just been said is merely an indication of the main spheres of theoretical interest. We shall look at some of the other ideas that are prominent in modern discussions of organization in the following section. Current work on organization theory differs in three fundamental respects from the work done before: firstly, in the much wider scope of its content; secondly, in being based on a much larger number of disciplines; and thirdly, in combining more abstract speculation with a generally more rigorous and scientific treatment of the data which research has produced. The variety of disciplines in which organization theorists have been trained helps to explain differences in their willingness to accept the validity of various kinds of data; in the levels of abstraction on which they work; in the kind of language (e.g. specialized, non-specialized, verbal, symbolic, mathematical) they use to express their ideas; in their propensity to describe or prescribe; and in the classes of phenomena (e.g. individual behaviour, group behaviour, organizational subunits, organizational wholes) with which they deal. A large number of modern organization theorists have continued with the task of humanizing the formal organizational structure which the human relations theorists began, but there is as yet no common bond to hold the fragments of modern theory together in a cohesive form, although a few attempts have been made, as by March and Simon for example, to synthesize the mass of available material into a comprehensive theoretical frame.

In a review of organization theory it is as necessary to stress the evolutionary and complementary character of organizational thought as it is to show the differences between schools. Despite the contrasts between the modern theory and its predecessors that theory is itself a product of the past in several important respects, especially in its original dependence on the evidence of earlier research to support or disprove particular theoretical propositions, and in its adoption of a number of ideas derived from human relations theory. The links between scientific management and classical theory, and between the latter and human relations theory, have already been mentioned. It is always part of the work of each generation to look critically at the ideas and methods of its forebears, and an examination of the merits and demerits of inherited, as well as of newly propounded, theories, is essential to the continuous process of refinement and selection; but some of the arguments about the value of alternative theories of organization have tended to become rather sterile, and to degenerate into mutual denigration at times. It seems clear at present that modern organization theory, vigorous, rapidly changing and faceted as it is, has not yet made the earlier theories of organization redundant, but it has certainly led to a more critical assessment of their scope and value, and in that way, among others, has had a most beneficial effect.

14.2 Systems theory and the firm

We saw in the first chapter that a system is a conceptual or physical entity consisting of interacting or interdependent parts, and that it can be classified in one or more of a number of ways. Kenneth Boulding has devised a classification in which systems are ranked on nine levels, starting with the simple static system at the lowest and rising through elementary dynamic, animal, and human systems to transcendental systems at the highest level of all. Social systems (human organizations), of which the business enterprise is an example, are envisaged as probabilistic open systems of the penultimate order of complexity according to Boulding's scale.

All open systems have an input, internal processes for transforming the input, and an output, a fundamental property of the system being its dependence on other systems in the environment for its survival. Analysis of the system enables us to identify the nature of the input, the pattern of the transformation activities, and the means by which output is converted into the necessary input for the sequence of activities to be sustained. In the case of a firm its input consists primarily of units of human and material resources to which money values are attached: these resources are used in the firm's internal processes to produce an output of goods or services whose sale generates a money income from which the cost of the input resources is met. The series of input–transformation–output actions constitutes a dynamic structure, consisting in its simplest form of a single cycle of events: larger structures are made up of greater numbers of cycles comprising event systems of varying degrees of complexity.

An open system has a composite energic input and expends energy in the conversion processes and disposal of its output. Biological systems are inherently prone to dissolution, because although a given quantity of input may be assured it is eventually incapable qualitatively of preventing the decay of complex living tissue. In social systems, however, this tendency to decay may be postponed for a long period by the reduction of entropy. A social system can alter its input and change its conversion and export activities, both qualitatively and quantitatively, so as to survive for an indefinite length of time. It can import more energy than it uses at one stage and store the surplus in a reserve on which it can draw if the amount of energy expended exceeds the current energic input. The firm, for example, converts its output into money, and when money income is greater than money outlay it accumulates funds which both protect it against the potentially damaging consequences of a deficit incurred at a later time and enable it to grow. The fact that social systems have an enhanced ability to survive does not, of course, mean that all survive indefinitely: many firms go out of existence each year, sometimes after a very short life.

An open system's input consists not only of energic units in the conventional sense of physical and mental work, but also of information about its environment and its performance in relation to the environment. A firm using budgetary control, for instance, receives information about the expected behaviour of customers and competing concerns which is relevant to its sales forecast, and compares actual sales with expected sales during an operating period to which the forecast relates. Differences between actual and expected values (variances) are transmitted by a feedback process to a control point where corrective action can be taken to rectify the differences that have occurred. The system reacts to information in a discriminating way and is only able to accept information signals to which it is tuned. It has a selective mechanism (a coding device) whose character is determined by the kinds of activity that the system performs, and by accepting or rejecting information according to the adopted code the mechanism helps to perpetuate the activities that influenced its design.

Open systems which arrest the process of decay may survive for a while in a static state, the character of the system remaining unchanged. The survival of social systems, however, is frequently accompanied by adaptation and growth which alter the character of the system in any one or more of a number of different ways. Growth is usually associated with increased differentiation and specialization of activities, and as a firm grows it tends to employ not only more human and material resources, but different kinds of resources from before. It may incorporate new sets of activities which were previously external to it, such as the production of raw materials or the retailing of its goods; it may add new departments, extend the division of labour within departments, adopt new processes and diversify its product range; it may merge with another firm to form a larger and still more complex system, and in all cases there is a strong tendency for growth beyond a certain size to cause the character of the firm to change.

The open system view of the firm emphasizes environmental influences more specifically than either the rather mechanistic treatment of the classical school or the semi-closed system analyses of some members of the human relations school, and provides interesting possibilities for studying the enterprise in comprehensive terms. By viewing the company as a complex open system, and analysing the cycles of activities performed, the nature and purpose of its component parts, the degree of interdependence between them and the reciprocal ties between the system and its environment can be elucidated, together with the system's potentiality for growth, adaptation, self-regulation and survival.

The analysis of the company in system terms clarifies the import, conversion and export activities essential to the achievement of its primary task, emphasizes the necessary relations between these three sets of basic activities in each subsystem of the firm and between one subsystem and another, and indicates the kinds of boundary control called for between different parts of the system and between the system and its environment. The effects of a change in any of the activities on the whole system's performance can be more clearly identified, and this helps to ensure that company needs are more fully and continuously met. System analysis is particularly helpful in showing what information the firm and its subunits require to function effectively, and assists in the design of appropriate information-handling processes and communications networks. It can also cast light on the suitability of different groupings of tasks. For example, marketing is the function embracing the export activities of the firm and it is pertinent to ask what are the essential marketing tasks, whether they should be grouped in a single subsystem or located in different places in the firm, and what are the probable net advantages of each alternative arrangement. In many companies product design and development; packaging design; price, credit and discount policy; advertising; market research; after-sales service; and other activities that have a direct connexion with the firm's ability to export goods to the environment, are the responsibility of different departments and sections. System analysis may suggest that efficiency would be increased if these activities, or a number of them, were grouped under the command of a marketing manager responsible for their coordination and the improvement of their contribution to the exporting work of the firm.

Within the framework of systems theory it is quite possible to look at the enterprise in different ways, select certain aspects of the system for detailed analysis, and lay individual stress on, or attach particular value to, certain elements of its character or behaviour. The Barnard-Simon theory referred to in the previous chapter is an instance of the selective use of system analysis, and it will be recalled that the Cyert and March theory of decision making was propounded in system terms. Argyris's recent work is clearly influenced by systems theory, and another interesting illustration of the theory's application to social organization can be found in an essay by E. W. Bakke.[1] As a final example of the variety of approaches to be found,

[1] E. W. Bakke, 'Concept of Social Organization' in *Modern Organization Theory*, ed. M. Haire, Wiley, 1959.

a very brief synopsis of one of the major theoretical arguments of Likert can be given.

In *New Patterns of Management* Likert has described a model of the enterprise conceived of as an interaction-influence system whose main features are these. Within the structure there are processes for collecting information about the firm's internal condition, and about the environment and the system's connexions with it; a communications subsystem; a decision-making subsystem; means of translating decisions into action; influence processes on which the system relies to elicit cooperative effort; and 'attitudinal dimensions', or measures of the favourable and unfavourable attitudes towards the enterprise, its employees and its constituent parts. Likert is mainly interested in the effects of organizational doctrine and methods of motivation on the nature of internal activities and human relations, and he tries to show that if motivational forces are punitive in character, and designed to cause fear, the firm's work will be adversely affected by the resulting hostility and suspicion of its employees. Different motivational forces, and different methods of communication, decision making and control, distinguish the non-punitive from the punitive enterprise, and influence attitudes in ways that are generally favourable to the firm.

The biological concepts of homeostasis and viability are frequently introduced in systems treatments of the firm, and call for some explanation if their significance in this context is to be understood. The notion of the viability of a firm, of its capacity to live, grow and survive, appears to be derived from the Malthusian and Darwinian theories of natural selection from a continuously increasing population in an uncertain environment. It has been variously suggested that firms may survive because they are adopted by an environment over which they have only minimal control, because they adapt themselves to environmental changes and exercise some control over their rate and direction, or because they are adopted and adaptive in different degrees.

In an organization that is correctly designed to fulfil a specific set of purposes in accordance with the precepts of classical theory, the people occupying positions in it are assumed to be rationally motivated and controlled, and to act in rational ways to ensure organizational survival. The symmetry and logic of its structure and processes, and the employment of properly qualified people to do its work, give an organization its strength and eliminate serious danger of malfunctioning and irregular performance. Many modern theorists would say that this is an insufficient explanation of the firm's ability to survive, and that it understates the effects of organizational friction and the effort needed to deal with dysfunctional behaviour and environmental change. The effective maintenance of the 'aggregated role structure' on which viability certainly depends is more likely to be achieved if the dysfunctional effects of mechanistic organization are recognized and remedied. It is important to discover which factors threaten, and which improve, the chances of survival, especially the things that a firm can control or react to by its own volition. It is necessary to explain both the fact that firms may survive by achieving a given result in a variety of ways (the principle of equifinality), and that many firms are not content to survive at a constant level, but aim for ever more ambitious goals, frequently taking action which exposes them to greater uncertainty, rather than less.

Homeostasis is the preservation of a steady internal state in the face of external change. Living organisms maintain stability by adaptive responses to certain stimuli, and it may therefore be asked whether an open system like the firm has the same responsive characteristics. Boulding, in considering this problem, suggested that if we postulate some preferred condition for the firm, like a certain structure of assets, we can envisage a series of data, collected at frequent points in time, which would give a dynamic picture of the firm and show how differences between preferred and actual states provided stimuli to corrective action which preserved the preferred condition. Organizational systems and subsystems are certainly designed to behave in a self-regulating way in many cases, but the control (adaptive) mechanism has to be built into the system by a human agency, it does not develop naturally in a biological sense. The preferred state has to be defined by people in the firm: it has to be conceived in the human mind. The control mechanism also has to be designed, or selected, and operated by people in the firm, and their minds direct the forces that govern corrective action. But biologically speaking the mind is a supernatural thing and cannot be fitted into the explanation of homeostasis at all. Homeostasis presumes an ideal state, but in a social system we need to know how that state was determined and understand how one conception of the ideal state may eventually be replaced by another. The idea of homeostasis cannot be applied literally to complex social systems, because they have the ability to grow and modify their structures, and acquire a new character if they choose.

In his book, *Cybernetics and Management*, Stafford Beer drew the outlines of a cybernetic factory, whose design was based on the fact that it was theoretically possible to construct an industrial control machine which could deal with rapid changes in conditions and learn from experience in such a way that it would be virtually guaranteed to develop towards, and ultimately maintain, a predetermined system state. To begin with, the machine would aim for a preferred state that was arbitrarily fixed by 'limited human intelligence'; its mutation process would be uneconomical at first, and its adaptation to the environment would be slow. But repeated experiences would increase its efficiency and diminish the arbitrariness with which the preferred state was defined. The machine would develop the capacity for rapid learning, purposive selection from alternatives, and 'directed mutation'. It would have the ability to seek an 'optimum homeostatic strategy' and adapt itself swiftly and efficiently to environmental change.

Beer expressed an unshakable belief that a machine of this kind could be produced, although much more research and extensive development would be necessary before it became a reality. The cybernetic factory would, he argued, have several advantages over the managerially controlled factory of today. The machine would be able to find workable (satisfactory) solutions to problems more quickly than managers, and would suffer neither from emotion nor distraction from the decision-making task. In the time taken for a human being to reach a decision, conditions often change so greatly that the relevance of the decision is reduced: if the machine could decide as effectively as, and influence action more quickly than, a man it would be superior to him for that purpose. When he wrote, however, Beer did not apparently envisage more than a cybernetic machine for a manufacturing plant, and even if this were produced and used to direct an automatic production line there would still be many tasks which only human beings could perform, and many problems which only 'limited human intelligence' could solve. Since Beer's book appeared the rapid advances in computer technology have brought much closer the possibility of operating units of the kind he had in mind, and it is obvious that their creation will call for some fundamental changes in the attitudes of both managers and workers, and in their methods of work. The introduction of less far-reaching computer systems for decision making and control has shown already their profound effects on conventional role patterns and traditional procedures, and has intensified the search for different, and more appropriate, organizational designs.

Systems theories of organizational behaviour seek in many cases to explain how equilibrium is achieved and maintained. Equilibrium denotes stability and is generally treated as an organizational good, whereas instability is a potential threat to the viability of a system. Equilibrium is, of course, dynamic, not static: static equilibrium is incompatible with environmental change, and any firm which persisted in trying to maintain a fixed state would destroy its prospects of survival. Equilibrium can be achieved at different levels, in different ways and in different conditions, and an organization has alternative courses of action to choose from as it seeks to preserve an established equilibrium, or move from one equilibrium state to another.

An increasing number of organization theorists see the company as a dynamic, stable, adaptive, viable, open system. They hope that the systems concept may prove to be a unifying one, and that by studying the enterprise within the framework of systems theory it will be possible to learn more about its character and behaviour by comparing them with the character and behaviour of other systems whose properties are known, although the danger of drawing inferences about complex systems from a knowledge of simpler ones is well recognized. But as yet it is still too soon to say whether systems theory will indeed be the means of integrating the ideas of organization theorists trained in different disciplines, and of combining the diversified and not always easily related results of their work.

14.3 Conclusion

In recent years the interest in organizations, and especially in the business enterprise, has increased at an unprecedented rate, and there has been a stream of valuable information about the operations of the firm and the behaviour of its employees which now puts this particular organization in a substantially different light from that in which it formerly stood.

The multidisciplinary approach to business has been a rewarding one, although not devoid of danger. It has led in many cases to an intensive illumination of special problems and aspects of business behaviour that were hardly considered or recognized before, but it has also produced some confusing and contradictory results at times. Communication between different specialists in the theoretical field has not always been easy or complete, and the non-academic student of business has sometimes found it difficult to relate to his existing knowledge and to each other the diverse and novel ideas with which he has been presented, and assess their real importance for his work. We emphasized in the first chapter that, while it is desirable to have specialized insights into the company, it is necessary to keep in mind a picture of the organization as a whole. A similar view has been expressed by other people, like Mechanic and Mosson for example, the latter of whom observes that an 'approach to administrative processes which concentrates on abstracting certain aspects of them will never be able to provide a sufficiently deep or a sufficiently complete understanding' of an organizational entity.[1] The results of multidisciplinary theorizing and research need to be more thoroughly reconciled and integrated than they have been so far, and a major objective of organization theorists (especially in multidisciplinary teams) is the construction of a truly general theory of organizational behaviour that is realistic and tractable, and has predictive value.

The construction of such a theory would seem to be difficult because of the number of variables to be handled and the complexity of their relationships. March and Simon itemized 206 variables in the course of their review of organizations and, although this should not be regarded as either a complete list or a list of equally important factors, it indicates the problems that have to be faced. A careful selection from the numerous variables must be made for the sake of tractability, but the actual choice and the way the variables are weighted and combined are bound to affect the scope and predictive value of the theory. To go into this matter more deeply now, however, would take us too far afield, and might easily cause the reader to lose sight of the solid nature of existing achievements in conjecturing the nature of what may be achieved in the future. For the newcomer to business administration the important thing to stress is the wide range of valuable knowledge about the firm that we have, and it is hoped that our own discussion of the subject will have helped to demonstrate both the extent of current business theory and the scope for its useful application to business practice.

In *The Economics of Welfare* Pigou observed that in the study of any subject one

[1] T. M. Mosson, 'Management Theory and the Limits of Common-sense', *Management International*, 4, no. 1, 1964, 25–37.

may be searching for light or fruit, pursuing knowledge for its own sake or for its expected practical use, and most business students of organization theory will judge the value of their efforts to understand it by the quality of the fruit. For those who seek it intellectual satisfaction can indeed be found in speculating about the nature of organization, and pure theoretical work is indispensable to the development of the subject; but the businessman, actual or potential, will probably be looking for tools to help him solve real organizational problems. Happily there is no inherent incompatibility between a search for fruit and a search for light. Business people, in whose domain most of the research and theoretical tests must take place, and academic students of business can combine their resources to extend the boundary of our knowledge of organizational behaviour and increase the area in which this knowledge can be usefully applied.

There is a large and constantly growing body of scientific knowledge about business which managers can use to improve company performance, and which those outside business can study if they wish to increase their appreciation of the way a company works. In *The Mayor of Casterbridge* Henchard observed of his own trade that, although 'strength and bustle build up a firm . . . judgment and knowledge are what keep it established'. How much more profound the general truth of this statement has become in the complex and rapidly changing environment of the twentieth-century enterprise need hardly be said. Many people have contributed to our knowledge of the activities of the firm—economists, engineers, lawyers, mathematicians, political scientists, psychologists, sociologists and others besides. Without their efforts, and especially the increasing collaboration between them, the recent advance of business studies, in which the development of organization theory has played a major part, would have been made less rapidly and on a narrower front. There is still much to be learnt, undoubtedly, but our understanding of the company has been greatly increased in a comparatively short time by the work that has been done.

Our concern in this book has been with a particular kind of economic and social organization, one type of open system, the joint-stock enterprise. It is an institution developed for the efficient use of scarce resources to achieve economic ends, which is sanctioned and, to a limited extent, shaped and regulated by law. But the modern company has a great deal of discretion to decide what it shall do and how it shall do it within the parameters of the law, and bears a considerable responsibility as a result of the freedom it enjoys. In the past its responsibility has been thought of as being mainly, if not entirely, to the shareholders, but that view of the company is changing and there is a more widespread readiness nowadays to acknowledge the claims of other organizational participants. The very big question of the broader social responsibilities of business, however, is one that we have largely, and deliberately, ignored. It is a question that merits an extended discussion in its own right.

We have explored the relationships between a number of organizational variables

286

and efficiency, and our argument has been that the efficient achievement of economic goals must in the last analysis take precedence over other business aims. But we have also tried to show that the pursuit of greater efficiency need not be wholly inconsistent with the achievement of other social objectives, or entirely inimical to the employees' enjoyment of greater personal satisfaction in their work. Indeed, one of the most valuable results of organizational analysis has been to provide a scientific explanation of the effect on the attainment of economic ends of the company's ability to satisfy personal and social needs, and of the ways in which psychological and social forces can be harnessed more fully to increase the probability that formal objectives will be efficiently reached. One of our hopes should be that as we learn still more about the nature of organized work and man's behaviour in that context, and as new techniques of production and administration are developed and new organizational structures designed, any incompatibility between increases in efficiency and increases in participants' satisfaction will be progressively reduced, and a larger real income result.

Suggestions for further reading

ANTHONY, R. N., *Planning and Control Systems*, Harvard University Graduate School of Business Administration, 1965.

BROWN, W., *Exploration in Management*, Heinemann, 1960.

BURNS, T. and STALKER, G. M., *The Management of Innovation*, Tavistock Publications, 1961.

INTERNATIONAL LABOUR OFFICE, *The Enterprise and Factors Affecting its Operation*, I.L.O., 1965.

LEAVITT, H. J., *Managerial Psychology*, 2nd edn., University of Chicago Press, 1964.

LITTERER, J. A. (ed.), *Organizations: Structure and Behavior*, Wiley, 1963.

MCGREGOR, D., *The Human Side of Enterprise*, McGraw-Hill, 1960.

RICE, A. K., *The Enterprise and its Environment*, Tavistock Publications, 1963.

SIMON, H. A., *Administrative Behavior*, 2nd edn., Collier-Macmillan, 1965.

WOODWARD, J., *Industrial Organization: Theory and Practice*, Oxford University Press, 1965.

Select bibliography

ACTON SOCIETY TRUST, *Management Succession*, 1956.

ALLEN, L. A., *Management and Organization*, McGraw-Hill, 1958.

ALLEN, L. A., *The Management Profession*, McGraw-Hill, 1964.

ANTHONY, R. N., *Planning and Control Systems*, Harvard University Graduate School of Business-Administration, 1965.

ARGENTI, J., *Corporate Planning*, Allen and Unwin, 1968.

ARGYLE, M. and SMITH, T., *Training Managers*, Acton Society Trust, 1962.

ARGYRIS, C., *Personality and Organization*, Harper and Row, 1957.

ARGYRIS, C., *Integrating the Individual and the Organization*, Wiley, 1964.

BAKER, B. D., *A Board of Management instead of a Managing Director*, British Institute of Management, Winter Proceedings no. 9, 1950.

BARNARD, C. I., *The Functions of the Executive*, Harvard University Press, 1951.

BARNARD, C. I., *Organization and Management*, Harvard University Press, 1956.

BATES, J. and PARKINSON, J. R., *Business Economics*, Blackwell, 1963.

BEER, S., *Cybernetics and Management*, English Universities Press, 1959.

BLAU, P. M. and SCOTT, W. R., *Formal Organizations*, Routledge and Kegan Paul, 1963.

BRECH, E. F. L., *Management, its Nature and Significance*, 3rd edn., Pitman, 1953.

BRECH, E. F. L., *Organisation, The Framework of Management*, 2nd edn., Longmans, 1965.

BRECH, E. F. L. (ed.), *The Principles and Practice of Management*, 2nd edn., Longmans, 1963.

BROWN, J. A. C., *The Social Psychology of Industry*, Penguin Books, 1954.

BROWN, W., *Exploration in Management*, Heinemann, 1960.

BROWN, W. and JAQUES, E., *Glacier Project Papers*, Heinemann, 1965.

BURNS, T. and STALKER, G. M., *The Management of Innovation*, Tavistock Publications, 1961.

BURSK, E. C. and CHAPMAN, J. F. (eds.), *New Decision-Making Tools for Managers*, Mentor Executive Library, 1965.

CARLSON, S., *Executive Behaviour*, Strombergs, 1951.

CARTER, C. F. and WILLIAMS, B. R., *Industry and Technical Progress*, Oxford University Press, 1957.

CHAMBERLAIN, N. W., *The Firm: Micro-economic Planning and Action*, McGraw-Hill, 1962.

COOPER, W. W., LEAVITT, H. J. and SHELLY, M. W. II (eds.), *New Perspectives in Organization Research*, Wiley, 1964.

COPELAND, M. T. and TOWL, A. R., *The Board of Directors and Business Management*, Harvard University Graduate School of Business Administration, 1947.

COPEMAN, G. H., *Leaders of British Industry*, Gee, 1955.

COPEMAN, G. H., *The Role of the Managing Director*, Business Publications, 1959.

CROZIER, M., *The Bureaucratic Phenomenon*, Tavistock Publications, 1964.

CYERT, R. M. and MARCH, J. G., *A Behavioral Theory of the Firm*, Prentice-Hall, 1963.

DALE, E., *Management: Theory and Practice*, McGraw-Hill, 1965.

DALE, E. and URWICK, L. F., *Staff in Organization*, McGraw-Hill, 1960.

DALTON, M., *Men Who Manage*, Wiley, 1959.

DRUCKER, P. F., *The Practice of Management*, Heinemann, 1955.

EDEY, H. C., *Business Budgets and Accounts*, Hutchinson, 1959.

EDWARDS, R. S. and TOWNSEND, H., *Business Enterprise*, Macmillan, 1958.

ELBOURNE, E. T., *Fundamentals of Industrial Administration*, ed. H. McF. Davis, 4th edn., MacDonald, 1947.

EMERY, F. E. and TRIST, E. L., 'Socio-Technical Systems' in *Management Sciences Models and Techniques*, **2**, Pergamon Press, 1960.

ETZIONI, A., *A Comparative Analysis of Complex Organizations*, Free Press, 1961.

EUROPEAN PRODUCTIVITY AGENCY, *Human Relations in Industry*, (Report of the Rome Conference), E.P.A., 1956.

FAYOL, H., *General and Industrial Management* (trans. C. Storrs), Pitman, 1949.

FLORENCE, P. S., *The Logic of British and American Industry*, Routledge and Kegan Paul, 1953.

FLORENCE, P. S., *Ownership, Control and Success of Large Companies*, Sweet and Maxwell, 1961.

FOLSOM, M. B., *Executive Decision Making*, McGraw-Hill, 1962.

FRASER, J. M. and BRIDGES, J. M., *The Industrial Supervisor*, Business Publications, 1964.

GORDON, R. A., *Business Leadership in the Large Corporation*, Brookings Institution, 1947.

GOULDNER, A. W., *Patterns of Industrial Bureaucracy*, Free Press, 1954.

GOWER, L. C. B., *Modern Company Law*, 2nd edn., Stevens, 1957.

GRANICK, D., *The European Executive*, Weidenfeld and Nicolson, 1962.

GREENWOOD, W. T. (ed.), *Management and Organizational Behavior Theories*, South-Western Publishing Company, 1965.

GULICK, L. H. and URWICK, L. F. (eds.), *Papers on the Science of Administration*, New York Institute of Public Administration, 1947.

HAAS, H. VAN DER, *The Enterprise in Transition*, Tavistock Publications, 1967.

HAIRE, M. (ed.), *Modern Organization Theory*, Wiley, 1959.

HAIRE, M. (ed.), *Organization Theory in Industrial Practice*, Wiley, 1962.

HANIKA, F. DE P., *New Thinking in Management*, Hutchinson, 1965.

HARBISON, F. and MYERS, C. A., *Management in the Industrial World*, McGraw-Hill, 1959.

HARRIS, R. and SOLLY, M., *A Survey of Large Companies*, Institute of Economic Affairs, 1959.

HOLDEN, P. E., FISH, L. S. and SMITH, H. L., *Top Management Organization and Control*, McGraw-Hill, 1951.

HUMBLE, J. W., *Improving Managerial Performance*, British Institute of Management, 1965.

HUNERYAGER, S. G. and HECKMANN, I. L. (eds.), *Human Relations in Management*, 2nd edn., South-Western Publishing Company, 1967.

INTERNATIONAL LABOUR OFFICE, *The Enterprise and Factors Affecting its Operation*, I.L.O., 1965.

JOHNSON, R. A., KAST, F. E. and ROSENZWEIG, J. E., *The Theory and Management of Systems*, 2nd edn. McGraw-Hill, 1967.

JONES, E. D., *The Administration of Industrial Enterprises*, Longmans, 1926.

KATZ, D. and KAHN, R. L., *The Social Psychology of Organizations*, Wiley, 1966.

KIMBALL, D. S. and KIMBALL, D. S., JR., *Principles of Industrial Organization*, McGraw-Hill, 1939.

KOONTZ, H. (ed.), *Towards a Unified Theory of Management*, McGraw-Hill, 1964.

KOONTZ, H. and O'DONNELL, C., *Principles of Management*, 2nd edn., McGraw-Hill, 1959.

KOONTZ, H. and O'DONNELL, C. (eds.), *Readings in Management*, McGraw-Hill, 1959.

KRUISINGA, H. J. (ed.), *The Balance between Centralization and Decentralization in Managerial Control*, Stenfert Kroese, 1954.

KRUPP, S., *Pattern in Organizational Analysis*, Holt, Rinehart and Winston, 1961.

LEARNED, E. P. and SPROAT, A. T., *Organization Theory and Policy*, Irwin, 1966.

LEAVITT, H. J., *Managerial Psychology*, 2nd edn., University of Chicago Press, 1964.

LEAVITT, H. J. (ed.), *The Social Science of Organizations*, Prentice-Hall, 1963.

LESIEUR, F. G. (ed.), *The Scanlon Plan*, Wiley, 1958.

LEWIS, R. and STEWART, R., *The Boss*, Pheonix, 1958.

LIKERT, R., *New Patterns of Management*, McGraw-Hill, 1961.

LITTERER, J. A. (ed.), *Orgnizations: Structure and Behavior*, Wiley, 1963.

LUPTON, T., *Management and the Social Sciences*, Hutchinson, 1966.

MCBEATH, G., *Organization and Manpower Planning*, Business Publications, 1966.

MCCARTHY, W. E. J., *The Role of the Shop Steward in British Industrial Relations*, H.M.S.O., 1966.

MCGIVERING, I. C., MATTHEWS, D. G. J. and SCOTT, W. H., *Management in Britain*, Liverpool University Press, 1960.

MCGREGOR, D., *The Human Side of Enterprise*, McGraw-Hill, 1960.

MCGUIRE, J. W., *Theories of Business Behavior*, Prentice-Hall, 1964.

MCGUIRE, J. W. (ed.), *Interdisciplinary Studies in Business Behavior*, South-Western Publishing Company, 1962.

MADEHEIM, H. (ed.), *Readings in Organization and Management*, Holt, Rinehart, 1963.

MARCH, J. G. and SIMON, H. A., *Organizations*, Wiley, 1958.

METCALF, H. C. and URWICK, L. F. (eds.), *Dynamic Administration, the Collected Papers of Mary Parker Follett*, Pitman, 1941, repr. 1952.

MILLER, D. C. and FORM, W. H., *Industrial Sociology*, 2nd edn., Harper and Row, 1964.

MILLER, E. J. and RICE, A. K., *Systems of Organization*, Tavistock Publications, 1967.

MILLER, H., *The Way of Enterprise*, Deutsch, 1963.

MILWARD, G. E. (ed.), *Large-Scale Organisation*, MacDonald and Evans, 1950.

MINISTRY OF LABOUR, *The Training of Supervisors*, H.M.S.O., 1954.

MINISTRY OF LABOUR, *Report of the Committee on the Selection and Training of Supervisors*, H.M.S.O., 1962.

MOONEY, J. D. and REILEY, A. C., *Onward Industry!*, Harper, 1931.

MOORE, F., *Manufacturing Management*, Irwin, 1953.

NATIONAL ECONOMIC DEVELOPMENT COUNCIL, *Management Recruitment and Development*, H.M.S.O., 1965.

NATIONAL INSTITUTE OF INDUSTRIAL PSYCHOLOGY, *The Foreman*, Staples Press, 1951.

NATIONAL INSTITUTE OF INDUSTRIAL PSYCHOLOGY, *The Place of the Foreman in Management*, Staples Press, 1957.

O'SHAUGHNESSY, J., *Business Organization*, Allen and Unwin, 1966.

PARKER, S. R., BROWN, R. K., CHILD, J. and SMITH, M. A., *The Sociology of Industry*, Allen and Unwin, 1967.

PARKINSON, H., *Ownership of Industry*, Eyre and Spottiswoode, 1951.

PENROSE, E. T., *The Theory of the Growth of the Firm*, Blackwell, 1959.

POLITICAL AND ECONOMIC PLANNING, *Thrusters and Sleepers*, Allen and Unwin, 1965.

PUCKEY, W., *What is this Management?*, Chapman and Hall, 1945.

PUCKEY, W., *Management Principles*, Hutchinson, 1962.

PUCKEY, W., *Organization in Business Management*, Hutchinson, 1963.

READ, A., *The Company Director*, Jordan, 1955.

REDFIELD, C. E., *Communication in Management*, University of Chicago Press, 1953.

Report of the Committee on Company Law Amendment, Cmd. 6659, H.M.S.O., 1945.

Report of the Company Law Committee, Cmnd. 1749, H.M.S.O., 1962.

RICE, A. K., *The Enterprise and its Environment*, Tavistock Publications, 1963.

RICHARDS, M. D. and NIELANDER, W. A. (eds.), *Readings in Management*, 2nd edn., South-Western Publishing Company, 1963.

RICHARDSON, F. L. and WALKER, C. R., *Human Relations in an Expanding Company*, Yale University Labor and Management Center, 1948.

ROETHLISBERGER, F. J., *Management and Morale*, Harvard University Press, 1949.

ROETHLISBERGER, F. J. and DICKSON, W. J., *Management and the Worker*, Harvard University Press, 1939.

RUBENSTEIN, A. H. and HABERSTROH, C. J. (eds.), *Some Theories of Organization*, Irwin-Dorsey, 1966.

RUBNER, A., *The Ensnared Shareholder*, Macmillan, 1965.

SAMPSON, R. C., *The Staff Role in Management*, Harper, 1955.

SAYLES, L. R., *Managerial Behavior*, McGraw-Hill, 1964.

SAYLES, L. R. and STRAUSS, G., *Human Behavior in Organizations*, Prentice-Hall, 1966.

SCHELL, E., *Technique of Executive Control*, McGraw-Hill, 1957.

SCOTT, W. G., *Human Relations in Management*, Irwin, 1962.

SCOTT, W. H. and others, *Technical Change and Industrial Relations*, Liverpool University Press, 1956.

SEABORNE, A. E. M. and THOMAS, L. F., *Subjective Standards in Industrial Inspection*, H.M.S.O., 1964.

SEYMOUR, J., *Company Direction*, MacDonald and Evans, 1954.

SHELDON, O., *The Philosophy of Management*, Pitman, 1924.

SIMON, H. A., *Administrative Behavior*, 2nd edn., Collier-Macmillan, 1965.

SLOAN, A. P., JR., *My Years with General Motors*, ed. McDonald, J. and Stevens, C., Sidgwick and Jackson, 1965.

STARR, M. K. (ed.), *Executive Readings in Management Science*, Collier-Macmillan, 1965.

STEWART, R., *The Reality of Management*, Heinemann, 1963.

STEWART, R., *Managers and their Jobs*, Macmillan, 1967.

TAYLOR, F. W., *Scientific Management*, Harper and Row, 1964.

THURLEY, K. E. and HAMBLIN, A. C., *The Supervisor and his Job*, H.M.S.O., 1963.

URWICK, L. F., *Elements of Administration*, 2nd edn., Pitman, 1947.

URWICK, L. F., *The Load on Top Management*, Urwick, Orr and Partners, 1954.

VICKERS, C. G., *The Art of Judgment*, Chapman and Hall, 1965.

WEBER, M., *The Theory of Social and Economic Organization* (trans. A. M. Henderson and T. Parsons), Oxford University Press, 1947.

WEDDERBURN, K. W., *Company Law Reform*, Fabian Tract 363, Fabian Society, 1965.

WHYTE, W. F., *Men at Work*, Irwin-Dorsey, 1961.

WHYTE, W. H., *The Organization Man*, Cape, 1957.

WILLIAMS, B. R. and SCOTT, W. P., *Investment Proposals and Decisions*, Allen and Unwin, 1965.

WILSON, C., *History of Unilever*, Cassell, 1954.

WOLF, W. B. (ed.), *Management*, Wadsworth Publications, 1964.

WOODWARD, J., *Industrial Organization: Theory and Practice*, Oxford University Press, 1965.

Index

Index

Thompson, R. E., 159
time-span capacity, 134–6
Townsend, H., 241
training of foremen, 102–3
Trist, E. L., 27
Tube Investments Limited, 241

Unilever Limited, 78
unity of command, 61, 119, 144
Urwick, L. F., 107, 108, 144, 148, 149, 150, 151, 189, 272, 273

value, theory of, 11
variance, 222
Veblen, T., 136
viability, 282
Volkswagen Company, 217

Vorstand, 236
vote gearing, 37
voting agreement, 39
voting rights, 33, 47
voting trust, 39

Walker, C. R., 164
Webber, O. F., 183
Weber, M., 140, 273
Western Electric Company, 26, 274
wheel network, 132–4
Whitehead, H., 67
wide structure, 162–3
Williams, B. R., 175
Woodward, J., 19, 96, 113, 119, 122, 123, 124, 125, 136, 160, 182, 203, 237
work, 110–12, 170